Fighting to Save
Our Urban Schools . . .
and Winning!

LESSONS FROM HOUSTON

Fighting to Save Our Urban Schools . . . and Winning!

LESSONS FROM HOUSTON

DONALD R. MCADAMS

Teachers College, Columbia University
New York and London

Published by Teachers College Press, 1234 Amsterdam Avenue, New York, NY
10027

Library of Congress Cataloging-in-Publication Data

McAdams, Donald R.
Fighting to save our urban schools . . . and winning!: lessons from Houston /
    Donald R. McAdams.
        p. cm.
    Includes bibliographical references (p.   ) and index.
    ISBN 0-8077-3884-0 (alk. paper)—ISBN 0-8077-3885-9 (alk. paper)
        1. Education, Urban—Texas—Houston—Case studies.   2. Educational
    change—Texas—Houston—Case studies.   I. Title.
    LC5133.H8 M32 2000
    370'.9173'2—dc21   99-052194

ISBN 0-8077-3884-0 (paper)
ISBN 0-8077-3885-9 (cloth)

Printed on acid-free paper

Manufactured in the United States of America

07   06   05   04   03   02   01   8   7   6   5   4   3   2

To my wife, Anne,
my children, Shaun, Daniel, Laura, and Hanna,
and the parent activists of the Houston
Independent School District

Contents

Acknowledgments   **xi**

Introduction   **xiii**

1. The Battle for *Beliefs and Visions*   **1**

Board and Superintendent   1
The Battle for *Beliefs and Visions*   6
The Departure of Joan Raymond   10

2. Empowering Houston's Schools   **16**

Building Board Unity   16
Hiring a New Superintendent   18
Empowering Houston's Schools   23

3. The Great 32 Percent Tax Increase   **32**

Developing the *Blueprint*   32
Petruzielo Recommends a Tax Increase   34
Houston Fights over HISD Taxes   36

4. Neighborhood Wars   **46**

Constituent Service   46
What Went Wrong at the Rice School?   49
Changing School Attendance Zones   53

A Neighborhood Middle School for Bellaire?   57
Reflections on Neighborhood Wars   58

5. **The Long, Bumpy Road to Accountable Schools**   **62**

Measurement Complexities   62
Petruzielo's Problems with the Board   63
Accountability for Rusk Elementary   67
The Texas Accountability System   71
Establishing the HISD Accountability System   74
Reflections on Accountability   83

6. **Some Accountability for Employees**   **86**

An Unworkable System   86
Petruzielo's Initiatives   92

7. **The Wonderful Cacophony of a Free People
    Disagreeing**   **104**

What if HISD Needs a New Superintendent?   104
The Desire of the Board of Education   107
All Hell Breaks Loose   109
Confrontation with the TEA and a Lawsuit   114

8. **Decentralizing the School District**   **122**

Petruzielo Won't Decentralize   122
Implementing the Hook-Haines Plan   127
Decentralizing the School District   133

9. **Improving District Operations**   **140**

Fraud in the Alternative Certification Program   140
Peer Examination, Evaluation, and Redesign   146
Reflections on Improving District Operations   154

10. The Demise of the Reform Board **157**

The Dynamics of the New Board 157

The Board Splits over Jobs 163

We Don't Want Your Children 168

11. The Voters Determine the Future of HISD **176**

Rod Paige Makes a Decision 176

Fallon and Friends vs. Paige and Friends 177

Preparations for Board Elections 181

Board Elections 182

12. Stop HISD Bonds **191**

Preparations for the Bond Election 191

The Bond Election Campaign 198

Public Response to the Bond Failure 202

HISD Response to the Bond Failure 204

13. 228 Ways to Save a Bundle **211**

Sharp Is Coming 211

The Texas School Performance Review 214

Response to the TSPR 218

HISD's Six-Month Report Card 226

14. A New Beginning for HISD **229**

Paige's New Beginning for HISD 230

The Reforms of 1996–1997 232

A New Beginning for HISD 244

15. Lessons from Houston **248**

Three Waves of School Reform 248

Houston Achievements 252

Lessons from Houston 255

Children Come in Last 259

What Is to Be Done?   262
A Final Note on Houston   263

Epilogue   **267**

A Note on Sources   **271**

References   **273**

Index   **283**

About the Author   **294**

Acknowledgments

I wish to acknowledge Paula Arnold, Ron Franklin, Cathy Mincberg, Rod Paige, Laurie Bricker, Kelly Frels, Susan Sclafani, Leonard Sturm, Mary Murphy, Hilda Poindexter, Robert Stockwell, Melanie Markley, Bruce Bolger, Andrew Price Woolley III, Marvin Hoffman, and H. Jerome Freiberg, who read all or parts of my manuscript and made many valuable suggestions. I frequently accepted their advice. Sometimes I did not. They share no responsibility for my words. I wish also to thank Nancy Brock of HISD board services for helping me locate board documents.

My biggest thank you, and all my love, goes to my wife Anne. She has cheerfully carried an extra family burden on top of a busy career so I could serve on the Houston Independent School District Board of Education, and then she has given even more time so I could write. Without her encouragement and support, this book could not have been written.

Introduction

This book is the story of an intrepid band of school reformers who, against all odds, turned around one of the nation's largest urban school districts. It is a story of leadership and luck, with larger-than-life characters and the unexpected twists and turns of a novel. But it is all true.

In Houston, the reformers are not beaten down by an unyielding educational establishment. In Houston, the reformers win. Student achievement is up. The drop-out rate is down. Administrative costs have been reduced. And numerous management changes have improved operational effectiveness. Houston is in the midst of one of the most successful reforms of an urban school district since the publication of *A Nation at Risk* in 1983.

What are the lessons from Houston? Urban school reform is hard work, and it takes time. There is no silver bullet. School reformers who push one reform or another as the key to revitalizing urban schools misunderstand the magnitude and complexity of urban school districts.

Liberals are right. Urban schools need more money, a lot more, but more money without fundamental change is more money wasted.

Conservatives are right. Charter schools and private school vouchers are needed. But some public oversight of charter and voucher schools is also needed, and charters and vouchers alone will only slowly and minimally improve education for a small percentage of urban children.

Urban schools need money, and charters, and vouchers. They also need a focused, aligned, academic curriculum for all students, high standards, assessment on high-stakes standardized tests, and school and teacher accountability for results. School communities need to be empowered. Parents need to be involved. Management systems need to be decentralized. Business functions need to be outsourced. And contracts should be signed with alternative educational providers. Urban schools need all this, and a lot more.

Urban school reform must be broad and deep. And everything must be done with strategic intent and with a focus on the organization as a whole. Urban schools are parts of very large, complex, open, and dynamic systems called school districts. It is almost impossible for schools to flourish in districts that are dysfunctional. Whole school reform models are important, but the focus of urban school reformers must be school districts.

All the reform initiatives mentioned above have contributed to the improvement of the Houston Independent School District (HISD). We have empowered school communities, decentralized the district, put into place a school accountability system, strengthened teacher accountability, developed and deployed a core curriculum with special emphasis on reading, outsourced most major business functions, approved more than 20 school charters, and even created our own modified voucher program.

How has this happened? Leadership and luck. In the late 1980s the business leaders of Houston determined to make the improvement of HISD one of their highest priorities. They have maintained this focus throughout the 1990s. Working very loosely, and sometimes at cross-purposes, with parent activists, they have helped elect and support strong, reform-minded trustees.

The luck is that in 1989 and again in subsequent elections, tough, talented school reformers have sought election to the board of education. These trustees and a nontraditional superintendent are the strategists and fighters who have led the fight to reform Houston's public schools. Business leaders and parent activists have usually been their close allies. And school administrators and teachers have responded magnificently to the challenges of change.

I have been privileged to be a part of this reform as a member of the board of education. I was elected in 1989 and am now two years into my third four-year term. It has been an education, an education I wish to share with all those who care about America's urban schools.

This book is the story of Houston's fight to save its public schools, 1990–1997. It is not based on interviews with the major participants. It does not reflect multiple points of view. It is my recollections and reflections, supplemented by public and private documents and newspaper clippings. As a literary device to carry the narrative, I have frequently summarized my conversations with others in dialog, placing the essence of the conversation within quotation marks. The quotation marks do not indicate that I have recordings or notes of these conversations.

The Houston story is about the clash of superintendents and business leaders with huge egos, the weakness and demagoguery of board members, the hardball tactics of a tough teacher union leader, the politicization of state education officials, the hyperbole of community activists, and the apathy of voters. It is also about a great city that through all this manages to pull itself together and significantly improve its public schools.

I have tried to tell the story chronologically, because that is how it happened. The great reform battles described chapter by chapter were always influenced by what had gone before, and over time people changed and alliances shifted. But a straight chronology would be unreadable. At any given time, almost all the reform issues, which I usually try to confine to one chapter, were on the table. So, inevitably, there are flashbacks and flashes forward.

Chapters 1–3 are basically narrative chapters that cover the election of the reform board in 1989, the writing of the board's vision statement, the forced departure of one superintendent, the hiring of another, the implementation of shared decision-making in every HISD school, and a great citywide battle over a 32 percent increase in school property taxes.

These chapters illuminate several critical reform issues common to all urban school districts: board dynamics, board–superintendent relationships, how sunshine laws inhibit superintendent selection, the difficulty of implementing effective shared decision-making, and the core issue for so many urban districts: what comes first, money or reform.

Chapter 4, "Neighborhood Wars," is a collection of stories that illustrate the constituent service required of urban school trustees and the neighborhood conflicts that occupy so much of their time. All too often, the underlying issues are class, race, or property values. This is democracy at the grassroots. It is not always pretty. But in this chapter are found the only true heroes in this book, the parent activists who have no other interest than the welfare of children.

Chapters 5 and 6 focus on school and employee accountability. No issue is more central to reform than accountability, and no reform is more difficult to implement. Student and employee assessment issues and appropriate interventions are complex, and the stakes are high. Only ethnic and tax issues generate more passion.

These two chapters show how difficult it is to force administrators and teachers to accept accountability and how easy it is for school reformers to work against each other. A bitter, unnecessary fight over accountability between board members and some business leaders for a time threatened the fragile board–business alliance that was just beginning to form.

Chapter 7 resumes the narrative with an account of the key event in the reform of Houston's public schools—the selection of a nontraditional superintendent who shared the board's vision for reform. The selection process and the superintendent's ethnicity sparked a huge public controversy that pitted Hispanic activists and the Texas Education Agency against the board of education. Every city has its own ethnic politics. In Houston, ethnic politics almost ended the tenure of a great reform superintendent even before it began.

Chapters 8 and 9 examine management issues: the decentralization of central office functions to district offices and schools and the redesign of more than a dozen major district operations. These chapters show how poorly HISD had been managed, describe the indispensable contribution made by Houston business leaders to management improvement, and demonstrate that the chief obstacle to management improvement is politics.

Chapters 10 and 11 resume the narrative with particular focus on board dynamics and the electoral process. In these two chapters the board splits into two loose factions, and the superintendent finds himself unable to advance his reform agenda. Board elections save the day. With a lot of help from business leaders, a narrow reform majority reemerges on the board. Issues that focus on race and class divide the board, but the real issue is jobs and the power of the Houston Federation of Teachers.

Chapters 12 and 13 are topical chapters that describe two major events that dominated news coverage of HISD during 1996: a performance review of the district by the state comptroller of public accounts, and a failed bond election. Both events demonstrated how negatively the public viewed HISD, and both gave various centers of power the opportunity to leverage the district for their own agendas.

But out of defeat came victory. Chapter 14 describes how the superintendent and board reformers used the defeats of 1996 to push the board in 1997 to approve a wide range of aggressive reform policies. The board agreed to reduce its role in management. It approved public school choice, numerous district charters, a contract with a for-profit educational provider, and even modified vouchers. Significant improvements were made in instruction and assessment. Employee accountability was increased. And contracts were signed with private companies for the management of most major business functions.

The last chapter places the Houston experience in national context, summarizes Houston's achievements, and draws lessons from Houston.

Implicit in the Houston story from Chapter 1 is what I consider to be the core issue in urban school reform: governance. Urban schools are centers of conflict. Schools are where we send our most precious possession, our children. They affect our neighborhoods, our property values, and our tax rates. Schools are at the center of America's obsession with race, so schools are the major arena in this country for ethnic politics. Schools are about the core values of society. Everyone who wants to change or protect the status quo wants to influence the schools. And public education is big business. Schools are about vendors, contracts, and jobs. School reform is not reasoned debate about children, curriculum, teaching, and learning. It is political combat. Everyone is for school reform. But nearly everyone has another agenda.

Schools are in the middle of the political arena subject to direct democratic control. No wonder school reform is difficult. We must find some way to give urban school districts strong, stable, apolitical leadership. We must get special interest politics out of the schools.

The most powerful lesson from Houston is that business leaders and parent activists can work together to recruit and elect competent trustees committed to change. If those who have the most to gain from good schools don't work together to elect reform trustees, special interests will dominate school board elections and schools.

We Americans complain a lot about government, but most of the time we get what we deserve. If we want good schools for our children, we have it in our power to give it to them.

1

The Battle for
Beliefs and Visions

The reform of the Houston Independent School District (HISD) began with
the board elections of 1989. Somewhat by accident, the elections brought together a core of school reformers who shared the same beliefs and visions for
urban schools. We were convinced that poor, urban children could learn and
that it was the school's responsibility to see that they did. Far too many HISD
schools were failing, and the district's powerful central bureaucracy seemed
unable or unwilling to improve them. Within six months, we had bonded as
a small band of warriors determined to do whatever necessary to turn the
district upside down. The superintendent, Dr. Joan Raymond, had a different opinion.

BOARD AND SUPERINTENDENT

Superintendent Joan Raymond

Joan Raymond was a single white woman in her mid-50s. She had been educated at Rippon College, De Paul University, and Northwestern University,
made her reputation in Chicago, and then became a superintendent in Yonkers, New York. She came to Houston in 1986 at the height of her powers.
And her powers were considerable. She was smart, informed, and decisive.
Always impeccably dressed and heavy with expensive jewelry, her medium-
cut frosted hair perfectly coiffured; her every word spoken with absolute confidence; her long, polished nails tapping always tapping, on every available
hard surface—she was a commanding personality.

The downside was that Dr. Raymond had to be in control of everything
she touched. She dominated every conversation. And every issue, no matter
how small, was a personal battle she had to win. She could be charming, and

she had her network of supporters within HISD, but much of her power was based on intimidation. When mistakes were made, heads rolled.

The business leaders respected Joan Raymond. She was that tough lady from the North who was cleaning up HISD. And most of HISD's nine trustees believed Dr. Raymond's strengths outweighed her weaknesses. She successfully obtained the full restoration of HISD's state accreditation, which had been lowered in 1985, and she provided leadership for a successful $300 million bond election in March 1989. But privately, nearly everyone who knew Joan Raymond agreed that she had significant weaknesses. She was a great person with great flaws. But this could not be said publicly. You were either for Joan or you were against her.

Board Elections of 1989

Every two years five, or four, of HISD's nine trustees were elected to four-year terms. Each trustee represented a single-member district. The districts in the West were mostly white and middle to upper middle class. The other districts were mostly Hispanic or African American and medium- to low-income.

The 1989 board elections attracted considerable public interest. Five trustees faced reelection. Two of them appeared to hate Joan Raymond. They opposed nearly everything she proposed. The business leadership of Houston wanted them off the board.

A well-managed HISD was essential for Houston's economic growth. It served nearly 200,000 students—nearly 50 percent Hispanic, about 35 percent African American, 12 percent white, and 3 percent Asian—in 235 schools. It employed about 27,000 people and had an all-funds budget of nearly $1 billion per year. It was also problematic. Fifty-five percent of the students were poor, 24 percent could not speak English, and 10 percent had learning disabilities. Student performance, on average, was well below state and national standards. Most business leaders believed Joan Raymond was bringing order and discipline to HISD—strong trustees who would support her needed to be elected to the board of education.

Four new trustees were returned. Paula Arnold and Rod Paige, both well-known community leaders with strong backing from the business community, replaced Raymond's two critics. Ron Franklin, an up-and-coming trial attorney, used his own money to defeat a Raymond supporter. My own election was a fluke.

In 1986, I moved to Houston to work at the American Productivity & Quality Center. Two years later, I filed in the Republican primary for an open seat on the State Board of Education. At the quality center, I was receiving an education in quality management. As a former university professor, I had firsthand experience with unprepared college freshman. And as president of an independent liberal arts college in Texas, I had failed to reform a teacher education program, in part because the Texas Education Agency (TEA) supported the status quo. I believed the nation's schools needed improvement and that with my background in education and management I would be able to shake up the TEA. I was itching to become a school reformer. But it was not to be. I came in fourth in a field of five.

But just a few months later, the incumbent HISD trustee for the district in which I lived announced that he would not seek reelection. As soon as this was known, the parent leaders in the district reactivated Public Education Patrons (PEP), a powerful coalition of parents and school activists who had united four years earlier to elect the incumbent. Some of these school activists were friends I had made during my unsuccessful run for the State Board of Education. Within a few weeks some of the PEP leaders were encouraging me to file for election and seek the PEP endorsement. Whoever won the endorsement, they assured me, was certain to win the election.

I received the endorsement. That, essentially, was the election. The other serious candidates withdrew. Only four fringe candidates remained in the race. The business leaders of Houston took the lead in raising $30,000 for direct mail, telephone banks, yard signs, and so forth. I had hundreds of volunteers hosting receptions, addressing mail, walking blocks, and passing out cards on election day at every polling place in District Five. I was elected with almost 70 percent of the vote.

The New Board of Education

All four new trustees felt a strong need to get acquainted, develop good working relationships, clarify views about school reform, and come to a consensus about an agenda for HISD. Almost immediately we, along with Cathy Mincberg, who had just been reelected for her third term, began planning a board–superintendent retreat for the weekend following our first board meeting. Ron Franklin offered his father-in-law's ranch northwest of Houston near Cat Springs.

January 4, 1990, was an exciting day for me and the new trustees. A large crowd packed the board-room gallery. TV cameras and news reporters were everywhere. The five newly elected board members took the oath of office. Cathy was unanimously elected board president. Later, at a huge reception in the administration building atrium, the HISD senior staff, school principals, and others introduced themselves to the new trustees. Joan Raymond looked uncomfortable.

The next day we met at Cat Springs, four new trustees and four returning trustees. Only one board member, Tina Reyes, was absent. Cat Springs was not a working ranch. It was a vacation house, hidden in trees and scrub at the end of a long dirt track. Two bedroom wings and a great room with a kitchen at one end and a stone fireplace at the other embraced a large patio and swimming pool. Long glass doors opened onto the patio and to the morning sun. Nearby were some outbuildings and a paddock with horses waiting to be ridden.

We rode the horses, but mostly we talked. We talked while cooking and eating spaghetti and garlic bread. We talked on a walk down a long, dirt track in the dusk. We talked over long, slow drinks around a crackling fire. I learned that all the trustees were long-time community leaders with significant power bases and extensive networks.

We were all quite different. We had all sought election to the board for different reasons. But it was clear that the four new trustees and Cathy Mincberg wanted significant change, that we intended to be involved, aggressive trustees, and that we were compatible, perhaps even potentially cohesive.

Joan Raymond frowned. She fidgeted. She tapped her nails on the arm of her chair. Joan did not like what she was hearing. She did not deny that HISD could be improved, but she insisted that she had already made great improvements and would make additional changes as they were needed. "I'm an experienced superintendent," she said, "one of the best in the country. I'm in control. I know exactly what needs to be done. Just leave things to me."

Joan's strongest supporter on the board, Melody Ellis, concurred. Melody, a young African American woman with a doctorate in education, had been the board president the previous year. Her brother Rodney was a powerful and effective Houston city councilman and later a prominent state senator. Melody was slim and attractive, with waved black hair, huge eyes, beautiful teeth, and a very sharp tongue. When she became upset, her tongue got even sharper.

Melody was upset now. "You're neophytes," she said, glaring at Paige, Franklin, and me. "You should keep your mouths shut for at least a year. HISD is a complex organization. You should concentrate on learning about HISD rather than giving directions to the superintendent."

The Appointment of Felix Fraga

Soon after the retreat, before any planning for reform could begin, the board was dragged into a controversy. Tina Reyes, sister of the most powerful Hispanic politician in the city, City Councilman Ben Reyes, resigned her seat on the board. State law gave the board the authority to appoint Tina's successor, which is what the business leadership of the city wanted. They wanted a trustee who would support Joan Raymond. Their candidate was Felix Fraga.

Felix appeared to be the perfect candidate for an appointment to the board. He was a social worker in his mid-50s from a large Mexican American family that had been prominent in Houston for generations. Felix had a full head of wavy, black hair and a broad smile and firm handshake for everyone. He had been a college baseball star as a young man and remained lean and fit. Felix loved everybody. His political philosophy was say yes to everyone. Once he endorsed two candidates who were running for the same position. Who could be opposed to Felix?

The Hispanic community activists. Though only 25 percent of the voting population served by HISD was Hispanic, almost 50 percent of HISD's students were Hispanic, and Houston's Hispanic population was increasing rapidly. The Hispanic activists believed that 50 percent of HISD's leadership and workforce should be Hispanic. Joan Raymond was not hiring Hispanics fast enough. She was not sensitive to the needs of Hispanics. The Hispanic activists did not want the appointment of an establishment Hispanic who would support Joan Raymond. They wanted an opportunity to elect one of their own.

Houston's Hispanic community was divided. Mexican Americans, who lived mostly in the east and north of Houston and were a rich part of Houston's history, had the political power. Central Americans, many of them recent immigrants, lived mostly in the southwest and had almost no power. Business and professional families were scattered throughout the city.

Hispanics had few natural centers of power. The Catholic bishop stayed out of politics, and Hispanic elected officials frequently feuded among themselves. It was a field ripe for demagoguery. The activists, which is what they liked to be called, took it upon themselves to represent the needs of Houston's oppressed Hispanics.

For a week the controversy flared. At the last minute a compromise was struck. The business community got the Fraga appointment. In return, the Hispanic activists received a commitment that Fraga would resign his seat in a few months, at which time the board would call a special election. Felix was appointed on February 13, and on August 11 was elected, unopposed, in a special election.

Felix Fraga's appointment to the board strengthened the reformers. Felix did not appear to have a reform agenda. His priority was increasing the percentage of Hispanics employed by HISD. But Felix wanted schools to get better, and he had no commitment to the status quo. Now five of the nine trustees were new. There appeared to be a solid majority for the restructuring of HISD. So where should we begin?

THE BATTLE FOR *BELIEFS AND VISIONS*

Writing *Beliefs and Visions*

The priority was a <u>mission statement</u>. Board president Mincberg appointed Rod Paige as chairman, me, and herself as a committee of three to prepare a draft for board approval. Almost immediately there was conflict with Joan Raymond. She was adamant that board members not meet to work on the vision statement unless she was present.

We reformers wanted Raymond's best critique in advance of any public discussion. We genuinely valued her knowledge and experience. But we insisted that first we meet alone to sort out our own thoughts and come to a consensus. We knew from our retreat and numerous public and private statements what Raymond believed. And we were convinced that if we met with her, she would dominate the discussion, pit us one against the other, and leak information to discredit our ideas.

So we met alone, over Raymond's strenuous objections. Night after night we met in Rod Paige's home, a pleasant brick house in a black middle-class community. There in jeans and sweatshirts, amidst stacks of books and papers and a flickering computer terminal, we considered the current state of American education and the needs of Houston. We argued educational philosophy. We considered management issues. We dreamed about a district where every school was a center of learning.

The work was stimulating. I had extraordinary colleagues. Cathy Mincberg, still in her 30s, had already served eight years on the board. She had taught biology in one of Houston's premier high schools and earned a doctorate in education from the University of Houston. She was an active leader in the Jewish community and had close ties with business, ethnic, and community leaders throughout the city. Her husband, David, at some later time was elected chairman of the Harris County Democratic Party.

Cathy, with her short-cropped brown hair, glasses, and conservative business suits, was the picture of a corporate woman. But she had a hint of music in her voice and, as a full-time mother of three (later four), frequently had a child in tow. Cathy was extraordinarily bright, with broad knowledge and a common-sense practicality that made her the perfect strategist. As board president, she was our official leader. By virtue of her character, ability, energy, and experience, she was also our natural leader.

Rod Paige, an African American in his mid-50s, was dean of the School of Education at Texas Southern University. He was a big man, tall and powerfully built like someone who spent a lot of time in the gym. He had been born and raised in Mississippi, the son of a high school principal, and earned his doctorate in physical education from Indiana University. Rod made his early career as an athlete, and he had enjoyed a distinguished career as a university football coach, athletic director, and education professor. He was also a Republican activist and long-time civic leader. Like Cathy, he had cordial relationships with many of Houston's major political players.

You could see both the country and the city in Rod. He always wore cowboy boots and used lots of homespun expressions, but he also wore conservative double-breasted suits, usually with a handkerchief in the pocket, and he could debate ideas with anyone.

Rod must have always been an intellectual. He read and seemed to remember everything about education reform. In fact, he seemed to read and remember everything about everything. When I teased him about staying up all night reading, he laughed and acknowledged that sometimes he did. And he did not just read. Rod had the philosopher's ability to understand complex issues and relate them back to general principles. Rod was our intellectual leader, and in time he became the heart and soul of our commitment to school reform.

Adopting *Beliefs and Visions*

At last, after many weeks, we had a document to show our colleagues. With minor changes, they loved it. The same could not be said for Joan Raymond. Her first response was to rewrite the entire document. We rejected her draft. There were numerous phone calls and meetings. Negotiations became bitter. No compromise was possible. We were determined to adopt the document and give it the full force of board policy.

On June 18, 1990, in the Lanier Middle School auditorium, before a large gathering of school personnel, community leaders, parent activists, and media representatives, the board of education approved unanimously the *Declaration of Beliefs and Visions*. It was a festive day, full of promise for HISD. I noted with amusement that immediately after the vote, Joan Raymond, who had no choice but to voice her support for *Beliefs and Visions,* passed up the refreshments and the media to hurriedly leave the building and slip into her black, chauffeur-driven Lincoln Town Car.

Beliefs and Visions was introduced with a foreword that expressed the confidence of the board in district personnel and asked for help from the community. HISD's problems were systems problems, not people problems. And successful restructuring would not be possible unless business, labor, and civic leaders worked together with parents, educators, and the school board in a new coalition of support for public schools.

Additional introductory language acknowledged the challenges of urban education and committed the board to increased student achievement, reduced drop-out rates, safer schools, more parental involvement, less regulation of schools, greater district responsiveness to school communities, and an improvement in the district's image. "We do not believe that we can respond to these challenges by modifying the traditional public education structure. The time has come for dramatic restructuring and reform."

The heart of the document was the board's vision for the future, outlined under four headings.

I. HISD *exists to support the relationship between the teacher and the student.* "The personal and face-to-face contact between teacher and child is the central event that the education system exists to support. The district's structure, governance, and policies must promote the quality of this relationship." Teachers would have to redefine their roles and relationships to create more effective learning environments. The district would have to provide professional levels of compensation, empowerment, and accountability for its teachers, administrators, and other educators.

II. HISD *must decentralize.* The traditional management pyramid would be turned upside down. Decision-making would be placed as close as possible to the teacher and the student.

The board would provide guidance and support to local schools by establishing clear goals, high standards, and effective systems of evaluation, while at the same time giving schools maximum freedom to develop and implement the methods that best achieved these goals.

Central office would become an enabler rather than an enforcer. Its new role would be training, consulting, providing resources, and evaluating.

Schools would be the units of accountability and improvement and have control over budgets, curriculum, teaching methodologies, and personnel. They would be responsive to their communities and specifically provide parents and members of the community with formal, structured inputs into decision-making.

III. HISD *must focus on performance, not compliance. District-level policies must focus on educational outcomes rather than on the fine details of the educational process.* School evaluation would be based on improvement trends. Innovation would be encouraged with specific incentive systems to reward improvement.

IV. HISD *must require a common core of academic subjects for all students.* All students would be required to complete a core of academic courses and meet high standards so that on graduation they could enter college or the workforce fully prepared to be successful and not need remediation.

The document concluded with a commitment by the board to a participative change process. We accepted our responsibility as elected trustees to mandate change, but we acknowledged that effective reform had to be built from the bottom up.

> The reality is that unless teachers and principals are at the center stage of any restructuring efforts, and unless they buy into and are trained for the new structure, the effort will fail. Those who will be most affected by restructuring must be involved in designing the new structure, and changes must be implemented in careful stages.

The final sentence in *Beliefs and Visions* was a directive to Joan Raymond: "The general superintendent shall initiate a process for the development of a plan to implement the beliefs detailed in this declaration."

Project 10

As a board, we were pleased with our work. But a clear description of a desired future state was not enough. We needed an implementation plan. For this we needed Joan Raymond. We did not want her simply to announce an implementation plan. We wanted her to initiate a process for the development of a plan, a process that would include teachers, principals, parents, and community leaders.

But this was not to be. The summer went badly. Joan did not want to decentralize. Shared decision-making seemed contrary to her nature. She seemed genuinely uncertain what to do next. She did not initiate a process to participatively develop an implementation plan. Rather, she hired a consultant. The consultant's concept paper became the superintendent's plan.

She called it Project 10. Project 10 proposed to convert 10 percent of the HISD schools to school-based management and shared decision-making in a two-year process. Volunteer schools accepted for the project would receive extensive training and technical assistance. "Successful portions of Project 10," said the plan, "may be used in subsequent years to bring additional schools on-line in accordance with established procedures" (Wright, 1990, p. 1).

Wonderful! In two years we would improve 25 to 30 schools and then see how to apply successful innovations to additional schools. Meanwhile, what about 200 plus other schools? What about curriculum? What about central office? At this rate we might implement *Beliefs and Visions* in 10 years! Long before then, Joan Raymond would have a new board of education.

At the same time that Raymond matured her plans for tepid reform, she launched an aggressive initiative to reassert her control over the board. Tensions mounted. There was growing confusion among HISD employees. Board members began to talk bitterly about her management style. A coup was brewing.

THE DEPARTURE OF JOAN RAYMOND

The Cabal Is Formed

I do not know who first put forward the idea that Dr. Raymond must go. My guess is that it started with a conversation between Rod Paige and Ron Franklin shortly after Cat Springs.

Franklin was a University of Texas Law School graduate and already, not yet 40, a very successful trial lawyer with his own firm. Looking at Ron, you could see why he had made a lot of money. He was trim, with clean, strong features; always perfectly dressed for the occasion; and clear, confident, and direct in his speech.

Ron was rich, but he was not your ordinary lawyer from River Oaks (the most exclusive residential area in Houston). For one thing, he was a Democrat, connected with some of the top Democrats in the state. But what made Ron different was his fierce sense of social justice and fair play. He was no reformer in the Whig tradition. He was a radical. He wanted revolutionary change, now.

Ron came to a boiling point quickly. He was incisive and succinct. When he went after an issue he would stretch his neck and slightly turn his head, then fix his eyes on yours. Then, with a rare combination of emotion and logic, he would fire one salvo after another. From the beginning, Ron Franklin and Joan Raymond clashed. They were fire and ice.

Sometime in the summer, Rod and Ron shared their views with Cathy Mincberg. And soon Cathy, and then Rod, were talking to me. Cathy had been close to Joan, and she found it difficult to work against her. But she came to agree with Rod and Ron that Raymond would never implement meaningful reform in HISD. Eventually I came to the same conclusion.

I was the fourth vote. Franklin, Paige, Mincberg, and McAdams were prepared to fire Joan. What now? Who would be the fifth vote? We knew the stakes were high. If we tried to fire her and failed, HISD would be in chaos. Where were the votes? Who could we trust? We decided to approach Felix Fraga and Wiley Henry.

After quite a bit of persuasion, Felix agreed to support Joan's termination. We all knew Felix tended to agree with whomever he had talked to last, so two of us pushed him. "Felix, you know Joan is a fighter. There might be considerable pressure on you to change your mind. What if the pressure is intense?

"I'm committed," Felix responded. "My feet are in concrete."

Wiley Henry also agreed that Joan must go. Wiley, an African American in his mid-40s, had served three terms on the board. He had grown up with the late U.S. Representative Mickey Leland, played football in the National Football League for the Dallas Cowboys, and now worked for the city of Houston.

Wiley still looked like a football player—massive neck and arms—but he was not an intimidating man. Though he knew what he believed and could not be pushed, he was courteous almost to the point of being deferential. And his broad grin was for everyone, friend and foe alike. Now there were six votes.

Negotiations

What was the next step? We wanted a quiet, behind-the-scenes settlement. A public controversy would disrupt the district, damage Raymond's career, and make it more difficult for us to hire a new superintendent. We wanted Joan to find another job discreetly and depart with honor.

We debated alternative approaches. Finally we decided that Paula Arnold, who was close to Joan, should begin the negotiations. Meanwhile, we pledged our absolute confidentiality.

Paula, a white woman in her late 30s, was a social worker and long-time community activist in liberal causes. She had a master's degree from the University of Texas Health Science Center, Houston, and in recent years had worked in real estate for one of Houston's richest men, Walter Mischer. Paula was tall—very tall—but perfectly proportioned and attractive. Later I learned she had been a high school homecoming queen.

Paula had been elected to the board on the platform "I can work with the superintendent." She had attracted significant financial support from the business elite of the city to defeat one of Raymond's critics on the previous board, and during her year on the board, she had developed a close personal friendship with Joan.

Paula wanted school reform and eagerly embraced *Beliefs and Visions,* but she would not, could not, work against Joan Raymond. Paula had to feel right about an issue before she would act. And she did not feel right about pushing Joan. Paula was the perfect ambassador to treat with Joan on behalf of the board.

So Paula went privately to see Joan. Subsequently, accompanied by Cathy and Ron, she went to see Joan again. Joan was told she had lost the confidence of the board. Paula, Ron, and Cathy urged her to go quietly and pledged to make her departure as easy as possible. Joan refused. Then time ran out.

It was late October. Joan's year-end evaluation was due. Though state law allowed a confidential evaluation in closed session, Joan had always insisted on an open evaluation. Would she opt for a closed evaluation this year? No, she said, it must be open.

Joan had called the board's hand. If we gave her a positive evaluation, it would be impossible to turn around and fire her. If we gave her a negative evaluation, it would be impossible to arrange a quiet, friendly departure. If we backed away from an evaluation, we would violate her contract and put ourselves in an awkward situation. Joan was refusing to agree to a quiet departure at a later date and challenging us to make the first move.

The superintendent of HISD was, after the mayor and a few professional athletes, the most recognizable person in Houston. Everyone knew Joan Raymond. She was that tough woman with the iron hand who had the impossible job of maintaining order in Houston's schools. She had a much higher public approval rating than did the board of education, and she had powerful friends among Houston's business leaders. She believed she could turn the board. She was willing to risk a public controversy and her career to keep her job.

The Battle Is Joined

Very well, we responded, let the evaluation be posted. The battle was joined.

Joan counterattacked on two fronts: she worked the board directly and she worked her business allies to work the board indirectly. "Please don't do it," she told us. "The district will be paralyzed. My career will be ruined. Finding a successor will set off a race war between blacks and Hispanics." The message to business leaders was, "An inexperienced board is trying to fire me. They have no idea what is at stake. If they succeed, there will be chaos in HISD."

The pressure was intense. Two of Houston's business leaders, the ones who had raised most of the money for my election, invited me to lunch to inform me politely but firmly that the board would be making a terrible mistake if it pushed out Raymond. Rod said he was called personally by Mayor Kathy Whitmire. The messenger was different for each trustee, but the message was the same.

On November 8 the board met in closed session to consider the superintendent's evaluation. All nine board members were present. The discussion was vigorous, at times angry. Joan's counterattack had turned Felix Fraga and Wiley Henry. No conclusion was reached. We pledged ourselves to keep our discussion confidential and say nothing that would indicate that the superintendent was in trouble.

Board members kept their vow of confidentiality. But somehow the secret was out. Both of Houston's major newspapers, the *Houston Chronicle* and *The Houston Post,* were picking up gossip downtown and pushing board members for information.

The board met again on November 13. Once again we were unable to reach a conclusion. But this time tempers flared and Ron Franklin, Cathy Mincberg, Rod Paige, and I told our colleagues we would have to speak candidly with the press.

When we reconvened in open session, we faced a huge press corps. Cathy stated that she was going to post for board action on November 16 regarding "consideration of the superintendent's evaluation and employment." She then invited questions. Ron Franklin's comment was succinct and unequivocal: "I would like to see her gone right now" (Houston Independent School District Board Minutes, November 13, 1990, pp. 1–3).

That evening and for the next several days the television stations and the newspapers were full of the Joan Raymond story. On November 15, a *Chronicle* editorial laid out the situation and blasted the board for creating chaos (p. A36). The trustees had "messed up the superintendent's post in the same way as Casey Stengel's immortal contention that a certain player had messed up center field so badly that no one could play the position." Raymond's evaluation had been turned into an "effective disaster." The "terribly mishandled affair" would damage the trustees, the community, the schools, and the children. HISD presented "a picture of disarray and contention." And buying out Raymond's contract would cost an estimated $600,000. "If that were not bad enough, the succession to Raymond would provoke a bitter political fight between the black and Hispanic communities, each feeling a member of their race is due the post."

Evaluation and Resignation

The next day, November 16, the board met to determine the fate of Joan Raymond. The halls were full of spectators, reporters, television camera crews, and HISD employees. The gallery was packed. Some of the city's movers and shakers were standing against the back wall. Many of the employees were wearing "I Support Joan Raymond" buttons.

Just a few minutes before the meeting was scheduled to begin, I learned that Felix and Wiley would not support termination. So much for the concrete around Felix's feet. But Ron had been working on them and reported that they might support a negative evaluation.

In a closed session discussion they did just that. The discussion was angry and a bit frantic. Everyone was talking at once. Melody Ellis, Olga Gallegos, and Paula couldn't believe what was happening. "Please don't do this," Paula begged. "You're going to ruin the district."

A few minutes later, in open session, I made the motion. The board was "dissatisfied" with the performance of the superintendent and wished to re-evaluate her on or before March 1, 1991. The motion was seconded. There was a pause. I felt certain that if Joan made a spirited defense, Wiley and Felix would change their minds yet again and the motion would fail. But Joan said nothing. At last Cathy called for the vote. The electronic display behind the large, horseshoe-shaped table lit up. There were six green lights for the motion and three red ones against it. There was a gasp from the gallery. Joan Raymond was finished.

Joan was a fighter, but she knew the battle had been lost. She could not be an effective superintendent with four key board members in open opposition and two more who would support a negative evaluation. She had passed up the opportunity to go quietly on her own terms, her career undamaged. Now her only option was to seek a buyout of her contract. She determined to get as much money as she could, and, after winning over Felix and Wiley, she did.

Not quite two weeks later, on November 27, the board accepted Dr. Raymond's resignation, effective August 31, 1991, and bought out her contract for $425,000. The vote was taken in open session after a long closed session meeting characterized by shouting, charges of dishonesty, and frequent use of the f-word. Ron, Rod, Cathy, and I voted no. We were unwilling to go over $300,000.

Once again the city was in an uproar. Those who supported Dr. Raymond blasted the board for forcing out an effective superintendent. Others blamed the board for wasting taxpayers' money on an extravagant buyout. The *Houston Chronicle* worried about a divided and ineffective board and a possible racial battle over the selection of Joan's successor. Nevertheless, concluded the *Chronicle* editorial, "[We] do not mourn Dr. Raymond's departure. Her tenure has been an authoritarian and secrecy-bound affront to the people for whom she works—the taxpayers" (November 28, 1990, p. A18).

The controversy did not die down quickly, but it was over for Joan. She continued on as a lame duck through the end of the school year in May, hinting until near the end that she could be talked into staying.

The Controversy at Wesley Elementary

Unfortunately, Joan's last days were marred by a controversy that brought national attention to HISD and left her looking the fool. In April 1991, someone reported that a teacher at Wesley Elementary had cheated on the Metropolitan Achievement Test. Nearly all of Wesley's students were black and poor. The test scores, said the informer, were too high for poor, minority children. The teacher cheated.

Joan dispatched two HISD administrators to investigate. They moved the students to the library and spent nearly a day asking questions and searching through materials. They found nothing.

Joan immediately apologized for the intrusion, but it was too late. The teacher was embarrassed, and the principal, Thaddeus Lott, was a hero.

Thaddeus was an experienced black educator who had been principal at Wesley for 16 years. He was a maverick. He ignored the district's reading curriculum, which leaned strongly to whole language learning, and pushed his students hard with rigorous direct instruction in phonics. He required intensive drills in arithmetic. He demanded absolute conformity to strict rules of conduct. And he got results. Year after year students at Wesley performed as well as or better than students in many of the schools in affluent, white neighborhoods.

George Scott, an associate with the Tax Research Association of Houston and Harris County, was furious. HISD administrators were trying to intimidate Thaddeus because they were jealous of his success. "We've got to free Wesley," he said. "Probably the single best thing that HISD could do right now is put a restraining order on HISD administrators and keep them out of Wesley. If they are not going to come there to help, stay the hell out of the way" (*Houston Chronicle*, April 15, 1991, p. A1).

The next day the *Chronicle* editorialized that Joan Raymond also owed an apology to Thaddeus Lott and the children (April 16, 1991, p. A12).

The controversy would not go away. Outraged residents from the Wesley community packed the school board chamber a few days later charging that the district was trying to discredit the neighborhood by false implications of cheating. "You ought to be ashamed," said one community member. Residents applauded and cheered. Some carried signs that said "We Don't Cheat," and "How Dare You, HISD."

For a month, news reports, op-eds, and letters to the editor kept the story alive. Then, on June 6, the story was aired on ABC *PrimeTime*. Wesley Elementary students performed on camera. Gayle Fallon, president of the Houston Federation of Teachers, HISD's largest teacher union, accused HISD administrators of being racists and said that Joan Raymond had privately called Mr. Lott a clown.

Joan's interview with *PrimeTime* reporter Chris Wallace was a disaster. She claimed to be a supporter of Lott, but acknowledged that she had not visited the school before last year. Wallace asked her, "Didn't you ever just want to go over and pat him on the back and frankly see how the program works?"

Raymond's answer was, "Well, he has been patted on the back a lot."

A few days later Joan Raymond was gone.

2

Empowering Houston's Schools

The 5–4 board decision on November 27, 1990 to buy out Joan Raymond's contract removed the major cause of board disunity. Joan was still superintendent, but she was history. Nevertheless, hard feelings remained, and board unity was not assured. Without board unity it would be difficult to hire a strong superintendent. Board members did not need the stinging rebuke of the November 28 *Chronicle* editorial to know that board unity was priority number one.

BUILDING BOARD UNITY

Choosing a Board President

It was time to think about our next move—the selection of the board president for 1991. The HISD board president was a powerful person under normal circumstances. He or she presided over board meetings, served informally as the superintendent's chief advisor, and represented the board to the media. Most importantly, board members expected the board president to be fully informed on all matters and to advise them on complex policy issues. By custom, board members deferred to the president. Now the board president would be even more powerful. He or she would fill some of the power vacuum created by a lame-duck superintendent and be first among equals in selecting HISD's next superintendent.

Who would be board president for 1991? Ron Franklin, Cathy, and I wanted Rod Paige, and he was willing to serve. But Wiley Henry also wanted the position, and he had strong support from Melody Ellis, Felix Fraga, and Olga Gallegos. Paula Arnold was the swing vote. However she voted, the board would be split and the divisions on the board would deepen, perhaps become permanent. There was only one solution. Paula herself must seek the presidency. The pro-Raymond trustees saw her as one of them. Ron, Cathy, Rod, and I saw her as a reformer who, now that Dr. Raymond was leaving, was one of us. Paula agreed to seek the position. Rod and Wiley agreed to stand down.

But at the last minute there was a back-room fight. Melody Ellis announced that she had reassembled the bloc of four votes for Wiley. Rod would have to vote for Paula or his fellow African American, who also happened to be the senior member of the board. Paula was furious and Rod was in a tough spot.

Melody's strategy failed when Paula announced that she would withdraw and support Rod. Melody could not stand the thought of Rod being board president. Wiley, for the second time, withdrew. A few minutes later, Paula was unanimously elected board president. HISD watchers breathed a sigh of relief. It looked like the board of education had come together.

The Board Retreat at Walden Resort

It had not. In anticipation of her election as board president, Paula had planned a board retreat for the next evening. Because Melody Ellis refused to be Ron Franklin's guest at Cat Springs, the board met at Walden Resort on Lake Conroe, an hour's drive north of Houston.

I arrived late. I could hear the shouting even before I entered the room. The board members were sitting on a sofa and easy chairs in a sort of half circle in the living area of a hotel suite. Ron and Melody were going back and forth with insults and accusations. Other board members were breaking in. The issue was not Joan. It was the integrity and good faith of board members.

Finally, after one bitter exchange with Melody, Ron angrily stalked out of the room and returned to Houston. The meeting broke up a bit later with most of us convinced that board unity was impossible.

The next morning, things looked better. Ron returned. Everyone behaved well. And the retreat ended on a fairly positive note.

Such was Paula's initiation to board leadership. As it turned out, she was the perfect choice for board president. She was a healer, and she provided very effective leadership for several complex and sensitive issues.

Redistricting the Board of Education

The redistricting of HISD's nine trustee districts to accommodate the 1990 census data turned out to be a major battle. Operating under the federal Voting Rights Act, HISD was required to draw trustee district boundaries to maximize minority representation on the board. Hispanics wanted the board to turn Paula's seat into a safe Hispanic seat or the Texas Legislature to increase the number of trustee districts from 9 to 11, or maybe even 13.

During the spring of 1991, Paula was in constant negotiations with Hispanic activists, legislators, representatives of the U.S. Department of Justice, and the law firm hired by HISD to assist with redistricting. She and other board members were involved in endless meetings, public hearings, and phone calls and letters to legislators. It soon became clear that even if the board approved grotesque boundaries for all nine districts, it could not create a third safe Hispanic seat. Hispanics were scattered too widely throughout the city. Also, the leadership in the Texas Legislature declined to increase the number of board seats. The compromise results of this complicated and frequently acrimonious controversy was that Paula's seat became significantly more Hispanic.

Paula had always had excellent relationships with Houston's Hispanic leaders. She went regularly to Belize with a humanitarian medical and social service team and she spoke passable Spanish. Paula had always acted in support of Hispanic issues. From this time forward she did her best to act, in effect, as a Hispanic representative.

Board Unity at Last

Paula's second achievement as board president was to bring unity to the board. No dramatic event marked the achievement of board unity. It just emerged gradually. Board members, without Joan Raymond pitting one against another, became ever more friendly.

Felix loved everyone. Wiley carried no grudges. Olga Gallegos, who had consistently supported Dr. Raymond and looked to Melody Ellis for leadership, was an older, quiet woman who seemed happy to put the conflict behind her. Olga's husband, the first Hispanic captain in the Houston Fire Department, had recently died. Later, her son Mario would become the first Hispanic state senator from Houston. Only Melody remained angry. But Melody was irrelevant, and she knew it. She finished out her term, which ended that year, and moved to California.

HIRING A NEW SUPERINTENDENT

Paula's third priority was leading the board in the search for a superintendent who shared our vision. Joan Raymond had warned us that hiring such a person might not be easy.

Problems with the Open Records Act

I did not want a traditional superintendent. An experienced leader from some other walk of life would, I believed, be a more effective reformer. But few of my colleagues shared this opinion, and Texas law required a superintendent to have a superintendent's certificate.

Also, because of the Texas Open Records Act, we were going to have to limit our consideration to candidates willing to have their names made public. Successful superintendents did not usually want their boards to know they were considering a move.

The Open Records Act created a wonderful market for executive search firms. Here is how it worked. The board wrote the job qualifications and described the ideal candidate. The search firm reviewed its files, called its network, and confidentially interviewed candidates. It then presented the board with a short list of candidates who were willing to have their names released to the public. These were either candidates who believed they had an excellent chance of being offered the job or candidates who could afford to be turned down.

Then the interviews and the public scrutiny began. As soon as a candidate decided he or she was not likely to be offered the job, he or she withdrew, citing some personal problem heretofore unmentioned. The board was then left to appoint one of the remaining candidates as the new superintendent.

Sometimes the process worked reasonably well. Sometimes the process did not work at all. The search firm, obliged to produce a politically correct short list, added candidates who were really second drawer. If the first drawer candidates were unacceptable or withdrew, the board was stuck. A second search made nearly everyone angry and seldom attracted strong candidates.

The search process in Houston did not go well, but it was not a disaster. Paula took the lead in identifying and hiring a reputable search firm. The firm assisted us in involving the public in writing the job qualifications. Then, after some searching, the firm brought us four names.

We had asked for a long list of the best candidates in the nation. The search firm insisted, however, that top candidates would not allow their names to be on a long list. So we got a short list. It was also a weak list. But of course, it was politically correct: two whites, one African American, and one Hispanic.[1]

Ethnic Considerations

Now we had to consider the ethnic issue that Joan Raymond had predicted would be problematic, the issue that had so worried some of Houston's business leaders and the *Chronicle* editorial board.

There were strong feelings in both minority communities. Many in the black community believed that, because of the rapidly growing Hispanic population, the next time the superintendency was vacant, it would be filled by a Hispanic. This time it was their turn. Many in the Hispanic community believed that because the HISD enrollment was nearly 50 percent Hispanic, the time had come for a Hispanic superintendent.

For the most part, Houstonians of different races got along fairly well. The tone for race relations was set, to a great extent, by the peaceful desegregation of HISD. There was no violence at the time and little residual rancor. Nevertheless, the experience left black Houstonians justifiably suspicious of white intentions and Hispanic motives.

Whites hung on to a segregated system as long as they could, from 1956, when the first desegregation lawsuit was filed in federal court, until the 1970s, when the court ordered significant rezoning and paired 24 white and black schools. Many whites were outraged. In West Houston some tried to form a breakaway school district. There was also a secession movement in the city of Bellaire, a suburban white enclave in Houston's Southwest. From 1968 to 1973 the white population of HISD dropped from 54 percent (of 245,000 students) to 44 percent (of 225,000 students). In 1981 the percentage of whites was 26 percent.

During the 1960s Hispanics, who were classified by HISD as white but attended mostly Hispanic neighborhood schools, remained silent. But because black and Hispanic neighborhoods were adjacent, the paired elementary schools were mostly attended by black and Hispanic students. Now there were disruptions and boycotts by Hispanics and a request to the court to recognize Hispanics as an "identifiable minority group," and issue a new desegregation order designed to achieve racial balance between the three ethnic groups.

The judge, Ben C. Connally, was not impressed: "Content to be 'White' for these many years, now, when the shoe begins to pinch, the would-be Intervenors wish to be treated not as Whites but as an 'identifiable minority group.' In short, they wish to be 'integrated' with Whites, not Blacks" (*Ross v. Eckels,* May, 24, 1971, p. 8).

By 1991, all this was ancient history. Houston's schools had been integrated to a large extent by a very successful system of magnet schools, and in 1981 the court declared HISD a unitary (integrated) school system and determined that further judicial intervention was unnecessary (*Ross v. HISD,* June 17, 1981).

Nevertheless, the 1970 desegregation decree, with a few very significant amendments, remained imbedded in numerous HISD policies. The school attendance zone boundaries ordered by Judge Connally remained in place. Ethnic considerations continued to dominate every decision. And Houston's African American leaders, many of whom had lived through the desegregation of Houston and HISD, had excellent memories.

Houston's black community was diverse. There were areas that were desperately poor; there were strong and politically active working-class and lower-middle-class communities; and there were large, affluent middle- and upper-middle-class communities, particularly around Texas Southern University, one of the largest, historically black universities in the United States. Politically, the black community was mature, fairly unified, and powerful. African Americans voted in reasonable percentages, and through the black churches, the black vote could be mobilized quickly. If a dozen key pastors and the local chapter of the NAACP agreed on an issue, the rest of the black community would likely support it.

Given the history of HISD desegregation, the rapidly growing Hispanic population, and black political power, many Houstonians wondered how African Americans would respond to the selection of a Hispanic superintendent, or how Hispanics would respond to the selection of a black superintendent.

The Backroom Deal

On June 7, 8, and 9, 1991, the board interviewed the finalists for HISD superintendent and introduced each one in separate receptions to the leading citizens of Houston. One candidate stood out: Frank Petruzielo, associate superintendent in Dade County, Florida.

Petruzielo, a man in his late 40s, exuded energy and self-confidence. Though short, he was a very large man, with thick, wavy, silver hair; a bold, handsome face; and a powerful, beefy handshake. He moved quickly, spoke in a torrent of words filled with colorful metaphors and, because of his size, constant movement, and large gestures, occupied a great deal of space. Frank was quick, articulate, and knowledgeable about every aspect of education.

He began his career as a high school English teacher in Florida, obtained a doctorate in education from Nova University in Fort Lauderdale, and worked his way up the administrative ladder in Dade County Public Schools. He had been the board's chief labor negotiator for several years and most recently had directed the implementation of shared decision-making in 154 Dade County schools, the largest school empowerment reform in the nation.

None of the other three candidates matched Frank. The Hispanic candidate should not even have been on the list. His personal qualities and experience did not even come close to the requirements given by the board to the search firm. Despite the extraordinary efforts of Paula Arnold and Cathy Mincberg to add strong minority candidates to the list of finalists—they had even traveled to California and Washington State to encourage highly regarded minority candidates to apply—this was the best the search firm could do.

Immediately the maneuvering began. The white board members preferred Frank. One Hispanic board member spoke to me glowingly about the Hispanic. The black board members, pointing out that the search firm had brought us a weak list and that Faye Bryant, a black deputy superintendent, was doing an excellent job as interim superintendent, suggested that the search be closed and reopened in six months.

Suddenly the Hispanic candidate withdrew for personal reasons. Some of Houston's Hispanic leaders called Paula. They knew that the pool of qualified Hispanic superintendents was small. They preferred Frank Petruzielo over the alternatives. A backroom deal was in the making. We are willing to support Frank, they said. What can we get in return?

Paula, with help from Cathy and with Ron's approval, handled the negotiations. I was out of town on business, but Cathy called and briefed me. Commitments were made. The deal was sealed. Frank would be HISD's next superintendent. The black trustees knew nothing about these negotiations and were caught by surprise.

The board had previously agreed that no decision would be made until after board members visited the school districts of acceptable candidates. Now this commitment was abandoned. The board offered Frank the superintendency, subject to positive visits by board members to Dade County. Frank Petruzielo had in effect been elected superintendent.

The Hispanic community leaders and board members were pleased. They got a superintendent that seemed to understand Hispanic needs and specific commitments from white board members to support an increase in the number of top-level Hispanic administrators, extraordinary efforts to recruit bilingual teachers, and a new high school in a heavily populated Hispanic part of the city. It was easy for the white board members to make these commitments, because they were things that needed to be done. Subsequently, all the commitments were kept, though the aggressive recruitment of bilingual teachers led to a great scandal in HISD's Alternative Certification Program and the high school is just now being built.

African Americans had reason to be furious. Frank had the votes to be superintendent—that was not the issue. But the board had changed the rules in the middle of the process. And African Americans had been excluded from the deal. They were losing the superintendency and getting nothing in return.

There were a few days of tension and some fiery talk in the black community. However, tensions gradually eased. The black trustees exerted quiet leadership behind the scenes to restore calm. With their help, Frank Petruzielo made all the right comments and symbolically attended a Sunday service in a black church, where he was pictured in the local papers sharing an embrace with one of the leading black pastors of the city and Houston's most famous principal, *PrimeTime* star Thaddeus Lott.

The crisis was over. Petruzielo was formally and unanimously elected superintendent on June 20. The three African Americans on the board expressed their unhappiness with the process, but all of them made complimentary remarks about Petruzielo.

The story of Frank Petruzielo's selection as superintendent is not a pretty one. It demonstrates the ethnic tensions that existed in Houston and on the HISD board. Why, after all, had white and Hispanic board members excluded black board members from the negotiations? Why had they changed the rules in mid-process? Because they feared an open and prolonged process that seemed clearly destined to end with a white superintendent would stimulate protests and agitation by black community activists.

This was my first education in ethnic politics, and I did not like the way I felt. I had betrayed Rod Paige. Supporting Frank Petruzielo's selection was not the issue. I had been openly enthusiastic about Frank from the moment I met him. But I had kept something important from Rod.

Rod was one of the core reformers. He deserved to be in the loop. But because he was an African American, we, the white trustees, had treated him differently. We had given him reason to mistrust us, rationalizing to ourselves that we were doing him a favor by not putting him in the position of knowing something he could not share with the leadership of his community.

We all apologized within days, and Rod graciously accepted our apologies. He never spoke of it again, and I never had any reason to believe that my relationship with him was weakened.

I came away from the experience with a great deal of respect for the black leadership of Houston. They had made their point about the process, but then dropped the issue and graciously accepted the Petruzielo selection. But they did not forget.

EMPOWERING HOUSTON'S SCHOOLS

Frank Petruzielo officially began his superintendency August 31, 1991. It had been a year and a half since our board retreat at Cat Springs. But at last we were poised for action. The board was united. We had a superintendent who said he knew exactly what to do. It was time for another board retreat.

The Right Man for HISD

Once again we went to Cat Springs. It was July. In the ranch country west of Houston, July is hot. We spent a lot of time around the pool. During the day a camera crew from one of Houston's TV stations arrived by helicopter to film the new superintendent. Frank was already a Houston media star.

We talked mostly about school reform. We knew where we wanted to go. Frank said he knew how to get there. *Beliefs and Visions* was at the leading edge of the latest thinking on school reform. We were going to implement what everyone was talking about. Restructuring, alignment, or systemic reform was in. The so-called second wave of school reform had begun. All over the nation the focus of school reformers was shifting from academic standards to structural issues. Houston was going to be a laboratory for the nation.

Almost immediately Frank was everywhere doing everything at once, and always with the widest possible participation. The input of every conceivable stakeholder was solicited before any decision was made. Frank was always establishing standing and ad hoc committees. He was always meeting with people: breakfasts here, lunches there, speeches, conferences. Decision-making was time-consuming. Yet Frank, who had enormous energy, took on everything and finished nearly everything on time.

The contrast with Joan Raymond was striking. Gone was the black Lincoln Town Car and personal chauffeur. Frank asked for a Ford Explorer and drove himself everywhere. In no time he was familiar with all parts of the city. Nearly every day he was in a different HISD school.

The public loved Frank. The newspapers praised his first budget for cutting administrative waste. The staff liked his dynamic personality and participative management. The reformers on the board were excited. After Frank's powerful opening address to principals and other administrators at the Lamar High School auditorium on July 26, I leaned over to Ron Franklin and said, "Let the revolution begin." He grinned. There was no doubt about it. We had hired the right man.

Frank Petruzielo's *Blueprint*

At the heart of Frank's *Blueprint: Houston Schools of Excellence,* as it came to be called, were two interacting restructuring initiatives. At the schools, shared decision-making committees would be established. These committees would develop and implement comprehensive, multiyear school improvement plans focused on improving student achievement. School performance would be reported, along with the results of community surveys, in school report cards. At the same time, a broad-based educational excellence steering committee, coordinating the work of four task forces, would develop and recommend policies to support the schools' improvement initiatives.

Putting together the steering committee was a significant diplomatic victory for Frank. For several years the Greater Houston Partnership, the business elite of Houston, had been studying public education reform. With substantial business money and excellent leadership by Dr. David Gottlieb, an executive with Mitchell Energy Company, the partnership had produced a first-class report. *A Framework for Educational Excellence 1990*, released in April 1990, put forth, with supporting research, 12 principles for student achievement.

Eager to see their recommendations adopted by Houston-area school districts, the partnership had spun off a not-for-profit organization to carry forward the banner of school reform. The organization, the Greater Houston Coalition for Educational Excellence, chaired by Gordon Bonfield, a senior Tenneco, Inc. executive nearing retirement, expected to be a major player in the reform of HISD. Frank could not reject their initiative, but his marching order was *Beliefs and Visions*.

In a wise move that removed a potential conflict and brought into the planning process some of Houston's most informed and committed business leaders, Frank invited the coalition to take joint ownership of the Houston Schools of Excellence Steering Committee. Gordon Bonfield joined Frank as cochair, and a business executive from the coalition board joined an HISD administrator as cochair of each of the four task forces: Attracting, Retaining, and Training the best Teachers, Principals, and other Staff; 21st Century School Facilities and Programs; Partnerships; and Increasing Productivity through Technology and Reduction of Paperwork/Bureaucracy. The steering committee launched a year-long examination of these issues, broken down into scores of specific sub-issues, to prepare policy and resource recommendations for the board.

Shared Decision-Making

The school-empowerment process was formally launched on November 8 and 9, 1991, at Frank's first annual HISD Schools of Excellence Convention. Principals, teachers, and selected parents from every HISD school joined with administrators at the Stouffer's Hotel for two days of planning. Over 2,000 people were in attendance. Working from resource notebooks an inch thick, the school representatives listened to speakers lay out principles and outline assignments. Then they met in groups to discuss implementation.

The priority objective of the convention was to provide training for principals and their school representatives in the structure and process of shared decision-making and the development of school improvement plans. The notebook outlined a straightforward but flexible methodology. Schools were to form a school improvement team, develop a mission statement, and agree on a model for shared decision-making.

The size, membership, name, responsibilities, and operating policies of the shared decision-making committees were not specified, but all shared decision-making committee models had to fit a pattern. They had to describe membership, duties of members, and procedures for voting; establish processes for the establishment of subcommittees; establish processes for communicating with all members of the school community; establish a process for submission of issues by members of the school community; consider decision-making in the area of budget, personnel, and curriculum; and define the areas of use of the administrative veto.

The shared decision-making committee, as soon as it was in place, was to develop a school improvement plan. The plan was to be based on community needs (determined by a community survey), school climate issues (such as clean, safe, and attractive facilities and grounds; student discipline; effective use of technology; staff effectiveness; and parent/community support), and student learning outcomes. The student learning outcomes had to include the nine academic excellence indicators established by state law, which included standardized state tests, graduation rates, academic progress of students with special needs, etc. School improvement plans had to have specific goals, methods of measuring success, and action plans for implementation, including waivers needed from HISD policies and state regulations.

The training was thorough, as far as it went. The notebook included detailed instructions and numerous examples of shared decision-making models and school improvement plans. But there was no training in team building, conflict resolution, and consensus decision-making.

There was much confusion, and the confusion continued for at least a year. Some of the confusion was inevitable. Frank determined that Houston would not implement shared decision-making and school-based management in phases. Every one of Houston's 235 schools would do it at once. And there was no blueprint for schools. Each was free to design its own system, provided certain principles were followed. These turned out to be very wise decisions, and they appealed to the bold reformers on the board, though we did not fully understand or appreciate them at the time.

I learned later that the traditional pattern was to phase in school empowerment a few schools at a time, as Joan Raymond had cautiously planned to do, and give schools significantly more direction. Houston was breaking ground in school empowerment. We were doing it right. Yes, there was confusion at the beginning, but school communities became stakeholders in their shared decision-making systems and began to gain experience in self-management. Change throughout the district reinforced change at each school.

Another reason for confusion was changing state requirements. On December 2, the board approved Frank's *Blueprint;* established the Houston Schools of Excellence Steering Committee, with its supporting task forces; and required the establishment of shared decision-making committees and the development of school improvement plans at every school. Principals were given directives on how to proceed. Then, on February 6, 1992, the board had to change its policies.

To accommodate a reinterpretation of state law by the Texas Education Agency, HISD had to revise its policy to define the membership of school shared decision-making committees. The revised policy specified that the professional staff membership would consist of two-thirds classroom teachers and one-third members of the school-based professional staff. In addition, the school's parent organization would select a minimum of two parent representatives and the principal would appoint a minimum of two community residents. Many of the details regarding elections and terms of service were also specified. Many schools had already formed their shared decision-making committees and were busy developing their school improvement plans. They had to start over.

Frank tried to do things right. Dozens of training sessions on school improvement plans were held throughout the district. Numerous memoranda were sent to principals providing background information, directions, sample school improvement plans, and other useful information. Nevertheless, many schools had to rewrite their school improvement plans. Some had to rewrite them twice.

The process worked like this. School improvement plans were first reviewed by the geographic area superintendents and a small staff from central office who had expertise in personnel, budget, and educational programs. Then the school improvement plan was presented to a large, multirepresentational schools of excellence oversight committee. The oversight committee determined if the school improvement plans were in compliance with district, state, and federal policies, regulations, and guidelines. The committee also reviewed the shared decision-making committee models and all requests for waivers. Imagine all this for 235 schools! Confusion abounded.

At one point board members had to intervene. The original timeline required schools to submit their school improvement plans by April 1. Most schools were not going to make it, and as March passed, cries of pain were coming in from all over the district.

"Frank," some of us said, "we know we told you we wanted everything done yesterday, but you need to slow down." On March 20 Frank sent out a memorandum to all principals extending the deadline to April 27.

School-Based Budgeting

The next step in school empowerment was a new school-based budgeting sys-tem. Heretofore schools had been assigned specific staff positions based on enrollment. Teachers, assistant principals, counselors, librarians, office secre-taries, and other ancillary staff were assigned in increasing numbers as school enrollments reached increasing plateaus. For example, every 500 students brought a counselor to a middle school or high school. Additional dollars were assigned for specific functions, and principals could not transfer funds from one function to another without central office approval.

Principals were not happy with this micro management. Many activists in the minority communities were convinced that the formula favored schools in the white areas of HISD. In addition, over time, all manner of political deals had been made to increase resources at certain schools. Squeaky wheels had been oiled.

In the spring of 1992, while schools were struggling with shared decision-making and school improvement plans, Frank began the budget change process by asking an ad hoc committee of principals and central office administrators to review the formula for determining how many staff posi-tions and dollars a school received and the guidelines for school spending au-thority.

The committee, and subsequent committees in following years, made certain that the allocation formula accounted for all the variables that made individual schools unique. The *Allocation Handbook,* a thick document ap-proved annually by the board, became one of HISD's most important docu-ments.

The *Allocation Handbook* not only improved equity in school funding, it improved flexibility in school spending. Schools were given block grants rather than money for numerous line items and budgets for staff numbers rather than staff positions. Now a principal and shared decision-making com-mittee could transfer money from one function to another without central office approval. They could even trade one position for another, provided there was no incumbent in the position.

The new school-based budgeting system was put into place with numer-ous memoranda to principals, training sessions for principals and shared decision-making committees, and the establishment of budget analyst posi-tions to assist principals in understanding and managing budget transactions. The new budget system was a great success. Most principals not only believed they were being funded fairly, they had much greater authority over how to spend their money. They loved it.

Shared decision-making committees, school improvement plans, and school-based budgeting—these were Frank Petruzielo's three greatest achievements. He implemented them in 235 schools in one year.

A Staunch Advocate for Urban Education

Frank's first year, 1991–1992, was essentially a planning year, and it was chaotic for many schools. But things went much better in 1992–1993. Frank started his second year with another district-wide convention, this one at the George Brown Convention Center. The convention, held on October 9 and 10, was well attended, and most participants were enthusiastic. School leaders had put their shared decision-making committees into place. They had developed school improvement plans. They had significant control over their budgets. They were ready to roll. And indeed 1992–1993 was a year of significant school improvement.

In April 1993 the Texas Education Agency conducted a massive accreditation evaluation of HISD. It was a performance-based accreditation, a new accreditation methodology mandated by the legislature that focused on educational outputs rather than educational inputs. HISD was the first large district to be evaluated under the new accreditation standards. Over 200 educators from the TEA and school districts throughout Texas examined HISD operations and 114 selected schools. It was a period of intense activity.

The accreditation report, released in July, was glowing. "A massive, extensive transformation has occurred in the HISD schools," it said. District and campus improvement plans and school-based shared decision-making were praised. The school-based budgeting system was cited as "an efficient system for decentralizing . . . budgets," and called "innovative" and "effective." Many of the team members indicated that "they would replicate the HISD budgeting system in their school districts."

One statement by an HISD employee, identified as typical of the multitude of unsolicited comments made to the team, was quoted: "The schools have changed more during the past 18 months than during the previous six years."

Positive results on the state-mandated criterion-referenced test, the Texas Assessment of Academic Skills (TAAS) were also praised. "Houston ISD schools are improving and the improvements are systemwide." Seventy-two of the 114 schools visited were cited for improvement in the percentage of students passing all three TAAS tests—reading, writing, and mathematics.

In summary, said the report: "Principals and teachers are fully involved in the transformation of the schools, and campus improvement plans guided by site-based decision making are operational in the schools. Houston ISD schools are positioned to become some of the best schools in Texas and probably in the nation." "HISD is 'winning' its quest to improve student achievement in the schools."

The hero of the report was Frank Petruzielo. His *Blueprint* was praised. He was called "vigorous," "visionary," "a man with firsthand knowledge and application expertise." His responses to questions were called "exemplary." He was, in short, "a staunch advocate for urban education, site-based decision-making, and quality education in an urban setting." "Many, many TSIIs [team members], most of whom were principals, forwarded unsolicited comments to the chair of the visit that indicated . . . they wished they worked for someone like him." (Mora, July 28, 1993; Texas Education Agency, Department of Accountability, July 28, 1993, pp. 56, 61, 147, 149).

Of course all of us were happy to receive good news, especially since the media regularly bashed HISD. Publicly we all rejoiced with Frank. But some board members believed that the accreditation report was the product of a TEA team made up of school administrators and state bureaucrats who, in a very negative climate for public education, had every incentive to make one of their own look good and claim victories wherever they could find them.

By July 1993 some board members were disillusioned with Frank. In the great controversy over his 1992–1993 budget and the struggle for accountability, described in Chapters 3 and 5, Frank had revealed inflexibility, a rough and controlling management style, and a hot temper. Several board members believed they had been treated with disrespect, and one said he had been threatened with assault. A majority of the board believed Frank had fooled the TEA.

I still supported Frank. I had seen his flaws up close, but I was impressed with his achievements and believed he deserved the accolades he received. I knew, however, that Houston's schools had not changed that much. Frank's critics were right about that.

Most schools in my trustee district adapted quickly. Parents were already involved. But throughout HISD, there were many schools that had gone through the motions of school empowerment without changing anything. Though school objectives were now explicit, a new structure for decision-making was in place, and action plans were adopted, parents were still not involved, and action plans were not sharply focused on improving student achievement. Even a year later, by which time thousands of school waivers from state regulations had been approved by the board and passed on to the TEA for approval, board members could not help but notice that few waivers involved issues of real importance.

Except for schools where strong principals and active communities seized control, central office bureaucrats still ruled with an iron hand. Services were still not efficiently delivered to schools. And because of state statutes and district policies, principals still had great difficulty evaluating teacher performance and removing ineffective teachers from their schools.

Much remained to be done. Nevertheless, the empowerment of Houston's schools had begun, and it had begun with a bang. All over the nation systemic reformers were talking about empowering schools. In Houston we were doing it. Every school had a shared decision-making committee. Every school had a school improvement plan. Every school had fairly equal access to resources and significantly more control over its budget. If Joan Raymond had remained superintendent, the board would still have been arguing with her about the need to change.

NOTE

1. Two strong African Americans withdrew their names at the last minute, and a strong Hispanic candidate refused to be considered.

3

The Great 32 Percent Tax Increase

Dr. Petruzielo's second restructuring initiative, developing and implementing the *Blueprint: Houston Schools of Excellence,* failed. The schools of excellence steering committee and four supporting task forces established to develop the *Blueprint* did their work well, but the recommendations crashed in the summer of 1992, a casualty of the fight over a huge tax increase. This battle was the turning point of Frank's superintendency.

DEVELOPING THE *BLUEPRINT*

The Educational Excellence Committee

The committee and the four task forces got off to an excellent start. They were cochaired by an HISD administrator and a business leader. The membership of the task forces was almost perfectly balanced among HISD administrators, principals, teachers, employee organization representatives, parents, business leaders, civic and community leaders, and content experts from business and academia.

The first task force, attracting, retaining, and training teachers, principals, and others, was going to tell the board what needed to be done to provide the children of Houston with effective teachers and principals. The second task force, 21st Century School Facilities and Programs, was going to describe for the board the facilities and programs required for schools of excellence. The third task force, partnerships, was going to design the best possible policies and procedures for building effective school/community partnerships. The fourth task force, increasing productivity through technology and reduction of paperwork/bureaucracy, was going to recommend what HISD needed to do to come into the information age.

Throughout the winter and spring of 1992 the task forces met regularly. Everything seemed to be on track. The task forces would have carefully crafted, coordinated recommendations ready for the board by June. As school communities worked to establish shared decision-making committees and develop school improvement plans, the task forces were preparing the blueprint for transforming the environment in which schools operated.

The *Blueprint* Is Not *Beliefs and Visions*

Everything seemed to be on track, but it wasn't. Frank and the task force leaders were trying to fine-tune the existing structure. They were not trying to change the paradigm. They had failed to grasp the philosophical core of *Beliefs and Visions*.

The board member who first and most clearly recognized this was Rod Paige. Rod was board president in 1992. He had been unanimously elected to replace Paula Arnold on January 16, just a few minutes after two new board members had been sworn in.

Melody Ellis had chosen to vacate her seat. Elected in her place was Arthur Gaines, a retired HISD administrator who had spent his entire career in HISD. Arthur, an African American, was trim and distinguished-looking with a full head of snow-white hair and a warm, friendly smile. Arthur walked slowly, and talked slowly and carefully with perfect diction. His manner was almost courtly.

Arthur had been a teacher, principal, assistant superintendent, and deputy superintendent. He had been one of the first black assistant superintendents in the district and had lived through the long years of desegregation. He had a reputation for being a real operator, a master of the inside bureaucratic game of influence and turf. One thing for certain, Arthur had seen it all.

The other new board member, also an African American, was Carol Mims Galloway. She had defeated Wiley Henry in a very close election. Carol, a long-time community activist and full-time employee of the Houston Federation of Teachers (HFT), was a stout, handsome woman in her early 50s. She dressed sharply, usually in bright colored suits; wore lots of heavy jewelry; and almost always wore, inside and out, heavy plastic sunglasses.

Carol radiated warmth, but she was a tough union infighter. Her job as a union recruiter took her into schools nearly every day. She was plugged in tightly to the internal politics of the district, and her boss, HFT president Gayle Fallon, was the most powerful and politically connected teacher union leader in Houston.

The election of Arthur and Carol significantly changed the dynamics of the board. But it took a while for the new patterns of power to emerge.

Rod began complaining about Frank's *Blueprint* in February. As board president, he was attending some of the meetings of the educational excellence steering committee. He was frequently in attendance when Frank spoke at business, civic, or community luncheons. And, of course, Rod read everything.

"Don," he said to me with increasing frequency and vehemence, "Frank never talks about *Beliefs and Visions*. All he talks about is his *Blueprint*. And his *Blueprint* is not right. It's just traditional 'fix the parts' school reform. It's not systemic change. Frank isn't restructuring HISD along the lines of *Beliefs and Visions*. He doesn't understand."

Rod was right. The *Blueprint* was not bad. It was just not *Beliefs and Visions*. The two were not incompatible. HISD needed everything Frank proposed in his *Blueprint*: trained teachers, adequate facilities, technology, and community partnerships. But with all this, HISD would just be a more effective traditional public school system. *Beliefs and Visions* asked for much more. It demanded accountability, decentralization, a new core curriculum, and a structure and culture that focused everything on the relationship between the teacher and the student. Frank's *Blueprint* proposed to improve the existing system. *Beliefs and Visions* proposed to change it.

Frank had missed the point. This was not surprising. He had spent his entire adult life in public education. He knew how the old system worked, so he set out to make it work better. It was surprising that almost no one noticed. No one on the task forces, to my knowledge, asked the fundamental question, "Are we working on the right issues?" The task force members, like Frank, were stuck in the old paradigm. To my knowledge, only Rod Paige and Cathy Mincberg recognized that Frank's *Blueprint* was incomplete.

Rod and Cathy raised questions, but that was all they could do. The *Blueprint* had been approved by the board on December 12, 1991. No one had asked the right questions then. Now 180 business leaders, parents, and HISD personnel were preparing recommendations for the board. The train was coming down the track.

PETRUZIELO RECOMMENDS A TAX INCREASE

The educational excellence steering committee planned to submit its recommendations to the board on June 18, 1992. Immediately following, Frank intended to present his 1992–1993 budget. To begin the implementation of the recommendations, the budget would ask for a significant increase in spending and local property taxes.

Petruzielo's Strategy

Frank was open and enthusiastic about his strategy. The board would support a large tax increase. We had told him that at Cat Springs the previous July. We knew HISD was underfunded. We saw the needs in the schools. The Coalition for Educational Excellence would also support a large tax increase. They had helped develop the recommendations the tax increase would fund. And the coalition leaders would sell the budget and tax increase to their peers in the business community.

But just as the educational excellence recommendations were coming together, Frank's plan began to unravel. In a board workshop on May 21, Leonard Sturm, the district's chief financial officer, announced that due to reductions in state revenue, the state was withholding $23.5 million promised for 1991–1992 and $50 million promised for 1992–1993. In addition, declining HISD tax rolls would reduce local tax revenue by another $15 million. HISD faced an $89 million shortfall. Even a status quo budget would require a 20 percent tax increase in local property taxes.

The next day's newspapers quoted Frank and Paula Arnold, calling it a crisis. It seemed obvious to board members that Frank would not be able to go forward with his spending plans. We were wrong.

The week of June 8, in preparation for the June 18 board meeting, Frank began sharing his budget plans with board members. The current ad valorum property tax rate was $1.05 per hundred valuation. Frank was going to recommend a 49 cent tax increase to $1.54, 21 cents to replace the $89 million shortfall and 28 cents to fund the educational excellence task force recommendations. We were astounded. A 47 percent increase was unthinkable.

"Don't do it," we said. But Frank was confident. "I've already run this by the business leaders. They'll support it."

What Frank had run by *some* business leaders was his intention to recommend to the board a budget requiring a significant tax increase. But only the Coalition for Educational Excellence leaders knew that Frank was planning to recommend a tax increase of 47 percent. Frank was counting on them to sell his budget to the real powers, the chief executive officers of Houston's largest corporations.

Petruzielo's Strategy Fails

No such luck. During the week of June 15, Frank met with the powers of Houston. The meetings were disasters. Everywhere he went Frank told Houston's leaders what he was going to do and then swept aside their objections.

All week long the telephones rang. Everyone, it seemed, was talking about HISD taxes. Most were angry. Thursday morning Houston's newspapers informed the city in bold headlines that Superintendent Petruzielo intended to recommend to the board a 47 percent increase in local property taxes!

The reaction was predictable. One state representative, conservative Republican John Culberson, called the proposal "outrageous and disgraceful," and said he expected "a genuine taxpayer's revolt in Harris County" (*Chronicle,* June 18, 1992, p. A30).

Frank refused to back down. That afternoon at the board table, he first presented the Educational Excellence Task Force report. HISD suffered from a teacher shortage, excessive teacher turnover, low salaries, and inadequate resources for staff development needs. HISD facilities were overcrowded and many schools were in need of repair. Business/community partnerships with HISD needed to be rationalized and more effectively managed. And HISD was way behind the times in providing information technology for instruction or the conduct of school business. Fifty specific recommendations followed. Almost all cost lots of money.

The task forces had worked hard. Their findings were accurate. Their recommendations were sound. Everything that they said needed to be done, needed to be done. They probably needed to be done in every urban school district in the nation.

Frank's strategy was brilliant, almost. He had invited the Greater Houston Coalition for Educational Excellence to become his partner in school reform. How could they refuse? He had put into play a very participative process. What could be more fair? He had let the data speak for itself, knowing in advance what the outcome would be. Now he was going to let the coalition leaders make the case that HISD needed significant additional resources.

But Frank made one terrible error. Rather than allow the city several weeks to debate the educational excellence recommendations publicly while he privately negotiated with board members and Houston's business elite about the size of the budget and the tax rate, Frank immediately presented his budget. The educational excellence recommendations were lost in the roar of opposition that followed. They were hardly ever mentioned again.

HOUSTON FIGHTS OVER HISD TAXES

Ire against HISD at Fever Pitch

The budget came to $991 million. Frank acknowledged without apology that it would require a tax rate of $1.54 and announced that he would ask the board to approve the budget on July 16.

The city almost exploded. George Scott, now president of the Tax Research Association of Harris County (TRA), said no. The Taxpayers Coalition of Greater Houston said, urge your HISD board member to protest strongly. *The Houston Post* said "Ouch!" (June 19, 1992, p. A26). The *Chronicle* said "Taxpayers should not be fooled" (June 19, 1992, p. C14).

The harshest critics of Frank's budget were state representative John Culberson and businessman Charles Miller. Culberson said he sensed "tremendous outrage" and asserted that the proposed budget would destroy the credibility of trustees and the goodwill Petruzielo had built up during his first year in Houston. He said he would personally organize a tax rollback effort if the board approved the tax increase (*Houston Post*, June 21, 1992, p. A1).

Miller, president and CEO of Transamerica Asset Management Group Inc. and former chairman of the Greater Houston Partnership, had been named in 1989 to chair the Governor's Select Committee on Public Education. He was viewed by most of Houston's business elite as one of the two or three business leaders they could trust to monitor public education and tell them the truth about what was going on. Miller was "outraged," "flabbergasted." He said he might submit an alternative budget for the board to review (*Post*, June 20, 1992, p. A1).

Most board members equivocated. They acknowledged the need, but indicated they would have to check with their constituents before making a decision one way or the other. Only Arthur Gaines said no. Carol Galloway and I said we would likely vote to approve Frank's budget.

I was an enthusiastic supporter of Frank. There was growing evidence that he had a temper problem, and it was true, the *Blueprint* was really not *Beliefs and Visions*. But Frank was putting into place the structure for school empowerment at breakneck speed. Maybe school empowerment was enough for the first year. Accountability—which was at least talked about in the recommendations—decentralization, the core curriculum, and the rest would be next year's priorities.

Meanwhile, I could not argue with any of the educational excellence recommendations. So Frank had rejected my advice to recommend a lower tax rate. So he had rushed his budget recommendation. The battle had been joined. I believed Frank needed support.

On June 21 I made the case for the tax increase in an op-ed in the Sunday *Chronicle* (p. E1). HISD had low administrative expenses, and they were going down. HISD had a very low tax rate and low per pupil expenditures; and in spite of tax increases totaling 54 percent since 1987–1988, HISD spending per student in constant dollars had increased less than 1 percent per year. HISD needed $89 million just to replace a shortfall in promised state aid and local tax revenue. HISD facilities needed an additional $11 million for such things as heating, ventilation, air conditioning, roof repairs, drainage, resurfacing, painting, vehicle and heavy equipment repair, etc. HISD also needed an additional $28 million to staff six new schools and cover increases in health insurance, utility and transportation expenses, and other operating expenses over which it had little control.

This $128 million would not move HISD forward; it would keep HISD from falling backward. Frank wanted to move forward. He wanted an additional $50 million to pay teachers in the upper range for Texas school districts. And he wanted $30 million to strengthen academic programs.

The next Sunday, July 5, Charles Miller took his shot at the proposed budget in a *Chronicle* op-ed (p. E1). He called it "incredible" and "unconscionable." The tax increase, he said, would hurt the economy, which was still recovering from the oil bust depression of the 1980s, and in any case, HISD could not effectively use that much new money. "Even well-run organizations cannot absorb and effectively manage huge, immediate increases in revenues."

Two state representatives, John Culberson (R) and Ron Wilson (D) wrote a letter to the assistant state auditor requesting an audit of HISD because they did not believe HISD had actually reduced administrative positions by nearly 300 in the 1991–1992 budget.

A group of Hispanic activists opposed the budget because they believed it did not direct sufficient funds to predominantly Hispanic schools. They charged that Frank became defensive and arrogant when they questioned him about district priorities.

Even the employee groups began to back away from the proposed budget. HFT President Gayle Fallon said the salary schedule, which gave beginning teachers the largest raises, showed how little Frank cared about experienced teachers. Houston Association of School Administrators Executive Director Irene Kerr said that the small raises for central office administrators was unfair.

Meanwhile individual board members were scheduling public meetings throughout the city to obtain direct input from voters. Everywhere angry crowds blasted Frank's budget proposal.

Late in the afternoon of July 2, the full board held a public hearing. It was a circus. A capacity crowd, mostly hostile, cheered while taxpayer after taxpayer told the board that the proposed tax increase was exorbitant, that money alone wouldn't solve the problems of public education, that HISD wasted too much money on administration, that HISD was stealing from the working men and women of Houston, and so forth. A fair number of parents and HISD employees spoke in support of the tax increase. Most were jeered at, some were insulted. The front page headline in the next day's *Chronicle* was "Ire against HISD at fever pitch."

Within a few days the newspaper editorial boards hit HISD again. The *Post* called the tax increase a "terrible idea." It was "ill-timed" and "divisive," and would lead to a rollback referendum if the board approved it (July 4, 1992, p. A28). The *Chronicle* essentially repeated Charles Miller's arguments: there was insufficient accountability for performance improvement in Petruzielo's plan; the HISD bureaucracy could not wisely spend that much new money in one year; and HISD had a rich property tax base of business and commercial property and did not need a tax rate as high as the suburban school districts to raise the same amount of money per student (July 5, 1992, p. E2).

Somehow the *Chronicle's* editorial board had missed the fact that under the state's new school finance law having high property value was no longer an advantage. A penny of tax effort yielded approximately the same amount of money per student regardless of a school district's property value. Also, Frank was not proposing a huge increase in program spending. Spending would go up 20 percent, and much of that would go into pay raises for teachers and principals.

Shortly after Frank had presented his budget recommendations, Paula Arnold and Arthur Gaines suggested that increased taxes and spending be phased in over several years. The July 5 editorial in the *Chronicle* made the same recommendation, and within a few days several school board members concurred. The partnership was also known to be in support of a three-year phase in.

Also, talk of a rollback referendum was growing. Under state law, school districts were allowed to raise taxes by 8 percent without risking a rollback referendum. The base for calculating the percentage increase was the previous year's tax rate, adjusted for increases required to offset state funding losses, changes in the state school finance law, and lost property value.

No one knew for certain what tax rate would trigger a rollback option. Harris County property values would not be certified until the fall. The best guess was about $1.34. So, if HISD raised taxes to more than $1.34, plus or minus four or five cents, 10 percent of the qualified voters could sign a petition calling for a rollback referendum. Tax increase opponents were confident they could get the required signatures.

It was clear to nearly everyone that the $1.54 budget was dead. Still, Frank would not budge. He told the press: "I'm going to recommend what I think is right and what we need in order to be a good school system. If for any reason the board believes it is in the best interest of the public to move in a different direction, I'm going to work with them as cooperatively as I know how" (*Chronicle*, July 10, 1992, p. A1).

The last week before the scheduled vote a few voices came forward with op-eds in support of Frank's budget. The strongest case was made by Tom Friedberg. Friedberg was cochair of the educational excellence task force on partnerships, a member of the board of the Houston Coalition for Educational Excellence, chairman and president of Ranger Insurance Company, and a long-time volunteer in one of HISD's middle schools.

His article was long and packed with data. It refuted, in my opinion, every point made by Charles Miller, George Scott, the newspaper editorials, and others. It also made the case for funding urban schools (*Chronicle*, July 12, 1992, p. G1).

But all Friedberg's numbers meant nothing to most people. Only one number had stuck in the public's mind: 47 percent. Board members knew that if they approved Frank's budget, taxpayers would revolt.

As the *Chronicle* put it in yet another editorial on the HISD budget, "If the HISD trustees defy the obvious strong opposition to such an enormous increase, the schools stand to lose that which they must have—the public's support" (July 10, 1992, p. A28).

The *Chronicle* was right. Whatever the need, regardless of the fact that Houston's suburban school districts were raising property taxes into the $1.60 to $1.80 range with little or no apparent opposition, the people of Houston would not support a significant tax increase for HISD.

Petruzielo's First Budget Rejected

On Tuesday morning, July 14, the partnership board finally spoke. They wanted consideration of the budget delayed. They asked HISD to adopt a three-point program emphasizing annual student performance goals, administrative accountability, and consequences for not meeting objectives. And they called for noninstructional expenses to be cut.

Board president Rod Paige, who had carried a tremendous burden as the link between Frank, board members, the partnership, and other centers of power, immediately called board members to share this information and count the votes. They weren't there. The front page headline in next morning's *Chronicle* read: "HISD board will not back Petruzielo's tax hike." Frank called the partnership decision "real unfortunate."

Knowing how the board would vote, Rod urged Frank to withdraw his budget. Frank refused. Let the board take the responsibility for the continued neglect of HISD facilities, a lower teacher pay raise, and fewer new academic programs, he said. And then let the board tell him where to cut.

So we voted. Frank's budget was rejected eight to one. The only yes vote was mine.

"I am disappointed for the children because what was brought to the table was responsible, and it was needed," Frank told the media. "However, I'm not daunted" (*Chronicle*, July 17, 1992, p. A1). The next day he left town for a previously scheduled two-week vacation.

Petruzielo's Second Budget Rejected

The $1.54 tax rate was dead, but the budget battle was not over. The lead story on the evening news and in the next day's newspapers was that though the board had rejected the 47 percent tax increase, a large tax increase was still unavoidable. Olga Gallegos and Carol Galloway said they would support $1.47. Rod Paige predicted it would be $1.40 or slightly more. Ron Franklin said he would not go below $1.34. Paula Arnold, who was very close to the business leaders, put out the lowest number. She said $1.32 might be enough.

For two weeks everyone in Houston took a vacation from the HISD budget. Then Frank returned. This time he was going to do it right. This time he would take advice from business leaders, employee group representatives, and board members. Meetings were scheduled with everyone.

"Look," he said in his individual conversations with trustees, "I'm not stupid. I lost once. I don't want to lose again. This time, you tell me in advance your spending priorities and exactly what tax rate you'll support. I want to be absolutely certain that the budget I recommend is approved."

A consensus emerged fairly quickly. The board would support an all funds budget of $953 million, which would require a tax rate of $1.44. Employee pay raises would be, on average, 10 percent rather than 13 percent, but with a salary schedule that would satisfy the employee groups. Another $20 million would be saved by dropping summer school and cutting back after school programs, technology, and planning and training costs for school communities.

Board support was not unanimous. Paula Arnold and Arthur Gaines opposed going over the rollback rate, which was still assumed to be about $1.34. But Frank had commitments from everyone else.

The budget was officially unveiled on Monday, August 10. Frank announced that a public hearing on the budget would be held on Thursday, August 13, after which he would ask for the board's approval.

At the same time he announced that, in response to the calls for accountability from the partnership, school and employee accountability would be HISD's highest priority. HISD would begin publishing an annual progress report on every school and every classroom. A blue-ribbon committee would be formed to review the reports and recommend schools to be recognized for outstanding progress or for intervention by a team of administrators and teachers. And employee groups had agreed to work with the district to develop a teacher evaluation system that would link a teacher's evaluation to improved student performance.

The reaction to Frank's revised budget was swift. TRA president George Scott complained that Frank had failed to set aggressive performance goals as promised. He called the budget "continued mediocrity." The partnership issued a statement saying they were "firmly opposed," citing lack of performance objectives and long-term planning (*Post,* August 12, 1992, p. A1). The *Post* called it a "break-the-taxpayer increase" (August 12, 1992, p. A18). The *Chronicle* said it was a "railroad job" (August 12, 1992, p. A20).

Board support collapsed immediately. Rod counted noses and determined that Frank did not have the votes for $1.44. The public hearing and budget presentation to the board scheduled for Thursday were canceled. Frank announced that he would present a third budget to the board for consideration on August 27.

Frank felt betrayed. Publicly he said the criticism of the TRA and the partnership was a "significant disappointment." He pointed out that HISD was doing more than any other school district in Harris County on the issue of accountability and proposing a tax rate 20 cents or more below the average Harris County rate. Claims of poor accountability, he said, masked the real reason the two business organizations opposed the budget. They just didn't want to pay the taxes (*Post*, August 12, 1992, p. A1).

Privately, he wondered what had happened to the board. Had they not committed themselves to $1.44?

Petruzielo's Third Budget Accepted

The newspapers reported that same day that Dallas had raised its tax rate from $1.29 to $1.39. Austin's rate was going up from $1.47 to $1.56. And San Antonio trustees were considering a budget that would raise the rate from $1.41 to $1.51.

By now it seemed obvious to many that the partnership would, in effect, set the tax rate for HISD. The magic number for them, it appeared, was some where between $1.32 and $1.35.

My parent activists were furious. Who were these men, all rich, almost all white, mostly residents of the suburbs, men who sent their own children to private or suburban schools and had no complaints with suburban tax rates of $1.60 to $1.80? Who gave them the authority to set the tax rate for HISD's poor, minority children? Who elected them? What was the matter with board members? Had they no guts?

Employee groups were also furious. Were board members puppets whose strings ran downtown to the partnership?

Frank did not have much time. School was starting in a few days. By law, school district budgets had to be approved by September 1.

Within a few days Frank made a decision. Rather than reduce spending further, he decided to revise upwards estimated revenue from local property tax and dip into HISD's reserve funds. There were risks in this, but it appeared that HISD's tax rolls were nearly $1 billion higher than the original estimate by the Harris County Appraisal District, and Joan Raymond had always maintained a healthy reserve in HISD's fund balance.

On Tuesday, August 25, Frank held a press conference to present his third and last budget. The tax rate was $1.385, an increase of 32 percent. Projected spending was $954 million, an increase of 13 percent. HISD would have an additional $90 million: $40 million for employee pay raises that averaged 10 percent, over $10 million for deferred maintenance at schools, and virtually all of the rest for academic programs.

The TRA and the partnership immediately announced that the tax rate was still too high. They believed noninstructional spending could be cut sufficiently to get the tax rate down to $1.34. The *Chronicle* said the budgetary process was "miserable." The superintendent and board had shown an "arrogant disregard of the public." And thanks only to the partnership, there was some progress in setting out performance standards (August 27, 1992, p. B18).

This time, however, the board was prepared to stand with Frank. Parents and employee groups were exerting tremendous pressure on board members to support $1.385, and calculations by finance chief Leonard Sturm indicated that $1.385 (the number actually turned out to be $1.384) would place the tax rate below the rollback referendum trigger point.

The public hearing on the revised budget was on Thursday afternoon, August 27. Again the board chamber was full. Again there was cheering and heckling. But this time supporters of the budget outnumbered opponents three to one. And this time the board approved the budget by a vote of nine to zero. There was thunderous applause, mixed with boos and hisses.

Frank, who was clearly relieved, said he would not recommend another tax increase until the public acknowledged measurable improvement in student achievement. "We'll deliver," he promised (*Post*, August 28, 1992, p. A1).

The great tax battle was over. The taxes paid by the owner of a $100,000 home would go up $251 per year, but HISD would still have a tax rate 20 cents below the average for Harris County school districts, and weighted HISD per student spending would still lag $270 per year behind the county average. The Houston economy would not collapse under the weight of this additional tax burden, as critics had predicted, and there would not be another tax increase for six years.

Petruzielo and the Powers of Houston

The tax battle of 1992 left Frank with wounds from which he never recovered. It was the defining moment of his superintendency. Up until June 1992 he had been popular. He had been praised for his first budget because 300 administrative positions were cut and the tax increase of 5 cents was lower than expected. He was the new superintendent who was going to empower school communities, decentralize the district, introduce accountability, and significantly improve student performance. Television viewers saw him regularly on the evening news. He was articulate, energetic, full of ideas.

Only the insiders saw his inflexibility, his temper, and his ego. These personal flaws contributed not a little to the negative blast that greeted his first budget. Employee groups, who had the most to gain, were not supportive. HFT president Gayle Fallon accused him of stonewalling. Lee Barnes, Houston Education Association director, said Frank insulted people who disagreed with him (*Chronicle*, July 19, 1992, p. D1). And most board members, none of whom felt any ownership of the budget, spent the summer reflecting public opinion rather than trying to shape it.

Frank had also turned off TRA president George Scott long before his first budget was announced. They had engaged in a shouting match in Frank's office, and Frank openly referred to Scott as a loose cannon.

Finally, Frank alienated many of Houston's business elite. As some of them reported to me later, he did not try to sell his budget to them by presenting HISD's needs and asking for advice. Rather, he informed them what he was going to do and asked if they had any questions. When some of them challenged his views, he dismissed them as uninformed. As Rod Paige, who was privy to some of the key meetings between Frank and business leaders, told me, "Frank's problem is that he always thinks he's the big elephant. He doesn't recognize that no matter how big an elephant he is, sometimes he's not the biggest elephant in the room."

Frank's relationships with the power brokers of Houston, which had never been warm, turned to ice the week of June 15, 1992. From that week onward, Frank was privately despised by some of the most powerful men in the city. What Charles Miller said openly, most of them said privately. The newspaper editorial boards followed suit, giving everyone license to treat Frank with ridicule and scorn. His popularity bounced back somewhat, but never fully recovered.

The tax battle of 1992 showed Frank at his best and worst. He was courageous and tough. He was also arrogant, unable to take advice, and unlucky. If HISD had not faced an $89 million shortfall, Frank could have obtained all he wanted for HISD with a tax rate of $1.33. For all his personal flaws and strategic mistakes, that might have been doable. Fortune was against him.

Frank's view of all this was that he didn't play politics. He told people, all people, the truth about what was right for Houston's children. As he told the press following the rejection of his first budget, "I didn't play the game on this budget." "The definition of 'political' in this town is asking people, and then following their advice. I am not able to do that. In this job, I have to recommend what I think is right. If the board supports it, that's fine. If they don't support it, I'm going to roll with the punches and be a professional and do the best I can" (*Chronicle*, July 19, 1992, p. D1).

Frank was right about one thing. In Houston, the superintendent traditionally sought the advice of the business leaders first and then proposed to the board what the business leaders recommended. In Houston, power was diffused, but business leaders were the primary power brokers. They funded candidates for elective office and they expected to be heard when their interests were at stake. Homeowners paid only 30 percent of HISD's taxes. Business paid the rest. Historically, business leaders had determined how much they would pay, and historically, they had kept HISD's tax rate low.

Houston Education Association Director Lee Barnes, an African American, spoke for many school people when he said, "I think personally, the Greater Houston Partnership—a bunch of Anglo men—is not going to vote to support additional moneys to educate African American and Hispanic students. That's the bottom line, you know. If it were out in Cy-Fair or Clear Creek, they would be digging in their pockets, handing out more money" (*Chronicle*, August 26, 1992, p. A1).

The great tax battle of 1992 was not Frank Petruzielo's finest hour. It was not a very good hour for anyone else, either.

4

Neighborhood Wars

There were nine HISD trustees. Each one of us was expected by our constituents to represent his or her interests. Most of the parent activists in the district I represented supported my efforts to reform HISD. They were interested in vision statements, the goings and comings of superintendents, board unity, budget and tax issues, and especially new district policies that affected their schools. They understood that reforming HISD would take time.

But most parents saw school reform in terms of their child, their school, their neighborhood, this year. Not surprisingly, parents did not always agree with the school's assessment of their child's needs. Sometimes parents disagreed among themselves about what was best for their school. And what was good for one school or neighborhood was not necessarily perceived as good for another.

CONSTITUENT SERVICE

Trustee District Five

My trustee district, District Five, was in southwestern Houston and included West University Place, Southside Place, and Bellaire, three small adjacent cities completely surrounded by the city of Houston. The population of District Five in 1990 was about 125,000 people: 72 percent white, 17 percent Hispanic, 7 percent African American, and 4 percent Asian.

Within District Five were some very upscale neighborhoods, some that were solid middle class, many older working-class homes, and lots of large apartment blocks. Most of the apartments were along the northern and western edge of the district. They were filled with new immigrants from Central America, sometimes with several families to an apartment unit.

There were two major demographic trends affecting schools in District Five. One was the gentrification of West University Place, Southside Place, and Bellaire. Young professional families were buying small, old houses on prime lots and replacing them with large, expensive homes. Many of these families had young children. The result was growing enrollments in neighborhood schools.

The second trend was a rapidly growing population of mostly poor Central Americans in the north and west that was overcrowding schools—one elementary school had over 1,300 students. When Hispanic enrollments reached 50 percent or more, neighborhood whites began seeking other educational options for their children.

Located in District Five were one high school, four middle schools, and 17 elementary schools. These schools served about 22,000 students, of whom about 36 percent were Hispanic, 32 percent white, 25 percent African American, and 7 percent Asian.

Most of these schools were excellent, among the best in Texas. Bellaire High School, with about 2,900 students, was one of the finest high schools in the nation. Every year students from Bellaire won national awards and 30 to 40 seniors were selected as National Merit Scholar Finalists. In the main, the schools were clean and well managed. Teachers cared about students. Parents were involved. And test scores were excellent.

Nearly every school community in District Five had an agenda. Most wanted more money for their school. HISD was seriously underfunded. The public believed that schools had enough money, but public school parents knew better. Their schools needed stage curtains, hot water in the boys' shower room, sidewalks, new air-conditioning systems, new roofs, and more temporary buildings or entire wings. Many wanted additional teachers for academic enrichment—Suzuki violin or foreign language study, for example. Some school communities didn't like their principals. Others were upset about a particular teacher.

Constituent Complaints

As board member for District Five, it was my responsibility to respond to the needs of these communities and the dozens of individual constituent complaints that came in monthly.

"My child has been missed by the school bus three days in a row."

"My child deserves an A in Dance but has been given a C because the teacher is prejudiced against Irish folk dancing."

"HISD has not provided my child with speech therapy as required by federal law."

"My child's history teacher has covered only half of the textbook this semester."

"A teacher watched and did nothing as my white middle school girl got roughed up in the hallway by a much larger black girl."

"The girls' track coach won't let my daughter compete in an upcoming track meet."

"HISD refuses to place my child in a gifted program because of racial bias."

"My child's calculus class is being taught, in effect, by the smarter students in the class because the teacher is incompetent."

And on and on and on.

Many complaints were valid. Some were not. Most parents were polite. Some were rude. Occasionally there were threats.

Constituent service was time-consuming and sometimes frustrating. When HISD employees were not doing their jobs, a quick call to the superintendent would usually get results. But if extra dollars were needed, I almost always failed. Every school had needs. Other trustees were sure to object if one of *my schools* appeared to be getting more than its fair share.

Personnel issues were also out of my control. By law, personnel was the responsibility of the superintendent. Superintendents, and superintendents alone, could recommend persons for employment or termination. Boards of education could only approve or disapprove. All I could do with constituent complaints about employees was pass on to the superintendent what I was hearing and make an attempt to evaluate the credibility of the source.

Sometimes it was clear that a principal did not have the confidence of his or her community. What then? Key parents would begin to call me or take me out to breakfast or lunch. Organized letter-writing campaigns would generate scores of letters.

Parent activists were persistent. For several years the leadership of one elementary school was a group of five women I called "the gang of five." They did everything together. For a period of almost a year they scheduled frequent breakfasts with me at the Bellaire Coffee Shop to remind me kindly but firmly of the 20 reasons why they wanted a new principal. It got to the point where we could order breakfast for each other.

My standard course of action when a principal was under fire was to urge parents to communicate their concerns directly to the area assistant superintendent, the principal's boss, and the superintendent. I would also pass on directly to the superintendent what I was hearing. Nine times this happened. Nine times principals were moved. Eight times communities were happy and I was given credit I did not deserve.

But there was one spectacular failure. It was the forced retirement by Joan Raymond of Myrtle Lee Nelson, a popular Bellaire High principal. It led to a firestorm and a petition with over 6,000 signatures to the board of education demanding the reinstatement of Ms. Nelson. The board stood with Joan— under Texas law it really had little choice—and the retirement stuck. But the legacy was bitterness in Bellaire for years.

WHAT WENT WRONG AT THE RICE SCHOOL?

Project Renewal

Overcrowding was a citywide problem. A dozen or so new schools were needed, mostly in Hispanic areas. Also, because HISD had deferred maintenance on its schools, many schools needed such essentials as new roofs, new air-handling systems, and other renovations to comply with building codes. To meet the most pressing needs, the voters of Houston had approved a bond issue of $300 million in March 1989. This money would fund Phase A of a two-phase construction project named Project Renewal. The voters would be asked to approve bonds to fund Phase B in four or five years.

Many of the schools in District Five were scheduled to receive significant amounts of money for Phase A of Project Renewal. But what should have been a source of satisfaction became for many schools a source of frustration. Those schools that were scheduled for renovations were frequently disappointed. They received roofing, air handling, plumbing, and other repairs that were difficult to see. The school communities had supported the bond election, believing they would receive enough money to make a difference in their schools. But two years and one million or more dollars later, many schools still looked old and small.

District Five was scheduled for two major projects. The first, an $11 million classroom wing for Bellaire High School to replace numerous temporary buildings, generated some controversy. The second, a new school to relieve overcrowding at, mostly, West University Elementary, set off a series of controversies that continue to this day.

Selecting a Site for the School

What made the establishment of the relief school problematic was the decision made by Joan Raymond and George Rupp, then president of Rice University, to make the school a laboratory school affiliated with nearby Rice University. It was a great idea. But once the school acquired a second agenda it became a battleground.

First, to accommodate Rice University, which did not have a traditional teacher education program and did not prepare teachers for elementary teaching, the school became a K–8 school. A K–8 school required more land and more money, and for almost 18 months there was controversy over where the school should be built.

One potential location, just west of West University Place in the city of Bellaire, angered many Bellaire residents. They objected to a school being built in their city that would serve many West University children and maybe not have much space for them. At a town hall meeting in Bellaire on October

4, 1991, a large, angry crowd gave me a hostile reception unequaled by any I have had during my years on the board. What really made people angry was that large portions of Bellaire were zoned to two mostly Hispanic elementary schools north and west of Bellaire. "Bellaire residents," said speaker after speaker, "should be zoned to Bellaire schools."

The land that was finally purchased for the new school, an acceptable but not ideal site south of West University Place in the Mark Twain Elementary attendance zone, upset the Mark Twain community. Mark Twain was small, old, and in poor repair. It was scheduled to receive $1 million plus from Project Renewal for renovations. The Mark Twain community wanted to use this money and the $5.7 million needed to buy the identified property to build the new school on the Mark Twain site. This would save HISD money and give them a beautiful new school.

The Mark Twain community made a good case. They had done a lot in previous years to improve their school and currently were involved in an ambitious multimillion dollar redevelopment project to replace aging apartments around the school with a recreational and learning corridor.

But the Mark Twain site was too small for a large K–8 school. West University parents by the hundreds were making it absolutely clear that they would under no circumstances accept the Mark Twain location. And a new school on the Mark Twain site would result in a net loss of 500 desks for Southwest Houston. The site selection committee and the board said no.

The next challenge was getting the board to approve the contract for the property. Nearly $6 million was a lot of money to spend for property for a K–8 school. In other parts of Houston $6 million would buy property and almost build a school. One minority board members suggested HISD build the school where property was less expensive and bus children from West University Place. Most of the others voiced their concern that this expensive school would serve only rich, white children.

Again and again I argued that the rich children were no less deserving of a neighborhood school than poor children. Again and again I pledged that the school would be ethnically balanced and serve children from every trustee district in HISD. Now the school had a third agenda.

Planning and Opening the School

Planning began almost immediately. HISD officials, Rice professors, and over 100 parents and community leaders from all over the city began meeting regularly to decide what should happen in the new school. What should students be taught? How should students be taught? What were appropriate roles for parents, teachers, Rice faculty? How should the school be governed? In the end, the committee produced a magnificent plan.

The school was to offer dual language instruction in Spanish and English, multigrade classes grouped in clusters that would allow children to learn at their own speed and move easily from one grade level to another, mathematics as the unifying theme in the curriculum, intensive application of information technology in all instructional and administrative activities, school uniforms, and underlying everything a commitment to broad participation in decision-making.

Building on these ideas, the architects submitted a brilliant design. Stories and pictures began to appear in the press. People began to talk about the school. Unfortunately many people, especially in West University Place, assumed that because Rice University was involved, the school would be a selective admissions school for the gifted and talented.

By early 1993, the big question was, Who would get to go to the new school? Some West University parents were wondering if there was still going to be room for them.

The school opened, at last, in August 1994. Over 7,000 students applied for the 1,300 positions. A very complex process was used to select the students for admission. Random selections were made by grade level, attendance zone address, ethnicity, and other criteria.

There was enormous controversy as soon as the process was announced and then again when the names were chosen. Parents in an older, affluent community just to the east of the school were angry because their children did not have access to the school except through the citywide lottery. Private school parents were angry because, except for students in kindergarten and sixth grade, the first grade of middle school, only students currently enrolled in HISD were eligible for admission. Leaders from some of the neighborhood schools were angry because the new school had pulled more students from their schools than they had anticipated. Principals from nearby schools were angry because the new school appeared to be getting extra resources. Many parents were angry because Rice University had been guaranteed eight desks per grade level for the children of Rice employees. And there were charges that the lottery was fixed and so-and-so got in because of backroom influence.

Gradually the controversy subsided and The Rice School/La Escuela Rice: an HISD School for Professional Development, as it was officially named, began to settle down to the routine of teaching and learning. The start-up principal, Kaye Stripling, was a talented and experienced HISD administrator. She had recruited a school full of HISD's best teachers. Most parents were delighted. Soon after school opened, *Texas Monthly* named Kaye Stripling one of 20 most influential Texans. The Rice School was "an oasis in the desert of public education," the triumph of an individual principal who had heroically overcome the dead hand of a broken and ineffective bureaucracy (Swartz, 1994, p. 102).

What Went Wrong at the Rice School

But there were problems. Dr. Stripling was not able to complete the first year. In the spring, she was unexpectedly promoted to a district superintendency. The relationship with Rice was not working well. Some African American parents charged that black students were not being treated fairly. A group of angry, mostly white parents complained that multigrade classrooms were not working. Their children, most of whom performed above grade level, they said, were being held back by children performing below grade level. Other parents said that instruction in mathematics was inadequate.

Under the leadership of a new principal, the second year went fairly well, but at the end of the third year there was an explosion. The problems of the first year had not been resolved. Affluent white parents from West University Place were pulling out by the hundreds. The rain forests and the whales admittedly were important, they said, and everyone recognized that diversity was a priority; but reading, writing, and arithmetic were being neglected. Many minority parents complained that West U. parents were trying to run the school and that they were treated like outsiders. Nearly everyone agreed that the bold curriculum called for by the planners was either not in place or not working well.

Meanwhile the partnership with Rice had almost completely collapsed. Rice, under a new president, was a cautious partner at best. And in numerous ways—some subtle, some not so subtle—the HISD bureaucracy made it clear that the Rice School was an HISD school. Rice would be tolerated. It would not be embraced.

Something had to be done. In June 1997, the superintendent announced that he was changing the entire leadership team at the school and placing the school in the alternative district, the management unit responsible for HISD's special purpose and citywide magnet schools. He also dispatched the district's chief education officer to begin discussions with Rice University on ways to strengthen the partnership between Rice and HISD.

There was a huge cry of outrage from hundreds of Rice School parents. Most of the dissatisfied parents had pulled their children out of the school. Most of those who were left were reasonably satisfied. Almost all of them loved the principal, a wonderful woman who had served with distinction in her previous assignment.

For a few weeks everyone was talking about the failure of the Rice School. Who was to blame for the mess? "What Went Wrong at the Rice School?" trumpeted the headline on a cover article in the *Houston Press*. There were a dozen answers. The three that stood out were the school's multiple agendas, unreasonable expectations by parents, and student diversity.

The school was roughly one-third Anglo, one-third Hispanic, and one-third African American. But ethnicity was not the issue. Many HISD schools were ethnically balanced. The issue was class. Other HISD schools with city-wide enrollments had admission standards. The Rice School did not. Because family income correlates with student performance, the other schools, in effect, favored middle-income minorities over poor minorities. But at the Rice School there was a combustible mix of affluent whites and largely middle- or low-income blacks and Hispanics.

"It wasn't just diversity in terms of ethnic and racial differences," said Richard Tapia, a professor of computational science and applied mathematics at Rice University and an active Rice School parent. "All of a sudden, the differences were greatly magnified by the parts of town they came from. That's what was hard to handle." The gulf between affluent, privileged children from West University Place and crosstown children from low-income neighborhoods was extraordinarily difficult to bridge in mixed-age classes (Fleck, 1997, p. 17).

In September 1997 a new principal was hired and negotiations were under way with Rice to strengthen the partnership with HISD. The superintendent and board were not going to back away from the original plan: dual language instruction, multigrade classes, mathematics as the unifying theme in the curriculum, and intensive application of information technology. For all its critics, the Rice School had not failed. It was magnificent in many ways. But it had not met our great expectations. We were going to try again.

Someday someone will write a book about the Rice School. Its story captures almost every dynamic of urban education: neighborhood rivalries, board politics, teaching and learning issues, school and district management issues, resource issues, the challenges of school partnerships, parents struggling to find what is best for their children, and issues of race and class. Let us all hope the book has a happy ending.

CHANGING SCHOOL ATTENDANCE ZONES

Within a few months of my election to the board, I knew that attendance zone boundaries in District Five were a problem. Nearly every school community was dissatisfied, and for good reason. Except for one or two minor changes, the school attendance zones ordered by the court in September 1970 as part of the desegregation of HISD had not changed. Twenty years previously neighborhoods had been divided to maximize integration. For 20 years neighborhoods had wanted to be reunited.

In addition, Houston had changed. Many communities had been transformed. New ones had come into being. Numerous major thoroughfares and interstate highways had been built. The geography and demographics of Houston had changed almost beyond recognition.

Soon after my election to the board, I suggested to Joan Raymond that attendance zone boundary lines needed to be redrawn.

"I won't touch attendance zones boundaries with a 10-foot pole," she responded. "I did that once in Yonkers, and it was the worst experience of my life. Never again."

Frank Petruzielo's arrival provided the opportunity to try again. Frank was willing to take on anything. He readily agreed with board members that the time had come to examine the attendance zones, not just for new schools being built, but for all of Houston's schools. He began at once.

By November 1991 an attendance boundary committee was at work. Nearly 100 parents and community leaders from all over the city were meeting with HISD officials to review the desegregation of Houston's schools and the establishment of existing attendance zones; review student transfer policies; examine data on enrollment, school capacity, and demographic projections; and look at maps.

Meyerland Wants Bellaire High

Then, almost overnight, there was panic in Meyerland, a large, prosperous white community just to the south of Bellaire High. Frank wanted to align elementary, middle, and high school attendance zones so that as much as possible all students from any given elementary school would attend the same middle school and middle school students would move together as a group into high school. Improving the purity of feeder patterns, in the jargon of school people, would keep student and parent communities together from grades K through 12, facilitate curriculum alignment, and provide management units that could be held accountable for results.

Shortly before Christmas a document labeled "draft," which showed what attendance zones would look like if a pure feeder pattern system were put into place, was distributed to the committee. The document showed Meyerland being moved from Bellaire High to Westbury High. Bellaire was one of the crown jewels of HISD. Westbury was not.

Meyerland panicked. For a decade or more, Meyerland had lived in fear that one day it would be zoned out of Bellaire. I had already met once with Meyerland residents to assure them that this would never happen. But who could believe an HISD trustee? The draft document was cited as proof that Meyerland was going to lose Bellaire High. Property values would plummet.

Immediately after the holiday, the avalanche of phone calls and letters began. They continued for months. I received over 500. Some were abusive.

Nothing I could say could convince the Meyerland residents that Meyerland was not in danger.

Meyerland did not relax until the board meeting on May 21, when the attendance boundary committee recommendations, which explicitly recommended no change in the Bellaire High attendance zone, were adopted by the board.

Bellaire Residents Want Bellaire Schools

Throughout the winter and spring of 1992, while Meyerland stood guard to maintain its position in Bellaire High, other communities pressed their agendas for change. On April 29, the attendance boundary committee recommendations for Southwest Houston were presented at a public hearing at Johnston Middle School. The large auditorium was packed. Ten school communities received the zoning changes they wanted. Hundreds of people went home happy.

But not everyone. One small, outlying section of the city of Bellaire was still not zoned to a Bellaire school. It was zoned to Cunningham Elementary, a 95 percent Hispanic school just blocks away but not in the city of Bellaire. The residents wanted Condit, a 50 percent middle-class white school which was a mile away but in Bellaire. "Bellaire residents should go to Bellaire schools," they said. They had a point. Bellaire children played together in city-sponsored sports and summer programs. Why not let them go to school with their friends. I agreed to do what I could. Frank Petruzielo agreed. And the board voted the change on May 21.

Westwood Wants Westbury High

Another neighborhood, Westwood, in the far south of my district, was part of a large white area that in 1970 had been rezoned by the court from Westbury High to Madison High. Twenty years later Madison was 1 percent white and Westbury was a thoroughly integrated school, about 50 percent black, 25 percent white, 15 percent Hispanic, and 10 percent Asian. Now the residents of this area wanted to be zoned back to Westbury. The attendance boundary committee concurred, but somehow left Westwood in the Madison zone. The residents of Westwood were not pleased.

On May 12 I went to a meeting at the home of one of the Westwood community leaders. Rod Paige, who was board president that year and the trustee for District Nine, which included Madison High, agreed to join me. There was a large crowd. The people were wonderful. They were polite. They served cookies and punch. And they made their case with numbers.

"Westwood," they said, "is an integrated community. Whites, blacks,

Hispanics, and Asians live happily together in almost perfect balance. [The faces in the room confirmed the truth of the statement.] All of us want to be rezoned from Madison to Westbury. Westbury is our neighborhood high school. It is closer than Madison."

How could we say no? Rod and I agreed to do what we could.

But Frank refused to change his pending recommendation to the board. "The change makes sense, but my top black administrators will not support it. Some of them were here in the 1970s. To them, it is a step backward. I just can't go against them. But I have no problem if you make an amendment at the board table. I can see the merits of your case, and I won't take it personally."

And so the Westwood community leaders and I made our plans for May 21. I lobbied my colleagues, especially the other two African Americans on the board. The Westwood community leaders prepared a large multiethnic group of residents to sit in the gallery and three speakers, an African American, Hispanic, and Asian, to address the board.

The plan was executed perfectly. The presentations to the board were data-based and unemotional. My amendment carried unanimously. Another community was happy.

Braeburn Neighbors Want Herod

The third request for an additional attendance zone change came from a prosperous middle-class community immediately to the south and west of Braeburn Elementary. Braeburn had once been a strong, middle-class, mostly white school. Residential homes filled the southern half of the zone and upscale apartments the northern half. But during the 1980s oil bust the apartments emptied, rents fell, and Central Americans crowded in. By 1990 Braeburn had over 1,000 students, only 5 percent of which were white.

Some white activists from the southern part of the Braeburn zone wanted their neighborhood rezoned to Herod Elementary, an outstanding school in a white neighborhood to the south. Within days of the April 29 meeting at Johnston a petition was circulating in the Braeburn neighborhood. Virtually every homeowner signed it. It was presented to the board at the May 7 board meeting.

This was one request that I could not support. Herod was overcrowded, and the area that wanted to be rezoned to Herod included the blocks directly across the street from Braeburn to the west and south. Moving this neighborhood to Herod would acknowledge that middle-class white children were not expected to go to a school filled with poor Hispanic children, even when the school was directly across the street.

Without my support the petitioners had no chance with the board. Their request was denied.

The rezoning of Houston's schools in 1992 was a great victory for Frank Petruzielo. Throughout the city, thousands of children were shifted from overcrowded to underutilized schools. Scores of neighborhoods were reunited. Feeder patterns were rationalized, laying the foundation for the decentralization of HISD in 1995 into 11 geographic districts built on high school feeder patterns. Frank accomplished what Joan Raymond would not even attempt, and he did so with a participative process that kept neighborhood wars to a minimum. What could have been months of controversy, laid out before the city on the nightly TV news and the front page of the newspapers, hardly got any coverage at all.

A NEIGHBORHOOD MIDDLE SCHOOL FOR BELLAIRE?

Shortly after the failed attempt by HISD to acquire property in Bellaire for the West University relief school, a group of Bellaire parents organized themselves into the Bellaire Area School Improvement Committee, or BASIC. They hoped to improve Bellaire area schools and turn around the negative opinion in Bellaire toward HISD.

BASIC's first achievement was a magnet program for gifted and talented children at Jane Long Middle School, a large middle school west of Bellaire. The western half of Bellaire was zoned to Jane Long, but few Bellaire residents sent their children to Long. It was less than 10 percent white. It was an *unacceptable* school. There was no middle school magnet for gifted students in southwest Houston. The leaders of BASIC believed that a gifted magnet at Long would help Long build an academic reputation and attract students.

The gifted magnet at Long was one of the eight new magnets funded by Frank Petruzielo's 32 percent tax increase. When school opened in August 1992, Long also had a new principal. The new principal turned out to be extraordinary. The magnet for gifted children was successful. In a few years Long showed dramatic improvement in appearance, discipline, and test scores.

But Long was never going to be acceptable to many Bellaire parents. As one parent told me, "I don't care how good the gifted program becomes. I don't care what you do to Jane Long, I will never place my daughter there with all those Hispanic boys."

Even before the gifted magnet had been approved for Long, some BASIC leaders were looking for another solution. Then someone had an idea. Why not turn Gordon Elementary into a small middle school?

Gordon was a small school in the northeast quadrant of the city of Bellaire that had been closed as a neighborhood school for lack of enrollment several years before. It was now an overflow school for overcrowded, almost totally Hispanic schools to the west.

Many Bellaire residents liked the Gordon proposal. Gordon Middle would be within the city of Bellaire. It would be small, about 500 students. And because it would primarily serve Bellaire students, it would be at least 50 percent white.

The proposal generated controversy. The Gordon champions were mostly Bellaire residents who lived west of the Interstate 610 loop that ran north-south right through the middle of Bellaire. They were zoned to Jane Long Middle School. Bellaire residents who lived east of the 610 loop were zoned to Pershing Middle School, an acceptable middle school east of Bellaire that was about 40 percent white. The parent activists who lived in the Pershing zone were not certain they wanted to abandon Pershing for a small school that would be less than full service. It might not have music, sports, and maybe even be deficient in science labs.

At my request, Dr. Petruzielo established a Gordon use committee as a subcommittee of the attendance boundary committee for 1992–1993. The committee met from December through March. It was all-out war. The pro-Gordon people from the Jane Long zone and the anti-Gordon people from the Pershing zone had little affection for each other. Both groups arranged meetings with me to tell me how the other group was dishonest and mean-spirited.

The major hurdle had always been the disposition of the children currently at Gordon. They could not be pushed back on their home schools. My constituents from the overcrowded schools that supplied students to Gordon had already made it clear to me that it was unacceptable even to think about putting up more temporary buildings on their campuses.

Sometime in February, the Gordon champions came up with a solution. HISD should buy an empty commercial building they had located just north of Jane Long and renovate it for an elementary school. This new school would empty Gordon and in addition relieve some of the overcrowded schools that fed Gordon.

Frank's staff liked the idea, but unfortunately, on close examination the building proved to be inadequate. The Gordon proposal was dead. In April 1993, the board reaffirmed that Gordon would continue to be an elementary school. The Gordon champions and many people in Bellaire were furious. They would be heard from again.

REFLECTIONS ON NEIGHBORHOOD WARS

There were many other neighborhood wars. There will always be neighborhood wars. In urban school systems resources are inadequate, parents and communities put their own children first, and quality education is defined not only by curriculum, teacher effectiveness, and facilities—it is also defined by the race and class of the students in the classroom and the school.

Overall, ethnic enrollments in District Five were almost perfectly balanced. But in fact there were two types of schools: those that had become 90 percent plus minority and those that remained at or near 50 percent white. In the first group, with two exceptions, academic achievement was low and parent support almost nonexistent. In the other schools, the "acceptable" schools, white parents were very involved and test scores were good. What was really going on?

Most of the white children in District Five schools were there because their parents wanted them there. Many of these parents could afford private school tuition, but they believed in public education. As long as HISD could provide reasonable assurances that their children were safe and receiving high quality academic instruction, they kept their children in public school.

These parents wanted their children to go to school with minority children, but not too many minority children. And they wanted those minority children to be mostly from middle-class homes. Also, they wanted their children separated into ability groups for instruction.

For most white parents, class was more important than race. Many of the African American students who attended schools in District Five did not live in District Five. They were bused or driven in from black areas of Houston on magnet transfers designed to integrate schools in white neighborhoods. Magnet transfers were voluntary. African American parents who sought magnet transfers for their children were frequently middle-class parents who were involved in the education of their children. Very poor black children were more likely to stay in their neighborhood schools. The African American enrollment in District Five schools was fairly stable and by and large acceptable to white neighborhoods.

Hispanic enrollment was at the root of many of the neighborhood wars in District Five. The Hispanic enrollment was growing rapidly, and few Hispanic students were middle class. Many of them were recent immigrants from Central America. Many did not speak English.

Hispanic students were not bused into neighborhood schools. They lived in apartments located within the attendance zones of the schools they attend. As they crowded into neighborhood schools like Cunningham, Braeburn, and Jane Long, these schools became unacceptable to white parents.

School administrators knew the magic numbers. A white, middle-class community would support an elementary school that was up to 50 percent minority. For middle and high schools, which grouped classes somewhat by ability, the minority enrollment could exceed 70 percent. Asians did not count as minorities. Middle-class blacks were more acceptable than poor Hispanics. As percentages rose above these numbers, the white students quickly disappeared and soon the school was 90 percent plus minority. Only poor or exceptionally dedicated whites remained.

Where did the white students go? Many were able to obtain transfers to magnet programs in other HISD schools. This was the great game in southwest Houston. Hundreds of children from middle-class homes in the zones of "unacceptable" schools transferred to "acceptable" schools. Most of those who failed to obtain a transfer either sent their children to private school or moved.

During my first election campaign, at a coffee meeting in a home zoned to Jane Long Middle, I learned that the host and hostess were giving their elementary child cello lessons so that years later she would be able to obtain a magnet transfer from Jane Long to the excellent music magnet at acceptable Johnston Middle. There were plenty of violinists, they pointed out. Cellists were always in short supply. Several years later the family moved into the Johnston attendance zone.

The transition of a school from acceptable to unacceptable was not just a problem for parents; it also reduced property values. Now homeowners were angry. Being rezoned from an unacceptable to an acceptable school could increase property values by $5,000 to $10,000. The Meyerland community leaders who feared that Meyerland might be rezoned from Bellaire High to Westbury High were concerned about more than quality education.

All this may sound fairly negative, but consider the numbers. White communities would support schools with minority enrollments up to 50 percent. Was this true 30 years ago? In the 1960s the voters of HISD and the school board members who represented them would not accept any blacks in a white school. When Judge Connally ordered the integration of HISD in 1970, his definition of an integrated school was a racial mix of at least 90 percent one race and 10 percent another. White parents had come a long way.

Furthermore, white middle-class parents who wrote off some schools as unacceptable were not necessarily racists. They wanted their children to be safe. They wanted effective instruction and high academic standards. It was a fact, after all, that the instructional materials and teaching methodologies chosen to meet the needs of poor children frequently did not meet the needs of middle-class children. This certainly was a core issue at the Rice School.

Most of the public school parents I knew in District Five were true believers in integrated public schools. Almost all took an interest in their children's education. Most volunteered some time in their neighborhood school. Some, the school activists, were exceptional. I called them the PTO mothers. They were usually wives of professional men with excellent incomes. Some had professional degrees themselves. They had put their careers on hold to be full-time homemakers. And as their children grew older, some became practically full-time, unpaid school employees.

The PTO mothers volunteered time to chaperone students on field trips, assisted teachers in the classroom, worked in the office, and managed events like fall concerts, show choirs, carnivals, auctions, Christmas programs, and fundraising walkathons. Some programs attracted nearly 1,000 parents. These PTO mothers (and sometime fathers) helped raise $30,000, sometimes up to $100,000, per year for teaching materials, computers, stage curtains, or whatever the school needed. And they didn't just serve their own children. If a field trip—for example a visit to a museum—required money from each student, they raised the necessary money to pay for the children, usually minority children, who otherwise could not go.

These PTO mothers made schools successful. They demanded effective teaching, high academic standards, and strong leadership. They were towers of strength to effective principals. But if principals were ineffective or the bureaucracy did not respond to programmatic or facilities needs, they took action. They called their trustee, took him out to lunch, organized letter-writing campaigns, or circulated petitions. They knew how the system worked, and they got results.

If there is a hero in my story, it is the PTO mothers (and fathers). Unlike all the other players—vendors, ideologues of the left and right, ethnic leaders and activists, teachers, administrators, superintendents, business leaders, board members, and other elected officials, they had only one agenda: children.

Yes, they sometimes got into neighborhood wars over a principal change, the location of a new school, attendance boundaries, or pet projects that would benefit their neighborhood at the expense of another. Most of them saw school reform in terms of their child, their school, their neighborhood, this year. They could make life complicated and sometimes painful for their trustee. But without them, it was difficult to build an effective public school. And without them I could not have been an effective voice for reform on the board of education, for they were my political power base.

5

The Long, Bumpy Road to Accountable Schools

Accountability was at the heart of the national school reform agenda. It was a central tenet of *Beliefs and Visions*. Nearly everyone believed that public schools should be accountable. Public education critics wanted to know how students were performing and what was going to be done about low performing schools. Some HISD critics wanted to see the heads of school administrators on a platter.

The great budget battle of 1992 put accountability on center stage. Charles Miller, the Greater Houston Partnership, and the newspaper editorial boards hammered Petruzielo again and again throughout the summer because specific accountability measures were not part of his budget recommendations.

As the dust from the budget battle cleared and 1992 drew to a close, board members recognized the priority for 1993 was a comprehensive accountability system. We had clearly stated in *Beliefs and Visions* that "the individual school must be the unit of accountability and improvement" and that "school evaluation must be based on improvement trends." In 1992 we did not have an instrument for measuring school improvement. In 1993 we would.

MEASUREMENT COMPLEXITIES

When I came on the board in 1990, HISD measured student performance with a state-mandated, criterion-referenced test, the Texas Educational Assessment of Minimum Skills (TEAMS). HISD also tested students with a norm-referenced test, the Metropolitan Achievement Test (MAT). In addition, many high school seniors took one or both of the national college admission examinations, the Scholastic Aptitude Test (SAT) or the American College Test (ACT).

SAT and ACT scores could be compared from one year to the next, but the

SAT and ACT were college admission tests that measured the performance of a self-selected group of students. They could not be used to evaluate high schools, let alone middle and elementary schools.

TEAMS and MAT scores could not be used, either. In the fall of 1990 the Texas Education Agency (TEA) replaced the TEAMS with a new, more difficult, criterion-referenced test, the Texas Assessment of Academic Skills (TAAS), and in the spring of 1991 the MAT was given for the last time because the TEA announced that beginning in 1992 school districts would have to use a state, norm-referenced test, the Norm-referenced Assessment Program for Texas (NAPT).

The two new Texas tests, the TAAS and the NAPT, would solve our measurement problems. The TAAS was tied directly to the Texas curriculum. It assessed whether a student had or had not mastered the curriculum's essential elements in reading, writing, and mathematics. A student either passed or failed. With the TAAS, we could compare student passing percentages from year to year to measure school improvement. The NAPT would make possible an even more sophisticated method of measuring school improvement. With the NAPT we could track student cohorts, comparing grade level performance year after year of the same students or groups of students.

The TAAS and NAPT could be used for accountability for the first time in 1992–1993. Since the first administration of the TAAS in 1990, the TEA had changed something every year—either the passing standard, the time of year the test was given, or the grade levels that were tested. Not until the summer of 1993 would there be stability in the TAAS, and then not much. Valid year-to-year comparisons would be possible for only grades 3, 7, and 11. Also, because the NAPT was given for the first time in 1992, it would be possible in 1993 to measure grade level improvement. In 1993, then, there would be no excuse. HISD could put into place a comprehensive accountability system. It could, and it would. On this point, the board was unanimous.

"Frank," we said again and again, "this is the year for accountability. We expect to receive at the earliest opportunity your recommendations for a thorough, comprehensive accountability system built on the principles in *Beliefs and Visions*."

PETRUZIELO'S PROBLEMS WITH THE BOARD

We were expecting a lot. Accountability meant standards, measurements, and consequences. Accountability would threaten administrators and teachers. Implementing a comprehensive accountability system would challenge a strong superintendent with a team of loyal administrators, the goodwill of employees, the full confidence of his or her board, and broad community support. Frank had none of this. The tax battle of 1992 left him without any support downtown. Within HISD his critics were legion. Board support was uncertain.

Petruzielo Loses Two Sacred Cows

Frank's problems with the board began just a few months after his arrival in August 1991. Paula Arnold and Cathy Mincberg observed that he did not seem to take them seriously, perhaps because they were women. When they voiced concerns, he either ignored them or suggested they were being manipulated by others. By early 1992, HISD administrators and principals were also unhappy. Frank, they said confidentially and with some trepidation to board members, had a temper. He allegedly shouted at his senior staff, humiliated them in front of others, and used abusive language.

Also, said Frank's critics, two high-ranking administrators that Frank had brought with him from Florida were abusing their power. Frank hotly denied the charges against his friends. They were excellent administrators doing what needed to be done without regard for the entrenched power centers in the HISD bureaucracy. That was the reason the old guard was complaining about them.

Both administrators had the standard one year contracts given to new administrators. Their contracts could not be renewed without board approval. Rod, Cathy, and Paula, who were especially close to HISD employees, rejected Frank's defense. They determined to oppose renewal of the contracts.

On May 21, 1992, Rod fired the opening shot in the campaign by formally reading into the record what became known in HISD as the "sacred cow letter." He charged that some central office administrators were abusive, disrespectful, rude, impolite, and unprofessional when interacting with employees of lower rank. These administrators were damaging employee morale, reducing productivity, and impeding the achievement of the goals of *Beliefs and Visions*. "It is my wish," said Rod, looking directly at Frank, "that administrators who conduct themselves in this fashion be put on notice that there are no sacred cows in this district" (HISD, May 21, 1992, p. 119). Frank fought hard for his friends. But it was no use. In a brutal closed-session board meeting on July 2, the board refused to renew the contracts of the sacred cows. Only Ron Franklin and I stood with Frank. From that moment on, it was clear that Frank did not have the full confidence of the board.

Petruzielo's Performance Evaluation

As the summer of 1992 turned into fall and the time for electing next year's board president and Frank's annual performance evaluation approached, it was clear that 1993 was going to be a challenging year. The board presidency was not a trivial issue. A strong president who supported Frank could provide him with some needed coaching, push for a less negative evaluation, and perhaps heal the rift between Frank and the board. As it happened, I was elected board president.

My first challenge was Frank's evaluation. It did not go well. Board members insisted that in addition to filling out the formal evaluation instrument that ranked Frank numerically on a wide range of performance criteria, they be given the opportunity to give Frank confidential feedback in private sessions. Rod and I were to be witnesses, and I was to bring all the comments together into a document for the board to approve at the upcoming board retreat.

The private feedback sessions began well. As a diplomat would say, exchanges were frank, open, and constructive. Then it was Arthur Gaines's turn.

Arthur had little use for Frank. He frequently goaded him in closed board sessions. Frank, remarkably, kept his cool. But not this time. It was in the evening on January 19. Since I had a previous appointment, Paula and Rod were the witnesses.

Arthur's view of what happened is that he had some positive things to say, followed by some negative comments. Specifically, Frank had a temper and abused people. Arthur proceeded to give examples. Frank exploded. "He threatened to come across the table and strike me," asserted Arthur. "I demand that he be written up for insubordination."

Rod and Paula confirmed the essential truth of Arthur's story. Rod felt as strongly as Arthur that Frank should receive an official reprimand. I knew that if I documented the incident, Frank would be set up for possible non-renewal of his contract, which expired in midsummer of 1995. I determined to do nothing.

The board retreat was scheduled for Friday evening and Saturday, February 5 and 6, at a private beach house in Pirates Cove on Galveston Island. Unfortunately, once again it would not be at Ron Franklin's ranch at Cat Springs. Arthur refused to be Ron's guest. The two had clashed repeatedly, mostly over Frank.

On Friday evening the board met without Frank. The conversation was angry and dark. But with morning came a brighter mood. Perhaps it was the pounding surf and the sunlight streaming in through the high windows. Maybe it was Frank, who arrived shortly after dawn. He was cheerful, flexible, and extremely well-prepared. Soon we were into significant issues: facilities needs and plans for a bond election, HISD's legislative agenda, and of course, accountability.

We were casually dressed, sitting in a loose circle in comfortable, family-room chairs. We all had our say about accountability. Paula said it best. She was sitting directly across from Frank, looking him squarely in the eye. "Frank," she said, "this is the year. Priority number one, above all else, is accountability. It must be done. Do you understand me?"

"It will be done," Frank replied. "I understand perfectly. Accountability is my priority as well as yours."

We then moved to Frank's evaluation. Frank was given the tabulation of his numerical evaluations. They were not good. Frank acknowledged that he had room for improvement. He was gracious and noncombative. He had apologized to Arthur before. He apologized again. He asked, almost pleaded, that he not be given an additional evaluation statement. "Can't we just leave it at this and go forward?"

Several of us spoke in agreement. We did not want to force the issue. Whatever Frank's problems, the accomplishments of his first year were significant. If the board divided again and once more drove off a superintendent, the damage to HISD would be incalculable.

The retreat ended on a positive note. The board had not split over Frank.

The Women Authority Figures

But the larger issue of board and employee dissatisfaction with Frank's leadership would not go away. Employees continued to complain to board members about Frank's controlling and abusive management, and Cathy and Paula continued to feel that Frank did not take them seriously.

In late May, Frank's friction with board members became public knowledge. In an interview with the *Post* Frank was asked if he, as some of the women on the board charged, had trouble with female authority figures? Frank lost his composure. "That is absolutely nonsense from my standpoint. I think the problem is their problem. I don't think it's my problem. . . . I think that is a very malicious observation and has political and self-serving overtones" (May 24, 1993, p. A1).

Cathy and Paula were furious. They demanded that I do something. This time I had to act. With the assistance of the board's attorney, I prepared a letter of reprimand. And with Rod as a witness, went to see Frank. The letter, which charged Frank with making disparaging remarks about board members, confronting staff and others in an abrupt or aggressive manner, and making small issues the subject of unpleasant confrontations, in effect put Frank on probation.

Frank completely disarmed me. He did not make excuses. He apologized freely, committed himself to work better with board members, and agreed to discuss all these matters with the board in the closed session. The letter stayed in my pocket. Only Rod and I ever saw it.

That afternoon at the board meeting the women trustees had a surprise for Frank. Just after the opening ceremonies, Cathy, Paula, Olga Gallegos, and Carol Galloway, one by one, slipped away from the board table. In a moment they were back, each wearing a white T-shirt with Female Authority Figure written in large black letters across the front.

Everyone roared, even Frank. The women had made their point. The crisis was over. Later, in the closed session, Frank apologized and made commitments. "I will do better," he said. "You'll see." The women trustees seemed satisfied.

As far as I could tell, Frank kept his promises. From that point onward he was a better listener and significantly more flexible. He ignored negative remarks. He frequently laughed at himself. Perhaps the female authority figures had gotten his attention.

ACCOUNTABILITY FOR RUSK ELEMENTARY

Perhaps. Or maybe it was because about this time HISD's TAAS scores were announced to the public. Overall, there was significant improvement. Also, about this time, the TEA accreditation report came in, praising Frank as a visionary urban school reformer. Remember, he was called "vigorous," "visionary," and "a staunch advocate for urban education."

Still, there was no recommendation on accountability. It was now June. Then suddenly there was hope. On June 3, the day the women trustees wore their Female Authority Figure T-shirts, Frank showed that he was willing to intervene decisively in a low-performing school.

Petruzielo Reconstitutes Rusk

Rusk Elementary had just under 400 students, most of which were Hispanic. Many were transients who lived in the Salvation Army shelter or Star of Hope Women and Family Shelter. These were probably Houston's most disadvantaged students. Test scores were awful. Twice in the previous year, teachers and parents had addressed the board because of concerns about the curriculum and student discipline. Representatives of the Salvation Army and the Star of Hope had also complained to HISD about the way teachers were treating homeless children (*Post*, June 5, 1993, p. A1; *Chronicle*, June 8, 1993, p. A13).

Frank's explanation to the board in closed board session was that the principal and a group of teachers from the HFT were at each other's throats. The TEA accreditation team described Rusk as a school that had totally failed. The team had suggested, picking up a phrase from Frank's accountability pledge to the partnership the previous summer, that Rusk be reconstituted.

"I'm ready to move in, clean out the entire professional staff, and start over from scratch," said Frank. "We've probably got a dozen schools that need the same treatment. Under state law and board policy, I have the authority to transfer personnel. I don't need the board's authority. Nevertheless, I won't take such action without your support. Do I have it?"

Most board members were enthusiastic.

The next morning, Frank, trailed by reporters and television cameras, went to Rusk. All professional staff, he announced, were being transferred out of the school. He was going to appoint a new principal. Teachers who wished to stay at Rusk could reapply for their position.

The reconstitution of Rusk was a huge news story in Houston and in national education journals. Reconstituting a school was considered a drastic measure. It almost never happened, anywhere. The employee groups hated it. The public loved it. Frank was famous.

What Really Happened at Rusk

Almost immediately the real story came out. Two years previously Rusk had been given a new principal, Johana Thomas, a close friend of board member Olga Gallegos. The rumor was that Olga had *obtained* the position for her friend. Within months, reported HFT president Gayle Fallon in a column printed a week later in the *Post*, teachers were complaining about the instructional program, lack of student discipline, and violations of state and federal guidelines for bilingual education, special education, and Chapter 1 programs. Nothing was done. Why? "In almost every meeting between the Houston Federation of Teachers and Petruzielo, the union was told he understood the problems at Rusk but that he would not take action because he would lose the support of a board member" (June 10, 1993, p. A21).

On Thursday afternoon, June 17, in a closed board session, the rest of the story came out. Two documents, leaked to the press that morning, confirmed that Gayle was telling the truth.

In March 1993, the principal had been given a less-than-satisfactory performance evaluation by her immediate boss, Area Superintendent José Hernandez. In two areas he had found her to be *below expectations*, and overall he rated her as *meets expectations*. In HISD, this was a poor performance evaluation. Then, a short time later, the performance evaluation was changed. All ratings were changed to "meets" or "exceeds" expectations and the overall evaluation was "exceeds expectations." Both Hernandez and his boss, Deputy Superintendent Lloyd Choice, had signed the revised evaluation.

The obvious question was, how can a principal be given an "exceeds expectations" evaluation three months before the school is reconstituted? The more interesting question was, why was the original evaluation changed? The answer, it appeared, was Olga Gallegos. She pressured Frank, who pressured

Lloyd Choice, who in turn pressured José Hernandez. She may have also pressured Mr. Hernandez directly.

It was unbelievable, but apparently true. Accompanying the changed evaluation was a memo by José Hernandez addressed to Lloyd Choice indicating that a copy had been sent to Olga Gallegos. The memo, dated March 19, read: "As per our discussion . . . Thomas' appraisal has been changed to reflect an Exceeds Performance Expectation rating" (*Post*, June 19, 1993, p. A27).

Board members were stunned. The closed session was brutal. Again and again Ron Franklin, with contempt in his voice and fire in his eyes, pushed the administrators involved for answers. They had poor memories and no explanations. Frank, looking very uncomfortable, said nothing. And Olga? She claimed she had never seen the memo and had no knowledge of Ms. Thomas's evaluation.

The newspapers reported all the details the next day. Frank and other HISD personnel refused to comment, saying personnel matters were highly confidential. Olga told the *Post* that she had no involvement in Ms. Thomas's evaluation and had not seen the Hernandez memo until the board meeting on June 17.

The same news story that carried Olga's denial also quoted several Rusk teachers. They said Ms. Thomas used her connection with Olga to scare teachers, that teachers felt in jeopardy, that Olga was always invited to school functions, and that Ms. Thomas gave out tickets to Olga's fund-raisers. "It was never said we had to go to that fund-raiser, but you got the idea that it was in our best interest. It was just kind of understood" (*Post*, June 19, 1993, p. A27).

Now I understood. Frank had been caught in the middle. Rusk was not performing. A core of union teachers were blaming the principal. Undoubtedly, the principal was blaming the teachers. Olga herself, in several conversations urging me to support Ms. Thomas, argued that Ms. Thomas was the victim of a plot by Gayle Fallon. So what was Frank to do? Carol Galloway, a full-time employee of the union, and Olga were two of his supporters on the board. He could not afford to alienate either one. So he did nothing until the TEA came to town. Then, as likely as not, he suggested discreetly to the TEA that they suggest formally to him that Rusk be reconstituted. Frank was no fool.[1]

The reconstitution of Rusk worked. Improvements could be seen almost immediately. The new principal, Felipa Young, ended up rehiring 5 of the 20 Rusk teachers and bringing 5 more with her from Briscoe Elementary, where she had been principal. The rest were hired from throughout HISD.

A year later, Rusk was a different school. The Salvation Army, which a year earlier was about to stop sending students to Rusk—they were "crying and asking not to go back"—now said Rusk "is the one stable influence in some of these kids' lives." Arthur Andersen, an accounting firm which the year previously was about to pull out of its partnership with Rusk—our volunteers were "on pins and needles" when on campus—now had 30 volunteers on campus tutoring Rusk students. "It's a clean slate," said Charlotte Williams, Arthur Andersen's community involvement director. A sixth-grade teacher, Robert Reich, one of the five Rusk teachers rehired by Ms. Young, said, "It's been a terrific year." The best measure of the change at Rusk, said Reich, are the student journals. One child wrote, "Last year Rusk was the dumbest, silliest place to be, but now it's No. 1" (*Post,* May 19, 1994, p. A31). In 1995 a large number of Rusk parents and staff asked the board to make Rusk a K–8 school. The sixth graders did not want to leave.[2]

The reconstitution of Rusk also left its mark on HISD. We all learned that when a school was really dysfunctional, just changing the principal was not enough. Frequently a cadre of trouble-making teachers also needed to be removed. Otherwise the new principal had little chance of success.

We also learned that formal reconstitution was not needed to give a school a new start. In the years that followed, quite a few low-performing schools had large numbers of professional staff transferred out and dispersed throughout the district to make way for a fresh beginning. But never again was a school formally reconstituted.

The Death Penalty, Gayle Fallon, and Me

The reconstitution of Rusk also had a significant consequence for me, personally. It ended my cordial relationship with HFT president Gayle Fallon. We continued to work together, but only as business required. Gayle, a short, heavy white woman, was a former teacher who had made her career as a labor leader by mastering the art of confrontation. She had grown up in the East, majored in political science at American University, and had been arrested in civil rights demonstrations during the 1960s. Gayle kept her hair short, dressed down as a rule, and walked with a bit of a swagger. She was smart. She did her homework. And she could be intimidating.

Because she always knew what was going on and was quick with a sound bite, Gayle got lots of media attention. The media loved controversy, and Gayle made everything controversial. Gayle had also developed some good relationships with two or three of Houston's most powerful business leaders. Gayle was by far the most powerful union leader in HISD and a major player in the district.

Gayle's priority, as far as I could tell, was HFT membership. And the way to build membership was to make teachers afraid that something terrible was about to happen to them. So Gayle thrived on controversy and hyperbole. Strong language was her trademark. Principals could not be trusted. HISD administrators were frequently liars. Board members were, on occasion, fascists.

Reconstituting a school was a wonderful issue for Gayle. It threatened teacher job security. Of course, no Rusk teachers were fired. They were all placed in other schools. But, charged Gayle, their reputations had been ruined. Frank, she said, was a political coward (*Post,* June 5, 1993, p. A1). Olga's political patronage was the rule rather than the exception. "It is not a problem with just one board member—it is a district tradition among past and present board members" (*Post,* June 10, 1993, p. A21).

And me? I was blasted for referring to some of the teachers at Rusk as troublemakers and describing the reconstitution of Rusk as the death penalty.[3]

THE TEXAS ACCOUNTABILITY SYSTEM

The reconstitution of Rusk was a victory for accountability, but it was not a district accountability system. It was now June, and still Frank had not acted. Every time I asked him about accountability he responded, "I have people working on it." Now his excuse was that HISD needed to wait and see what the Texas accountability system looked like. It would be announced in just a few weeks.

The Texas Legislature had been working on accountability throughout the spring.[4] The public wanted it. Powerful groups like the Texas Business and Education Coalition demanded it. The Greater Houston Partnership officially listed it in its legislative agenda. Public schools throughout the state were going to be held accountable for student performance. Low-performing schools were not going to be tolerated.

But how, exactly, should the state measure student performance? And what could the TEA really do about low-performing schools? The issues were complex. The Economic Education Policy Center had the answers.

The Educational Economic Policy Center

The Educational Economic Policy Center (EEPC) was the brainchild of Charles Miller, the Houston business leader who had led the charge against Frank's 1992 budget. It had been established by the Texas Legislature in 1990 to examine the efficiency of the public school system and to make recommendations to the legislature. It was organized as a consortium of major Texas universities and housed in the Lyndon Baines Johnson School of Public Affairs at the University of Texas at Austin.

The EEPC's first major report to the legislature, *A New Accountability System for Texas Public Schools,* was submitted to the legislature in February 1993. It emphasized strongly that schools should be the unit of accountability and that annual student improvement should be the basic performance measure for elementary and middle schools and successful course content mastery the basic performance measure for high schools. The report, which came to three volumes, was cogent and thorough. In his letter of submittal to the governor, lieutenant governor, and speaker of the house, Miller called it "the best work to date in the field of educational accountability" (EEPC, 1993, vol. I, unnumbered first page).

The key point regarding student performance measurement, emphasized again and again, was that the only fair, accurate measure of improvement was year-to-year comparisons of grade level performance by the same students. It would be unfair, said the report, to measure changes in performance by taking snapshots of unrelated groups of students.

The measurement proposal was built around the Norm-referenced Assessment Program for Texas, the NAPT. "The NAPT, and not the TAAS, allows adjacent grades to be equated in order to assess year-to-year progress. *Without year-to-year progress that is assignable to a grade or campus, campus level accountability has limited meaning*" (EEPC, 1993, vol. I, p. 20, emphasis in original).

The second volume of the EEPC report provided a detailed discussion of specific measurement requirements, changes, and enhancements in school performance data.

The third volume focused on sanctions and rewards. Schools and school districts that failed to meet state standards and expected improvements were automatically in conditions of academic failure. A third year of academic failure led to academic bankruptcy. At this point, the commissioner of education could suspend the certificate of the principal or superintendent for not less than two years. This really was the death penalty.

The HFT supported the EEPC proposal. They liked the measurement system. Cohort tracking was fairer to teachers than snapshots of unrelated groups. Also, the proposal adjusted expectations to match student performance levels. Student cohorts with higher performance levels would be expected to make greater gains than student cohorts with lower performance levels. This took some of the heat off teachers in low-performing schools. Finally, teachers liked the idea that when sanctions fell, they fell on administrators, not teachers.

Principals and superintendents viewed things differently. They were determined to kill the proposal. Their lobbyists went to work. By May the EEPC proposal was in trouble in the Texas Legislature.

I knew nothing of this battle raging in Austin until May 8, when Darv Winick explained it to me over breakfast. Darv was a management consultant with a Ph.D. in industrial psychology. He was very close to Charles Miller and had enormous credibility with Houston's business elite. Darv was probably the best networked business/education guru in Texas.

Over coffee and toast Darv brought me up to date. The conclusion of the conversation and the point of the meeting was this: HISD, the largest and most powerful school district in Texas, was helping to kill the EEPC accountability proposal. Houston's business leaders were very upset. Frank and the board needed to reverse their position quickly.

That very day I talked to Frank about my conversation with Darv. He saw things quite differently. "Don," he explained, "I know all about the EEPC proposal. I don't have a big problem with it, and I'm not opposing it. I'm just not supporting it. I can't. The Alliance [the lobbying group of large Texas school districts] is strongly opposed to it, and these school districts are helping us with our legislative agenda. I can't go against them. Our silence is already upsetting the Alliance."

When I pushed him, Frank became angry. "Why should I do anything for Miller? He bashes me at every opportunity. Nothing I could do would ever make him happy. No. I'm not going to work against the Alliance. They are our friends, and we need them. If you don't believe me ask Paula." Within a few minutes Paula Arnold, who was spending full time in Austin pushing HISD's legislative agenda, confirmed Frank's viewpoint.

I informed Darv. He was not pleased.

The Educational Economic Policy Center proposal failed. The sanctions were unacceptable to the superintendents and administrators' lobby and, as it turned out, the measurement system, excellent in theory, could not be put into practice. It depended on the NAPT, and the NAPT was technically flawed. The results from the statewide 1993 administration of the NAPT were unusable. The NAPT itself was discarded and never given again. Texas had no norm-referenced test to measure the grade level improvement of student cohorts.

The Texas Accountability System

The accountability legislation approved by the 73rd Texas Legislature was not exactly what the EEPC wanted, but it was comprehensive and a great tribute to Charles Miller and the ideas of the EEPC. For the first time in Texas history, district accreditation was tied directly to student performance, and schools and districts that did not meet minimum performance standards were subject to severe sanctions.

The accountability measures were complex. School districts and schools were to be measured by student TAAS performance levels, drop-out rates, attendance rates, the results of college admissions tests, and eventually end-of-course examinations. Performance indicators were to be disaggregated by race or ethnicity, sex, and socioeconomic status. District and school performance and performance ratings would be published in an annual report, and campus report cards would be provided to parents.

Districts and schools that failed to satisfy accreditation criteria were subject to a list of sanctions. The most severe sanctions were the appointment of a master to oversee the operations of a district, the appointment of a board of managers to exercise the powers and duties of a board of education, the annexation of a district to one or more adjoining districts, and even the closure of a school. There was much, much more (TEA, Office of Accountability, June, 1993).

The final state accountability system, based on this legislation, was developed by the TEA and promulgated by Commissioner of Education Lionel R. "Skip" Meno. Based on the percentage of students who passed all three TAAS tests—reading, writing, and mathematics—it placed schools in one of five categories—exemplary, 90 percent; recognized, 65 percent; acceptable, 40 percent; unacceptable, 20 percent; and clearly unacceptable, those below 20 percent. There were additional requirements for ethnic subgroup performance, and schools were required to improve by 10 percent of the difference between their previous year's pass rate and 90 percent. Because it was based on the TAAS, year-to-year improvement had to be measured by taking snapshots of unrelated groups. The state accountability manual was long and complex. It was difficult for school officials to understand. The public never did (TEA, Office of Accountability, July, 1993).

Frank presented the state accountability system to the board on June 17. The board response was critical. We were committed to measuring and rewarding performance improvement. It was fairer. It was a principle of *Beliefs and Visions.* The state system took into account performance improvement, but the primary emphasis was on performance level. HISD, even if it showed significant annual gains in student achievement, would look bad for many years.

Frank assured us that his proposals would be ready soon. "Don't worry. I've got people working on it. You'll be pleased."

ESTABLISHING THE HISD ACCOUNTABILITY SYSTEM

Petruzielo's Unacceptable Proposal

The rest of the summer of 1993 was fairly quiet. Frank did not propose a tax increase, and the budget for 1993–1994 was approved on July 22 with minimal controversy. Still, there was no accountability recommendation from Frank.

Then, the week before school started, Frank brought forth his plan. "Here is my draft recommendation," he informed me. "If you are O.K. with it, I'll present it to other board members at agenda review next Monday and recommend it for approval on Thursday."

The document was three and one-half pages long. The first page summarized the commitment to accountability in *Beliefs and Visions* and Frank's accountability commitments of the previous summer. The actual proposal had five parts, each just a few sentences long.[An accountability committee would identify low-performing schools using the state's performance categories. Area superintendents would establish technical assistance teams to provide assistance to schools in the unacceptable and clearly unacceptable categories. The teams would conduct school audits in low-performing schools, assist principals, and coordinate the delivery of services to the school. Schools would make monthly reports on progress to the superintendent. And low-performing schools that did not make progress might be restaffed or contracted out to private vendors.[5]

I could not believe it! Frank was proposing that HISD do what the state required; that area superintendents do their job; and that where improvement did not occur, schools *might* be restaffed or contracted out. That was it.

I was furious. I called Frank. He was out of the city for a long weekend, so I talked with Susan Sclafani, his de facto chief of staff.

"Tell Frank he has failed," I told Susan. "Tell him the board is taking charge. I want to meet immediately with a representative group of principals. If Frank won't develop an effective accountability system, the board will."

Sometime later I learned how Frank described the situation to Gayle Fallon: "We have a problem." I and my management team have developed an accountability plan, but McAdams says it's not punitive enough. The plan doesn't show how to fire people. So McAdams has taken the responsibility for developing an accountability system away from me. He says the board will do it (*Thomas v. HISD*, pp. 52–53).

Developing Standards and Measures

To me, Frank was all apology and cooperation. Immediately on his return, the administrative wheels began to spin. On Wednesday, August 25, a large, representative group of principals, central office administrators, and research specialists met in the superintendent's conference room. Frank was in the chair. I was at his side.

Frank opened the meeting by inviting the principals to share candidly with me their concerns about accountability. "Tell Don what you have been telling me." For nearly an hour they talked about the unreliability of standardized tests, student mobility, parental responsibility, the state laws and board policies that restricted their ability to evaluate and remove ineffective teachers, inadequate support from facilities management, lack of resources, and so forth.

But, finally, they agreed. HISD needed its own accountability system. The state had already put into place an accountability system that focused on performance level. HISD could establish an accountability system that emphasized performance improvement or do nothing and let the public label most schools as failures.

The serious work began. We started with a blank slate, agreed on principles, and then responded to drafts prepared by HISD's research specialists. We met four times in the next several weeks.

The document evolved. At first it was complex. We considered goals and objectives, guidelines, assumptions, available indicators of school performance, sources of data, evaluation criteria, decision rules, hypothetical examples, rewards and consequences, and system management. The principals were fabulous. They had excellent ideas and worked with enthusiasm. Frank came to the meetings, but said little.

At these meetings the fundamental philosophical decisions were made. All students would be expected to reach the same standard. We would make no exceptions and accept no excuses from poor, minority schools. Schools would be evaluated on progress. Because of the limitations of the TAAS, progress would have to be measured by comparing grade performance in the current year with same grade performance in the previous year. Schools with lower performance would be expected to make larger gains than schools with higher performance. Issues beyond the control of the schools, such as extraordinary mobility or significant changes in school populations due to attendance boundary changes, would be taken into account in determining school progress. There were others.

Our biggest problem was measurement and scoring. We were committed to a measurement and scoring system we could explain to the average parent in 60 seconds. The TEA had written a small book to describe the state system. We knew most teachers, let alone parents and the general public, would never understand it. The HISD system had to be accurate and fair. It also had to be stable and simple. Cynical critics of public education would never believe we were making progress if our accountability system changed every year and was so complex they could not understand it. Finally we agreed on a measurement and scoring system that assigned schools points for meeting or exceeding expected gains. It was complex. No one was enthusiastic about it.

The second week of September I began to push the document with key stakeholders. On September 8, one of HISD's educational research specialists and I had a long breakfast with Darv Winick. At noon I had lunch with Gayle Fallon. The next morning I met with Lee Barnes, director of the Houston Education Association. What struck me most forcibly about these conversations was the difficulty I had explaining our measurement and scoring system. It had to be simplified.

Later that morning, Ron Franklin, Cathy Mincberg, and I solved the problem. We did not need to give schools points for meeting or exceeding expected gain. This added an unnecessary step. We had already come up with expected gains in TAAS scores for schools in each of the five TEA performance levels: 8 percent increase in pass rates for schools with passing rates 20 percent and below; 6 percent for schools with pass rates between 21 and 39; 4 percent for schools between 40 and 64; and 2 percent for schools between 65 and 89. Schools that achieved the state standard, a student pass rate of 90 percent, would be expected to maintain pass rates above 90 percent.[6]

All we needed to do was give an acceptable progress rating to schools that achieved their expected gain. Schools that doubled their expected gain would receive a recognized progress rating. Schools that tripled their expected gain would receive an exemplary progress rating. There would also be two ratings, unacceptable progress and no progress, for schools that made less than expected gains or slipped backward.

By bringing together these five performance progress ratings with the five TEA performance level ratings into a 25-cell matrix, we could place every school in the district into one of the cells in the matrix and show instantly its performance progress and its performance level.

Within a few days we had worked out some of the details and filled in the names of the schools. The completed matrix was a revelation. Eight elementary schools had TAAS pass rates of 90 percent or more. Four were located in upper-middle-class residential communities, but had significant minority enrollments. The other four schools were in poor neighborhoods. All four were predominately minority and poor. Twenty-nine elementary schools had increased their TAAS pass rate by 12 percent or more. Almost every one was in a poor neighborhood. So much for the idea that less should be expected from poor children.

We had another meeting with the ad hoc principals group to obtain their approval. They were enthusiastic.

We did not have a complete accountability system. We had nothing on rewards. We had still not worked out the details on consequences for low-performing schools. But we had an accountability rating system. We had something we could propose to employee groups, community leaders, and others, and with modifications take to the board for approval. There was no time to lose. Accountability needed to be in place by election day, for accountability was likely to be the number one issue in the board elections.

Board Elections

I had pretty much decided to seek a second term by November 1992, but as late as March 1993, I was still not totally committed. School board work was taking nearly 20 hours a week, and the personal abuse was beginning to tell. But the reform of HISD had just begun. And so, in April, I decided to run again.

In conversations with parent activists and neighborhood and downtown business leaders I determined that I had strong support, but one key person was noncommittal: Charles Miller. Sometime in the early summer the rumor began to circulate that Miller was planning on running strong candidates against incumbent board members. We had raised taxes. We supported Frank. We had opposed the Educational Economic Policy Center accountability proposal. And we had done nothing about accountability for HISD. In early September I learned that Miller had found a candidate to run against me.

Keith Rudy, a management consultant with an M.B.A., was a man of about 35 from a very prominent Houston family. His father, a wealthy land developer, had been one of Mayor Kathy Whitmire's closest advisors. Keith was tall, good-looking, articulate, and politically connected. With Charles Miller's help and his father's connections, he could raise significant campaign dollars. He might also attract support from those people and communities that were unhappy with me for one reason or another. Keith would be a very tough opponent.[7]

Sure enough Keith attracted support from the losers in the neighborhood wars. The Braeburn to Herod rezoning champion became his campaign treasurer. The Gordon champions, who had failed to get HISD to turn Gordon Elementary school into a small middle school for Bellaire, mobilized all their resources for Keith. The friends of Myrtle Lee Nelson, still angry about her forced departure from Bellaire High School, went after me with flyers, receptions, and card pushers on election day. And Gayle Fallon put the full resources of the HFT and the AFL-CIO at Keith's disposal.

The election consumed me for nearly two months. It required extensive recruitment and organization of volunteers; fund-raising; preparation and mailing of campaign literature; assembly and erection of yard signs; numerous receptions at private homes; visits with newspaper editorial boards; candidate forums and debates; visits to school carnivals; and endless breakfasts, lunches, meetings, and phone calls. The campaign produced dozens of little crisis points, interesting encounters, and angry exchanges.

I was reelected with 53 percent of the vote. Keith received 36 percent. Paula Arnold, Rod Paige, Ron Franklin, and Cathy Mincberg were also reelected. In the past four years we had raised HISD property taxes 59 percent! Yet Paula and Rod had only token opposition. Ron, who appeared to have the toughest opponent, a right-wing Republican activist, won easily. And Cathy did not even have an opponent.[8]

The Board Approves Standards and Measures

Accountability was a major issue in my election. Not surprisingly, I wanted the board to approve an accountability system for HISD before election day.

Gayle Fallon and Charles Miller wanted just the opposite. Within days of my breakfast with Darv Winick on September 8, Darv, Charles Miller, and Gayle Fallon were stirring up opposition in the business community to our proposed accountability plan.

On September 20, at a meeting in the superintendent's small conference room, Al Haines, president of the chamber of commerce division of the partnership and our primary contact with Houston's business leaders, urged Cathy, Ron, and me to drop accountability completely until after the election. "Employee groups have not been adequately consulted. Some business leaders are critical of the timing. Board members look like they are suddenly interested in accountability because they are up for reelection. This issue is too important to be politicized by pushing it through during an election campaign."

"Unbelievable," I responded angrily. "Miller gets Keith Rudy to run against me, using HISD's lack of action on accountability as an issue, and then wants us to sit back and do nothing about accountability until after the election."

Ron was more upset than I. "Who are these unnamed business leaders," he almost shouted, leaning forward onto the table and glaring at Al. "I want to know who they are. I want to talk to them. We've been pushing for accountability all year. We've been criticized ever since I've been on this board for not having accountability. Now we're doing it. I want to know who is complaining and why."

Al, a bit nervously, refused to answer. The meeting ended on a sour note.

After Al left, Cathy, Ron, and I agreed on a plan of action. We would have to make certain our board colleagues understood exactly what we were proposing and were strong in support. And to counter Miller's critique of our accountability system, Cathy, who did not have an election opponent, would brief as many opinion leaders as possible.

For a few weeks Cathy was very busy. She briefed and obtained input from key constituents all over the city: business executives; elected officials; employee organization leaders; ministers; leaders of community-based organizations, ethnic groups, and civic clubs; editorial boards; television reporters; and so forth—53 briefings in all.

Meanwhile Charles Miller was doing his best to slow us down. Our accountability proposal was scheduled to be approved at the October 7 board meeting, still a month before the election. On October 5, Miller and three of Houston's most influential minority leaders, Kirbyjon Caldwell and Jodie Jiles African Americans; and Michael Solar, Hispanic, sent a letter to all board members.

The language was diplomatic, but the message was clear. Miller and friends did not like the proposal and they objected to the process. We should adjust expectations for schools, expecting less, not more, from low-performing schools. Our expected improvement percentages were arbitrary and not statistically valid. Writing scores were unreliable. The performance improvement of a school could not be captured in one number. Frank, not the board, should have developed the policy. Teachers had not been consulted and would not accept it. And pushing accountability through quickly to satisfy others implied that we did not believe in it ourselves. We should delay consideration.

We did not. On October 7, Frank formally recommended the accountability system on first reading. Graphics specialists had prepared large posterboards for the board meeting showing the accountability matrices for high schools, middle schools, and elementary schools with school names inserted.

Gayle Fallon spoke against the motion: "This is brought to us like the tables being taken down from the mountain."

There was a spirited discussion between Gayle and several board members. Paula told Gayle she was disappointed in Gayle's response but not entirely surprised. "We cannot create a system that says it's okay for low-income minority children not to do as well, and I will not support a system that says it's okay for those kind of kids not to be provided the same opportunity and not to be expected to achieve at a high level of achievement."

Cathy disputed Gayle's position that the best predictor of future performance was past performance. This, in effect, she said, lowered expectations for poor minority children.

Ron agreed with Gayle that the accountability system was not perfect, but added: "I've been on this board for four years waiting for a measure of accountability. This is the first one, whether it has come down from the mountain or not, that I've seen that has gone out there that the public can look at, understand, and start to believe that this district is committed to accountability" (HISD, October 7, 1993, pp. 25–31).

The motion passed. Only Carol Galloway, who, remember, was employed by the HFT, voted against it.

The public reaction was positive.[9] The only critics quoted by the media were Gayle Fallon ("We feel no ownership") and Charles Miller and friends ("Oversimplified, questionably fair, too punitive and extremely top-down") (*Chronicle*, October 8, 1993, p. A26).

The Board Approves Responses and Consequences

Following the board action on October 7, accountability ceased to be an issue in the board elections. The development of an accountability system, however, was far from over. The board had only approved on first reading part one, standards and measures. Part two, responses and consequences, remained to be developed.

The board leaders had asked Frank to prepare recommendations on responses and consequences for board approval before the election. But Miller's opposition was spreading through the business community. We reluctantly concluded that we should delay further action on accountability until after the election.

Development of a full and complete accountability system, however, proceeded at full speed. At the October 21 board meeting, Frank presented a status report on part two, responses and consequences. It was masterful.

Fifteen schools had been targeted for intervention. These schools had TAAS pass rates below 20 percent and had made no progress. Frank met with the principals of these schools on October 14. Subsequent meetings that would include representatives of the shared decision-making committees were scheduled. Parents and community leaders were being identified and recruited as volunteers to assist in the schools. Public forums had been scheduled. School intervention teams, which included mentor principals, had been appointed. Complete data on school performance was being collected. Every aspect of school life was being examined. Over 100 specific questions were being asked about instructional programs and school climates. Revised school improvement plans were being written.

At the same time a multipronged initiative had been launched to develop proposed rewards, sanctions, responses, and consequences for all schools. Meetings were underway to gather input from the district advisory committee, the superintendent's ad hoc principals advisory committee, the partnership advisory committee, employee organizations, the Houston Business Advisory Council, the Greater Houston Coalition for Educational Excellence, the Houston Business Education Committee, Houstonians for Public Education, and the Houston Council of PTAS. In addition, every area and central office department had been directed to develop and implement department improvement plans, and customer surveys were being prepared to assess the scope, quality, and timeliness of services provided by central and area offices to schools.

With or without a second reading on standards and measures. With or without formal approval of responses and consequences, HISD was, in effect, putting into place an accountability system. The organization was acting as if it were a done deal. Indeed, it was.

Business Leaders Drop Their Opposition

A few days after the election I received a call from Cathy Mincberg. Charles Miller and a few others wanted to meet with selected board members. The meeting took place in the morning on November 8 at a neutral location, the conference room of a Houston law firm. Present were Charles Miller and one or two other signers of his letter of October 5, Darv Winick, Cathy, Paula Arnold, and me.

Everyone was pleasant, but there was a lot of tension in the room. Charles and Darv went over the same points raised in the letter.

We disagreed. Employee groups had been involved. The board's role was appropriate. Our rating system was fair. Snapshots of very large groups were statistically valid. Our expected gain percentages were not pulled out of thin air.

Paula was a real champion. I had seldom seen her so tough.

Then came the threat. "Your plan won't work," said Miller. "If you don't make needed changes, we'll just keep picking away at it until it fails."

We smiled. Our body language said "pick away." The meeting was over.

Not quite a month later, on December 3, Frank, Paula, Cathy, Arthur Gaines, and I met with the partnership's education committee. The education committee was a large group of Houston's most prominent business leaders, the ones the rest of the business community looked to for leadership on education issues. The meeting had been called by Al Haines, president of the chamber of commerce division. I expected a shoot-out with Charles Miller and Darv Winick.

The room was full, the questions tough, the discussion vigorous. But Miller was not present, and Darv said little.

We responded to many of the same issues that had been raised in our meeting with Miller and friends. Frank was confident and articulate. He made it clear that he accepted responsibility for the accountability system and that he appreciated the assistance the board had provided in its development.

In response to the charge that there had been insufficient public input into the accountability system, we agreed to hold public hearings on accountability throughout the city. Tom Friedberg, a Coalition for Educational Excellence director and the business leader who had so ably defended Frank's budget the previous summer, volunteered the coalition as the sponsor for the public hearings.

That was it. The committee members seemed satisfied. The accountability controversy was over. For nearly six months Houston's school reformers had been needlessly fighting among themselves over accountability.

The partnership education committee adjourned on a positive note. We all agreed there should be more communication between the superintendent and board and the business leaders. Many cordial and supportive comments were made as people headed for the door. Al Haines smiled. "You know what this means, don't you?" he said to me privately. "The controversy over accountability is over. You can put this issue behind you." We never heard another negative word about our accountability system from Charles Miller, Darv Winick, or any of the other business leaders. And within a year, we were working closely with Charles and Darv on other important reform issues.[10]

Six town hall meetings were held throughout the city, on January 24, 25, 26, 27, and February 15 and 16. Overall, about 1,200 Houstonians attended. At the beginning of each meeting an HISD representative explained the proposed accountability plan. Public response followed. Most comments were general complaints about HISD. Few speakers had anything specific to say about our accountability system.

On March 24, 1994 the board received a full report on the public hearings and approved on first reading the complete accountability system. With minor revisions on part two, responses and consequences, the accountability system was approved on second reading on May 19.

REFLECTIONS ON ACCOUNTABILITY

The road to accountable schools was long and bumpy. Why? Because the issues were complex, far more complex than the public or even active school reformers realized. Because the TEA, with all the best intentions, kept changing student assessment systems. Because Frank Petruzielo, without strong support from Houston's business leaders and board members, was unwilling to take on the bureaucracy and the teachers unions with a strong accountability system of his own design. Because key business leaders failed to understand that, given the limitations of the TAAS, snapshots of same grade performance was the only method available to HISD for measuring improvements in student achievement. Because Gayle Fallon worked tirelessly against accountability, charging that the proposed measures of student performance were unfair and that the HFT had not been sufficiently involved. And finally, because board leaders, namely me, had failed to understand the dynamics of the situation and establish direct communication and working links with a broad base of business leaders.

But in spite of all these obstacles, HISD had, at last, accountable schools. No other reform during my years on the board did more to improve school performance. School accountability drove accountability upward and downward through the system. Accountable schools needed authority. HISD would have to decentralize management authority by moving significant resources, numerous professional staff, and responsibility for decisions from central office to area offices and schools. Accountable schools needed timely, effective support from administrative service providers: HISD would have to examine, evaluate, and review every process that delivered services to schools. And accountable schools would require accountable principals and teachers. HISD would need to develop effective personnel management policies.

NOTES

1. My interpretation of Frank's inaction on Rusk is confirmed by Gayle Fallon who said under oath that Frank repeatedly told her that he understood the problems at Rusk, but that he could not take action. Given the opposition he had on the board, he could not afford to lose the support of a board member who consistently voted with him. He might even find it difficult to get his contract renewed (*Thomas v.* HISD, October 17, 1995, pp. 134–135).

2. Throughout the entire Rusk controversy, Johana Thomas said nothing. Instead she sued. She lost. She is still employed at HISD in an administrative capacity.

3. In a breakfast speech on June 3, I likened reconstitution to the actions of the National Collegiate Athletic Association when it closed down a college football program for a period of time and required it to start over again from scratch, what sports writers called the death penalty. My comments received wide publicity. Gayle objected and I responded (Fallon, June 17, 1993; McAdams, June 22, 1993).

4. Equity in school finance was the top education priority of the 73rd Legislature. In spite of equalization attempts spanning several decades, school districts that were property rich could raise many more dollars per student with a low tax rate than school districts that were property poor could raise with a very high tax rate. The only way to equalize funding was to take property tax money away from property-rich school districts and give it to property-poor school districts. Critics called all such share-the-wealth plans "Robin Hood." Throughout the winter and spring of 1993, Texas was embroiled in a great controversy over Robin Hood. The school finance issue was finally settled—following the defeat by the voters of a constitutional amendment to allow, in effect, a statewide property tax—by Senate Bill 7, which was subsequently ruled constitutional.

5. I discovered later that the recommendation had been prepared by a handful of administrators. No principals were involved.

6. We had selected these percentages for expected gains because we recognized that the closer a school came to achieving a 90 percent pass rate, the more difficult it would be for the school to improve its pass rate. Also, the TEA accountability system expected schools to improve each year by 10 percent of the difference between their current pass rate and the 90 percent goal. The 8 percent, 6 percent, 4 percent, and 2 percent growth targets almost exactly met this requirement.

7. I had two other opponents, a young Rice University graduate student whose major concern was HISD's sex education curriculum, and a political organizer for Lyndon LaRouche.

8. Charles Miller tried, but failed, to find a candidate to run against her.

9. A local education writer, Eric May, said it best with a sports analogy.

A coach taking over a football team that went 0–10 last season has a big problem on his hands, but if the coach brings last year's winless team to a 3–7 mark for this season, then his job would be secure. According to the state-mandated rationale, both seasons could be labeled "clearly unacceptable," while the HISD rationale would give a favorable rating to the improved season (*Chronicle,* October 12, 1993, p. A17).

10. In 1996 *Texas Monthly* placed Miller on its list of 20 most impressive and influential Texans for his leadership in school accountability. More than any other business leader, he was responsible for ramroding accountability through the Texas Legislature in 1993 (Curtis, 1996). He has continued to be a powerful advocate for school reform in Texas and an ally of the reformers on the HISD board to this day.

6

Some Accountability
for Employees

HISD's accountability system for schools put considerable pressure on school professionals to improve student performance. Parents, communities, and district administrators were all watching and could easily track student achievement. But[without accountability for employees, how much accountability could there be for schools?]

For many years, accountability for employees had been a joke. Performance evaluations were almost meaningless. During my first board election campaign one of the most frequent complaints I heard from parents was that HISD either couldn't or wouldn't fire incompetent teachers.

AN UNWORKABLE SYSTEM

HISD's employee management systems were unworkable because the political power of employee groups had, over the years, led to state laws and board policies that gave job security a higher priority than job performance. All too often, jobs came before children.

Employee Organizations

Almost all administrators, half or more of the teachers, and maybe a third of all other employees were members of one of 10 employee groups.[1] The four employee groups that had the most significant impact on district policies were the Houston Association of School Administrators, the Congress of Houston Teachers, the Houston Education Association, and the Houston Federation of Teachers.[2]

All of the employee groups sent representatives to regular *consultation* meetings, chaired by senior HISD administrators. Consultation was not required by law. Texas was a right-to-work state, and public employees did not have collective bargaining rights. The Texas Education Code did, however, provide for voluntary consultation with teachers on wages, hours, and conditions of work. Though the code was explicit that consultation did not limit or affect the power of trustees to manage and govern schools, HISD board policy gave employee groups significant rights and privileges.[3]

Employee groups were concerned about many issues: salary schedules, benefits, employee contracts, involuntary teacher transfers, performance evaluations, merit pay, grievance policies and procedures, termination policies and procedures, criminal background checks, drug use tests, safety committees, no-smoking policies, and so forth. At the root of most of these issues was the core issue of job security.

Passing the Trash

Job security was also at the core of any meaningful attempt to improve student performance. The issue, simply put, was what should be done with ineffective teachers and incompetent administrators? In my experience, the overwhelming majority of district employees were honest, competent, hard-working people who did their best and really cared about children. As Rod Paige often said, "We have better teachers and employees than we deserve." Still, not all teachers taught effectively. Some were not competent. Some were lazy. Some who had once been high performers had burned out. And a very small number were corrupt. The same could be said for principals, other HISD employees, and employees in all large organizations.

Who could be trusted to evaluate employees fairly and weed out ineffective and even corrupt ones? Obviously the only ones who could do this were other employees. This meant that at every level in the organization, supervisors had to be able to evaluate their direct reports and make employment-related recommendations—in other words, exercise power.

In HISD, trusting others to exercise power was extraordinarily difficult. The basic premise of the teacher unions was that principals must not be given much discretion in the exercise of power. They would abuse it. They would unfairly reward employees who sucked up and unfairly punish employees who spoke up. (Teachers, of course, would never do this to students.) Board policies must enable teachers to protect themselves from abusive principals.

The administrators' association carried the argument up one level in the organization. Principals must be free to exercise power in schools, but area superintendents must be watched carefully lest they abuse their power over principals.

Over the years, state law, board policy, and administrative practice had reinforced these views to the point that at every level of management, managers had responsibility, but when it came to evaluating employee performance and making employment-related decisions, they had almost no authority. The system was dysfunctional. Ineffective employees, even negligent or destructive employees, were seldom fired. They were just transferred to another work location.

Usually an appropriate job was found for such employees. Sometimes jobs were created for them. The favorite dumping ground for failed school administrators was the textbook warehouse or some other position in facilities management. Many times the transfer worked. The employee performed well in the new location. He or she had been a round peg in a square hole or a teacher out of sync with his or her principal. But sometimes the transfer did not work, and those making the transfer did not even expect it to work. They were just, in HISD lingo, "passing the trash."

The numbers were not trivial. At any given time up to $6 million in payroll were being wasted on employees who had been parked in nonjobs. Who could guess how many other employees who had been transferred to appropriate jobs were still ineffective.

Professional Contracts

State law required that all new teachers receive one-year probationary contracts for three years. Then, at the option of the district, they could either be given a continuing contract or not be rehired. Continuing contracts were almost automatic. Board policy did not require any peer review or administrative evaluation of classroom management, content knowledge, or teaching effectiveness, beyond the worthless Texas Teacher Assessment System evaluation. And once teachers received continuing contracts, they had almost as much job security as tenured university professors.

What about administrators? Under the Texas Term Contract Nonrenewal Act (TCNA) all administrators who held a position that required an administrator's certificate from the state received a contract that could not be terminated or nonrenewed without due process—which meant in effect innocent until proven guilty with extensive rights of appeal. So if HISD wanted to terminate the contract of an administrator it believed was ineffective or just let the contract expire and not issue a new one, it had to prove that the administrator was ineffective. This was not always easy to do. In effect, after one year on a probationary contract, administrators were given lifetime contracts.

The TCNA applied only to certified administrators who managed educational activities: principals, special education administrators, assistant superintendents, etc. However, HISD had for many years given all administrators contracts under the TCNA. Accountants, lawyers, and administrators in personnel, data processing, transportation, maintenance, and so forth all had, in effect, lifetime contracts.

Terminating Contract Employees

How difficult was it to fire an administrator or a teacher with a continuing contract? On paper the process appeared fairly simple. The work supervisor documented unacceptable behavior or poor performance, held a conference with the employee, and recommended termination to his or her own supervisor. The employee was notified that the superintendent intended to recommend his or her termination to the board, and if the employee did not appeal, the board approved the termination. HFT president Gayle Fallon frequently scoffed at the notion that firing incompetent teachers was difficult. She claimed any skilled principal could fire an inadequate teacher in three or four easy steps.

The reality was quite different. The Texas Education Code listed many reasons for termination, but except for obvious moral failures such as falsifying documents, theft, or abuse of a child, most were difficult to prove. The reason most frequently given by a work supervisor for recommending the termination of an employee, because it was the easiest to prove, was repeated failure to comply with official directives and established school board policy.

Consider, for example, a teacher who frequently failed to meet his or her class. The principal could write a memo directing the teacher to meet scheduled appointments, document that appointments had not been met, send two or three additional memos, and then, if the teacher continued to miss appointments, convene a conference for the record and proceed with termination proceedings.

But this seldom happened. Few principals were willing to write up a teacher at the first or even tenth failure to perform adequately. Instead they would talk to the teacher about the problem and encourage the teacher to change behavior. This *soft* approach preserved the team atmosphere of the school and no doubt frequently worked. Behavior improved.

Writing up a teacher was a high risk act. It was seen by the teacher as a declaration of war, a clear signal that the principal intended to build a case for termination. If the teacher were not a member of the HFT or HEA, he or she quickly joined. And now the guerrilla warfare began.

The unions knew exactly what to do. The teacher, and perhaps other union teachers in the school, might begin immediately to undermine the principal. They could spread rumors, stir up parents, and in general make life miserable for the principal.

The teacher might also begin filing grievances against the principal. Grievances were official complaints that required formal hearings with many of the trappings of a trial. Level I grievances were heard by the principal. Appeals to Level II were heard before the area superintendent. Level III hearings were held before a senior administrator. Finally, grievances could be appealed to the board. Grievances put the principal on the defensive and required an enormous amount of time. Once a principal had been grieved, the teacher could charge that additional write-ups were retaliation.

Sometimes, as soon as the principal wrote up a teacher, the union would come to the school and get in the principal's face. The union representative might assert that the principal was violating state or federal law, not following board policy, or discriminating against the teacher because of race, sex, or age.

Gayle Fallon was an especially effective intimidator. She bluffed with total assurance. She could be loud and abusive. And she seemed to enjoy getting into people's faces. She even boasted how she used her smoking habit to intimidate. Her tactic was to "walk into an administrator's office, rearrange some of the papers on his desk, set up an ash tray and fire up the longest cigarette she could buy, 110 millimeters" (Berryhill, 1995, p. 17). An insecure principal, or one not fully conversant with the Texas Education Code or board policy, might back down.

The official termination process began with a conference for the record, a meeting with the teacher and his or her union representative. Following this, if the principal determined that termination was unavoidable, he or she would officially inform the teacher that a termination recommendation was being forwarded to the area superintendent. The area superintendent, if he or she supported the principal, in turn forwarded the recommendation to the superintendent. The superintendent, following state law, then asked the board for authorization to give notice officially to the teacher of the district's intent to terminate.

While all this was happening, the union might push the area or general superintendent to transfer the teacher to another school in return for some concession by the teacher. Sometimes the union would work on a board member. It was common knowledge in HISD that Joan Raymond and Frank Petruzielo frequently made such deals with Gayle Fallon. Gayle herself bragged about her ability to meet behind closed doors with Raymond and Petruzielo and settle grievances and disputes privately (Berryhill, 1995, p. 17). When this happened, it demoralized the principal and sent a message to all principals that it was better to make your own deal with Gayle than have the carpet pulled out from under you by the superintendent.

If the board approved the superintendent's recommendation to terminate a teacher, the superintendent sent an official letter to the teacher outlining the reasons for termination and informing the teacher of his or her right of appeal. The teacher had 10 days to appeal to a committee of district employees—

usually senior administrators and one or two teachers—or directly to the board. The teacher could also appeal to the committee and then appeal the committee's decision to the board.

If the teacher appealed to the board, the board sat as a court and conducted what amounted to a formal trial—attorneys, witnesses, rules of evidence, a court reporter, the works. A hearing could take two or three days.

Board members served without pay. All of us had other responsibilities. It was impossible to get all nine board members to schedule two or three days for a hearing. It was difficult enough to get a quorum of five. The staff in the board services office spent scores of hours scheduling and rescheduling termination hearings. Sometimes hearings remained unscheduled for up to six months. Meanwhile, the teacher was still drawing a salary.

The clincher was that state law required a majority vote of the full board, not just a majority of a quorum, to terminate a contract employee. Since Carol Galloway was a full-time HFT employee and quite open about her commitment never to terminate any employee under any circumstance, this meant that at least five of the remaining eight board members had to be scheduled, sit through a day or more of testimony, and then all agree that the teacher deserved to lose his or her employment with HISD. Holding the five votes was difficult. If the teacher accused the principal of racism, and this happened, holding the five votes for termination was very difficult.

At last, if the board voted to terminate, the teacher was taken off the HISD payroll. The case, however, was not necessarily closed. The teacher could appeal to the commissioner of education, and if the commissioner upheld the decision of the board, the teacher could file a wrongful termination suit in state court. Lawsuits were not infrequent.

The system was unworkable. Gayle Fallon knew this and used it to her advantage. In a small school district with 500 or so contract employees, a board of education could easily handle two or three termination appeals a year. But there was no way the HISD board could handle the dozens of appeals that Gayle could easily generate. On more than one occasion she threatened openly that if the superintendent and board did not work with her on teacher termination issues, she would simply appeal every case to the board and tie it up in endless termination hearings.

Of course many terminations did not follow the path outlined above. Sometimes the HFT or HEA recognized that a teacher really was incompetent and successfully encouraged him or her to resign. Sometimes principals did abuse their power. Some teachers were signaled out for unfair treatment. Every case was different. But the pattern I have described was not unusual.

PETRUZIELO'S INITIATIVES

Soon after the new board began working together in 1990, we sat to hear our first teacher termination appeal. It was an eye opener. From that moment board members began to clamor for a better approach. Nothing happened for a year. Joan Raymond did not seem to hear us, and within several months all our energies were focused on the battle for *Beliefs and Visions.*

Professional Standards

With Frank Petruzielo, things were different. Even before he officially assumed his responsibilities as superintendent in August 1991, Frank established a department of professional standards with an executive director reporting directly to the deputy superintendent for personnel. The mission of the department was to conduct employee misconduct investigations, provide training and technical assistance to principals and other work supervisors regarding employee discipline issues, track cases to ensure administrative action on all investigated cases, generate termination notices, monitor employee appeals of disciplinary actions, track temporary reassignments of employees pending investigations or disciplinary actions, track judicial proceedings of criminal charges against employees, and monitor the discipline process.

The professional standards department and its executive director, Hilda Poindexter, became an immediate target for Gayle Fallon. Publicly and privately she complained that the department was violating teachers' rights. Repeatedly Frank told me to ignore Gayle. "She hates Hilda," Frank said, "because Hilda knows what she's doing and is very effective. She's as smart and tough as Gayle."

It was true. No longer could Gayle, who had been through numerous grievance and termination hearings, intimidate inexperienced principals. Hilda, a former principal herself, was training them, providing technical advice from day one on how to avoid procedural errors, coordinating support from HISD's legal office, and holding the principals' hands through the long, complex termination process.[4]

Quietly, behind the scenes, while public controversies raged, Hilda Poindexter and the professional standards department began to improve HISD's management of problem teachers and other employees. In 1992–1993 the department handled 162 cases and 31 employees were terminated or resigned in lieu of termination. The numbers went up every year. In 1996–1997 the department processed 410 cases and 180 employees were terminated or resigned or retired in lieu of termination.

Hearing Officers

Frank's second initiative to strengthen personnel management was the establishment of a system of professional hearing officers to hear teacher termination appeals. Frank had a two-pronged strategy.

Strategy one was to change the Texas Education Code to allow boards of education to delegate to professional hearing officers their appellant responsibilities. This would require legislation. By February 1993, the process was underway. Friendly Texas legislators were guiding HISD's legislation on hearing officers through the arcane legislative process. The bill added the following words to the section of the Education Code that described teacher termination hearings: "Such hearing may be conducted by a hearing officer designated by the board of trustees. The record of the hearing by the hearing officer and the recommendation of the superintendent shall be forwarded to the board of trustees for action."

Gayle Fallon, not surprisingly, opposed the legislation. She would accept hearing officers only if teachers retained their right to appeal hearing officer decisions to the board.

Strategy two, in case strategy one failed, was the establishment of a voluntary hearing officer system in HISD. The HISD system would have to allow contract employees to appeal hearing officer decisions to the board, but this would still be a big improvement. Most employees facing termination, Frank believed, would prefer an experienced attorney over a committee of administrators. And how many employees, having lost an appeal before an impartial hearing officer, would appeal again to the board?

Employee groups accepted Frank's proposal, as did board members. It was a win for everybody.

It took a lot of negotiation at consultation meetings to work out the details, but on November 30, 1992, the board approved the new hearing officer policy. Employee groups and board members would nominate hearing officers for formal approval by the board, and hearing officers would be selected from a list in numerical order. But the employee and the administration would both have the right to strike two names. Appeals by administration or employees would be heard by the board, but the hearing would be limited to the record developed before the hearing officer and oral argument. No new evidence could be introduced.

Frank fairly quickly obtained nominations for hearing officers from employee groups, but board members did not have their names in until February. Frank was impatient with the delay. Sometime in late February he came to me as board president with a request that the board approve the list at the next board meeting.

I was ready to act as soon as the list was checked to make certain all the hearing officers were licensed to practice law in Texas and had no professional malpractice or legal charges pending against them. A vigorous discussion followed. Frank did not want any responsibility for checking the names: "Gayle will charge bad faith if administration tries to remove even one of her nominees. This is a board responsibility. Ask Kelly Frels [the board's outside legal counsel] to check the names."

Kelly agreed to check the names, but in order to handle a few termination cases that had been pending for months, board members agreed on March 5 to approve about 10 attorneys known personally to them. The other nominees, we all agreed, would be approved at the March 18 board meeting.

Three days later, I received a letter from Gayle crying foul. The board was trying to stack the deck with pro-management attorneys. "With the exception of two attorneys that board members requested that we include on our list, all of our nominees were rejected" (Fallon, March 8, 1993).

The next day, March 9, Gayle sent a letter to all the members of the Harris County delegation to the Texas Legislature attacking HISD's proposed hearing officer legislation and charging that in the matter of voluntary hearing officers the board was acting with bad faith. A copy of her memo to me was enclosed (Fallon, March 9, 1993).[5]

The Texas Legislature adjourned without acting on HISD's hearing officer legislation. Chalk up another victory for Gayle. By misrepresenting the actions of the HISD board she had helped kill the legislation she opposed. But the HISD hearing officer system, which was fully operational by mid-summer, was a great improvement. Most contract employees facing terminations appealed to a hearing officer rather than directly to the board. And appeals to the board took only 30–40 minutes.

Administrator Contracts

Frank's third initiative to strengthen personnel management was a proposal to link an administrator's performance appraisal to the length of his or her contract. HISD's system for evaluating administrators was almost worthless. Every administrator was given a performance appraisal annually by his or her supervisor and rated exemplary, exceeds expectations, meets expectations, or below expectations in seven managerial competencies, job-related competencies, and individual job targets. Most administrators received a final evaluation of exemplary or exceeds expectations.

State law allowed administrators to be given one-, two-, or three-year contracts, but in HISD almost every administrator received a three-year contract. And Joan Raymond, in one of her last acts as superintendent, had talked the board into extending the contracts of almost all administrators in mid-contract so that no contracts would expire before August 31, 1993.[6]

Frank moved almost immediately to change the system. In January 1992, he implemented a comprehensive administrative performance planning and appraisal system. By March 1992, he was talking about linking meets expectations performance evaluations to one-year contracts and giving three-year contracts only to those administrators who received exemplary or exceeds-expectations evaluations.

The word spread quickly through HISD, creating anxiety among many administrators. The issue could not be settled until the spring of 1993, thanks to Joan Raymond, so the talk went on and on, contributing in no small measure to the growing hostility between Frank and HISD's administrators.

On June 17, 1992, HASA Executive Director Irene Kerr wrote Frank a strong letter, with open copies to all HASA members and board members, setting forth the official position of the administrators. The letter charged that recommending one-year contracts for meets-expectations evaluations would redefine the traditional understanding of competent; exacerbate morale problems; "de-stabilize middle management leadership in the schools and in the central office"; make it more difficult to implement the reforms desired by the board; and damage HISD's credibility in the community.

The contract issue continued to simmer on the back burner as Frank, in January 1993, scraped through his own performance evaluation. Then, on April 21, 1993, he announced his final decision in a memorandum to all board members. He would recommend to the board three-year contracts for principals and senior staff with exemplary or exceeds-expectations ratings. Administrators who received a meets-expectations rating would be offered one-year contracts. They would also be offered training opportunities so they could improve their skills.[7]

Frank's announcement was not well-received by some board members. Employee complaints about Frank's controlling and abusive management style were at their peak. It was just a month later that Frank made the comment in the *Post* about the female authority figures. To some board members, Frank's decision to grant only one-year contracts to meets-expectations administrators was just a strategy to get his enemies. This is what Irene Kerr was saying.

On July 6, 1993, in closed session, Frank brought to the board his contract recommendations. The number of meets-expectations administrators who were recommended for one-year contracts came to 214, or 25 percent of all administrators. There was some discussion. For a few moments I was not certain how the board would respond. But the support was there, and in open session the board approved the new contracts.

It was a small step. The TCNA still made it difficult to nonrenew contracts. But at least Frank and the board were sending a message to all administrators that performance mattered and that exemplary and exceeds-expectations evaluations were not for everyone.

Gayle Fallon Kills STAR

Frank's fourth initiative was a new appraisal instrument for teachers that would link teacher evaluations with student performance. Again and again in teacher termination hearings board members were told that the teacher had positive performance evaluations. How could this be? The answer was the state-mandated Texas Teacher Appraisal System (TTAS). It was an appraisal system built entirely on process with no weight given to outcome. Under the TTAS, the assessor could only evaluate the teacher under carefully controlled circumstances in 13 areas, grouped together into five specific domains—instructional strategies, classroom management and organization, presentation of subject matter, learning environment, and professional growth and responsibilities.

The evaluation was scheduled in advance, and the appraiser could only consider the specific indicators enumerated in the TTAS instrument. For each indicator observed the appraiser had to award the teacher one point. "Evidence concerning the indicators for which credit is denied must be documented in the space provided." This was an actual quote from the TTAS instrument (TEA, no date, first page). The appraiser had to justify low scores!

It was almost impossible for a teacher to receive a poor evaluation. All he or she needed was one good lesson plan to follow on the day of the scheduled observation. I was told by HISD administrators that some teachers had been using the same lesson plan since 1986. Some even asked their students to help them receive a good appraisal in return for a suitable reward at a later date. If, in spite of all this, the teacher still received only a meets-expectations evaluation, he or she could grieve the appraiser!

Is it any wonder that 96 percent of HISD teachers were rated exemplary or exceeds expectations? As one HISD administrator told me with a shrug, "With the TTAS, a dead body in front of a class could likely get sufficient student attention to qualify for a satisfactory evaluation."

Nearly everyone acknowledged that the TTAS was a joke. It was not even indirectly related to academic content or student achievement. A teacher could be teaching bad science or history, or have every one of his or her students fail the TAAS, and still receive a clearly outstanding or exceeds-expectations evaluation.[8]

My first introduction to TTAS was at a board workshop soon after my election. I could hardly believe it. Now I understood one of the reasons why it was so difficult to terminate incompetent teachers. From that point onward,

I and other board members were determined to get rid of the TTAS. But how? It was state law.

Frank had a plan. It began with his 1992–1993 budget recommendation. In return for a significant teacher pay raise, teacher groups would support the development of an alternative teacher appraisal system, which would then be authorized by the upcoming 73rd Texas Legislature.

Frank's plan almost worked. The 13 percent spending increase in Frank's 1992 budget funded a 10 percent pay raise for teachers. The teacher groups, even Gayle Fallon reported Frank, promised to support the development of an alternative teacher appraisal system that linked teacher evaluations to student performance. And in the spring of 1993, the Texas Legislature authorized the TEA to grant school districts waivers from the TTAS.

Soon after the budget battle of 1992 was over, Frank, in anticipation of success with the legislature, established a committee to develop a new teacher appraisal system. The Teacher Development and Assessment Committee, chaired by HISD administrator Mary Murphy, was a large committee of over 50 people. The committee members were teachers, principals, assistant principals, central office administrators, TEA representatives, university deans and professors, and, of course, the teacher employee group leaders.

The committee held its first meeting on December 17, 1992. The opening presentation by Dr. Murphy made it clear that the goal was to plan, develop, and implement a teacher assessment model that linked teacher performance with student achievement. Shortly thereafter, in Dr. Murphy's words, Gayle began her filibuster. She made it absolutely clear that the HFT opposed any link between teacher appraisals and student performance.[9]

The committee met again on January 12, 1993, for general discussion. This time Gayle dominated the entire meeting. She spoke almost continually. She was abrasive. She was rude. She asserted again and again that teachers could not be held accountable for student performance.

A few days later, Dr. Murphy received a call asking her to meet with Petruzielo. To her surprise, she found Frank already talking with Gayle. Frank made explicit to Mary that she was to work with Gayle on the development of the alternative teacher appraisal system and appoint an HFT member as cochair of the committee. Subsequently, Dr. George Camp, a history teacher at Lamar High School and HFT member, was appointed cochair.

The teacher assessment committee met frequently during March and April. George Camp proved to be a very effective co-chair, and a wide range of very complex issues were resolved by work teams and in the full committee: How is knowledge and presentation of content measured? How is classroom management measured? How can a teacher be assessed on a daily basis rather than by the current, one-time dog-and-pony show? What are valid measures of student achievement? How and by whom should they be selected and weighted? What distinctions should be made between a new teacher and a veteran teacher? Is assessment for professional growth, contract status, or both? What about the variables beyond a teacher's control: student absenteeism, student mobility, parental involvement, overcrowded classrooms, undiagnosed learning problems, and so on? The committee considered scores of specific issues related to teaching and learning.

On May 25, the first draft of what was soon to be named STAR (System for Teacher Appraisal and Review) was presented to Frank. A second draft, with added graphics, was presented to Frank on July 15. A third draft was ready for the attorneys on August 16.

On September 1 a team of senior administrators met to review the final product. They had concerns. STAR was complicated and cumbersome and had tight timelines. It established two different systems, one for probationary teachers and one for continuing contract teachers. Some administrators wanted just one system. Most agreed that STAR included language that allowed teachers too many excuses for not demonstrating student growth.

All these issues, as well as the process for identifying schools to pilot the system, were discussed at a joint meeting of the management team and the full STAR committee on September 20. Consensus was reached. The document, after one more rewrite, would be ready for presentation to the board.

Frank introduced the presentation at a board workshop on October 21. STAR, he said, would increase accountability by linking student growth to teacher performance. It would encourage collaboration between teachers and administrators in working toward achievement of the goals of school improvement plans. It would move teachers into goal-setting, with emphasis on results. It would encourage teachers to be innovative and take risks. It would also recognize teachers who extended themselves in unpaid educational service to students, schools, and the community.

George Camp then presented the 35-page proposal. STAR proposed two systems for assessing teachers—one for teachers in their first and second year with HISD, which focused on the development of teaching skills; and one for teachers in their third year and following, which emphasized goal-setting and student growth.

The essence of STAR for experienced teachers was that the teacher would propose student growth goals, based on current student performance, that supported the school's improvement plan. Then the teacher and the appraiser would reach agreement on the goals. During the term, the appraiser could make as many unannounced visits as he or she wished, and the teacher and appraiser could conference on progress as needed. At the end of the year, the teacher would be evaluated on student growth as well as several other criteria, including service to the school and the community.

STAR was not a finished product. Nearly everyone acknowledged that the evaluation process was time-consuming and bureaucratic. Clearly STAR needed to be pilot-tested in a dozen or so schools before it became the district teacher appraisal system. Also, Frank believed that the focus on accountability needed to be sharpened. In his October 21 transmittal letter to the board, he recommended that, when appropriate data were available, there should be a "relationship between teacher performance and TAAS score improvement."

Some time around October 21 Gayle became a bitter opponent of STAR. Up until then she had been supportive. Mary Murphy had done as Frank had asked and *listened* to Gayle. Gayle's own HFT member, George Camp, had taken the leadership in developing STAR. But at the board workshop I could see Gayle's anger, and HISD administrators confirmed that she was determined to kill STAR by whatever means possible.

What had happened? For one thing, George Camp had a mind of his own and did not take STAR where Gayle wanted it to go. But that was not the whole story. Remember what was happening in October 1993. Gayle was in the midst of an all-out battle to defeat HISD's school accountability system. Frank, whether reluctantly or not, was working closely with the board on accountability. Gayle and Frank had been close in previous times, though I always believed that both were trying to use rather than help the other. From October 1993 onward, however, it was clear that Frank and Gayle were in conflict.

On November 6, four days after the board elections that returned all five incumbents to office, Gayle made her position on STAR explicit in a strong letter to Frank with copies to Texas Commissioner of Education Meno, the Greater Houston Partnership, HISD trustees, and HFT stewards. The federation had five demands. The key demand was that "test scores must not be a component in individual teacher assessments. . . . Should the items above not be found in the pilot assessment instrument, please remove the name Houston Federation of Teachers as well as Andy Dewey [HFT vice president] and Gayle Fallon from all sections of the document. Please also remove our names from any document that might even remotely suggest support for the instrument or for the waivers necessary to implement an alternative assessment."

STAR, after formal discussion in consultation, was approved by the board on November 18, 1993, for piloting in selected schools in the spring semester. The Congress of Houston Teachers and HASA supported STAR. The HEA and the HFT opposed it. Now all that remained was the granting of a waiver from the TTAS by the TEA.

Gayle had been beaten at the board table by a seven to zero vote (Carol Galloway was absent). Frank enjoyed immensely the board vote. At the first break following the vote he came up to me and whispered, "This is the way to get Gayle. You don't go after her in the press. You just keep pushing those green buttons."

Gayle had been beaten in Houston, but she would not be beaten in Austin. Within days of the board vote, the TEA decided to postpone consideration of waivers for locally developed teacher appraisal systems until after the state had established guidelines for evaluating waiver requests. In December, the State Board of Education appointed a 15-member State Advisory Committee for Teacher Appraisal to assist the agency with the development of the guidelines. The committee did not meet until March 1994, and then met infrequently. It was a classic example of a bureaucratic execution.

The board discussed the execution of STAR at the February 3, 1994, board meeting. We wanted to know from administration exactly what had happened in Austin and what we could do to pressure the TEA to act. Ron Franklin, recently elected board president for 1994, looked up at Gayle Fallon, who was sitting in the gallery. "Gayle, do you want to tell us about it?"

Gayle rose from her seat and moved to the podium:

> Well, because it links test scores to student performance. . . . What it does, it takes the campus goals, which were not necessarily developed by the teachers. They were very often sent up and handed back down with changes. They are told, "All of you have to improve your test scores by X percent because this is the campus goal." Then it says on STAR that you do your own goals, but one of your goals has to be the School Improvement Plan or the campus goal. So consequently if I'm the greatest teacher in the world and I improve 10 percent and you guys have dictated 8 percent, but everyone else is horrible and they drag my scores down, under the language that you have in STAR, I couldn't get a good assessment.

This was not true. Nothing in STAR said that a teacher's assessment would be linked to the school's performance. What it did say was that: "Student growth will be measured by a pre-assessment and a post-assessment of students over the learner objectives for a grade or course." After describing a wide range of pre- and post-assessment options it said: "Using the results of the pre-assessment and any other data that the teacher may accumulate, the teacher will set appropriate student growth goals linked to the school's improvement plans" (HISD, November, 1993, pp. 11, 12).

Now the discussion got interesting. Ron asked Gayle if she was saying that a teacher's evaluation was based on school performance.

"It's schoolwide performance that you're basing it on," she responded.

Cathy Mincberg objected. STAR was based on pre- and post-classroom tests.

"That's not in there," responded Gayle.

And then she added another point, and now I knew why the TEA had killed STAR. HISD, charged Gayle, had not followed the appropriate process for approving the waiver request to the TEA: "So, if we're going to play games on how we slide it through the bureaucracy, then we're going to play games in Austin, where it's a matter of Democratic politics."

Ron: "Translated: you killed it."

Gayle: "Translated: it's dead" (HISD, February 3, 1994, pp. 91–93).

The discussion continued without Gayle, but really, she had said it all. It was an election year. Democratic Governor Ann Richards was facing a tough reelection battle. Teacher unions were a very important constituency of the Democratic Party. Education Commissioner Meno was a Richards appointee.

STAR was dead. Teacher assessment was not resurrected until 1995, following the election of George W. Bush as governor and the replacement of Meno as commissioner of education.

Gayle had played the game brilliantly. She tried first to intimidate the Teacher Assessment Development Committee. Then she pressured Frank to put a gag on Mary Murphy and appoint an HFT member as committee co-chair. When George Camp and the committee, however, proceeded to develop an assessment process that linked teacher evaluations to student performance and Frank pushed for an even closer link between teacher evaluations and student performance, she was stuck. She could not win at the board table. She did not even try. All the incumbent board members had been reelected. But Gayle was still not beaten. There was always Austin, where as she put it, it was a matter of Democratic politics.

Along the way, Gayle, ever the resourceful union organizer, used the controversy over STAR to recruit members. Her assertion that STAR would link a teacher's evaluation directly to the TAAS scores for an entire school was not true. It did not fool the board, and it made George Camp furious. But it probably helped HFT recruit new members.

By the spring of 1994, the board reformers could see that at last HISD would have accountable schools. But accountable employees? The journey had hardly begun. The Department of Professional Standards and the voluntary hearing officer system were making it easier to fire the truly incompetent. But the new contract standard for administrators had minimal impact, and the death of STAR meant that the system for evaluating teacher performance was still a joke. Ineffective teachers facing termination could still claim their performance evaluations proved they were outstanding teachers.

The struggle to make employees accountable took place almost entirely outside the public's view. There was no involvement from the business community. The newspapers barely mentioned the issues. The television reporters did not even know they existed. Real school reform was boring.

NOTES

1. About two-thirds of all HISD employees provided services directly to students. They were either teachers, 54 percent of all employees; teacher aides, 8 percent; or principals, assistant principals, counselors, librarians, nurses, and psychologists, 6 percent. Almost all of the rest, nearly 32 percent, were low-paid clerical, maintenance, food service, and transportation workers. Central office administrators comprised less than 1 percent of the total workforce.

2. The Houston Association of School Administrators (HASA), with about 600 members, was the voice of principals and other administrators. The Congress of Houston Teachers, with about 1,500 members, was a professional association for teachers that emphasized its nonunion tradition. HASA and the congress had no links to national organizations. The Houston Education Association (HEA) and the Houston Federation of Teachers (HFT) were labor union locals affiliated with powerful state and national organizations. The HEA, with about 1,500 members, was the Houston chapter of the National Education Association. The HFT, with about 4,000 members, was the local chapter of the American Federation of Teachers and a member of the AFL-CIO. It is difficult to establish the exact membership for the various consultation groups. The numbers given are my estimates based on employee requests for dues payment through payroll deduction as of September 1995.

3. By board policy, the board, except in emergencies, could not act on any issue relating to wages, hours, terms, and working conditions until it had been formally discussed at consultation. Officially certified employee groups received representation at consultation and voted in proportion to their membership, and elaborate procedures, guaranteed by outside auditors, assured that consultation elections were fair. HISD also provided employee groups with some free administrative services. Organizational dues were collected through payroll deductions, significantly increasing membership; and employee group mail was delivered by HISD's internal mail service, a custom widespread in union shops even though this was a violation of U.S. Postal Service regulations. The delivery of employee group mail ended in February 1997 over the strenuous objections of the employee groups.

4. By the summer of 1995, the Department of Professional Standards had developed four distinct flowcharts to describe the processes used to resolve issues with problem employees; criminal charges against employees; employee misconduct reports alleging violations of the code of ethics or board policy; performance reviews; and demotions, returns to probation, terminations/nonrenewals, and suspensions without pay. This last flowchart had a possible 53 process steps and 28 possible decision points.

5. I considered it a cheap shot, and said so in a response to Gayle, with open copies to Frank, HISD trustees, and members of the Harris County delegation. "I know you are opposed to the HISD Board's legislative program regarding hearing officers, but to misrepresent the facts in order to make the Board look bad so that you can discredit our legislative program is a cheap shot" (McAdams, March 21, 1993).

6. As Dr. Raymond put it in her March 28, 1991, letter to administrators giving them the good news, "It is my hope that this action will provide a greater degree of stability during the transition period to a new superintendent, as well as an effective,

operating administrative structure that is in place when a new superintendent assumes responsibility." I was one of two board members who vigorously opposed this action.

7. Frank added a nice little dig at the end of his memorandum. The board had just concluded a thorough and rigorous evaluation of me, and so "just as the Board has high expectations and standards for my performance, so also do I have high expectations and standards for the performance of my staff."

8. How could such an appraisal system become state law? It was a reflection of the power of the teacher unions. While the public was clamoring for school reform and the Texas Legislature passing reform legislation, including a requirement that all teachers be assessed for performance, the teacher unions were intensely lobbying officials at the TEA and selected legislators to make certain that the actual evaluation instrument was worthless.

9. This information and what follows on the work of the committee is based on personal interviews with Dr. Murphy.

7

The Wonderful Cacophony of a Free People Disagreeing

The reelection of all five of the reform leaders on the board of education in November 1993 confirmed that the reform of HISD would continue. And there was reason for optimism. Shared decision-making was beginning to take hold in schools. School attendance boundaries had been rationalized without controversy. School accountability was becoming a reality. Accountability for employees was increasing, at least a little. Test scores were up, at least a little.

On the down side, though the 32 percent tax increase had made possible a significant raise for teachers, it had left a bitter taste in the public's mouth, and Frank was stonewalling attempts to decentralize the district. Decentralization was the board's next priority, and a public battle between Frank and the board seemed inevitable.

Suddenly there was a new priority. The board might have to elect a new superintendent.

WHAT IF HISD NEEDS A NEW SUPERINTENDENT?

Petruzielo Might Go to Florida

It was Sunday evening, November 28, 1993, the end of a pleasant Thanksgiving weekend. The phone rang. It was Frank: "I've got some news for you. I've been asked to consider the superintendency in Broward County [Florida]. For most of the years I worked in Dade County, I actually lived in Broward County. I've got family in Broward County, and my wife wants to move back to Florida. Professionally it's a good move. If the position is offered, I'll probably take it. The story will probably be in tomorrow's newspapers."

The next day everyone was talking about the possibility that Frank Petruzielo might leave HISD. HISD employees could talk of almost nothing else. Few seemed unhappy with the prospect. Privately most board members, school employees, and business leaders hoped he would go.

I had mixed feelings. I liked Frank, and on balance I believed he had been good for HISD. But ever since the great tax battle of 1992, except for a few bursts of energy, he seemed to be a reluctant reformer. Replacing him would be problematic, but if the new superintendent quickly earned the trust of the employees and the respect of the business leaders and moved forward aggressively with decentralization, Frank's departure would be a plus. HISD was better for Frank's coming. It would also be better for his leaving.

HISD Needs Paige

Broward County was supposed to make a decision early in 1994. Frank might be gone by March. The scenarios for replacing Frank ran through my mind. A search process like the one that brought us Frank? The only upside was that under an interim superintendent the board would have the opportunity to decentralize the district. No traditional superintendent, some of us had concluded, would ever voluntarily relinquish power.

The downside was huge. We would have to appoint an interim superintendent, select a search firm, and then wait for up to six months for the politically correct short list of finalists. Then the ethnic politics, which would have been going on from day one, would break into the open. We had been lucky to escape open ethnic conflict when we hired Frank. We would probably not be lucky a second time.

And even if we were lucky and avoided ethnic conflict, the new superintendent, whatever he or she said, might not embrace *Beliefs and Visions*. (I recalled Frank's *Blueprint*.) What would happen to decentralization? The new superintendent would also have to build relationships with Houston's business, political, civic, and ethnic leaders, something Frank had never done; and last but not least, manage a large, complex organization. The task was monumental. No outsider would be able to sustain the reform momentum. I was certain of it.

HISD needed an insider, someone who already understood the complexity of HISD, someone who already had the trust of administrators and teachers, someone who already had the respect of Houston's business, political, civic, and ethnic leaders, someone who had already embraced *Beliefs and Visions* and would move quickly to decentralize the district. HISD needed Rod Paige!

It hit me sometime in mid-December. Rod was perfect for the job. He had coauthored *Beliefs and Visions* and had been its heart and soul for three years, constantly reminding the rest of us where we had promised to go. He had been a civic activist for more than a decade and was widely respected by Houston's business, political, civic, and ethnic leaders. And as dean of the

Texas Southern University School of Education he had been active for years as a teacher and scholar. Rod had been in most of HISD's schools. He read almost everything. He was smart. He was strong. He had courage and integrity. He was an effective public speaker. He radiated warmth and sincerity. Why not?

The Do Little Strategy

Rod would be a great superintendent, but did he want the job, and could he be elected? A few days later on the phone I just dropped it on him. "Rod, let me tell you who I think would be the ideal person to replace Frank as superintendent."

"Who?"

"You."

There was a moment of silence. "Don, we shouldn't talk about this."

That was all I needed. Rod had not said no.

A few weeks passed. Board members talked a lot about whether Frank would go or stay. We recalled our experience with the search firm when Frank was hired. We speculated about interim superintendents. We talked about the stalled decentralization process. One day Cathy Mincberg called: "Don, I have been thinking about our conversations. The only way we're going to maintain our reform momentum, especially with decentralization, is to make Rod superintendent."

I told her about my phone conversation with Rod.

"We need to talk," Cathy said with urgency.

A few hours later we met in my office. We agreed there was a good chance Rod would take the position if offered, though we suspected he would be a reluctant candidate. We thought through all the pros and cons. We thought through all the possible scenarios. Would it look like the board was trying to put one of its own in the superintendent's chair so it could directly manage the district? How would the Hispanic activists respond?

We decided to call Ron Franklin. Ron's initial reaction was cool. He feared that Rod's election might spark controversy. "I'll give it some thought," he promised. A few days later he concurred.

From that moment Cathy, Ron, and I knew there was a good chance Rod would be HISD's next superintendent. We could count. Arthur Gaines and Carol Galloway were African Americans. Arthur for certain, and probably Carol, would support Rod. That made five votes.

We also knew we needed to speak and act with great caution. Any decision made by the board outside of a duly posted open meeting would be a violation of the Texas Open Meetings Act. If five or more board members met to discuss HISD issues, or if in groups of less than five we consciously went back and forth to predetermine the outcome of a meeting, we could go to jail. Also, a huge public controversy was almost certain if word got out that several trustees wanted to elect Paige superintendent. The less said, the better.

There was just one call that I felt I had to make. When and if the time came, I wanted Arthur to put Rod's name before the board. Arthur had lived through the desegregation of HISD. He and Rod were close friends. If anyone was going to put Rod's name before the board, it should be Arthur. A few days later I called him. Arthur was enthusiastic.

That was it. There was nothing more to do but keep quiet and wait. If Frank resigned there would be numerous complex issues to manage. It would be a mistake to try to manage them in advance.

It was against state law for a school board member to solicit employment with the district on whose board he or she served. And a school board member continued to be the legal trustee until his or her successor had been chosen and taken the oath of office. If Rod were to become superintendent, he would have to resign his board seat and wait until a successor was appointed or elected before he could even apply for the job. The voters in his district might insist on an election. That could take months and be very problematic. Also, Rod could not serve as superintendent unless he had a Texas superintendent's certificate. I did not know whether he had one or not. On top of all this, Frank might not get an offer from Broward County. No, there was no way to manage the process, and one would have to skirt the edges of the law to try.

THE DESIRE OF THE BOARD OF EDUCATION

Preparations for a Big Day

Meanwhile, there were other issues to manage. On December 7, Felix Fraga was elected to an open seat on the Houston City Council. HISD was going to get a new trustee. Once again there was discussion in the Hispanic community: an appointment or an election? This time the community, organized as the Hispanic Education Advisory Committee, chose the appointment of a caretaker, who would be appointed on January 20, 1994, and the election of a replacement on the next regularly scheduled election day, May 7.

The caretaker was to be José Salazar, a Houston Community College mid-level administrator with an M.S. in ESL/bilingual education from the University of Houston. José was a young man with sharp features, a big smile, and a fiery temper when provoked on Hispanic issues. He had been very active in Hispanic education issues, and just six months earlier had served as president of the grassroots group that officially adopted Rusk following Frank's application of the death penalty.

On January 6, Frank was offered the Broward County superintendency and immediately left for Fort Lauderdale. If he and the Broward County Board agreed on a contract, he would resign, effective almost immediately.

So, at the January 20 meeting the board would appoint José Salazar to fill the vacancy created by Felix's election to the city council; elect a new board president, who everyone agreed would be Ron Franklin; and most likely go into closed session to select an interim superintendent. January 20 would be a very big day for HISD.

What would happen in the closed session? None of us knew. The board might select an interim superintendent and defer other decisions to a later date. It might launch a full search or a search limited to Houston candidates. It might offer the superintendency to Rod Paige. The key person was Carol Galloway. I believed Carol would support Rod, but maybe not. Carol was a full-time HFT employee. Her boss, Gayle Fallon, and Rod Paige were on the opposite side of the fence on many issues.

The Board Makes a Decision

The January 20 board meeting opened to a full gallery buzzing with anticipation and rumors. Over the past several days I had shared with a few business leaders and parent activists my belief that Rod should be HISD's next superintendent. I knew Cathy, Ron, and Arthur had done the same, and leaks were inevitable.

The public meeting went as expected. José Salazar was appointed to fill Felix's seat, sworn in, and seated at the board table. Ron Franklin was elected board president and took the gavel. Then, after a presentation by the Houston Business Advisory Committee on decentralization, we went into closed session.

Frank was expected to sign a contract with Broward County within a day or two and be gone by February 1. The first agenda was an interim superintendent. But should we not settle on the process for selecting a superintendent before we selected an interim superintendent? A short-term interim could be almost anybody. A long-term interim superintendent would need to be selected with great care. Then Arthur spoke: "Mr. President, in my opinion Rod Paige would be an outstanding superintendent for HISD."

Discussion followed. (About this time Rod left the room.) I do not remember the order in which board members spoke, but when Carol Galloway said she supported Paige, we all knew the board had made a decision.

José Salazar erupted. "It looks like it's already been decided. This is outrageous." José was leaning forward in his chair, shaking, practically shouting. A cabal had conspired to elect Rod superintendent. No one had talked to him about Rod. No one had talked to Olga. The Hispanic community had been purposely excluded, insulted, humiliated.

Paula was upset. She had passed off comments to her in recent days by Arthur and Cathy in support of Rod as off-the-cuff comments, not firm commitments. She had no idea Rod was a serious candidate and already had such strong support. She agreed that Rod would make an excellent superintendent. But, she insisted, it would be unfair to the Hispanic community to select him without an open search process.

The discussion went back and forth. What should we do? Could we keep it a secret that five board members wanted Rod to be superintendent? If a search were held and Rod resigned his board seat and applied, would anyone else apply? Was there any process we could launch that ended in Rod's selection that would not rightly be called a sham? The fact was, no state law, no HISD policy, no board promise committed us to a search.

Finally it was decided. We would tell the public the whole truth: a majority of the board wanted Rod Paige to be the next superintendent of HISD. We could not offer him the job. He was a sitting board member. If he wanted the job, he would have to resign his board seat and apply for it.

The great sliding door dividing the board table from the gallery slowly rolled open. Arthur read the motion: "Mr. President and Board, I move that we express the desire of the Board that Dr. Rod Paige consider becoming the next superintendent of the District. We express this desire with the recognition that he would have to resign and have a successor sworn in prior to our being able to negotiate with him for the position" (HISD, January 20, 1994, p. 244). Five board members voted yes. Paula, Olga, and José voted no. Rod abstained.

ALL HELL BREAKS LOOSE

Hispanics Object to the Process

The public was stunned. No one had seen it coming, but initial reactions from HISD employees were positive. Rod's famous sacred cow letter had not been forgotten. Employees had passed it around and quoted it ever since. Business leaders also seemed pleased.

Hispanic leaders, as expected, were angry. The board had discriminated against the Hispanic community. The problem was not that five board members wanted Paige to be superintendent. It was the process. A formal search was mandatory. Hispanics had been "shut out." It had nothing to do with race. The Hispanic Education Committee, the group that had come together to nominate José Salazar for appointment to the board, claimed they would protest the appointment of anyone, even a Hispanic, elected directly by the board (*Chronicle*, January 22, 1994, p. A1).

The next day, Friday, January 21, board members gathered at a beautiful old bed and breakfast in Columbus, a small country town about one hour west of Houston, for our annual board retreat. (Cat Springs was still unacceptable to Arthur Gaines.) The argument began at once.

José was furious. We had contrived to exclude the Hispanic community from the process. We had insulted them, humiliated them. They would fight.

Paula was hurt and mad. She used the f-word a lot when she was mad. We heard the f-word a lot that evening. Cathy, Ron, and I, her friends, her partners in school reform, had shared their thinking with each other, but not her. "How could you f-ing do this to me?" she stormed, glaring around the large, old oak table covered with drinks and snack food. "Have I not always been loyal to you? Have I not always worked with you since the Joan Raymond deal? You'd better never, ever do this again to me. Do you f-ing hear me. I swear if you do, I'll f-ing create hell."

We continued late into the night over dinner, interrupting each other, shouting on occasion, going around and around over the same points. Once Rod reminded the group how he had been out of the loop two and a half years earlier when the decision had been made to hire Frank. Once José called me a racist, a man who wanted to hold minorities down because of my own personal insecurities.

Discussions continued all day Saturday. Meanwhile Ron, our new board president, José, Paula, and others were continually called away for phone calls. The press was insatiable. And the Hispanic Education Committee, meeting at Velia's Cafe, was organizing for a fight.

For the next few days the newspapers were full of the Paige controversy. Readers were shown headlines like, "Did HISD exclude 3 dissenters? Talks held in private some allege." "Members divided on superintendent." "Hispanics not happy with way HISD recruited a new leader." "Hispanics decry input on Paige pick." "Walkout, sickout mulled as protest." "Hispanics threaten HISD suit." "Group protests superintendent selection process." "Paige's HISD backers defend choice." An editorial in the Saturday *Post* called on HISD to "Do it again." The board's action was called "appalling," "arrogant," and "bizarre" (January 20, 1994, p. A28).

A big showdown was planned by the Hispanic Education Committee for Sunday evening. Between 175 and 200 people packed into Velia's Cafe.[1] For nearly two hours Ron and Cathy were queried, challenged, sometimes insulted, and almost continuously hissed and booed. "Shame on you," said one speaker. "Our children are not for sale," said another. "There is a deep rage in us," said a third.

Paula made it clear to the group that she did not approve of the process, but she affirmed that Rod would make an outstanding superintendent. There were five votes committed to him, she said. It made no sense to fight for a search. If Rod applied for the position, she would vote for him. Now the crowd directed its anger at Paula. She was a turncoat.

Apparently some had thought they could pressure at least two board members into reconsidering their support for Rod, but when it became clear that Ron and Cathy would not yield, the crowd became even angrier. Committees were formed: one to press a lawsuit against the board; another to collect signatures on a petition for a recall election against Paula; a third to manage a public relations campaign to pressure the board into launching a search process; and a fourth to look into possible school walkouts, boycotts, and other protest measures. Checks were collected. Lists of volunteers were started. Roman Martinez, who was a candidate for the Texas Senate, said several HISD employees had promised "to sing like canaries" about how the Paige selection was illegally stage-managed by the board (*Post,* January 24, 1994, p. A1; *Chronicle,* January 24, 1994, p. A9).

Two days later, on January 25, Ron responded to the *Post* editorial with an op-ed defending the offer to Paige. The board went into closed session prepared to consider all options, he said. After two hours of discussion it became apparent that a majority of the board wanted Paige to consider becoming superintendent. "The *Post* criticizes us for this process being 'secret,' " he concluded. "Would the *Post* prefer that instead of voting on this issue, we should have kept this information to ourselves? That we should have embarked on a selection process that would intentionally mislead the public and candidates for the superintendency?" (p. A15).

African Americans Respond

On the same page, Robert C. Newberry, a regular columnist for the *Post* and an African American, took his shot at the Paige selection. He concurred with the board that Paige was an excellent choice, though like everyone else he damned the selection process. Then he concluded, "[I]t's a race issue. Pure and simple."

The controversy in the media continued. Every day the television stations had another story on the Paige selection. Columns, op-eds, letters to the editor expressed the full range of opinions. More and more the central issue was race. Most letter writers were strongly supportive of Paige and disgusted by the ethnic politics.

The inevitable black backlash came almost immediately. On Monday, January 24, at a news conference, the Rev. J. J. Roberson, president of the Baptist Ministers Association of Houston and Vicinity, praised the board for its swift invitation to Rod. Hispanics, he said, were only upset because the board did not chose someone from their community. They once "thought they were white folks," he said. "Then they found out they were minority groups like ourselves. They've never really been with us. We fought our battles and they fought theirs. My suggestion to them is let's unite and have a united front. It's our time now; it may be theirs the next time." Blacks, he continued, would not sit idle while Hispanics challenged the hiring of Paige. "If all of us get in our pulpits and start talking, the Hispanics may as well start walking. We are going to talk about it in our pulpits. Our members are going to be talking about it on their jobs. Everywhere we go, we are going to have somebody talking about Rod Paige being superintendent of this school district" (*Chronicle,* January 26, 1994, p. A17; *Post,* January 26, 1994, p. A1).

That afternoon 25 black children picketed outside the HISD administrative office headquarters in support of Paige.

Throughout all this controversy, Rod kept his composure. His comments to the media were humble and conciliatory. He was meeting with everybody, including Hispanic leaders. "I respect the cordial way they've received me," he said. "Some were supportive, some less so, but all were respectful. . . . I think this is going to run its course, and then I think there will be peace and we'll work together in harmony" (*Post,* January 26, 1994, p. A1).

The next day he said he was "considering what is the path to take, because I don't want to be a part of a disruptive situation" (*Chronicle,* January 27, p. A18). A few days later, on Thursday, January 27, Rod announced his resignation from the HISD board and stated that he would consider the position of HISD superintendent if it were offered.

Important Appointments Required

Immediately a new set of wheels started turning. A person to replace Rod as the district nine trustee had to be found and sworn in before Rod could begin negotiations with the board. Also, Rod had to obtain a Texas superintendent's certificate. Meanwhile the board had to select an interim superintendent. On January 24, following just a few days of negotiation, Frank and the Broward County board agreed on a contract and Frank submitted his letter of resignation. The effective date was February 1.

A special executive meeting of the board was posted for January 31. José Salazar came prepared with a recommendation. He wanted Yvonne Gonzalez, an assistant superintendent in the campus management department, to be interim superintendent. I was opposed. There were easily a dozen or more school administrators who outranked Yvonne and by experience and ability deserved the honor of being named interim superintendent. Two of them were Hispanic, one a Panamanian and the other a Mexican American woman married to an Anglo. If we had to appoint a Hispanic, which everyone agreed we did, why not one of them? No, said José, they were not *real* Hispanics. Being Hispanic, apparently, was not enough. One had to be Mexican American and politically active. So Dr. Gonzalez was elected interim superintendent.

Poor José. He thought he was doing the right thing. But the Hispanic Education Committee was upset. Wednesday night at Velia's Cafe he was given a tongue-lashing. He was supposed to show his displeasure with the board by voting against everything.

"I am not a puppet," he told the group at Velia's. "Just because you are angry, I am not going to sit here and be vilified just because you want revenge."

Marcia Olivarez, cochair of the committee, retorted: "All I am hearing is an elitist attitude: 'The masses are asses and I can do it better' " (*Chronicle,* February 3, 1994, p. A19).

Replacing Rod on the board, which could have been difficult, turned out to be simple. Within days the black leadership of Houston had united behind Robert Jefferson. Jefferson, a short, heavy man with a very round head and almost no hair, was pastor of the Cullen Missionary Baptist Church. He had been active in his community for years and received the NAACP Unity Award for founding Ministers Against Crime, a coalition of black and Hispanic ministers established to combat violence in public schools. Jeff, as he was called, had been a PTO president, served on numerous school and civic committees, and was known by almost everyone. His endorsement letters were numerous and came from all the right people.

At the regularly scheduled February 3 board meeting, Rod officially resigned his position on the board and Robert Jefferson was elected trustee for District Nine. Paula voted no. José and Olga abstained. There was applause from a packed gallery, but not from the members of the Hispanic Education Committee, who sat together as a group and looked on in angry silence.

Paige Hired

Contract negotiations with Rod began immediately. On Monday, February 7, at another specially posted executive meeting, the board approved a contract with Rod. He would serve out Frank's term, which ended June 30, 1995, and receive the annual salary the board had been paying Frank, $147,000 plus benefits and perks. The vote was 6–2. Paula voted yes. José and Olga voted no. Members of the Hispanic Education Committee, watching from the gallery, told the press, "It's not over yet" (*Post,* February 8, 1994, p. A13).

CONFRONTATION WITH THE TEA AND A LAWSUIT

The TEA Investigation

Unfortunately Rod was not able to assume the superintendency immediately. The Texas Education Code required superintendents to be certified. Rod was not certified, but a 1984 statute allowed the commissioner of education to grant certificates to "outstanding educators." Rod certainly qualified, and no one expected Commissioner Meno to delay the issue of a temporary superintendent's certificate pending Rod's passing of the superintendent's examination.

Commissioner Meno, however, said he did not have time to examine Rod's credentials before leaving on a 10-day vacation. Then, on his return, he requested that the board formally request a waiver. TEA rules, he said, conflicted with the statute. He did not have the legal authority to act without a formal board request. So on February 17, the board voted to ask the commissioner to apply the law. "Normally we don't have to ask state officials to follow the law. They just do," said Cathy (*Post,* February 18, 1994, p. A25).

The next day, Friday, Commissioner Meno granted Paige a two-year superintendent's certificate, contingent on his passing within one year the state test to qualify as a superintendent. (Subsequently Rod passed the test on his first attempt with a very high score.) But at the same time, Meno announced that he was sending a TEA assessment team to Houston to investigate complaints about the Paige selection.

A week earlier the Hispanic Education Committee had filed an official complaint with the TEA asking for an investigation. The committee charged that the board had violated the Open Meetings Act, acted unethically by excluding three trustees and their largely Mexican-origin constituents from the process, and ignored affirmative action laws by failing to conduct a national search.

It seemed obvious. Meno had stalled on the Paige certificate to test the political waters. Then he responded, as bureaucrats frequently do, with a compromise. Paige got his certificate. The Hispanic Education Committee got its investigation.

But the Hispanic Education Committee was not satisfied.[2] And Sunday the League of United Latin American Citizens (LULAC) announced that it would ask the U.S. Department of Education's Office of Civil Rights to investigate Paige's appointment. LULAC also said because of the "continued insensitivity and arrogance on the part of the board," it was forming a blue-ribbon panel to study creating a separate school district of mostly Hispanic students (*Chronicle,* February 22, 1994, p. A13).

Tuesday, February 22, was Rod's first day on the job. He spent most of his day in schools and meeting with rank-and-file employees. "I felt good being out in the schools," he told the press. "I'm in my element, and I can see what my job really is" (*Post*, February 23, 1994, p. A13). "The highlight of any day is when I can spend it in school with the teachers and the children who seem to reinforce your energy" (*Chronicle*, February 23, 1994, p. A17).

That same day the TEA assessment team began its investigation. The team was led by Ruben Olivarez, executive deputy commissioner for accountability. Assisting him were James Vasquez, senior director and head of the TEA division that reviewed board actions; and Walter Chandler, recently retired as associate commissioner for accreditation and investigation. Chandler, an African American, was pulled out of retirement to give the team ethnic balance.

The team began its work by meeting Rod and Ron. That evening they met with the Hispanic Education Committee. About 75 people were present when Martha Almaguer pointed at the TEA officials and said, "If we have a walkout, and some child kills another child because it looks like a Black-Hispanic issue, I'm not taking responsibility. It's going to be your responsibility" (*Chronicle*, February 23, 1994, p. A17).

The next day the assessment team met with board members. My meeting was in the morning. Olivarez bore in like a prosecuting attorney. He asked leading questions, inferred ulterior motives. He suggested that Ron had voted for Rod as superintendent in return for Arthur's vote for him as board president and that Cathy had supported Rod in order to obtain the support of Houston's black leaders for her husband David, who had declared his candidacy for chairman of the Harris County Democratic Party. I almost laughed.

The assessment report and any actions by the commissioner, said Olivarez, would not be announced for several weeks. Most board members concluded that the news would not be good. Olivarez came across as an angry Hispanic activist. It looked like he had already made up his mind.

Meanwhile Rod's credentials had become public documents. Now it was not just the process. Hispanic activists charged that Rod was unqualified. Because his doctorate was in physical education, charged Tatcho Mindiola, a professor at the University of Houston, Rod was "the least prepared person to become superintendent in the history of HISD." Paige and the African American community were "being used by the White members of the board to pursue their own agenda." We were pitting Mexican and African Americans against each other to achieve our goals. We were willing to "flout the law and publicly scoff at the Mexican American community." We—Ron Franklin, Cathy Mincberg, Don McAdams, and Paula Arnold—suggested Mindiola, were *gringos*—"vicious manipulators who would do anything to gain their way" (*Post*, February 25, 1994, p. F2).

The Lawsuit

On March 3, the Hispanic Education Committee filed its long-threatened lawsuit against the board in state district court. The plaintiffs, the Hispanic Education Committee, the Texas Association of Chicanos in Higher Education, and four individuals: Marcia Olivarez, Guadalupe San Miguel, Alfredo Santos, and Rosemary Covalt, alleged that the board had violated the Texas Open Meetings Act and requested a permanent injunction enjoining Paige from serving as superintendent. There was another flurry of news stories and editorials, and then, for the rest of March, relative quiet.

The TEA Report

The assessment report of the TEA investigation team was released on March 30 (TEA, February 22–24, 1994). The main conclusion was that there was no evidence that the Open Meetings Act was violated, "However, given the number of meetings and contacts with most of the board members involved at one time or another, the facts do indicate a potential violation of the Open Meetings Act."

The report also concluded that Rod violated the Texas Education Code by applying for and soliciting the position of superintendent while serving on the board. The evidence? At the January 27 press conference where he announced his decision to resign his board seat and respond positively to the board's invitation, Rod said to the entire city of Houston: "By accepting the offer of the school board, I also extend my hand to my friends and colleagues on the board to work cooperatively with them. I am hoping they will advise me about the best forum for soliciting input from their individual constituencies."

Finally the report concluded that though the board had not violated any of its own policies or procedures, "the board's action does call into question whether or not they violated their affirmative action policy which is under the jurisdiction of the Office of Civil Rights."

Based on these conclusions, Commissioner Meno announced that he was referring the possible Open Meetings Act violation to the Harris County District Attorney and the possible civil rights violation to the U.S. Department of Education, Office of Civil Rights. He was strongly encouraging the board "to immediately develop and implement an open and appropriate search process for selecting an individual to serve as superintendent beginning July 1, 1995." He was revising Rod's temporary superintendent's certificate so that it would expire on June 30, 1995. And he was assigning James Vasquez to monitor HISD. "He will report to me on the board's progress in implementing my recommendations and provide technical assistance if requested by the district" (Meno, March 30, 1994).

I was stunned. Ron was outraged. He characterized the report as "bizarre" and "influenced by political pressure." "This is a sad day for the TEA, and for everyone who believes in local control of schools."

Rod told the press the report hit him "like a ton of bricks," but he knew he had done nothing wrong and intended to keep his focus on students and schools.

The Hispanic Education Committee was delighted. "What the TEA has done is prove we've not been frivolous with our allegations," said Marcia Olivarez. She went on to charge board members with "race-baiting" (*Post*, March 31, 1994, p. A1).

The Commissioner Backs Down

The next few days were tense. The newspapers were once again full of stories about the HISD mess. It seemed that everybody had an opinion, most of them unfavorable to the board of education. A *Post* editorial put the full blame for the "mess" on the board, saying the board had exhibited poor leadership, insensitivity, and arrogance (*Post*, April 1, 1994, p. A30). Board attorney, Kelly Frels, informed us that it would be wise for us to begin thinking about hiring personal lawyers. Meanwhile, we determined among ourselves that we would not comply with the commissioner's directive. We would not begin a search. We would ignore Mr. Vasquez. And we might file a lawsuit against the commissioner.

The dark clouds began to part almost immediately. The very next day, March 30, Harris County District Attorney John B. Holmes Jr., announced that his preliminary review of the TEA findings turned up no evidence of wrongdoing by either the board or Paige. "If this is all they have to show that he solicited that job," he said, referring to Rod's acceptance statement, "I am unimpressed. Somebody might want to point out to these folks, the TEA, that they are not immune from libel and slander" (*Chronicle*, April 1, 1994, p. A1).

At least I would not need a lawyer. But there was still the matter of Rod's certificate and Commissioner Meno's requirement that HISD conduct a search for a new superintendent. It was time for political action.

We had information that Houston Hispanics, including at least one highly placed HISD Hispanic administrator, were in direct contact with TEA officials. We knew several Hispanic elected officials and office seekers were making as much out of the issue as possible. We were convinced Meno was acting politically and that he, and maybe Governor Richards, had made a bad mistake. How stupid! It was an election year. Two traditional Democratic constituencies were on either side of a complex issue. Meno could have, should have, politely stayed out. Instead he had attacked HISD's first black superintendent.

The phone calls and meetings began immediately. Rod told the press he was getting so many calls he had put his phone in the refrigerator. The Reverend Bill Lawson, pastor of the Wheeler Avenue Baptist Church and perhaps Houston's most respected black leader, said the issue was "like a lynching because it does look like there is some kind of concerted attempt to get him out at all costs" (*Chronicle*, April 1, 1994, p. A1).

I do not know the details of this part of the story. The work in the black community was managed by Robert Jefferson and Arthur Gaines. They kept me informed and told me not to worry. They were going to inflict serious political damage on Governor Richards if Meno did not reverse himself.

Governor Richards really was on the spot, as *Chronicle* political columnist Jane Ely pointed out on April 3. After making fun of the school board as a bunch of political incompetents, she pointed out that George W. Bush might make an election-year issue of the HISD mess. Ann Richards was between "a really big political rock and a superhard political place." She either had to chew out Meno or "swallow whole" her commitment to local control of education. And she had to "walk an especially careful line among the minority voters vital to a Democrat's political fate" (p. E2).

The black offensive continued. On April 4, the Houston branch of the NAACP announced that it would intervene in the lawsuit filed against the HISD board by the Hispanic Education Committee. "The board's actions," said President Al Green, "were not only lawful, but also in keeping with its established policies" (*Chronicle*, April 5, 1994, p. A15). Also, a group of black ministers were organizing to demand the resignation of Commissioner Meno and possibly the abolishment of the TEA.

State legislators were also hammering Meno. Sue Schecter (D-Houston) sent a strongly worded protest to Meno with copies to Richards, the Harris County legislative delegation, and others. Debra Danburg (D-Houston) also sent Meno a letter decrying his "overreaching power play" and defending local control of schools. Harold Dutton (D-Houston) said he was drafting a letter to Meno and thought maybe it was time to "Make TEA DOA" (*Chronicle*, April 8, 1995, p. A25).

Two days later Commissioner Meno crumbled. On April 6, he sent a letter to Ron Franklin to "clarify" his letter of March 30. No, Mr. Vasquez was not a "monitor" under section 35.121 of the Texas Education Code. He was just available to observe and be helpful. And no, reducing the time of Paige's temporary superintendent certificate did not preclude Paige from qualifying for permanent certification or having his contract renewed. He said, "Any other interpretation of my previous correspondence would be incorrect." And finally, "I have no interest in influencing who the board selects [as superintendent] from a pool of qualified applicants." In other words, do whatever you wish.

The same day District Attorney Holmes announced that he had found no evidence of misconduct by the board and was discontinuing his investigation. "I think they're wrong," he said of the TEA allegations. "It's D.O.A." (*Post*, April 7, 1994, p. A1).

It was public humiliation for Commissioner Meno. A source in the governor's office said, "We relayed our feelings to him that this was a local school board issue. We had no business being in there, and he agreed." Richards's press secretary, Bill Cryer, said that any possible role the state might have played in the HISD superintendent selection was eliminated when Holmes found that no laws had been violated. "We believe it's over. All the questions have been answered. There's nothing left for the TEA to do." Was Meno pressured? asked a reporter. "I would not say that he was pressured," said Cryer, "I'd say we let him know what we thought" (*Chronicle*, April 7, 1994, p. A1).

The Paige selection controversy was over. Houston's black leaders, however, wanted to fire one more shot to show the TEA, Governor Richards, the Hispanic Education Committee, and anyone else who might have doubts that Paige was their man and that he better be left alone. A huge rally for Paige was scheduled for April 13 at the Mt. Hebron Baptist Church.

It was wonderful. The church was packed. A drill team of young people marched up and down the aisles, executing complex drills in perfect unison. A large choir filled the church with powerful gospel music. Minister after minister thundered against the TEA and the great injustice done to Rod Paige. Board members were introduced to sustained applause and allowed to say a few words. And Governor Richards's recently appointed secretary of state, Ron Kirk, an African American, assured everyone that Governor Richards was taking a personal interest in the situation.

A week later Commissioner Meno came to Houston and shared breakfast with Rod at one of HISD's elementary schools. Cordiality prevailed. The media gave the breakfast major coverage and then dropped the issue. The controversy was over.

The Lawsuit Dismissed

All that remained was the lawsuit. The Hispanic Education Committee, of course, did not go away. They had built their reputation as great fighters. They could not surrender now. So the lawsuit dragged on and on. It was moved to federal court at the request of HISD. Documents were produced and interrogatories answered by the defendants in May. Depositions were taken in July. Finally, in December, United States District Judge Lynn N. Hughes ruled. HISD's request for summary judgment was granted. All charges against the board were dismissed (*Hispanic Education Committee v. HISD*, December 27, 1994).

Judge Hughes's opinion was a complete vindication of the board. He pointedly noted that the undercurrent of complaint was that the board did not select a Hispanic: "Paige does not represent in a meaningful way all black people any more than the committee can claim to represent all Hispanic people."

He ruled that there was no discrimination, and informal discussions by trustees were not cabals to subvert public view of the selection decision. "Important decisions require preparation as well as visible decision, and the individual members of the board did not evade Texas law by conferring with one another, staff members, interest groups, and other individuals."

The complaint that segments of the community had been denied the right to speak was also rejected: "During the whole gaggle of events from the occurrence of the vacancy through to the appointment of the new superintendent, the board was subjected to the buffeting of letters, press conferences, speeches, meetings, and the rest of the wonderful cacophony of a free people disagreeing."

The Hispanic Education Committee, of course, appealed to the United States Fifth Circuit Court of Appeals. The case would drag on a little longer. The documents generated by the lawsuit already made a stack of paper five inches high. More briefs would be written. Legal fees would go even higher. But it was over. Everyone knew it was over. Except for a short story when the Fifth Circuit Court rejected the appeal in August 1995, the newspapers never mentioned the lawsuit again. Neither did anyone else.

José Salazar resigned from the HISD board on April 8 as he had promised. He was succeeded by Esther Campos, who was elected in a runoff election on May 31 by a very low turnout.

George W. Bush defeated Ann Richards in the November 1994 election, and soon after his inauguration as governor of Texas, Skip Meno was replaced as commissioner of education.

Rod, meanwhile, proved to be a brilliant superintendent. Within three months he had intervened in three schools. Within a year he was transforming the district. In time, nearly everyone acknowledged that Rod was an outstanding superintendent. Still, just as universally, the board members who selected him were damned for arrogance, stupidity, and worse for selecting him the way they did.

NOTES

1. The leaders had worked the phones for two days to get this turnout. I had to attend a wedding and was spared the event.

2. "It's unscrupulous of the TEA to immediately certify him," said Guadalupe San Miguel, a spokesman for the committee. "It's quite clear they really don't care

about the process" (*Post*, February 19, 1994, p. A28). Marcia Olivarez, cochairman, said, "I think that by sending out the assessment team, they are just trying to appease us. Why grant a waiver and send an assessment team at the same time? Why bother? If they had truly wanted to do the right thing, they would have sent the assessment team out weeks ago" (*Chronicle*, February 19, 1994, p. A1).

8

Decentralizing the School District

Decentralization, after accountability, was the second board priority for 1993. The second mandate of *Beliefs and Visions* was that "HISD must decentralize." "A highly centralized hierarchical system of governance cannot meet students' needs." "Schools are where decisions should be made." "Central office must turn the traditional management pyramid upside down and become an enabler rather than an enforcer." "Schools must be given control over budgets, curriculum, teaching methodologies, and personnel."

But it was not just *Beliefs and Visions* that made decentralization a priority for 1993. It was the Greater Houston Partnership. During the budget battle of 1992, the partnership had repeatedly charged that HISD was spending too much money on noninstructional activities. Board President Paige's response was: Show us the waste and we will eliminate it.

PETRUZIELO WON'T DECENTRALIZE

Formation of the Hook Committee

Following the approval of the 32 percent tax increase in August 1992, Paige began to talk with the partnership about a formal process whereby the best business minds of the city could look carefully at the HISD budget and recommend ways to shift money from administration to classrooms. The result was the Houston Business Advisory Council, formally established by the board at the first board meeting of 1993. The Hook committee, as we came to call it, after its chairman, American General chairman and CEO Harold Hook, was appointed by the partnership but accountable to the Board of Education. Its immediate focus was the budget.

Petruzielo resented the committee. Its very existence implied that the

122

board could not rely on him to manage the organization effectively and efficiently. But there was an upside for him. The board had blocked Frank's desire to privatize some facilities management operations. Frank recognized that he could use the Hook committee to get privatization back on the table.

In October 1992, the management consultancy Deloitte & Touche completed a management audit of HISD's facilities management and operations department. The audit recommended contracting several fairly small operations out to private vendors. Annual reoccurring savings would be $800,000. Fifty jobs would be at risk. Numerous other very large privatization opportunities needed further study.

Frank wanted to implement the Deloitte & Touche recommendations, but key board members had told him they did not want the report to see the light of day. It was a jobs issue. I knew nothing of this until after becoming board president in January 1993, and at first doubted Frank, but he was right. I canvassed my board colleagues and found almost no support for privatization.

The establishment of the Hook committee gave Frank an idea. "Don," he said, "The business community supports privatization. Why don't you officially request that I transmit the Deloitte & Touche Report to you. This will cover me with the board members who want me to bury it. Then you can unofficially transmit it to Al Haines [president of the chamber of commerce division of the partnership and the active agent on the Hook committee] and urge him to put the full weight of the Hook committee behind a strong privatization recommendation to the board." Within a few weeks the members of the Hook committee had copies of the Deloitte & Touche report.

The Hook committee began its work in February. The first step was an assessment. During the next several months, committee members visited 18 schools and talked with dozens of principals, area superintendents, budget analysts, and central office staff. Their focus was the budgeting process, but their findings focused on the district's organizational structure.

The Hook Committee Report

At a June 15 meeting in Al Haines's office, Al and Mr. Hook previewed for me their report to the board. They were overwhelmed by the diversity of HISD. Indeed, said Hook, "About all some of the schools have in common with others is that they serve children."

The good news was that shared decision-making was beginning to work and principals were very pleased with Frank's school-based budgeting. The bad news was that the central office was trying to manage schools with a highly centralized, unitary management structure. All significant decisions and many insignificant ones were made by the superintendent.

"No one, not even the most talented manager in the world, could effectively manage HISD the way it is currently structured," said Hook. "Frank is so bright and has so much energy that he almost makes it work. But many important matters are slipping through the cracks. Frank has an impossible job. Your number one problem is not obvious waste in the system. It's ineffective management because the system is so highly centralized. You pledged yourselves to decentralization in *Beliefs and Visions*. We can help you do it. We think this is the most valuable contribution we can make to HISD at this time. Do you think the board will support this priority?"

The Hook committee recommendations were presented to the board two days later. Hook launched into an extended discourse on management theory and organizational structure. Hook, a short man who was reasonably trim for his age and distinguished-looking with every silver hair in place and not a wrinkle in his expensive gray suit, turned out to be more than a CEO. He was a management theorist and philosopher. He talked about the organizational iron triangle; outlined the characteristics of dynamic, complex organizations; referred to the double feedback loops of adaptive systems; and briefly reviewed the history of management structures starting with Moses and the twelve tribes of Israel. All this was preamble. The point was, the Houston Business Advisory Council had no budget recommendations; the budget was a derivative problem. The core problem was structure.

The recommendations were straightforward. Building on decentralization statements from *Beliefs and Visions,* Hook stated that "HISD cannot function efficiently or productively in its current organizational mode." It needed to convert its current unitary structure into a multidivisional structure (Hook, June 17, 1993).

HISD is moving in the right direction, he said. School empowerment has begun. But HISD has a long way to go. "With some risk, I would say, if you track a hundred percent, you're more in the 10 or 15 percent range. . . . I think it should be said that even though 15 percent doesn't sound like a lot, that may be the toughest part that is behind you. . . . I think the superintendent should take a great deal of satisfaction. You know, it is a very difficult thing to turn around battleships" (HISD, June 17, 1993, pp. 2–13).

What was needed, Hook continued, was to shift significantly authority and responsibility to the schools and restructure the central and area offices to support adequately, monitor, evaluate, and if necessary intervene in school operations. Al Haines, elaborating on Hook's comments, emphasized that the Hook committee was willing to work with the board to help design the new organizational structure and suggested that intermediate management units, perhaps built around high school feeder patterns, might be appropriate.[1]

The Board Restructuring Committee

The board's response was enthusiastic. My response as board president (planned in advance with Hook, Haines, and other board members) was to appoint a committee of three board members to meet with two members of the Hook committee and the superintendent. We would invite Frank to bring members of his staff to assist with technical issues. This small committee would prepare specific recommendations on organizational structure for the board's consideration.

I knew I was dancing around a sensitive point. Frank already resented the Hook committee, and Hook had just diminished the significance of his achievements.[2] Now the board and the business leadership of Houston were preparing, quite openly, to restructure HISD, almost as if he did not exist.

The board restructuring committee began its work on July 12, 1993. The trustee members were Arthur Gaines, Cathy Mincberg, and me as chairman. Al Haines and Caroline Vetterling, a partner at Blazek & Vetterling, LLP, an accounting firm, represented the Hook committee. Frank usually brought with him his chief of staff, Susan Sclafani. We met early on Friday mornings in the board conference room once or twice a month from July through December.

We accomplished nothing. It was clear after one or two meetings that Frank had no intention of making major changes in HISD's organizational structure. He talked about how much he had accomplished. He defended the status quo. And he always had a reason why suggestions put forward by others were not needed or would not work. Frank was all-powerful within HISD. He was sounding more and more like Joan Raymond.

Al Haines and Caroline Vetterling became ever more frustrated. Cathy and I finally concluded that we would have to force Frank to accept an organizational structure designed by the board even if it meant a public battle at the board table. We believed we had the votes.

Then, just after Thanksgiving, Frank announced his job opportunity in Florida.

The Hook-Haines Plan

On December 1, 1993, Al Haines and I lunched at Prego, an Italian restaurant in the Rice University Village. We agreed that HISD must move forward with decentralization with or without Frank. We had talked before about the barriers to decentralization. The bureaucracy and the teacher unions would resist. Board members might not have the political courage to implement decentralization recommendations. Hook, said Al, had come up with a strategy to overcome the resistance. He wanted to run it by me.

Al commenced to outline the plan. Al, a tall, trim, middle-aged man with silver hair, was usually soft-spoken and laconic. His appearance fit his personality—focused, disciplined, and tough-minded, but not one to take risks. Today, however, his enthusiasm was carrying him forward in a torrent of words and animated gestures.

The board would create a task force of HISD administrators and others, supported by full-time consultants and loaned executives as needed. The task force, which Al himself would probably lead, would master the technical issues and recommend a new, decentralized organizational structure. The Hook committee would oversee the work of the task force and advise the board on structural, management, and financial issues. A third body, a commission on decentralization, would be created by the board to represent the community. The commission, comprised of 30 or so of Houston's leading citizens, would review the task force's recommendations, hold public meetings, solicit the widest possible input, and then bring the decentralization recommendations directly to the board.

Excellent. The task force would produce realistic recommendations that met the needs of schools. The Hook committee would guarantee the integrity of the process. And the stamp of approval by the decentralization commission would give the board political cover. The special interest groups would be powerless.

Al said he would work with Hook to flesh out the plan. It would be presented to the board as an official recommendation as soon as we knew what Frank was going to do.

Two days later, Cathy, Arthur, and I met with Al and Harold in Al's office. Harold laid out the strategy for Cathy and Arthur. Cathy liked it. Arthur expressed no reservations. Soon the other board members were on board. Rod and Ron were especially enthusiastic. To my knowledge Frank never knew what we were planning.

On January 6, Frank announced that he had been offered the Broward County superintendency. It was time to act. The Hook committee would officially recommend the Hook-Haines decentralization strategy at the next board meeting, January 20. The board would approve it. The decentralization of HISD would begin.

Everything went as planned. The Hook-Haines plan was purposely presented to the board and the public before the board went into closed session on January 20, 1994, to discuss the superintendency vacancy created by Frank's departure. We wanted HISD employees and interested Houstonians to know that decentralization came first. Whoever became HISD's next superintendent, HISD was going to decentralize.

Ron made all this clear when, in his first act as board president, he introduced Harold Hook. Hook once again ranged far and wide—the behavior of complex structures, cause and effect in the affairs of humankind, inner and outer environments, resources and choice, and even a story of two boys who asked a famous mountain-top sage if the bird in their hands was dead or alive. Along the way he outlined the structure and process for decentralization.

The immediate focus of the decentralization initiative would be: (1) a review of the budget process and format and the development of a comprehensive fiscal plan; (2) a review of the appropriate role of the central office, specifically the office of superintendent; (3) consideration of decentralization of functions and strengthening of site-based management; and (4) a review of alternatives such as privatization of service delivery and service support (Hook, January 19, 1994).

The board unanimously accepted the proposal.

The *Chronicle,* alone among Houston's media, noticed what had happened, perhaps because Ron Franklin and Rod Paige had the opportunity to visit with the editorial board the next day and explain the link between decentralization and the board's interest in Rod as superintendent. Their Sunday editorial, printed as the fury of the Hispanic Education Committee broke upon the city, said: "It is possible, just possible, that Houston is closer to getting a handle on its frustrating public school problems than it has been in years. The school trustees seem to have settled on a route, a process, and a person which offer a rational way to get from here to there" (*Chronicle,* January 23, 1994, p. E2).

IMPLEMENTING THE HOOK-HAINES PLAN

The decentralization process began at once. While the public focused on the controversy over Paige's selection as superintendent, board members, Rod, and Al Haines began putting into place the infrastructure for decentralization.

The Commission on District Decentralization

During the first weeks of March, Cathy, who had agreed to take the lead in putting together the decentralization commission, gave almost full time to the task. She did a magnificent job. She knew who was who in Houston better than any other board member. She asked all board members to suggest names. She worked tirelessly and successfully to convince several board members to back away from candidates with obvious political agendas. She guaranteed the proper ethnic, gender, occupational, and geographic balance.

Al Haines and retired Exxon U. S. A. president Randall Meyer were the chief recruiters. They came up with excellent suggestions. They spent hundreds of hours visiting some of Houston's leading citizens, explaining the opportunity, and making an appeal for commitment.

The board approved the decentralization commission membership on

April 7. It was a very impressive group, 34 of Houston's established leaders: men and women, African American, Hispanic, Asian, and white, business executives, nonprofit executives, educators, judges, ministers, a rabbi, law enforcement professionals, attorneys, and so forth.

At its kickoff meeting on May 4, the commission members elected as its chairman Alberto Gonzales, a partner at one of Houston's best-known law firms, Vinson & Elkins. Sylvia Brooks, executive director of the Houston Area Urban League, was elected vice chairman.

The Decentralization Task Force

The decentralization task force was also appointed by the board on April 7. Appointed chairman was John Cater, president and CEO of River Oaks Trust Company. Al Haines was appointed managing director.

There was already some controversy. Al had the best of intentions and had been working very hard to build consensus by meeting with key administrators, principals, and parent leaders. But he was giving the impression that he had already decided what the task force recommendations would be. The terrifying word "downsizing" was beginning to be heard around the district. Central office administrators were nervous. Some principals were stirring up parent leaders.

The heat was on Rod to protect the organization from the wild thinking of this business man who knew nothing about education. Rod was in a tough spot. He had problems enough with the Hispanic Education Committee and the responsibility of learning a new, very complex job. Now he subtly had to reassure the staff that he was in charge of decentralization and at the same time support Al.[3]

Soon after the board established the decentralization task force on April 7, Rod appointed the task force members. He selected principals and line and staff administrators who were smart, experienced, and tough. They would not roll over for Al or anyone else.

Named as full-time task force coordinator was Robert Stockwell, director of instructional development at the time. He was given an office, a secretary, a computer, a photocopy machine, and a fax. Robert was going to know more about decentralization than anyone else. He was going to pay attention to the nuts and bolts. He was going to make certain Rod knew everything, and he was going to protect and advance Rod's interests.

On April 21, Rod recommended and the board approved an interim organizational structure—pending the recommendations of the decentralization task force—that realigned the responsibilities and reporting relationships of his senior staff. Significantly, slipped into the middle of the recommendation was the statement, "The task force for district decentralization reports directly to the superintendent of schools." None of the board members commented on this statement. I am not sure that they noticed it. But the staff did. Rod had made his point. Now I knew that in addition to being a visionary, a diplomat, and a man with great inner strength, Rod was also a skillful bureaucratic infighter.

The task force met for the first time on May 9. Thereafter it met regularly on Monday afternoons. It got off to a rough start. There were communication problems and disagreement on the agenda, and HISD team members said Al appeared to hold a low opinion of educators.

About this time the *Post* zinged HISD with an insulting editorial that exacerbated the situation. Educators were blasted for incompetence and Al was quoted saying that the business groups might be wasting their time but should try. Yes, agreed the *Post*, and "they also should be tough and not kowtow to district bureaucrats" (*Post*, May 23, 1994, p. A16).

The task force was going through the expected early stages of team development: forming and storming. But in time the later stages, norming and performing, arrived. One by one controversial issues were resolved. The agenda was clarified. Communications guidelines were adopted. Guiding principles were established. By late June, the task force was a high-performing team.

In mid-June, the task force began interviewing employees. A particularly dramatic event occurred on June 27 when the task force staged an all-day open meeting to gather information from principals and central office administrators. School board members and members of the decentralization commission were invited. The difference between the principals' comments in the morning and the central office administrators' comments in the afternoon was night and day.

The principals were frustrated in their work. They complained about the time they had to spend on business matters. They said they needed more clerical help, greater assistance with budgets, quicker responses to maintenance problems, and fewer roadblocks when trying innovative instructional methods.

Mark Twain Elementary principal Joyce Dauber said maintenance was a constant headache:

> I spend much too much time calling maintenance to get repairs done that I should be spending in instructional time with my teachers. And I know we've talked about this at other meetings that we have looker #1, looker #2, looker #3, and maybe the 4th or 5th looker will finally fix the problem. But obviously this sounds familiar (laughter). We need to spend our time working with our children, and maybe the maintenance department is too big.

Arlene Brenner from Gordon Elementary described the frustration of meeting the needs of a child with a speech problem:

> A good example . . . is a case I had recently of a little bilingual child who was speech delayed, which in simple language means he didn't speak. It took two years to get the child tested, referred, and placed in the proper program. It wasn't through anybody's lack of care, but simply the process. One, he had to be identified, two, he had to be tested by someone who was qualified to test a child in another language, then the paperwork had to be processed downtown, several meetings had to be handled, transportation had to be arranged, the proper class at the closest location to his home had to be established, and then he had to be physically transferred there. It's a very long process. It's not a-typical.

Gloria Howard, principal of R. P. Harris Elementary, said she would just like to have her phone calls returned:

> One of the things that I find I spend a great deal of time with . . . [is telephone calls]. I need to call this department and that department, so I set aside time to do that. When I finally get through, I understand the lines are busy, I leave a message. No return. I call back again tomorrow. If I get busy with my kids, then I say I'll try again. I call. I leave a message. It gives the impression to principals that their time is not important. You can keep calling and calling, and that is most departments. I would not say all, but most departments do not return phone calls. This is so important because it saves us some time. When we make a call, it is urgent. It's not life threatening, but it is urgent and we expect to have those calls returned. (HISD, June 27, 1994, morning, pp. 6, 8, 14)

The comments of the central office administrators in the afternoon, and even more their body language, conveyed anxiety more than frustration. In the morning the principals lined up behind the microphone waiting to speak. There was frequent applause and occasional laughter. In the afternoon it seemed that no one wanted to say anything. The room was quiet. The few speakers were mostly defensive. They complained about poor communication and lack of resources (HISD, June 27, 1994, afternoon).

In August, task force members met with principals in each of HISD's 21 high school feeder patterns to obtain input on feeder pattern management. They began to debate the pros and cons of organizing management units around high school feeder systems.

The work was almost complete. It was time to prepare draft recommendations for presentation to the commission. There were many critical issues.

There was significant disagreement. But everything was coming together. The HISD employees and partnership staff were working as a team. All was not sweetness and light. But Al was no longer mistrusted. He was admired. His attitude had changed, too. He spoke with humility about HISD's complexity and the challenges of educational administration. He commented in tones of genuine respect on the talent and commitment of HISD administrators.

The Task Force Report

On September 13, the commission met to receive the task force's draft recommendations in the superintendent's conference room. Attendance was excellent and support enthusiastic. There were three major recommendations (HISD, August 26, 1994).

The first focused on school management:

> *Summary:* The management authority of the principal as leader of the school campus must be fully supported by district structure and operating procedures. The district's operating environment, policies, and procedures should be examined carefully and adjusted as needed to enable principals to exercise the management authority granted them by state law and HISD policy. Barriers to the management authority of the principal should be modified and/or eliminated.

Specific recommendations followed in the management of instruction, personnel, finance, information, community relations, and facilities. The point was that although the authority of HISD principals was adequately provided for in law and board policy, it was not fully supported by the district's procedures, processes, and resources.

The second recommendation outlined a new geographic area management system. All the schools that fed a particular high school, a feeder pattern, would be organized into one management unit.

> *Summary:* The manager of the feeder system should be accountable for the performance of the feeder and should have all the responsibilities and authority required to fulfill that accountability. Feeder systems can be managed most productively when managers are responsible for no more that 2 to 3 feeders which are geographically close and have approximately 20–25 total schools in the management units.

Following were specific recommendations that outlined the appropriate responsibilities, authorities, and reporting relationships of feeder pattern managers and criteria for grouping feeder systems into manageable units. On one point the report was very emphatic. Feeder pattern management units were not to become smaller versions of the old HISD, with power concentrated at the top. "*The authority of feeder managers should be exercised with the utmost respect for the authority of principals to operate their individual school campuses*" (emphasis in original).

The third recommendation dealt with organizational structure at the top:

> *Summary:* The structural framework of the school district should be reorganized to improve the effective management of the district and the efficient delivery of services to the schools. A new division of School Operations should be responsible for the core operating units of the district—schools and feeder systems—and encompass all services which provide direct instructional and educational support to the schools. Other key offices should be created for essential district-wide support functions.

Currently, said the report, there were problems. Some districtwide functions were fragmented. Some parts were in one administrative office, other parts in another. There was duplication of responsibility for some district functions. Employees in different departments had overlapping responsibilities. There were too many organizational layers within reporting channels and inconsistencies in the interpretation of *Beliefs and Visions*. Finally, there was confusion between what a job title connoted and what a position actually required.

A significant recommendation of the task force was that key administrators in the district serve at the pleasure of the superintendent. This was a major point. Recall that in HISD administrators had, in effect, tenure.

The responsibility for moving forward the decentralization recommendation now lay with the decentralization commission. Public hearings were held on October 11, 12, and 13 at three geographically dispersed locations. The meetings were well-attended. Several suggestions had merit, and a few minor changes were made to the recommendations (Haines, October 26 and 27, 1994; Stockwell, October 27, 1994).

The Board Approves the Report

On November 17 the full decentralization commission report was presented to the board by chairman and cochairman Al Gonzales and Sylvia Brooks.

All the speakers to the agenda item were positive, except for HFT president Gayle Fallon. Her concern was the usual one—bad principals. The new district superintendents would not have the same authority as the old area superintendents to keep bad principals in check.

> We have a real concern. I mean, decentralization, if it's done well, will be wonderful. If it's done poorly, it's not a new concept. It was done poorly in New York City in the early 1960's and resulted in the 100,000 member United Federation

of Teachers and the first massive teacher walkout the New York system had. It's your choice. (HISD, November 17, 1994, p. 13)

The report was unanimously accepted.

Publicly, I was enthusiastic like everyone else, but privately I was disappointed. Instead of boldly decentralizing the district by giving principals real control over money and personnel, as I had recommended to Paige in a July 19 memo,[4] the task force and decentralization commission had simply fine-tuned the existing structure. Schools would still be funded by the allocation formula developed under Frank. Based on enrollment and types of students, they would be assigned staff positions rather than given money. Goods and services would still be supplied from central office, rather than being purchased from central office or private vendors. And real personal management authority would continue to reside in central office.

Also, the decentralization commission made no recommendations on privatization and teacher contracts. Both issues were complex and politically explosive. The commission could have given the board the political cover to tackle both issues. For a moment in time, Houston's business leaders had a golden opportunity to restructure fundamentally one of the nation's largest school districts. But they did not.

I shared my disappointment with Rod.

"I know it's not what you wanted," he responded, "but it's a step in the right direction. And it's the best we could get at this time. Be smart, Don. Act grateful and declare victory. Moving in the direction you outlined in your memo is my goal as well as yours."

I believed at the time that the business leaders of Houston shied away from fundamental decentralization, privatization, and teacher contract issues because of lack of political courage. Later I had second thoughts. Maybe they believed the board would not accept radical decentralization. Within six months, I realized that was indeed the case.

DECENTRALIZING THE SCHOOL DISTRICT

Controversy over Feeder Patterns

Following the public hearings held by the decentralization commission on October 11, 12, and 13, it was fairly clear to everyone that feeder pattern management units were coming. The questions were, which schools would be in which feeder patterns, how would the feeder pattern units be grouped into management units, and who would be chosen to manage the new management units. Well before the board approved the decentralization recommendations on November 17, HISD employees and informed parents were buzzing about these issues.

Feeder patterns were determined by school attendance zones. Attendance zone boundaries had already been redrawn to the satisfaction of almost every community in Houston. In effect, the feeder pattern management units had already been established. What was there to fight about? The issue was race.

HISD had 21 general purpose high schools with geographic attendance boundaries. The decentralization commission had concluded that a manager for each feeder system was not practical. Feeder system managers should manage two or three feeder systems.

"It should be emphasized," said the commission report, "that *feeder systems will remain distinct management units of the district.* They are not expected to combine in any way with other feeders, except for management purposes; their goals, programs, needs, communities, and management teams will remain distinct" (HISD, November 17, 1994, emphasis in original).

With all this, it would seem that it would not matter to communities which feeder patterns were combined into administrative districts. But it did. In October, I began to hear from some Bellaire High parents. Bellaire High was being cut off from strong (significantly white) feeder schools. It was going to be grouped with academically poor (predominantly Hispanic) schools.

Each one of Bellaire's three primary feeder middle schools—Pershing, Johnston, and Long—had attendance zones that were divided between Bellaire and an adjacent high school. The fear was that Johnston and Pershing, both *acceptable* schools, would be in the Westbury High or Lamar High feeder systems, and Long, an *unacceptable* school, would be the only middle school in the Bellaire feeder system.

The second issue was, which high school feeder system would be combined with Bellaire? Would it be Lamar, a high-performing high school second only to Bellaire in percentage of white students, or Westbury? Lamar was naturally preferred.

On November 3, two of my closest parent advisors and friends from District Five took me to breakfast. "Don," they said, "the shared decision-making committee and many of the teachers at Bellaire are really stirred up about this feeder pattern issue. People have a lot of questions. You have to take this seriously. You have to reassure the Bellaire school community that Long will not be the only middle school in the Bellaire feeder system."

On December 1, Rod presented for board approval the feeder system groupings. The administration recommendation put Lamar and Reagan High together. Lamar was considered one of HISD's two premier general-purpose high schools. It was 38 percent white. Reagan was 84 percent Hispanic. Also, Davis High, 86 percent Hispanic, was paired with Kashmere High, which was 97 percent African American; and Milby High, 81 percent Hispanic, was paired with Sterling High, which was 85 percent African American.

Board members Robert Jefferson, Olga Gallegos, and Esther Campos were not happy with the pairings. No one used the r-word, but race was clearly the issue. Feeder systems predominantly of one race did not want to be grouped with feeder systems predominantly of another. The discussion was long and contentious. Rod was repeatedly asked to pull the item. He repeatedly refused.

Ron Franklin was disgusted:

> What I am not going to participate in, to be very blunt about it, is injecting political issues into an administrative issue. . . . If we want to put the whole map on the table and start, you know, massaging around the edges and doing what board members are so good at. You know, let's take a recess and come back in two weeks and see what weird design we can come up with. I don't think that's beneficial. Dr. Paige says vote it up or down. He says he's going to leave it on the table. I take him at his word. . . . Let's vote on it. (HISD, December 1, 1994, pp. 41–51)

The motion was approved, but almost immediately Rod had second thoughts. He knew he needed near-unanimous support for an issue of this importance. The board began to do exactly what Ron had denounced—make deals. The challenge was to maintain roughly equal numbers of schools and students in each management unit, keep together high schools that shared middle school attendance zones, and at the same time keep certain black and Hispanic board members happy by placing predominantly black and Hispanic high schools in different feeder patterns.

Four days later agreement was reached. All the high schools that were predominantly of one race were either paired on ethnic lines or stood alone.[5] The largest management unit had 27 schools and the smallest one had only 12. But board members were happy. The board approved the revised feeder system pairings with minimal comment at the December 15, 1994, board meeting.

Performance Contracts

Now personnel issues came to the forefront. Rod was going to appoint 12 very powerful school administrators. They would have many careers in their hands. The selection of the district superintendents, as it was decided they would be called, set off the HISD employee rumor mill like no other issue since I had been on the board. There was intense speculation about the names over the holiday season, but only Rod knew the names, and he said nothing.

Only two things were known for certain. The 12 positions would be filled by four African Americans, four Hispanics, and four whites. Rod had not said this would be the case. Everyone just knew it. Also, the 12 district superintendents would be offered contracts quite different from the standard contract offered school administrators in Texas. They would relinquish job security for salary increases.

Recall that the Texas Term Contract Nonrenewal Act required school districts to offer certified administrators contracts that could not be terminated or nonrenewed without extensive rights of appeal. Paige had already started withholding TCNA contracts from all new administrators hired for jobs that did not require an administrative certificate and offering them contracts similar to those commonly used in the private sector. He was determined to do the same for educational administrators.

The decentralization commission recommendations gave Rod the opportunity he needed. Cathy Mincberg was the champion on the board. On December 21, at a special board meeting called so Rod could proceed with district superintendent appointments during the holiday break, the board approved performance contracts for the 12 soon-to-be-filled district superintendent positions and all other new appointees who reported directly to the superintendent of schools. Only Carol Galloway voted no.

The new contracts were for one or two years and offered, on average, a 15 percent salary increase and the possibility of performance bonuses. In return for this, the new district superintendents waived their rights to appeal if their contracts were not renewed.

Naturally, these contracts infuriated the employee groups. "Our attorney has advised us that the proposed contract is void on its face," said Irene Kerr, executive director of the Houston Association of School Administrators (*Chronicle*, December 22, 1994, p. A32). HFT president Gayle Fallon expressed outrage at the pay increases that, she asserted, overpaid administrators and didn't help schools (*Wall Street Journal*, March 10, 1995, p. B1).

At the first board meeting of the new year, January 5, 1995, the board approved a new organizational chart, job descriptions for an executive deputy for school operations and district superintendents, and contracts for 12 district superintendents. One of the new district superintendents, Sylvia Macy, speaking for the group, pledged support, diligence, hard work, and total commitment to the realization of *Beliefs and Visions* and to Superintendent Paige. "We understand this is not business as usual. This is an opportunity to demonstrate accountability for the achievement of every student in every school. . . . Thank you for this opportunity and this great challenge" (HISD, January 5, 1995, p. 7).

The Eagle Lake Retreat

The new assignments were effective immediately. There was much to be done. The first step was team-building. The weekend of January 28, HISD held its first joint board and administration retreat since the days of desegregation. The retreat was at Eagle Inn in Eagle Lake, a small hunting and resort town about 60 miles west of Houston.

Rod and his direct reports and all the newly appointed district superintendents came together on Friday evening. They worked all day Saturday studying *Beliefs and Visions* and clarifying the roles and responsibilities of the district superintendents.

Saturday evening board members arrived. After a light meal, we assembled for a joint board and staff meeting. The setting was very informal. One by one the new district superintendents rose to share with us their commitments and concerns.

Within 45 minutes the central issue was on the table. It was the issue that had troubled the district superintendents all day. Would board members meddle in administrative matters? The district superintendents had accepted enormous responsibility. Expectations were high. Their contracts put them at risk for poor performance. Would they be free to exercise authority commensurate with their responsibility, or would board members lean on them to make constituents happy, hire friends, or allocate resources to pet projects?

The discussion was friendly but vigorous. Board members defended constituent service. Administrators acknowledged that they were not always customer-friendly. All agreed the line between constituent service and meddling was a fine one.

The next morning, board members met alone to develop responses to the questions and concerns of the administrators and to formulate questions and concerns for them. Then, after lunch, administrators and board members met together again. Trustees did not want district offices to become centers of power that told schools what to do. We wanted them to support schools, to make the entire HISD system work for schools and parents, and to improve student performance in every way possible. Again, we had friendly but vigorous discussion.

The day ended under the shade of large trees in the beautiful backyard of Eagle Inn. We gathered in a large circle around an open fire. Each one of us wrote on a card an old behavior that stood in the way of excellence. Then, one by one, we read our cards to the group and threw them in the fire. With commitments to embrace new behaviors that would benefit children and school patrons, we departed for Houston.

Staff and Budget Issues

Now the real work began. District superintendents needed office space, personnel, and resources. And it remained to be seen, once back in the workplace, how much real authority central office would let them have and how much real authority they in turn would devolve on to their principals.

A week later, at the annual black history celebration in the administration building atrium, I had the opportunity to talk with four or five of the new district superintendents. "How's it going?" I asked. "Are you getting settled into offices? What about staff and budget issues?"

All had the same answer. "Don't quote us, but things are not going well. We don't expect difficulties getting office space, but so far there is no evidence significant resources are going to be transferred to the district offices. Many in central office don't want to let go."

A week later, February 15, Cathy and I met Rod for breakfast at the Ritz Carlton. We hammered him fairly hard about central office resistance to decentralization.

Rod spoke eloquently. "Come on, you guys. Give me a break. It's not as simple as it looks. Many central office functions can't be transferred to the districts. Many customers are upstream, for example the Texas Education Agency and the U.S. Department of Education. Believe me, HISD is far more complex than I realized. As much as I thought I knew about it, I had only scratched the surface. Some central office resistance is just that, resistance to change, but some is legitimate. Furthermore, some of the district superintendents don't yet fully understand their own needs. Some of them are doing dumb things. Really, you need to trust me. I'm doing all I can to put real power and authority in the hands of the district superintendents. I want to give them the resources they need. I'm doing a lot more to push effective decentralization than you realize, and I do indeed plan to shift resources to the districts in next year's budget. But you've got to have confidence in me that I'm doing the best I can."

Six weeks later, in a formal report to the board, Rod outlined what had been achieved and what remained to be done. Offices for the twelve new geographic districts had been found. Professional staffs, 15 to 20 people for each district, were currently being redeployed from central office, and additional central office staff would be transferred to the district offices in the summer. Also, starting immediately, evaluation systems were being developed to enable employees at every level to evaluate their supervisors. These evaluations would become part of the employees' permanent personnel record.

By May 4, Rod was able to report to the board that the 12 district offices were fully operational. Much more was coming. We would see the complete recommendations integrated into the budget for 1995–1996 that he would present to the board in mid-summer.

It was happening. HISD was decentralizing at last. It had been almost two years since Harold Hook had told the board that decentralization was the priority and offered to help. It had taken the departure of Frank Petruzielo to make it possible. And it had required the active involvement of some of Houston's most prominent citizens to make it happen. Al Haines, mostly behind the scenes, had been the hero of decentralization. Rod Paige had been the leader.

Time would tell how well the new system worked and whether we could build on it to break forever the power of central office, but we had taken a great step forward. District decentralization supported the HISD accountability system. *Beliefs and Visions* was becoming reality. But just as everything was beginning to go so well, the board began to unravel.

NOTES

1. Hook also put privatization back on the table. In his remarks to the board, he said, "In the area of support services, looking to last year's Deloitte & Touche report, there is a methodology that deals with the whole field of privatization, and we would encourage revisiting that general subject." It was not much, but it was a start.

2. Following the board meeting Frank shared with me his irritation that Hook believed HISD had progressed only 15 percent of the way toward its goal of empowering schools and turning the organization upside down. "I take offense at that statement. He doesn't know what he's talking about. We've come a lot farther than that." He also reminded me that by state law, he had the responsibility of proposing the district's organizational structure to the board.

3. Again and again during this period, Rod reassured the staff that decentralization was not downsizing and that the board of education would have the final say on decentralization (Paige, March 28, 1994).

4. I had been reading Paul T. Hill's RAND report, *Reinventing Public Education*, dated April 1994 (subsequently published as Hill, 1995), which offered the best idea I had seen for reforming urban school systems. I found compelling his proposal to contract out the management of schools to a variety of public and private organizations, and believed the first step in this direction was a new school funding allocation system for HISD that would fund schools with dollars per weighted student rather than with staff positions.

5. Predominantly black school pairs were Kashmere/Wheatley, Jones/Yates, and Madison/Worthing/Sterling. Predominantly Hispanic school pairs were Austin/Furr and Davis/Reagan. Sam Houston and Milby, both predominantly Hispanic, stood alone, as did Lamar. The three remaining geographic management units were comprised entirely of ethnically balanced schools: Scarborough/Waltrip/Washington, Lee/Sharpstown, and Bellaire/Westbury.

9

Improving District Operations

The redesign of major district departments and operations was sparked by a scandal. It would have happened anyway. Rod Paige was knowledgeable about customer satisfaction and process improvement and committed to bringing quality management to the district, but it was a scandal in HISD's Alternative Certification Program that forced the issue.

The scandal was kept before the public for six months by one of Houston's major television stations. It demanded priority attention by the superintendent and board when the priority should have been decentralization, and it damaged further HISD's public image. The long-term consequence, however, was that redesigning district operations became a priority for Paige sooner rather than later, and sooner rather than later HISD began to improve the effectiveness and efficiency of its major operating systems.

FRAUD IN THE ALTERNATIVE CERTIFICATION PROGRAM

HISD's Alternative Certification Program (ACP) trained and certified as teachers college graduates who lacked teaching certificates. ACP interns could begin teaching almost immediately under the supervision of mentor teachers. After one year of training in teaching methods and classroom management, and with satisfactory performance evaluations and passing scores on the required state certification examination, they could become certified teachers.

Channel 13 Charges Fraud

On March 22, 1994, just one month after Paige's first day as superintendent, Wayne Dolcefino, the investigative reporter for Channel 13 ABC TV, charged on the evening Eyewitness News that HISD was defrauding Houston's Hispanic children. Dozens of unqualified ACP teachers from foreign countries were teaching bilingual education classes in HISD. Some of these teachers could not speak English. Some had not passed a basic skills test. Some had submitted fraudulent foreign college transcripts.

Dolcefino was more right than wrong. District administrators had discovered in December 1993 that someone had tampered with a transcript from a Mexican university. Subsequently Spantran, a Houston-based private evaluation firm specializing in education documents, had been hired to review all transcripts from foreign colleges and universities submitted by ACP interns. Out of 350 transcripts evaluated, Spantran had found 40 that were deficient. Some one had leaked this information to Dolcefino.

Within days of Dolcefino's March 22 report, the ACP was being investigated by HISD's internal investigators, the district attorney, and the U.S. Department of Immigration and Naturalization Services. But weeks passed and no findings were forthcoming. The issues were complex, and the files that needed to be checked were voluminous.

Meanwhile, Dolcefino kept up the heat on the evening news. On May 12, he reported that HISD was hiring criminals to teach children—an arsonist, a male prostitute, thieves, and a teacher convicted of beating two women. HISD, he charged, was continuing to cover up the extent of the scandal and refusing to clean house.

HISD needed to get the whole truth quickly and clean up the mess. On June 2, the board approved the hiring of the law firm Haynes & Boone to conduct a complete investigation.

The Haynes & Boone Report

The Haynes & Boone report was presented to the board in a long, closed session on August 11. A team of attorneys led by former U.S. Attorney Lawrence D. Finder had interviewed 215 individuals and reviewed all available documents. The work product was a 291-page report, a volume of appendices, three volumes of interview summaries, and nine large binders containing 370 exhibits.

The findings were shocking: Funds were improperly received, accounted for, and disbursed. Fraudulent or altered transcripts and degrees were submitted to the ACP with the assistance of, or deliberate indifference by, ACP staff. False written statements or certifications were made to the INS. There was a failure to return HISD property. There was subornation of false statements and witness tampering. And there were serious conflicts of interest. These were just the major findings.

Significant irregularities included the manipulation of tests and the interview process to guarantee that applicants passed, flagrant cheating, and the knowing admission of applicants who could not speak English or demonstrate basic skills and lacked equivalent degrees or minimum acceptable grade point averages. Also admitted were applicants who were friends or relatives of influential people, even though they did not meet minimal requirements or attend required training sessions.

The Haynes & Boone report also described in detail what appeared to be a scam that linked HISD with Laredo State University in Laredo, Texas, and a professor at the Universidad Autónoma de Nuevo León in Monterrey, Mexico, to obtain entry into the United States for unqualified ACP interns.

Two employees, concluded Haynes & Boone, were at the heart of the ACP scandal: ACP director Delia Stafford and clerk Patricia Moreno. Moreno was collecting money orders, payee portion left blank, from bilingual interns for fictitious immigration services—Haynes & Boone documented 16 cases—and accepting valuable gifts. One intern, reported an employee in the ACP office, gave Moreno a refrigerator so he could pass the basic skills test. There were also reports of personal services—yard work, baby-sitting, car washing, and so forth—provided by bilingual interns for Ms. Moreno and Ms. Stafford.

Where was the Texas Education Agency in all this? The TEA was periodically supposed to audit HISD's Alternative Certification Program to prevent program irregularities, and a major audit was conducted in February 1993. Haynes & Boone characterized the TEA oversight role as overly relaxed. "Some audit procedures were so lax that the TEA visits could not be expected to uncover even blatant regulatory violations" (Haynes & Boone, p. 220). Instead of thoroughly reviewing ACP bilingual files, the auditors reviewed only files preselected for them by Ms. Stafford. ACP staffers reported that Ms. Moreno kept a box of files under her desk for two months during the 1993 audit. She told them she was hiding them from the TEA.

It is not surprising that the TEA audit procedures were lax. Certain TEA auditors were close personal friends of Ms. Stafford. Haynes & Boone were told these auditors dined regularly with Ms. Stafford during audits and that one auditor stayed at Ms. Stafford's home when she was in Houston.

Six to 10 other employees, including several high-level administrators, shared responsibility for the mess, but the root cause of the problem turned out to be district politics and Frank Petruzielo.

In HISD, there were nearly 50,000 Spanish-speaking students with limited proficiency in English. In spite of extensive recruitment and a special $3,000 per year stipend for bilingual teachers, HISD had hundreds of vacancies. Something had to be done. Frank, finding himself in the possession of a large, effective program for the alternative certification of teachers, arrived at the obvious conclusion.[1]

In preparation for the 1992–1993 school year, he told Delia Stafford and everyone else in the chain of command that he wanted the ACP to gear up at once from 300 to 1,000 interns. He wanted every bilingual teacher vacancy filled. He did not care how it was done, and he did not care if the teachers could speak English. HISD could use the monolingual teachers in the early grades. He wanted results.

And so the ball began to roll. Ms. Stafford, without additional staff, handled the increased volume (the actual number of interns increased in 1992 to 750) by cutting corners and disregarding rules. But she got results. With success came Frank's favor, increased prestige, and a feeling of independence from other administrators. All agreed that Delia was Frank's favorite, that she was untouchable, and that it was not wise to anger her.

She was also reputedly close to two board members, Arthur Gaines and Felix Fraga. Felix, it turned out, had actually been meddling in administrative matters. The Haynes & Boone investigation uncovered a memo from Felix to Leonard Sturm, deputy superintendent for finance, requesting a salary advance for a bilingual intern. The memo was written on a computer in the ACP office.

Within the department, chaos and confusion reigned. Greed and opportunity led to fraud, cheating, the exploitation of powerless immigrant bilingual interns, and probably theft. A year later, when the ACP scandal was history, HISD could still not account for over $30,000 in blank money orders.

Senior administrators knew the ACP was spinning out of control, though there was no evidence they knew there was fraud, theft, and abuse of interns, but none had the courage to act. They were afraid of Frank. Bill Morgan, deputy superintendent for personnel, told Finder that the priorities were made clear to him just before Labor Day in 1992 when he objected to Petruzielo that the interns admitted to the program from Laredo State were not qualified. "F- Off," said Frank. It is "politically expedient" to get as many bilingual teachers as possible employed by HISD. "If you don't put them in the classroom, I'll get someone else to do it" (Haynes & Boone, 1994, pp. 209–210).

Monica Sandoval, assistant superintendent for multilingual education, reported that during the 1992–1993 school year she received complaints from principals about bilingual interns who could not speak English. In the fall of 1992, she personally raised the issue with Frank and all his direct reports at a cabinet meeting. Frank's response was that it was a nonissue (Haynes & Boone, 1994, p. 212).

Livy Wilson, assistant superintendent for staffing and recruitment, said he knew there were non-English speakers in the bilingual ACP, but Frank insisted they remain employed with HISD. Wilson said he was unpopular with Frank and could do nothing.

Bonnie Collins, executive director of staffing, said she informed both Livy Wilson and Bill Morgan as early as the fall of 1992 that there were problems in the ACP. She described Hal Blitman, who preceded Bill Morgan as deputy superintendent for personnel, as Frank's hatchet man who managed subordinates through terrorist tactics. Given the political climate at HISD, she was confident that her complaints would have met with intense harassment or reassignment designed to force her resignation. She had seen it happen to other people.

In Haynes & Boone's words, "[M]isconduct this pervasive and notorious could only occur in a system where high level managers were either complicitous or indifferent" (Haynes & Boone, 1994, p. 206). Administrators blamed each other. No one took personal responsibility. "The one and only thing all administrators we interviewed agreed on was that former Superintendent Frank Petruzielo and his chief assistant, Hal Blitman [one of the sacred cows], were intolerant men who used the threat of job security to obtain results." *"Superintendent Petruzielo Created an Environment of Fear and Pressure to Produce Numbers that Fostered Program Abuses"* (Haynes & Boone, 1994, p. 208, emphasis in original).

"That's nonsense from my point of view," said Frank later to news reporters, when a summary of the report was made public and he was reached by phone in Broward County, Florida. "There were any number of things that we did over a period of time that were designed to put in checks and balances and to create more accountability. But in some cases, I think some of those patterns had existed for a long period of time. It was never brought to my attention, that I can remember, that there were unqualified people being hired" (*Chronicle,* August 27, 1994, p. A1).

Frank also claimed he was in the dark about the cheating and questionable money exchanges. "I should have had people in the system and in the chain of command who should have known of the problems, and if they did should have made sure that I knew" (*Post,* August 27, 1994, p. A23).

At the press conference that followed the Haynes & Boone presentation to the board, Rod outlined the major findings of the report and announced that the board had approved his recommendation to begin termination proceedings against Delia Stafford and Patricia Moreno. He also indicated that he would recommend for discipline at the next board meeting 6 to 10 additional employees. These actions, and the district's nearly around-the-clock work to check the qualifications of all bilingual interns, he hoped, would bring the ACP scandal to closure.

More Revelations of Corruption

The controversy, however, was far from over. Three issues kept it alive until nearly Thanksgiving: the discipline of several administrators, the disposition of bilingual ACP teachers with incomplete credentials, and the confidentiality of the Haynes & Boone report. These were major issues that caused considerable pain to individuals and kept the district in turmoil, but in the end they had little impact on the reform of HISD.

But there were further revelations of wrongdoing. On August 28, Rod discovered that someone in the personnel department was apparently selling copies of the aptitude test required for employment. The district attorney was informed and an internal investigation was launched.

The next day Wayne Dolcefino struck again. He had been working on the same story. Acting on a tip, he had captured on video an HISD employee allegedly selling employment tests to potential employees. Transactions were filmed at three Houston restaurants. The employee offered copies of the aptitude test and correct answers for $200, a dictation test for $100, and a typing test for $50. The activity had apparently been going on for years.

"It was a very disturbing sight," Rod said of the video. "Any employee who uses his or her position for personal gain will be dealt with severely. I'm concerned about the ethics and integrity of our operation. Whatever it takes to straighten this out, we are going to get this done." Two clerical employees were suspended (*Post*, August 31, 1994, p. A21; *Chronicle*, August 32, 1994, p. A24).

More bad news came on September 29. Rod announced that criminal background checks had resulted in the firing of eight HISD bus drivers—one an alleged child molester. "We don't want these people anywhere near children," he told the press (*Post*, September 29, 1994, p. A29).

Cleaning Up the Mess

In addition to these problems, Rod had to clean up the ACP mess. It was no small task. The entire ACP record system was in disarray. Starting in late August, 10 staff members worked overtime checking documents and verifying the qualifications of bilingual ACP teachers. Most of the work was completed by early October, but it was not until mid-1995 that HISD finished checking all 1,743 of the ACP interns admitted from 1991 to 1994. Only nine interns with fraudulent transcripts were identified. They were fired. Another 174 resigned or dropped out of the program because of incomplete credentials.[2]

Within a year the ACP had completely recovered. Operating under a new staff in 1994–1995 and under the watchful eye of Rod and the TEA, the ACP adhered to the highest standards of record-keeping; established an advisory committee of teachers, administrators, and university professors; and made numerous program improvements. In addition the program was audited twice by the TEA and once by an external auditor.

Based on these audits, the State Board of Education approved in June 1995 the continuation of the ACP. Members of the State Board Personnel Committee praised HISD for the improvements that had been made in just one year and said the program was a model, not only for other alternative certification programs, but for teacher preparation programs everywhere.

The ACP scandal was a great embarrassment for HISD. The nearly 70 reports on the scandal broadcast by Channel 13 kept the issue before Houstonians for nearly seven months, further eroding public confidence in the school district. It was also a huge drain on resources. In addition to hundreds of thousands of dollars of staff time and $686,000 paid to Haynes & Boone (which caused another controversy), HISD paid over $250,000 in legal fees for other work related to the scandal.[3] But there was a silver lining, PEER.

PEER EXAMINATION, EVALUATION, AND REDESIGN

Decentralization was the most significant initiative of Rod's first year as superintendent. Redesigning major district operations and departments was a close second. Decentralization was driven by the board and the business leadership of Houston. Redesigning district operations was Rod's idea.

The Origin of PEER

Rod was no stranger to the works of Edwards Deming, Joseph Juran, and other quality gurus. Soon after he was elected to the board he enrolled in several seminars at the American Productivity & Quality Center. Subsequently he read widely on quality management and pushed a quality improvement initiative in the School of Education at Texas Southern University. Sooner or later, he would have pushed HISD into quality improvement. The ACP scandal dictated that it would be sooner.

Rod's immediate response to management breakdown was to suspend employees and launch an investigation to get all the facts. Obviously, the priority was to clean up the mess. But from the beginning he knew that replacing problem employees would not fundamentally improve district operations. The problems were systemic.

It was not that central office was one, large dysfunctional mess. On the contrary, many departments operated very efficiently. Some—finance and research, for example—were high performance organizations. And overall, the system worked.

The central office problem was the problem of central offices everywhere. Employees were far removed from customers. In schools, at least the schools I knew, customers were taken very seriously. In central office they were not. The prevailing view in central office was that central office existed to tell schools what to do. Meanwhile, there was no accountability, little risk-taking, constant battles over turf, and almost universal allegiance to the number one rule of all bureaucracies: cover your ass.

Central office needed to be redesigned. And Rod was ready to redesign it. Sometime in the early summer of 1994, he gave me a report on quality improvement in Montgomery County, Maryland, public schools (Montgomery County, 1993). The document described how teams of business volunteers from 16 major corporations and school district employees, using standard business tools, had analyzed and made improvement recommendations in 11 key operational areas. "This is what we need to be doing," said Rod.

The Haynes & Boone report in July provided the stimulus to act. One of its recommendations was that the personnel department be restructured. Rod responded almost immediately by asking YWCA Vice President Ann Gibson to chair a blue-ribbon panel of district employees and external human resources professionals to recommend policy and process changes that would professionalize every aspect of employee recruitment, hiring, assignment, and retention.

A second improvement task force, a spin-off of the decentralization task force, was appointed in mid-September. In July, Al Haines had obtained the pro bono services of Gary Goolsby and Rick Russler from Arthur Andersen to work with the task force, specifically to begin an analysis of financial management systems. In September, Goolsby and Russler, joined by staff from the partnership who had been working on the task force, were designated as an independent task force. Their mission was to conduct a customer survey of financial services to schools and then analyze and, if necessary, redesign all of HISD's financial systems.

A third task force was appointed a week later. Following the news release that HISD had identified and fired eight bus drivers with criminal backgrounds, Rod announced the formation of a panel chaired by Justice of the Peace Richard Vara to recommend policies and procedures for criminal background checks of all HISD employees.

On November 10, Rod announced another task force, this one to examine HISD's communications services. The task force, chaired by Ray Viator, the partnership's vice president of communications and one of the partnership staff who had been working with the decentralization task force, would examine internal and external communications policies and procedures and make recommendations to improve the district's public and community relations organization.

The Establishment of PEER

About this time Rod began to talk about launching teams of community experts and HISD personnel to review and redesign all major district operations.

The task forces launched so far were developing excellent recommendations. Why not formalize the redesign process? "There's so much that needs to be done," he told board members. "We need a formal structure and assigned personnel. I'm going to put together a coordinating committee and ask Bob Stockwell to manage the process. Bob already has an office and a small staff to coordinate the decentralization initiative. I propose to call the new project PEER—Peer Examination, Evaluation, and Redesign."

On November 21, PEER was formally launched with a major press conference. In his statement to the press, Rod linked PEER to the decentralization initiative and likened it to a physical examination. "When we go for our own periodic physical checkup, we find the best possible professionals, have them thoroughly examine and evaluate our condition, and take whatever corrective actions are required to improve our health. It has been a while since HISD has had a thorough checkup. We have been suffering a lot of pain, which is a symptom that something is wrong and must be corrected. It is time now to expand our use of specialists to improve HISD's health."

As part of PEER, Rod announced that every major functional area of HISD would in time be examined in order to improve the effectiveness and efficiency of service delivery to schools and students. Counting the task forces that had already been launched, a total of 13 would soon be at work. The newly appointed task forces would examine employee hearing procedures, legal services, parental involvement, staff development, child study and psychological services, exceptional (special) education, discipline management, transportation services, and counseling services. Subsequently, PEER task forces were appointed to examine plant operator procedures, reading instruction, gifted and talented programs, athletic programs, substitute teacher issues, and teacher incentive pay.

In the meantime every department was being asked to reassess its mission, reevaluate how well services were being delivered, determine where process improvements were needed, redesign processes, track and measure improvement, and maintain a commitment to continuous improvement.

This approach to process improvement, said Rod, was neither new nor radical. "Successful American private sector businesses use process redesign techniques every day to improve their operations. We believe that using the best available expert assistance, business processes, and techniques in use today, will improve HISD's performance. Houston's children and citizens deserve no less than the best educational system and performance possible."

Rod then described the management structure for PEER—a coordinating council composed of the heads of each of HISD's functional areas—and introduced the council chairperson, Bob Stockwell.

Finally, he concluded the press conference by stating that PEER was not a project with a finite life span. "This will become HISD's way of life. This is not a 'quick fix' situation. This effort will take time. However, with the expert assistance available to us, we will continue to improve!" (Paige, November 21, 1994).

Not surprisingly, press coverage of PEER was almost nonexistent. Channel 13's Eyewitness News ignored it completely, and all I saw in the newspapers was a small note.

PEER Reports

During the months and years that followed, Rod gave the board periodic reports on the progress of the PEER program. The number of volunteers involved and the scope of their work was impressive. By early February 1995, all 13 PEER task forces were deep into their work and some were nearly ready to make reports to the board.

The first PEER report was presented by the personnel task force on April 6, 1995. It described the personnel office as a "system bogged down in paperwork and inefficiencies making it difficult for those responsible for the function to adequately service customers" (HISD, April 6, 1995, p. 1). Nine recommendations and a proposed organizational chart followed.

The report concluded with a point about the need for human resource professionals. For too long, the personnel department had been a dumping ground for problem employees or employees waiting to qualify for medical leave or awaiting special assignment or grievance hearings. "An organizational structure should not be allowed to exist which elevates employees into positions for which they are not qualified" (HISD, April 6, 1995, p. 5).

PEER reports on transportation and criminal history background checks were presented to the board in a special board workshop on May 4. HISD operated one of the largest student transportation systems in the nation: over 1,100 bus routes transported over 41,000 children every school day. The priorities were safety, user convenience, on-time service, and cost. It was a massive operation, and everyday everything had to go perfectly.

The PEER transportation task force, supported by the Texas Association of School Business Officials and chaired by the association's executive director, Bill Phipps, had been asked to analyze routing and scheduling, motor pool operations, vehicle repair, and safety. Their work was thorough. They visited the transportation facilities, interviewed selected personnel, conducted customer surveys, studied relevant written material, analyzed operational procedures, and compared HISD's efficiency of services with other school districts. Their report demonstrated complete mastery of school transportation issues.

Overall, the task force found HISD's transportation department remarkably effective, but improvement opportunities were many. Under 14 major areas of concern were hundreds of specific, detailed recommendations, including a new organizational chart, numbers of people required for specific functions, training needs, equipment needs, and work processes.

Administration had much to do, but the most important responsibility for improvement rested with the board. Consecutive HISD boards had starved transportation to keep taxes down and put money into popular spending areas. Politics had come first. Now a crisis was looming.

> As is the case with many budget-constrained organizations, support functions are sometimes targeted for reductions and/or provided insufficient funding to maintain the infrastructure required to provide that support. Maintenance of facilities and equipment often becomes a primary bank for satisfying more direct mission mandates because the results of such reductions are not immediate and readily apparent. However, this is often a cancerous process that ultimately can result in catastrophic failure of the primary function. Though the HISD vehicle maintenance function has not yet reached that extreme, it is the opinion of the Metro [Houston's metropolitan transit authority] participants in the evaluation that unless high priority is given to upgrading facilities, equipment, training, tools and equipment and preventive maintenance effectiveness, the organization is coming precariously close. Appearance, cleanliness, graffiti, missing nuts and bolts, loose wires, in-service breakdown may not be overwhelming reasons for that high priority but safety has to be. We would be remiss if we did not flag this concern. Quality, safety-oriented maintenance simply cannot be performed over sustained periods under the current conditions. Our review revealed many good folks doing the best job they knew how under the conditions, but it's not and cannot be considered good enough. (HISD, April 13, 1995, p. 38).

The report added the observation that in 1985 outside experts had made similar recommendations, but no action had been taken. "Similar treatment of these findings and recommendations can only result ultimately in a catastrophic, no-recovery maintenance program" (p. 38).

The second PEER report presented on May 4 dealt with criminal history background checks. For several years HISD had been checking all employee applicants for criminal backgrounds, but employment decisions were made on a case-by-case basis.

The task force recommendations were unambiguous. No one convicted of a felony or a misdemeanor involving moral turpitude would be hired by HISD. Those charged with criminal offenses that had been dismissed through deferred adjudication could be considered for employment with the district, but not if the charges involved violent crimes, crimes against children, or any charges involving deadly weapons or drugs. Current employees who were found to have a criminal record would be reviewed for continued employment by a committee. An employee convicted after the date of employment for any felony or misdemeanor involving moral turpitude would be subject to termination.[4]

On May 10, Rod hosted a breakfast for PEER chairpersons, the decentralization commission, the Hook committee, and members of the press to update everyone on the progress of the PEER program. Over 50 of Houston's leading business and civic leaders were in attendance. The PEER chairpersons presented reports. Rod showed how PEER, like decentralization, was part of an overall strategy to strengthen teaching and learning. Enthusiasm was high. There was no media coverage of the event.

The next PEER report was an interim report at the June 1 board meeting from the financial systems task force. This task force, a spin-off from the decentralization task force, was charged with eliminating or redesigning all administrative processes that impeded financial decision-making at schools.

Since September 1994, the task force had examined all financial operations, surveyed approximately 200 principals and administrators to assess current performance levels, and developed consensus among both process owners and customers on priorities. The priority issues that emerged were the requisition-purchase order process, the vendor payments process, the coordination of school startup supply orders, computer systems for financial reports and support, the availability and quality of warehouse stock items, fixed assets tracking system and inventory reports, processing activity funds receipts and disbursements, the development of a bid book on major commodities, processing technology supply expense transfers, and processing and payment of consultants.

With this information, process improvement teams of principals, finance administrators, and other central office personnel were creating process maps and redesigning work processes. Already, some low-hanging fruit had been picked. Procedural changes had been made to loosen internal controls but increase authority and accountability in the areas of consultant use, out-of-district travel, supplemental operating checks, money orders, and purchase orders under $500. Complete process analysis, benchmarking, and redesign of all processes was expected by September 1995.

There was no discussion of the report at the board table. None of my constituents ever spoke to me about the financial systems PEER task force. And the press missed it entirely.

By mid-summer 1995, the PEER program was running at full speed. At nearly every board meeting, another PEER task force reported its findings and recommendations. Some board members began to complain that we were taking too much time hearing PEER reports. We had important business to conduct. To accommodate the board, Rod instructed PEER teams to abbreviate their reports.

The PEER task force on staff development reported on June 15. The presentation was made by David Lindsay, manager of quality and purchasing for Lyondell Petrochemical and an examiner for the Malcolm Baldrige National Quality Award. The task force, formed in December, had chosen to focus just on instructional staff development. The objective was to design a system that enhanced job-related skills, knowledge, and behaviors which resulted in measurable improvements in student achievement.

The task force found that HISD had no identified philosophy for staff development and no system for identifying required teacher skills, other than the woefully inadequate Texas Teacher Appraisal System. HISD had no integrated structure and plan for staff development, no formal feedback and follow-up mechanism to assess the effectiveness of staff development activities, and no identification of best practices on which to build.

In addition, there were significant barriers to effective staff development. HISD did not provide adequate resources—money, materials, and time—for staff development. Campus needs were not assessed. Teacher input was not solicited. There was no system for teacher accountability. And staff development was not linked to expected student outcomes.

Specific recommendations laid out in detail exactly how HISD's staff development function should be organized, managed, measured, evaluated, and continuously improved.

The report concluded with some advice for administration and a request directed to the board. Success would require sustained application over a long period of time, three to five years. HISD must resist the tendency to react to short-term pressures that distracted from long-range improvement. It was essential that HISD put into place an audit process that demonstrated the link between staff development and student achievement. The task force wanted a written response from the board. Did we understand the recommendations and were we committed to implementing them?

Two additional PEER presentations were made on July 13, child study and psychological services and exceptional education. The first presentation was from the child study and psychological services PEER task force. This task force, led by Dr. Richard Griffin, a consultant with the Harris County Department of Education, began its work in December 1994.

HISD employed nearly 100 certified educational diagnosticians who tested students and diagnosed learning disabilities and about a dozen Ph.D. psychologists who followed up with children who were emotionally disturbed and responded to crisis situations. These professionals, organized into two departments, worked closely together and directly supported exceptional education, HISD's term for special education. They provided the assessments that were the starting point for the development of individual educational plans for students with learning disabilities.

The child study and psychological services task force found much to commend. Child study had been recognized recently by the TEA for its data-tracking system and for the recruitment and training of bilingual child evaluators through the Alternative Certification Program. Psychological services had been credentialed recently by the American Psychological Association as an approved predoctoral internship site, one of only three school-based training sites in the nation.

Still, there were concerns. There were staff shortages, inadequate work space, and communication barriers. Service delivery was delayed by inconsistent case management, turf issues, and role ambiguities within and across departments. In addition, over 14 percent of all referrals were not tested within mandated time lines, an unacceptably high number.

The task force recommended that the child study and psychological services departments be merged with the exceptional education department to improve effectiveness and efficiency of service delivery and that personnel be moved to the schools or at least to the administrative districts. An effective case management system was needed to coordinate referral and placement services. Also needed was a systematic and continuous monitoring system for federal compliance and quality control.

The exceptional education task force, organized in October 1994 under the leadership of David Topper, associate director for human resources at the University of Texas Health Science Center, Houston, reported next. Child study and psychological services diagnosed and prescribed. The exceptional education department delivered. It had responsibility for managing the delivery of special education services to over 20,000 students with physical or mental disabilities.

The task force findings were shocking. They included a lack of quality instruction for exceptional education students, limited use of best practices, insufficient staffing, and ineffective decision-making. Decisions regarding the individual education plans for exceptional education students were sometimes overridden by principals or by transportation considerations. There was no uniformity in interpreting policy. Staff development was limited, poorly planned, and poorly delivered. The organizational structure was highly centralized and at times dysfunctional. The department did not collaborate well with other areas of service and instruction. There were bottlenecks in the processing of information and students. Parents did not receive adequate and timely information on their children and available services. The work culture was reactive rather than proactive. Parents were viewed as adversaries rather than as partners. No one trusted anyone else. Exceptional education staff, perceiving inequities for themselves in resources and salaries, felt like second-class citizens and outcasts within HISD. Finally, there was no reward system to encourage or reinforce correct actions and no ownership of exceptional education at the campus level. The HISD accountability system served no purpose because 96 percent of exceptional education students were exempt from the Texas Assessment of Academic Skills test.

What was needed, said the task force, was a system that served all students according to need and recognized all parents as equal partners, to be treated with dignity and respect and valued for the vital information they could provide. Exceptional education services and programs should be provided in a decentralized manner and be the responsibility of all stakeholders. Accountability should rest at the campus level for all students, regardless of disability. And much more. Pages and pages of detailed recommendations followed.

Board members were stunned and visibly upset. Thousands of HISD's most needy children were not being served well. But there was no point in looking for someone to blame. The issue was the future not the past.

Paula Arnold asked for the floor. She recounted how before she had been elected to the board, she had been asked to serve on a task force to recommend improvements in public relations. "The problem," she said, "is that not one recommendation that committee made was acted upon."

Nona James, a parent on the exceptional education task force, asked to speak. She told the board about her fight to get appropriate services for her three disabled children. Though pleased with the report, she was concerned that the suggested changes would not be made. "Should they follow through with some of these proposals, it would be wonderful, but as a parent, it would have to be proven to me that it is going to be done" (*Chronicle,* July 15, 1995, p. A30).

REFLECTIONS ON IMPROVING DISTRICT OPERATIONS

PEER was and continues to be a great success. A sophisticated implementation structure assured appropriate follow-through and tracking. As of June 1997, PEER task forces had made a total of 394 recommendations. Forty-eight percent of these have been implemented, and the work continues. The fears of Nona James have not been confirmed. PEER has become the standard procedure for resolving complex management and instructional issues.

Even so, despite PEER, a major performance audit by the Texas comptroller of public accounts, and state-of-the-art management training for all administrators (both described in subsequent chapters), I remain pessimistic about the continuous improvement of district operations. District operations have improved significantly since 1995, but performance remains less than optimum. It is, in my opinion, almost impossible for a large, bureaucratic organization not subject to the discipline of the marketplace to remain at the cutting edge of effectiveness and efficiency.

This chapter illustrates why. Consider the obstacles to high performance. [Boards have an incentive to neglect infrastructure; pleasing taxpayers and employees is a higher priority. Continuous improvement requires a long-term commitment. Board elections are held every two years and superintendents turn over frequently. Because the media pays great attention to scandal and ignores nuts-and-bolts school reform, the public is uninformed and board members are off the hook on many of the issues that really matter. Special interest politics sometimes drive educational policy. Board members sometimes meddle in administration. And an all-powerful superintendent can intimidate senior administrators into going along with bad policy.]

These realities remain. In 1994–1995 a strong and reasonably united board, a strong superintendent, and hundreds of Houston's leading citizens worked together to begin the improvement of district operations. For a time we overcame some of the obstacles to high performance.

But Rod and a few trustees recognized even then that the best way to assure long-term continuous improvement was through aggressive contracting out of district operations to private vendors. Contractors wanting to obtain or retain our business would be subject to the discipline of the marketplace. Also, the more we could off-load responsibilities for noneducational operations, the more we could free up the superintendent and his staff to focus on HISD's core business, teaching, and learning.

But privatization would have to wait. By mid-summer of 1995, it was clear that the board was divided. *Beliefs and Visions* was becoming ancient history. Old-style urban politics as usual was gaining the upper hand. We had learned in 1990 that a reform board without a reform superintendent could do little. In 1995, we learned that a reform superintendent without a reform board could not do much more.

NOTES

1. Recall that extraordinary efforts to hire bilingual teachers had been part of the deal between whites and Hispanics that brought Frank to Houston. And during 1993, Frank's problems with the board made him dependent on the Hispanic trustees.

2. Most of the teachers had uprooted their lives and come to Houston in good faith. Termination was a significant hardship. Gayle Fallon said the HFT would sue HISD if any of its members were demoted or removed from the classroom. Subsequently the union sued. HISD paid six teachers a total of $65,455 to settle the case out of court in late 1996, but did not grant any of them teaching certificates.

3. Other legal fees were for the Delia Stafford termination, immigration services for ACP interns, and an unsuccessful court battle with Wayne Dolcefino over release of the names in the report.

4. These PEER recommendations did not just require management changes. They required policy changes by the board. Surprisingly, the policy changes were not passed immediately without dissent. Some board members were concerned that good people who had made just one small mistake might be barred from employment with the district. The issue was debated at board meetings on May 18 and again on June 1. Finally on June 15, with the addition of a review committee to hear appeals from applicants who were denied employment, the board approved the policy changes.

10

The Demise
of the Reform Board

The selection of Rod Paige as superintendent on February 3, 1994 was the most significant event in the reform of HISD. Rod had vision, courage, and integrity. Even Olga Gallegos and José Salazar, the two Hispanic board members who felt they had to vote against his selection, recognized Rod's personal qualities. What none of us fully realized at the time was that Rod also had considerable talent as an executive. He mastered complex subjects easily and could play the bureaucratic game as well as anyone. By June 1995, *Beliefs and Visions* was becoming a reality in HISD. Nearly everyone was singing Rod's praises.

But selecting Rod as superintendent had a significant downside. It was not the controversy over his selection—that had been expected. It was the loss of a reform majority on the board of education, which no one had foreseen. The replacement of Rod Paige and Felix Fraga with Robert Jefferson and Esther Campos fundamentally altered the dynamics of the board. Within eighteen months, the board had split, apparently on ethnic lines, and the continued reform of HISD was at risk.

THE DYNAMICS OF THE NEW BOARD

Not surprisingly, the board was divided by the selection of Rod as superintendent, but the divisions did not appear to be serious or permanent. Paula Arnold remained convinced that the process by which Rod had been selected was not fair to Hispanics, but she quickly got over her anger at Cathy Mincberg, Ron Franklin, and me for not including her in our discussions about Paige. Paula liked Rod, and we were all friends. Olga Gallegos and José Salazar, of course, could not afford to be too friendly with the board members who had so *arrogantly* excluded Hispanics from the superintendent selection process, but the fact was, Olga also liked Rod and was not one to fight. And José, whatever his views, would serve only until early June.

Robert Jefferson and Esther Campos

We all believed Robert Jefferson, Rod's replacement on the board, would be a good board member committed to reform. Jeff, as we called him, had been active as a volunteer in school issues, and he had been selected by the black leadership in Rod's trustee district with Rod's blessing. Jeff might not become a reform leader on the board, but certainly he would support Paige.

Our other new colleague, Esther Campos, a 63-year-old career HISD administrator who had retired as an assistant principal to seek election to the board, was sworn in on June 2.[1] Esther was a native Houstonian with a B.A. and M.A. from the University of Houston and a long history of involvement in Democratic politics. Esther was a short, heavy woman with short, dark hair. Most of the time she did not appear to be happy, and she was easily offended. But she was honest and very knowledgeable about HISD. Nothing in her career or campaign indicated that she would be a school reformer, but there was no reason to believe she would oppose the reform agendas explicit and implicit in *Beliefs and Visions*.

The Board Kills Creeping Privatization

For a month or so after Esther's election, the board worked together well. Ron Franklin provided excellent leadership as board president, and there were few reasons for disagreement. Our decisions regarding the Alternative Certification Program scandal were damage control, not school reform. And decentralization was not controversial because the decentralization commission was providing the board with excellent political cover.

But during the summer, an issue came up that divided the board. Rod was preparing his first budget and needed to cut expenses. Would the board support contracting out some operations in facilities management? At Rod's request, I prepared a resolution for introduction at the July 7 board meeting.

Following the customary whereases about HISD's core business and the need to be cost-effective, the resolution stated that the board supported contracting out selected support services where thorough analysis indicated taxpayers' money would be saved and the quality of service to schools would be maintained or enhanced. It also stated that HISD would give preference to vendors who offered employment to displaced employees and that should vendors be unable to employ all displaced employees, HISD would give priority to such employees for other job assignments within HISD.

I passed out the resolution with the explanation that I was trying to initiate debate, that I was flexible, and that I hoped we could vote on the resolution at the next board meeting in order to give the superintendent some direction. The discussion that followed made it clear that Esther Campos was the swing vote.

A few days later Esther and I had lunch. Esther seemed open to contracting out, but she made no commitments.

On July 24, the *Chronicle* carried a long story on privatization (p. C1). The headline read "HISD to ponder privatizing services: Critics say minorities will take big job hit." From the beginning, that was the issue—minority jobs. Two of the board member quotes that appeared in the article made this absolutely clear.

Carol Galloway: McAdams's proposal is "premature and imprudent." Any reduction in the workforce will directly affect minorities: "In many instances, these are the parents of our schoolchildren, and their employment is a vital component to the education of our young people."

Robert Jefferson: "I'm totally, totally, unequivocally against it. It is going to hurt black folk and Hispanic folk. Privatization is tagged 'lose jobs' for members in our churches and in our community."

Board member opposition concerned Rod. Our plans changed. Rod determined to write a new resolution that linked outsourcing to *Beliefs and Visions* and emphasized his sensitivity to the jobs issue. "In considering proposals for contracting services to private enterprise," said his resolution, "we shall be highly sensitive to staffing and personnel placement."

Discussion at the next board meeting began with employee group representatives speaking to Rod's resolution. They all adamantly opposed any outsourcing. Contractors would exploit employees. HISD would lose control of its workforce. Service quality would decline. Minority employees would lose jobs.

Trustees Galloway, Jefferson, Gaines, and Gallegos voiced strong opposition to Paige's resolution. Arnold and Campos voiced tepid support. At the end of the discussion, Ron announced that the resolution would be considered for action at a future board meeting.

The death of privatization came quite by surprise at the August 25 board meeting. The board had approved the 1994–1995 budget on August 11. This budget, Rod's first, funded 34 fewer positions in central office and facilities management. Rod was cutting costs. Now the board formally had to close the positions by approving a reduction-in-force resolution. This was standard procedure, and though some board members frequently grumbled about reductions in force, I had never seen a reduction-in-force resolution fail. After all, how could one argue that a job needed to remain open when the superintendent said that the work did not need to be done.

But there was something new in this reduction-in-force recommendation, a recommendation to close the audiovisual repair department. The eight employees in this department were mostly doing work that did not need to be done. They were repairing equipment that was either no longer used or could be replaced for less than the cost of repair. The recommendation of HISD's internal auditors, and now Paige's recommendation to the board, was to close the department, retrain the employees to repair computers, and send to outside vendors those few audiovisual items that it made sense to repair.

The audiovisual employees objected. They had comfortable, low-risk jobs. They did not want to be retrained to repair computers. For several days prior to the board meeting, they and the union leaders had been working on sympathetic board members. The superintendent, they said, was trying to slip privatization of the audiovisual department by the board by calling it "reduction in force."

The first speaker to the agenda item, Houston Education Association director Lee Barnes, put the issue squarely on the table. The audiovisual department should not be closed. And, he added, "The way this was done was really distasteful. You came in through the back door on this issue and called it budget reduction. It smells more like privatization." Board members picked up the theme. Carol opposed Paige's recommendation. Paula wanted it withdrawn.

Rod tried to explain. The recommendation came from middle management. It was completely incidental to the discussion about outsourcing. "If you ask us to develop an efficient operation and at the same time demand that we don't change anything, then that puts us in an impossible position."

But it was no use. Arthur Gaines referred to the proposal as "creeping privatization." He went on to describe the employees whose positions were being closed. "I cannot support this," he concluded, "because there are elements in the community which are strongly emotional about this, and I think you are going to hear about it."

Esther said she agreed with Gaines and Arnold. Jeff asked only procedural questions, but it was clear from his body language where he stood. The issue was lost (HISD, August 25, 1994, pp. 17–25).

A few minutes later Rod withdrew the entire reduction-in-force item. The audiovisual department positions never came back to the table. As Rod told me later, "It was not even about keeping jobs. We were committed to retraining the employees. It was about keeping specific jobs. The employees did not want to be challenged. They wanted to be comfortable."

A few days later, about 30 people, representing the NAACP and more than a dozen labor, religious, and civic groups, staged a press conference to denounce privatization in Harris County, the City of Houston, and HISD. "Privatization, outsourcing and the contracting out of services can lead to unnecessary layoffs that increase unemployment and welfare lines," said NAACP

Executive Director Keryl Smith. "Today, we're firing a warning shot," said Don Horn, secretary-treasurer of the AFL-CIO.

The message was stated most directly by NAACP president Al Green: "There are some persons here who are in the business of helping people getting elected to office. The converse of that seems to work quite well when they help people get into office who don't seem to take into consideration that there is a community to be served. You're going to hear a clarion call from the community to ask those persons to relinquish some of their power if they should move forward and displace workers unnecessarily" (*Chronicle*, August 30, 1994, p. A9).

So this was the emotional response from the community that Arthur had predicted. Well, it did not matter. Privatization in HISD was already dead.

The Del Lago Manifesto

By August, it was clear in many ways, some subtle and some not so subtle, that the board was becoming dysfunctional. Ever since the split over Joan Raymond's buyout, board members had worked hard to disagree politely, even in private, and always to treat the superintendent with respect at the board table. We had gone out of our way to keep discussions of race off the table, and not once had we voted on ethnic lines. But now, increasingly, board members were sniping at each other and challenging, almost insulting, Rod at the board table. Behind the scenes it was even worse. Some board members were pushing personnel recommendations on Rod. Angry comments were not infrequent. And more and more the race card was being played.

What was happening? For one thing, Robert Jefferson was not Rod Paige. Where Rod had been a board leader, mastering complex subjects, advocating positions, building coalitions, and effectively debating issues at the board table, Jeff was not even a good follower. He frequently came in late and left early, appeared to be unfamiliar with the agenda, and unpredictably changed his mind on important issues.

And whereas Felix Fraga loved everybody, Esther Campos seemed to have a chip on her shoulder. She insisted that the staff in the board services office address her as Mrs. Campos, rudely ordered them about, and became very angry over imagined slights.

At the August 25 board meeting, when the board was discussing in closed session the discipline for administrators implicated in the Alternative Certification Program scandal, she became very angry at Paula when Paula innocently suggested that she could assist Ron Franklin by translating into Spanish a public statement of the board president. "I don't translate," she fired across the table at Paula, and then refused Paula's repeated attempts to apologize.

But it was not just the new board members. Rod's departure from the board also seemed to change some of the old members. There seemed to be a sharp edge to every disagreement.

We need another board retreat, suggested Ron Franklin. The problem is that some of the board members are not committed to *Beliefs and Visions*. How could they be? Carol, Arthur, Jeff, and Esther were not on the board when it was adopted in June 1990. We need to rededicate ourselves to our mission.

So it was arranged. We met on September 16 and 17 at the Del Lago resort north of Houston. A Ph.D. in clinical psychology facilitated the weekend. He started us out with games and required us to select special names for the weekend. We were really going to get everything out on the table, and indeed, no one held back.

Paula challenged Esther on the translation encounter. She also was concerned that Olga and Esther were taking it upon themselves to speak for the Hispanics in her trustee district. Several of us put it straight to Arthur that he appeared to see everything through a racial lens. Carol told me she had considered me a racist because of my conservative views, but added that she had changed her mind when I had recently come to visit her in the hospital. Rod made an impassioned plea to all of us to stay out of personnel issues. And Ron shared his concern about the way some board members were *jamming* Rod at the board table.

The retreat ended in mid-afternoon on Saturday on a positive note, with warm expressions of friendship all around and unanimous commitment to a declaration of principles and a code of conduct. We called these two documents the *Declaration of Del Lago* and the *Del Lago Manifesto*.

First, in the *Declaration of Del Lago*, we agreed to dedicate ourselves to our central mission of educating students and the principles in *Beliefs and Visions*, to acknowledge our need to seek input from the communities we represented, to focus on our role as policy makers for the entire system, and to remind ourselves that our special interest was the children of Houston.

The *Del Lago Manifesto* hit the issues a little more directly:

We, the Trustees of the Board of Education of the Houston Independent School District Pledge to Uphold this Code:

1. Don't "jam" Rod at the table
2. Honor the integrity of closed sessions
3. Attribute disagreements to honest differences, not ulterior motives
4. Don't stereotype
5. Don't "mess in my district"
6. Don't squeeze Rod about personnel

7. Communicate
8. Keep the faith, i.e., *Beliefs and Visions*
9. Don't play the race card
10. KIDS, KIDS, KIDS = #1

THE BOARD SPLITS OVER JOBS

Gaines Elected Board President

What next? The implementation of the spirit of Del Lago would be in the hands of Arthur Gaines, for Arthur was going to be board president in 1995. Yes, it was a bit early to settle the board presidency, and some trustees were strongly opposed to Arthur. But Arthur had been running for board president ever since he had been elected to the board, and he had at least five committed votes. Arthur would be president. Rod said he would be king.

The months following the Del Lago retreat were exciting. Change, at last, was coming to HISD. In October, the decentralization commission held public hearings around the city unveiling its recommendations for a decentralized HISD. In November, HISD's school accountability results for 1993–1994 were announced to citywide acclaim.[2] Also, in November, Rod officially launched PEER. On December 15, the board approved the new feeder pattern alignments for district management units. On December 21, the board approved performance contracts for the soon-to-be-appointed district superintendents. And on December 27, Judge Lynn Hughes dismissed the Hispanic Education Committee lawsuit against Paige and the board of education.

On January 5, 1995, at the first board meeting of the new year, Arthur was unanimously elected board president. The newspaper article introducing Arthur to Houstonians as the new HISD board president was not encouraging. The headline said it all: "New HISD board leader self-avowed traditionalist." "At a time when the board he leads professes changes that tend toward the nontraditional," wrote the *Chronicle's* education writer Melanie Markley, "Gaines has been supportive of some trends, but resistant of others" (*Chronicle*, February 7, 1995, p. A15).

Fallon's Private War Against Paige

By contrast, the news coverage of Paige's first year as superintendent was very encouraging. Susan Besze Wallace, the *Post* education writer, in a special report headlined "Paige Two," contrasted the Christmas gift given to Rod by the HISD cabinet, a pair of black lizard Lucchese cowboy boots, with the Christmas gift given the previous year to Frank Petruzielo, a desk chair. The boots, she said, were a symbol of Paige's "professional-yet-downhome demeanor."

All the quotes about Paige in the article were positive, except for the comment of HFT president Gayle Fallon. Paige, she said, "is the most antiteacher superintendent we've had in the past decade. He has given them nothing" (*Post*, January 15, 1995, p. A1). Gayle went on to charge that the board, not Paige, was running the district. Privately she was saying that Rod was just a tool of the white board members.

The private war between Gayle and Rod was under way. The real issue was power. Joan Raymond and Frank Petruzielo had given Gayle special access. She could slip into the superintendent's office almost anytime she pleased and cut a deal. Rod insisted that Gayle be treated like all other employee group leaders. She could have her say on issues at consultation, and HFT member terminations and grievances would be settled like all other terminations and grievances, by established policies and procedures.

For a year, Gayle had been very discreet in her criticism of Rod. She was far too smart to be openly critical of HISD's first African American superintendent. But privatization and the 1994–1995 budget, which provided only a small salary increase for teachers, had given her the opening she needed. Now, directly, and through Carol Galloway, she was courting Arthur and Robert Jefferson. What could be more effective than to say that Rod was privately taking orders from the white board members?

Paige Strengthens the High School Curriculum

In January and February of 1995, Gayle's opposition seemed harmless. On January 27 and 28 the enthusiasm for reform at the Eagle Lake retreat had been palpable. Rod was building a team. Board member conflict had eased since the Del Lago retreat. And all of us promised to discard old behaviors and embrace new ones. On February 16, the board, with many words of praise, gave Rod a new, two-year contract. At the same board meeting, the board approved on first reading Rod's dream of a strong, academic, core curriculum for all high school students.

Rod had insisted that *Beliefs and Visions* include a requirement for a strong core curriculum. The reformers on the board had started pushing Frank to implement a new high school curriculum shortly after he became superintendent, and a core curriculum committee had been meeting since long before Rod became superintendent.

The problem was that the committee had been meeting, and meeting, and meeting. The reformers on the board were frustrated. So was Rod. The committee was told to finish its work. So, rather abruptly, a recommendation was prepared for presentation to the board.

The recommendation increased the number of credits required for a standard high school diploma from 21 to 24. The credits required for an advanced diploma were increased from 22 to 24. The additions to the existing curriculum were one credit of science, one credit in world geography, one credit in a second language, and one credit in computing. In addition, every student would be required to complete a coherent sequence of three credits of state-approved courses for career and technology preparation or three credits in a specialization consisting of state-approved courses in language arts, science, social studies, mathematics, foreign language, fine arts, and/or computing proficiency.

Before there was room for seven elective credits. Now, there would be room for only three. Also, there would be no "fluff" courses like consumer mathematics or language arts that could be substituted for solid English, mathematics, or science courses. No longer would there be any easy routes to graduation.

The new advanced diploma was similar to the standard diploma, except that it required three credits in a second language, one credit of fine arts, and offered more rigorous courses to meet the other requirements. The advanced diploma left no room for electives.[3]

There were many implications for staffing, scheduling, facilities, and of course budgets. HISD would need more teachers in foreign languages, science, computer science, and geography. Many current teachers might need to obtain certifications in additional teaching areas. And teachers in some elective fields would be left without students. HISD would need more science and language laboratories. The new standards would also require changes in the middle school curriculum.

Rod was taking a bold step. He was not asking the board for authorization to study how difficult it would be to implement the new graduation requirements or how much they would cost. He was not suggesting that approval be delayed until all implementation questions were answered. He was recommending that the board act immediately. He would provide the board information on funding and implementation at second reading.[4]

The question before the board, Rod said, was not "can we do this?" It was "how will we do this?" Administration would plan as carefully as possible and implement as thoroughly as possible. Maybe full implementation would have to be delayed in some subject areas in some schools. Maybe some of next year's ninth-grade students might not be able obtain all the required courses. If exceptions had to be made, so be it. It was better to act now and implement as effectively as possible, rather than to delay action until detailed plans existed for every implementation issue.

Rod's actions were for all students, but there was more to his haste and passion than his interest in all students. Rod was a proud black man, and I

had heard him complain time and again about performance comparisons between black and white high school students.

"How can you expect black students to score well on standardized tests
when they don't take academic courses?" he would ask. "The main difference
between high achievers and low achievers is the courses they take. If we expect
black students to perform as well as whites, we must accept no excuses and
provide no easy alternatives. We must make black students take the same academic courses that most white students take. If we do, in time, black students
will perform as well as white students."

Accompanying Rod's recommendation was a six-page research summary
from HISD's department of research and evaluation which proved this very
point. It contained 23 quotes from 16 research studies. The data were there
for all to see. Among HISD graduates the best predictor of SAT scores was not
race, it was the number of academic courses taken.

The Board Splits over Jobs

March and April of 1995 were generally good months for HISD. All 12 of
the new district offices were operational. Aggressive planning for a significant
transfer of staff and resources to the district offices, to be presented with the
1995–1996 budget, was under way. And a dozen PEER task forces were at
work. But behind the scenes board relationships were souring. Esther seemed
angry much of the time. Ron Franklin was frequently absent. And increasingly, Arthur was challenging Rod at the board table with, it seemed, the full
support of Robert Jefferson and Carol Galloway. So much for the Del Lago
Manifesto.

Stirring the pot was Gayle Fallon, constantly working directly and
through Carol to pull Arthur and Jeff her way on issues important to the HFT.
Board elections were coming in November. Carol, Arthur, Jeff, Esther, and
Olga—all five of HISD's minority trustees—were up for reelection. All five
represented districts in which organized labor had considerable clout. All five
were increasingly acting like a bloc on HFT issues.

Sometime in February or March Rod confided to me that he had made
a mistake supporting Jeff to succeed him on the board. "Jeff," he said, "has no
commitment to *Beliefs and Visions*. He doesn't understand what we're trying
to do. He takes his cues from Arthur and Carol. He's giving Arthur control
of the board. And Arthur is impossible. He wants to be king. He is demanding that the HISD police provide chauffeur service for him to HISD
events, pushing personnel appointments at me, and even giving employees
directives. I have refused to comply and gotten in his face a few times, but he
just responds by jamming me at the board table. Something has to change."

The first issue that showed the power of the new coalition was the old
issue of jobs. Rod wanted a policy change to allow administration to reassign,

retrain, and even remove personnel based on job performance rather than seniority. Because of decentralization and PEER, many central office departments were going to be reorganized. Some job descriptions and reporting relationships would change. In a few departments, for example information technology, some job skills had become obsolete and new job skills were needed. A new board policy was needed that would enable administration to match people with skills.

Rod's proposal, put forward in mid-March, was immediately attacked by the employee groups. Seniority, after all, was the most sacred of union cows. At instructional employee consultation on March 30, HFT called it a backdoor attempt to privatize. It would allow administration to "clear the top of the salary schedule" and replace employees at the top of the pay grade with new employees starting at base pay. It would be "politically dangerous." Representatives from three other unions agreed. The Houston Education Association charged that because most of HISD's noncontract employees were blacks and Hispanics, the proposed policy was an ethnic issue. HISD was "stripping people of color of their employee rights" (HISD, March 30, 1995, p. 2).

The issue was discussed again at combined employee consultation on April 4. The HFT said the proposed policy was a racial issue and that minority board members were unaware of its development (HISD, April 4, 1995, p. 1).

The union attack went public the next day. As usual, Gayle Fallon had the best sound bite: "If they get this policy in, it is open season, and patronage is alive and well. It's like if you work in the district for more than 20 years you should be worried. If you are not one of the in-crowd or not doing favors for people your job could be in trouble" (*Chronicle*, April 5, 1995, p. A20; *Houston Sun*, April 10, 1995, p. A1).

At the board meeting on April 6, 11 union representatives were signed up to speak to the agenda item, but they never spoke. Before the meeting began, Rod, discovering that he did not have the votes, withdrew the recommendation.

Something had to be done about the emerging antireform bloc on the board. I decided that Jeff was the key. Jeff owed Rod his seat on the board, and I felt close to Jeff. In February, he had invited me to preach from his pulpit at the Cullen Missionary Baptist Church. It was a wonderful experience. I determined to make an appeal to Jeff to listen less to Carol and Arthur and more to Rod.

On April 18, we met for lunch at Joe's Crab Shack on the South Loop. Jeff arrived nearly 30 minutes late, spent much of the time on his cellular phone responding to his beeper, and then abruptly left. We had only a few minutes to talk.

Amidst the constant interruptions I tried to talk to Jeff about the jobs issue, the growing polarization on the board, and Rod's need for support.

"It's Rod's fault," said Jeff. "He's not treating Arthur right. Arthur is the board president. Rod should brief him fully on all issues and be responsive to Arthur's advice. Arthur keeps me informed. Carol talks to me almost every day. I only know what I'm told. I was told that some of my church members' jobs were at risk. If Rod wants my support on an issue, he needs to brief me in advance. And you know what people are saying about Rod. He doesn't think for himself. He's just doing what you and Cathy tell him to do."

A few minutes later, after assuring me that he was always open to my views and that if I wanted to counter information he was getting from Arthur and Carol all I need to do was call, Jeff excused himself.

Now I understood what Rod was up against. Privately, the board was split. It was only a matter of time until the split became public.

WE DON'T WANT YOUR CHILDREN

River Oaks Wants a Neighborhood School

The issue that publicly split the board was the vote on River Oaks Elementary School. On March 2, 1995, Ron Franklin introduced at the board table a request of his neighborhood. River Oaks wanted a neighborhood school.

River Oaks was Houston's most exclusive neighborhood. The homes were not just large houses—many were estates. River Oaks residents paid about 9 percent of all the residential property taxes collected by HISD. River Oaks was almost 100 percent white.

Right in the middle of River Oaks was a beautiful elementary school on a large tract of land, but it was not a neighborhood school. In 1970–1971 the neighborhood had abruptly abandoned the school because of forced integration. HISD had responded by adding a magnet program for gifted and talented children from throughout the city, and in 1986, because there were too few neighborhood children to serve, closed the neighborhood component. Not everyone was happy with this decision, but River Oaks had become a community of older families. Those families with children could easily afford and almost always preferred private schools.

In recent years, however, a significant number of younger families with small children had moved into River Oaks. Many of these parents believed in public education. A group of them, said Ron, had conducted a door-to-door survey and determined that if HISD reopened a non-Vanguard component at River Oaks Elementary, a significant number of River Oaks parents would enroll their children.

Ron was committed to preserving the Vanguard program exactly as it was. He recognized that adding a neighborhood component was problematic. The issues were complex and needed study. All he wanted to do, he said, was to alert the rest of us to the discussion and state his view that if HISD could serve the neighborhood without in any way distracting from the Vanguard program, he would propose doing so.

Paula Arnold, Cathy Mincberg, and I responded positively. The other board members were either noncommittal or silent. Paula, Cathy, and I believed in neighborhood schools, and we knew that Vanguard programs for gifted and talented students selected from throughout the city could comfortably coexist with programs for neighborhood children. This was the pattern in HISD, which had 11 elementary Vanguard schools.

The Vanguard Parents Say No

The discussion at the board table unleashed a torrent of opposition from River Oaks Vanguard parents. On March 10, Ron met with about 100 of them. The message was loud and clear. No neighborhood component at River Oaks Elementary. It would "put the quality of the award-winning campus in jeopardy." It would require either expensive new facilities or the dilution of gifted classes with ordinary neighborhood children (*Post*, March 11, 1995, p. A26).[5]

The Vanguard parents were also working on other board members. I was getting letters and phone calls by the score. Just before the March 16 board meeting, I met with about a dozen Vanguard parents for nearly an hour. Rod, who strongly supported a neighborhood component for River Oaks Elementary from the beginning, had posted an agenda item asking the board to approve the neighborhood component, establish an attendance zone, and begin development of an implementation plan.

The parents were polite but firm. "River Oaks Elementary is nearly perfect as it is," they said. "HISD is meeting the unique needs of gifted children in an ethnically balanced school. Everyone gets along. Any change will be problematic. Neighborhood children will degrade the quality of the school. Also, many implementation issues have not been resolved. What will HISD do if there are only a handful of neighborhood children at a grade level, try to mix them with the Vanguard children? And what about the structure of the shared decision-making committee? Will there be one or two?"

The conclusion of the matter was that the Vanguard parents did not want neighborhood children in their school. "And remember," one parent said at the end of the meeting, "about 125 of your constituents are River Oaks Vanguard parents. We live in your district. We're well-organized. We'll help you get reelected if you help us keep River Oaks Elementary the way it is."

My colleagues were getting the same treatment, and five of them were up for reelection. I knew Rod's recommendation was in trouble. Sure enough, after a short discussion at the board table, it was clear that a majority of the board members had serious reservations. Rod withdrew his recommendation.

Class and Race Become the Issue

Throughout March, April, and May, the River Oaks issue simmered. HISD administrators, River Oaks community leaders, and Vanguard parents were studying implementation issues. Ron was working on board members. Rod was waiting for the right time to bring the issue back to the table.

Then class and race became the issue. In private conversations throughout the city people were saying that some minority board members did not want to open River Oaks Elementary to the rich, white children from River Oaks. On April 9, the *Chronicle* published an editorial which began, "A proposal to open the all-Vanguard River Oaks Elementary School to neighborhood children of average ability has been draped in the cloak of class warfare, rich against poor. Would that the issue were that simple" (p. O2).

The issue was not simple, but it was about class and race. River Oaks Elementary was a middle class school. Only 9 percent of the students qualified for free or reduced lunch. All the children were gifted by HISD's standards. And because it was a Vanguard school, River Oaks Elementary received additional money for academic enrichment.

For white parents it was a dream come true. The student population was 40 percent white, 30 percent African American, 28 percent Hispanic, and 1 percent Asian. White children could receive a high-cost, first-class education in an almost perfect ethnic mix, and all this with ethnic harmony. "See how well we get along," was the phrase I kept hearing.

No wonder the River Oaks parents, who made the point that they wanted to send their children to an integrated public school, wanted access to River Oaks Elementary. Would they have been as enthusiastic for the school if the minority children who had been labeled gifted by HISD had been mostly poor children with all the behaviors that frequently accompany poverty? But of course, the minority children labeled as gifted by HISD almost always came from middle-class homes.

The Real Issue at River Oaks

There was much more going on here than appeared on the surface. In fact, HISD's gifted program was really not just for gifted children. By state law children at the 95th percentile and up were identified as gifted, and children were tested for giftedness in kindergarten. This created a problem. At that age, some children identified as gifted were really just precocious. They were bright, yuppie children who had been force-fed an intellectual diet rich in books, music, museums, travel, and sophisticated adult conversation.

By third grade some of these children could be seen for what they were—bright, but not gifted. Meanwhile the gifts of other children, poor children in many cases, were emerging. But programs for gifted children were expensive, and positions were limited. By third grade every slot was filled. It was virtually impossible to create a vacancy. No principal wanted to tell the parent of a gifted child in an enriched educational program that his or her child was not gifted after all and was going to be moved back into regular classes.

A second problem was that HISD had ethnic guidelines for giftedness. Vanguard programs were expected to maintain at every grade level and in each class an ethnic balance of at least 65 percent minority (Hispanic and African American) and no more than 35 percent majority (white and Asian). Testing five-year-old children with the available instruments for determining giftedness did not yield that result. A significant number of white and Asian children who qualified at the 95th percentile were refused admission into preferred Vanguard programs to make room for African American and Hispanic children whose scores went as low as the 80th percentile.

Every spring, when the Vanguard acceptances were mailed to parents, I received calls from white and Asian parents complaining that their gifted and talented children had been discriminated against in Vanguard admission because of racial quotas. "How can HISD tell Mother Nature how she must distribute her gifts?"[6]

So, what was really going on at River Oaks Elementary? Because HISD sometimes identified precocious children as gifted, and then defined "gifted" quite broadly for minority children, River Oaks Elementary was not really full of gifted children. The River Oaks Elementary test scores were on the low side for Vanguard programs, and in the spring 1995 administration of the TAAS, eight neighborhood schools in my trustee district, all with significant minority enrollments—from 27 to 52 percent—had higher average test scores than River Oaks Elementary.

Class and race were issues at River Oaks Elementary, but even more fundamental was the elitist attitude of Vanguard parents and the issue of power. If River Oaks children were admitted into the school it would "dilute" the Vanguard program, and if River Oaks parents got involved in the school, the Vanguard parents would have to share power.

The Board Acts

By early June it was clear that the committee of school officials, Vanguard parents, and River Oaks community leaders established by Paige could not reach consensus on the future of River Oaks Elementary. The Vanguard parents did not want to work out a smooth transition. They did not want a transition at all.

Implementation had never really been the issue. The issue was, did the board support a neighborhood component. If it did, implementation plans could be developed for final approval by the board. If it did not, there was no need for school officials and parents to waste more time on implementation planning. Indeed, it was too late to make any decision that would affect the 1995–1996 school year. But Ron Franklin and his community were being worn down by the controversy. They wanted a decision.

The same agenda item that had been withdrawn on March 16 was posted for June 15. Once again, Rod was firmly and strongly recommending a neighborhood component for River Oaks Elementary. Advance media coverage was significant. Lobbying from both sides was once again at a fever pitch. Ron was lobbying board members for the neighborhood component. Carol Galloway and Arthur Gaines were leading the effort to keep out the neighborhood children. Ten citizens had signed up to speak against the agenda item. Eleven had signed up in support. The gallery was crowded and noisy.

Ron had pledges of support from Cathy, Paula, and me. He needed one more vote. Jeff, he believed, was that vote. But then, just a few minutes before the meeting was scheduled to begin, Jeff quietly informed Ron that he had changed his mind. He would vote against Paige's recommendation. Ron was visibly shaken.

About an hour later, following some preliminary business, a short presentation by administration, and quite a few emotional speeches from citizens, the board discussion began. Ron was the second speaker. He leaned forward in his chair, stretched his neck, and began speaking quietly, measuring his words to control his anger. He talked of his childhood in Houston, his education at the University of Texas, the hard work and good fortune that had made him a successful attorney, and his decision to dedicate his volunteer time to public education. He talked about River Oaks, the declining white enrollment in HISD, and the need to bring affluent parents back into public schools. Then, his voice rising, his eyes flashing, his body tense with controlled fury, Ron put the issue squarely before the board: Did the board care whether children from his neighborhood attended public school? If his community of 1,630 homes, which paid over $15 million in property taxes, could not be given 50 slots for 50 children who happened to be white, he wanted to know, today.

> Let me say one other thing about River Oaks. Despite what the audience may believe, despite what some board members may believe, not all River Oaks residents are there because of inherited wealth and trust funds. There are many people there who have followed the American dream, and because of a lot of hard work and some ingenuity, they have been successful and, yes, are affluent. If being tagged affluent and being tagged bright means you are no longer wanted in Houston's system of public schools, I need to know about that today, too. There can be no other explanation. (HISD, June 15, 1995, pp. 13–14)

Ron's speech was meant for the minority board members, but he did not look at them, and they did not look at him. They sat stiffly, showing no emotion, staring off into space. Ron's speech had not softened their opposition. It appeared to have hardened it. They were in stone.

The only revealing comment was made by Arthur. It was a question to Paige. But it put the real issue on the table.

> How do you answer a concern that there are those who feel that because of the power and prestige of the people who live in River Oaks, and who speak of it as "our neighborhood school," and that fact that we pay $15 million, that after a while they will dominate the school. How would you answer that? (HISD, June 15, 1995, p. 19)

A few minutes later, the motion failed. All four white board members voted yes. All five minority board members voted no. For the first time in my six years on the board, the board had divided on ethnic lines.

The board recessed. Rising from my seat at the board table, I bumped into two HISD district superintendents, one African American, one Hispanic. "I can't believe what the board just voted," they both said. "What a terrible mistake." A group of parent activists from my trustee district were standing in the hallway looking at one another in disbelief. One was crying.

Walking through the small board conference room on my way to the men's room, I passed Arthur and Ron. Ron was as angry as I had ever seen him. "You're a fraud," he shouted into Arthur's face.

"Back to you," responded Arthur smartly.

The River Oaks Vote Shakes the City

The River Oaks vote shook the city. A statement to the media by Ron quickly became the sound bite that for many whites summed up the issue: "The message to the River Oaks community is that 'we want your money but we don't want your children'" (*Chronicle*, June 16, 1995, p. A33).

Everyone was talking about the River Oaks vote. People were writing letters to the *Chronicle* editor, calling radio talk shows, writing Rod Paige and board members. Most of the letters were from people angry with the vote. Some were outraged. Rod received so many letters that he sent hundreds of community leaders an information packet on River Oaks and Vanguard programs (Paige, August 1, 1995).

Many of the newspaper letters and calls to radio talk shows called attention to the ethnic split on the board. No one did more to fan the flames of racial tension than *Chronicle* columnist Lori Rodriguez. Her column, entitled "Doing right at River Oaks Elementary," appeared in the June 24 *Chronicle* (p. A36). It was filled with misinformation and class and racial rancor. Nearly every statement made about HISD was incorrect: The board meeting was "racially charged." The fight was between the "overwhelmingly Anglo, overwhelmingly wealthy" residents of River Oaks who wanted wider entry into the school for their children and the "economically and ethnically mixed Vanguard parents" whose children had earned the right to attend River Oaks Elementary. "It was not a pretty fight, least of all on the part of Franklin, who insisted the board action sent a message to River Oaks residents that the district wants their money, but does not want their children."

She went on to impugn Paige's motives and independence. He was trying to please his white sponsors, the cadre of Anglo trustees who had gone behind closed doors to spearhead his appointment as superintendent. And she predicted some serious arm-twisting of minority trustees in the next few weeks to get them to change their minds. Minority trustees should "stand fast, stand courageous and stand for what they know is right."

Two Trustees Charge Money for Votes

A few weeks later the pressure on minority board members that Ms. Rodriguez had predicted, occurred, or so at least two board members claimed. On the front page of the July 13 *Chronicle* was a story headlined "Two HISD trustees say funds offered to alter vote." The news story described how, acting through an intermediary, Assistant Harris County Attorney Lana Shadwick had offered Esther Campos and Robert Jefferson $50,000 in campaign contributions if they would change their votes on River Oaks. If they did not change their votes, said Campos and Jefferson, they were told candidates would be recruited to run against them.

The intermediary, our former board colleague José Salazar, denied that money had been offered for a vote change. The River Oaks people had simply called him when they had trouble reaching Campos. They wanted to know why Campos had not been persuaded by simple logic to include neighborhood children in the school. "I know they are upset enough that they will help any candidate who runs against her," added Salazar.

That same day, Harris County district attorney Johnny Holmes announced that his office would investigate the allegations. Ms. Shadwick, speaking through her attorney, denied that she had made direct or indirect offers of money to Campos and Jefferson. But, added her attorney, "It is no secret that Shadwick and others are looking for candidates to oppose trustees who voted against opening River Oaks. . . . But absolutely, there has never been any discussion about financing anybody to change their vote or to make a run" (*Chronicle*, July 14, 1995, p. A1).

When asked about this statement, Esther affirmed her allegation. Jeff could not be reached for comment.

Exactly a week later, July 21, the district attorney closed the investigation. In response to direct questions by assistant district attorney Randy Ayers, Campos and Jefferson changed their stories. "They were both very clear that there never was any offer of any campaign contribution in exchange for changing a vote," said Ayers. Lana Shadwick's attorney claimed vindication (*Chronicle*, July 21, 1995, p. A1).

The River Oaks battle was over, at least for now.

NOTES

1. The election that placed Esther on the board was an embarrassment to the Hispanic community. Voter turnout was abysmal. Only 2 percent of the 58,000 registered voters in District Eight bothered to vote on May 7. In the May 31 runoff election, required because no candidate received more than 50 percent of the vote, voter turnout was 4.4 percent. Board members were disgusted. We could have appointed a trustee to serve until the next general election, just 18 months away, but the Hispanic Education Committee had demanded an interim appointment and an election. Board members remembered well the uproar from the same individuals in 1990 when Felix Fraga's appointment to the same seat had been considered; so, at great expense to the taxpayers, the board had called an election. This was the result. The Hispanic Education Committee, as *Chronicle* columnist Lori Rodriguez put it, was great at hooting and hollering about process, inclusion, and participatory democracy, but they were abject failures at mobilizing their apathetic community (*Chronicle*, June 4, 1994, p. A29).

2. "HISD rates 10 schools exemplary: District holding campuses to higher standard than state's" trumpeted the *Post* headline in the lead story on page one. "HISD schools with low rating decline to 3 from 15 in one year," said the headline in the more subdued *Chronicle* on page A34 (*Post* and *Chronicle*, November 11, 1994).

3. The new HISD graduation requirements were the requirements being considered by the State Board of Education for the school year 1999–2000. HISD would require them of next year's high school freshmen.

4. The new graduation standards were presented to the board for a second reading on April 6. Administration had determined that the new graduation requirements would not have a major impact on staffing patterns for at least a year, and additional staffing would be funded in future budgets. Forty-one additional science labs would be required at a cost of about $7 million, and over three years, 58 computer labs would be needed at a cost of $4.3 million. The cost of foreign language and world geography materials would be minimal.

5. This is my last citation from *The Houston Post*, which was last published on April 18, 1996. It was purchased by the *Houston Chronicle* and shut down immediately.

6. My repeated efforts to get this policy changed were not successful. By 1995, I had given up on the issue. But in 1997, faced with a reverse discrimination lawsuit in federal court, the board eliminated the ethnic guidelines. The development, implementation, and impact of the new policy, which grants a small advantage to minority children who qualify for free and reduced-priced lunch, is not described in this book. It is an extraordinarily complex and important story, but it is not directly related to the reform of HISD.

11

The Voters Determine
the Future of HISD

The River Oaks vote was in June 1995. In November, HISD voters would have the opportunity to elect six trustees. The only hope for *Beliefs and Visions* was election of a reform majority on the board of education. The voters would determine the future of HISD.

ROD PAIGE MAKES A DECISION

On Saturday morning, July 15, Rod and I met for coffee at a little coffee shop in Bellaire to talk about the November 7 board elections. Rod was unshaven and in sweats on his way to work out. It was exactly a month since the River Oaks vote.

We had both known for many months that Cathy Mincberg was resigning from the board. She and her husband were building a large house outside of her trustee district. When the family moved, Cathy would have to resign. It was a very difficult decision for Cathy, but the move was good for her family and long overdue. Cathy had determined to announce her resignation in time for a replacement to be selected at the November election.

An excellent replacement was standing in the wings. Laurie Bricker, an educational consultant and active HISD parent. She was sharp and had a strong political base. "Laurie will no doubt win that election," said Rod, "and she will be a good board member, but there will never be another Cathy. Cathy is a warrior. I can't tell you how much I'm going to miss her."

Ron Franklin was burned out. Since the River Oaks vote, we had hardly seen him. Ron was our heavy artillery. He could hit any target dead on with unbelievable power. I could see why he was so successful as a trial lawyer. Unfortunately, at the River Oaks debate, he tried to represent himself. But, as a rule, no one could match Ron for dissecting complex issues and then bringing emotion and logic together to deliver the telling blow. Ron, more than anyone, I believed, had provided the firepower in the back rooms and at the board table which had brought us so far.

Now we were losing Cathy. And Rod was right. It was not just Cathy's vote, it was her leadership. She was the master strategist who could see all sides of an issue. And she never missed anything. As Board Counsel Kelly Frels often said, "Cathy is just so danged smart." Cathy had a hard edge to her that made some people nervous. But Cathy could always come up with a plan, and she could nearly always make her plan work. Now we were losing her. The reformers no longer controlled the board. And with Cathy leaving, reform would be even more difficult. How were we going to move forward with *Beliefs and Visions*?

"I've had it with Arthur and Jeff," said Rod, leaning forward in his chair and poking my arm with his finger. "I've decided they must go. If good candidates don't appear to run against them, I'm going to recruit them myself. I can't go on like this."

This was very high-risk behavior. Such activity could not be kept secret, and if Arthur and Jeff were reelected, what then?

"I know," said Rod. "But I've got no choice. Arthur has put together a working majority. Right now *Beliefs and Visions* is dead. It's just urban politics as usual. You can't believe what is going on behind the scenes. It's worse than you can possibly imagine. I think Jeff will be the easiest to beat. He's never run an election, and that's my old trustee district. Arthur will be much more difficult. But I've got to try. If there's no change on the board, I may as well resign. I've given this a lot of thought. I know the risks. I'm prepared to take them." Rod jabbed his finger at me across the table.

"Who else knows about this?"

"Key leaders in the black community, Cathy, and Ron, and I'm going to talk to some of the business leaders downtown."

FALLON AND FRIENDS VS. PAIGE AND FRIENDS

The next five months were going to be political war, in fact the war had already begun. On one side were Gayle Fallon, the three African American trustees, and organized labor. On the other side were Rod Paige, the four white trustees, and the leadership of Houston's business community. Both sides, of course, brought in a large network of allies with a variety of agendas, many of whom did not understand the stakes. But the principals on each side understood very well what was at stake, control of Houston's public schools.

The war was fought on many fronts. One area of conflict was personnel management policies. Another was the 1995–1996 budget. In both cases the core issue was jobs.

HISD Makes War on Employees

By mid-summer Gayle Fallon and the three African American trustees—Gaines, Galloway, and Jefferson—had become close allies. They needed each other. Gayle needed the trustees to resist any policy changes or administrative actions that would increase employee accountability. The trustees wanted organized labor to support their reelection campaigns. During the spring and summer of 1995, the four of them met often to talk about how Paige and unfriendly board members like McAdams and Mincberg were trying to weaken the union. The issues were employee rights, decentralization, and privatization (*Dewey v. Paige*, November 22, 1995, Fallon deposition, pp. 101, 178, 206, 207).

On May 1, 1995, Richard Shaw, the secretary-treasurer of the Harris County AFL-CIO Council, accused Rod of making war on employees. In a letter to Rod, copied to board members, the partnership, the HFT, and the Transport Union Workers (bus drivers), he charged that "any attempt to eliminate or circumvent HISD's present policies and practices involving due process in disciplinary matters, whether it is to eliminate continuing contracts for teachers or to impose at-will employment on employees is a continuation of the practice of making war on your employees. Why does HISD continue to make war on its employees?"

On August 23, 11 HFT teachers filed a lawsuit against eight principals, three district superintendents, and Rod, claiming they had been involuntarily transferred to other schools because they had either filed grievances against their principals or, as members of their school's shared decision-making committee, been vocal critics of their principal. Gayle charged that the involuntary transfers, which were perfectly legal under state law and board policy, were having a "chilling effect" on protected speech (*Chronicle*, August 24, 1995, p. A37).

On August 30, a state district judge refused to grant the HFT teachers a temporary restraining order and the transfers were implemented. Also on August 30, another state district judge dismissed a lawsuit filed in March 1994 alleging that HISD and the board had breached the employment contracts of HFT members and violated due process rights by investigating employee wrongdoing through the professional standards department.

On September 6, Rod announced to the decentralization commission that he was moving 254 student evaluation specialists, psychologists, nurse consultants, behavioral coordinators, and other professional staff from central office directly into schools or one of the 12 district offices. The Gaines-Fallon coalition complained that decentralization was being forced on the district by the downtown business leaders and that Rod was just a tool of Houston's white business elite. As the *Chronicle* noted in a September 10 editorial, "There are political concerns and even talk that the changes are being wrongly forced on the district by the city's business community. Some of the off-the-record criticism also bears troubling ethnic and racial overtones" (p. C2).

Raise Salaries But Not Taxes

Inevitably, the 1995–1996 budget got caught up in reelection politics. Since the 32 percent tax increase of 1992, HISD had not had a tax increase and teachers had received only step salary increases. These raises, which averaged about 3 percent per year, were given only to teachers who moved up a step on the salary schedule.[1]

All five board members seeking reelection—Campos, Galloway, Gallegos, Gaines, and Jefferson—wanted a significant pay raise for employees, but they vehemently opposed a tax increase. By late spring, some of them were making the case that HISD had plenty of money to provide a teacher pay increase without raising taxes. All the superintendent had to do was wring the waste out of the system. These were the same board members who vigorously opposed privatization or job cuts.

Rod was furious. Since submitting his 1994–1995 budget recommendation the previous year, he had predicted that HISD would need a small tax increase in 1995–1996, and since February, he had been on record that his top budget priority was a teacher pay raise (*Chronicle*, February 3, 1995, p. A29; February 23, 1995, p. A23). Now he was trapped. There was no point in proposing a tax increase, he told me. Arthur and friends would kill it and take the credit in their reelection campaigns. They would also take the credit for a teacher pay increase or blame him for wasting money in inefficient operations if there were not one.

Rod needed to find $60 million. With guts and a little risk, it could be done. HISD had just won a lawsuit against the state, bringing in an additional $15 million in state aid. Staff cuts and privatization of two departments—workers' compensation and solid waste disposal—could save $10.2 million. And $35 million could be taken from the undesignated fund balance. This would reduce the fund balance from $75 to $40 million, risky for a district the size of HISD, and it would use nonreoccurring funds for a reoccurring expense, but it would provide the rest of the $60 million Rod needed.

On August 3, Rod announced his budget recommendation. Spending would increase by $60 million (2.5 percent), but there would be no tax increase. Thirty-five million of the $60 million would fund a 7 percent salary increase for teachers.[2] They would receive a 5 percent pay raise, and an additional 2 percent would be budgeted for incentive pay.[3] The old step increases would be replaced by a salary range, which would give administrators more flexibility in setting salaries. Also, the same performance contracts that had been approved by the board the previous December for district superintendents would be offered to principals.[4]

Rod's budget was approved on August 10, but not without a fight. Opposition from the HFT and the AFL-CIO forced him to withdraw his proposal to replace the automatic salary step increase with a salary range,[5] and some board members insisted that the district provide a larger pay increase for noncontract employees.

Rod had proposed a 3 percent raise for noncontract employees (bus drivers, food service workers, and others); the HFT wanted 5 percent. The board approved the 3 percent on August 10, but a few days before the next board meeting, Arthur posted a motion to amend the budget and provide the additional 2 percent by drawing down further the fund balance. "We've got plenty of money, plenty of money," he told the *Chronicle* (August 22, 1995, p. A13).

We all knew Arthur had five votes for the additional raise. Rod was angry, but resigned. Cathy, Paula, and I determined to fight. We came up with a plan to make Arthur cast a tough vote by linking the additional raise to privatization.

At the board meeting, before Arthur could make his motion, I moved to provide an additional 2 percent raise for noncontract employees and fund it with cost savings created by privatization of additional facilities management services. There were groans from the union people in the gallery, who had come to speak for Arthur's motion. Arthur was confused. "Would not that entail the loss of jobs?" he asked. "We have already had the city upset over that."

Discussion on the motion was brief. Caught in the trap, Arthur emphasized that the additional privatization would be held to just enough to save the $1.6 million needed to fund the additional pay raise, and that, most importantly, no personnel would be displaced. The motion passed unanimously.

Rod, who was sitting next to me at the board table, passed me a note. "Take credit for putting this on the table." And then he added with a whisper, "It's important. Otherwise Arthur will try to spin this defeat into a victory."

Sure enough, but it was Gayle who had the wit to do it. In the next issue of the HFT newsletter, she reported the board vote to her members as a great victory for Arthur. "Thank you, King Arthur (Gaines)! HISD Board President Arthur Gaines heard the pleas of the lowest paid HISD employees and reopened the budget," read the headline (*Federation Teacher*, September 1995, p. 1). The article went on to describe how Arthur, responding to the union, had reopened the budget, an unprecedented move, and obtained a raise for classified employees from 3 to 5 percent. "So thank you, Mr. Gaines!" Nothing was said about the additional privatization.

PREPARATIONS FOR BOARD ELECTIONS

Business Leaders Get Involved

Since our breakfast on July 15, Rod had been trying to recruit candidates to challenge Arthur and Jeff. He had also been talking discretely with selected black leaders and a small core of Houston's most influential business leaders. Within weeks there was a quiet buzz among Houston's political class about the upcoming HISD board elections.

On August 10, the day Rod's budget was approved, I was brought into the conversation. One of Houston's most respected business leaders had suggested we meet for lunch.

I outlined the situation. The board was divided. Mutual respect had given way to bitterness and anger. Some board members were meddling in personnel matters, demanding jobs for friends and even giving directives to employees. Gayle Fallon was allied with the African American board members against Rod. Rod could no longer count on support for his recommendations. The further reform of HISD was at a standstill. Everything that had been accomplished was at risk.

"This is not new information," responded my friend. "These points are being discussed by business leaders. Rod has already talked to several of us. Tragic isn't it. Houston's first African American superintendent. He's doing such a wonderful job. And minority children are the big winners. One would think the African American board members would be his strongest supporters. I can assure you we'll get involved in the board elections. I am confident we can raise significant dollars for Rod's candidates. But it's a very delicate situation. We can't recruit candidates. They'll have to spring from the communities. And we can't even fund them too openly. You know what'll happen. The incumbents will charge that the white business establishment is trying to tell the African American community who to elect. They'll call their opponents tools of white power. No, this must be handled very carefully. An African American quarterback needs to manage things. And that person shouldn't be Rod. A group of us are meeting tomorrow to decide what to do. Some prominent black leaders will be there. I'll let you know how it goes."

Five days later, on August 15, Cathy, Paula, Ron, and I met for breakfast to talk about the board and the coming elections. "If there're no changes on the board, I'll resign," said Ron, "I just can't go on. This River Oaks vote has taken a lot out of me. I'm not willing to spend another two years on the board watching Arthur play the race card at every turn and tear down all we've worked for. I'll announce my resignation right after the election, and then I'm going to write a strong op-ed for the *Chronicle* and tell this city what's been going on."

That same afternoon Cathy announced her resignation.

Desperately Seeking Candidates

Meanwhile, Rod was desperately trying to find candidates to run against Gaines and Jefferson. It was not easy. He was looking for successful professional people willing to give 20 hours a week for no pay and a fair amount of abuse, people who already had a political network and were willing to challenge an incumbent. I volunteered to help.

On August 17, I talked with an African American friend who was very knowledgeable about education and well-known throughout the city. "You'd be a great board member," I told him. "And I believe you could beat Arthur."

"I just can't," he responded. "I've talked to some of the key black leaders. They know Arthur's a problem. They'd be happy if he wouldn't seek another term. But they're not willing to work against him and split the black community. You have to understand, Don, splitting the black community is unthinkable."

The filing deadline for candidates was September 25. As the deadline grew closer and no strong candidates appeared, I grew increasingly worried. "You think you're worried," said Rod. "Do you realize what's at stake for me."

Jefferson Has a Problem

Jeff was the most vulnerable incumbent. And on September 18 he became more vulnerable. The *Chronicle* published an article with his picture and the headline "HISD trustee delinquent in his taxes" (p. A9). The article reported that Jeff had been five years delinquent in his school taxes and a defendant in a tax lawsuit when he was appointed to the board on February 3, 1994. He had paid his back school taxes one week later, but he still owed $4,011.65 to Harris County, the city of Houston, Houston Community College, and the Harris County Hospital District. Three days later the *Chronicle* blasted Jeff with an editorial that said: "It is somehow emblematic of the disarray of public education in this country that an official who helps to apportion the civic burden of public education was so little acquainted with, and so lax in meeting, his own responsibilities" (p. A34). Surely someone would challenge Jeff.

BOARD ELECTIONS

The Candidates

Someone did. At almost the last minute, Wayman Clyde Lemon, a young African American attorney, filed against Jefferson. As it turned out, Rod did not recruit him, but he enthusiastically supported him, as did the business community. Teddy McDavid, an African American woman who had recently retired from HISD as a fairly high-level administrator, was Rod's candidate against Arthur.[6]

Though she had four opponents, we all expected Laurie Bricker to be elected to Cathy's vacant seat. We also expected Esther Campos, who had drawn two opponents, to be reelected. Carol Galloway and Olga Gallegos had drawn no opponents.

So, most likely, the future of HISD would be determined by the outcome of Arthur and Jeff's elections. If both were reelected, Ron Franklin would probably resign from the board and there was a good chance Rod would resign the superintendency. The stakes were high.

October was a hectic month for the candidates and hundreds of volunteers. Arthur and Jeff were running effective campaigns. Gayle Fallon had brought into town an AFL-CIO campaign consultant to assist them. Teddy McDavid and Clyde Lemon were also running effective campaigns. The business leaders of Houston and a lot of River Oaks parents were raising considerable amounts of money to help them, and Rod was getting out the word as best as he could that McDavid and Lemon were his candidates.

On October 11, the *Chronicle* endorsed James A. Bonner, one of the other candidates running against Gaines. Gaines, said the editorial, "has shown a resistance to the swift and acute changes the district needs to make if it is to improve its below-average performance. Under Gaines' leadership, consensus on the board has tended to unravel rather than knit" (p. A26).

Four days later the *Chronicle* endorsed Clyde Lemon against Jefferson. "The incumbent in this race, Robert Charles Jefferson, neglected to pay his school taxes for several years prior to his appointment to the HISD board, an intolerable oversight for a person whose duties now require him to levy those taxes on his neighbors" (October 15, 1995, p. C2).

More Problems for Jefferson

More dirt on Robert Jefferson came out in the closed-session portion of the board meeting on October 19. Ron Franklin began asking questions of Rod and Jeff regarding a contract between HISD and the Coalition of Ministers Against Crime (COMAC), a group cofounded by Jeff.

COMAC had signed a contract with HISD in May 1994 to prepare youth under 21 who had dropped out of school for the high school equivalency exam, the General Education Development (GED).[7] The contract had been voided by HISD in November 1994 because an HISD audit had uncovered questionable business practices. Jeff, it appeared, had direct management involvement in the COMAC Academy and thus a serious conflict of interest. In addition, COMAC owed HISD $16,315 because it had collected for students who did not attend classes.

Ron wanted to know the full story. What were the problems at COMAC Academy? What was Jefferson's involvement? What about the $16,000?

The discussion became very heated. Jeff denied any wrongdoing. Paige stood up behind the board table, told Jeff to his face that he had betrayed his trust, and then, throwing his papers on the board table, strode out of the board room, slamming the door behind him. Arthur accused Ron of bringing up the issue during the election to embarrass Jeff and threatened Ron that if he ever sought election to public office he would pay the price: "What goes round comes round." Ron just glared at Arthur.

Then Jeff began begging Ron: "Please don't put this out before the public until November 8. I'm in the midst of a hard election. I may lose it anyway. But this issue will hurt me. I've done no wrong. I can answer all your questions, but it will be very difficult for me to defend myself on this issue during the heat of an election. Please, can you keep this quiet for three weeks?"

Ron continued to glare at Arthur. "O.K., I'll tell you what I'll do." His voice was measured and calm. "To show my good faith, to show that I'm not bringing this up just to embarrass Jeff, I will say nothing until November 8. You have my word. If it gets out, it didn't come from me. But after the election, I want the truth."

Will Black Houston Let Arthur Gaines Walk?

Several times during October, I saw Rod at lunches and dinners. He was not confident. "You can't believe what Arthur and Jeff are saying," he reported. "They're promising more money to school communities, no tax increases, and no job cuts. Amazing. They're saying they're the salvation of HISD. They're going to protect it from the power of the white board members and Houston's white business establishment."

On October 31, the behind-the-scenes maneuvering of Rod and some of Houston's business leaders to unseat Arthur and Jeff became public information. Someone had leaked a confidential memo to the *Houston Press*. Investigative reporter Tim Fleck knew everything (Fleck, November 2–8, 1995, p. 8). The Fleck article named Jim Edmonds, Louis Sklar, Ken Lay, and Bob Onstead, all heavy hitters among Houston's business elite, as members of a group determined to unseat Gaines and Jefferson because they had been "obstructionist" to the policies of Rod Paige. It cited Gayle Fallon claiming the campaign to defeat Gaines and Jefferson was an effort by big-business interests to take control of the board so they could influence the awarding of contracts for the next HISD bond issue. It identified McDavid and Lemon as the business community's chosen candidates, and summarized the strategy for electing McDavid and Lemon as outlined in a memo by Jim Edmonds.

The Edmonds memo, dated October 3 and stamped "Confidential," was a follow-up to the meeting on August 11 that my business friend had told me about at lunch on August 10. The focus of the memo was election strategy. It identified the candidates, gave the number of votes cast in the last board elections, mentioned a legal point about runoff elections, speculated on possible voter turnout, and then got into the nuts and bolts of the campaign.

Political situation

Arthur Gaines is a pretty formidable candidate, having pulled 57% of the vote against two opponents. Dr. Teddy McDavid, a former HISD and Texas Southern University educator and administrator, appears to be a competitive candidate. In her retirement, she remains actively involved in education and community activities. Her connections in the African American community are good and rival those of Arthur Gaines. In fact, people in the community have stated that Dr. McDavid should be very competitive with Arthur Gaines among their peers, a very good ballot-casting group that went rather solidly for Gaines in 1991. Although we suspect that neither is well-known, McDavid is behind on name ID and that will have to be corrected with mail, leaflets and yard signs.

Much of the above commentary also applies to Clyde Lemon in District 9. Lemon is an attorney and Marine veteran who is currently a member of the Texas Juvenile Probation Commission. Lemon holds degrees from Prairie View A&M and Thurgood Marshall Law, is an active Jaycee and screens candidates for the U.S. Naval Academy. He is married and has two children (both in HISD schools). Incumbent Rev. Jefferson, who has not been elected (he was appointed to fill out Rod Paige's term), has some vulnerability. You might recall seeing some of his problems recently surfacing in the *Houston Chronicle;* there may be more. Our chances in this race appear to be good.

Message

Without having the benefit of research, it appears our message or theme would be that both incumbents have been obstructionists to Dr. Paige, who, as the first African American superintendent, has consistently demonstrated strong leadership and keen attention to schools within the African American neighborhoods. In both Districts 4 and 9 we would highlight the excellent credentials of our candidates and point out any flaws that have already surfaced, or may turn up, on Arthur Gaines and Rev. Jefferson. Pointing out such negatives is important as incumbents aren't easily defeated, especially in low-income Districts where they have union backing. Voters will need specific reasons to vote against Gaines and Jefferson.

Budget

In the past, when we have been involved and have adequately funded Trustee races, we have been successful. Traditionally, school board races are fairly unsophisticated, poorly funded efforts. Our dollars have provided organization and well directed campaigns that include phone banking, voter ID, direct mail and street programs.

To achieve success, we must adequately fund these races. Our mechanism will be the creation of a specific purpose political action committee (PAC) called "Better Schools for Houston PAC." We will direct our financial efforts to the PAC so as not to cause any problems to the candidates. Also, the Better Schools for Houston PAC will directly retain its own consultants so we will know where and how our dollars are being spent. Dan McClung [a well-known political consultant] is already working on overlapping City Council races and Ken Calloway, the best black precinct organizer in Houston, is working on a precinct plan.

We have, if properly funded, the opportunity to make a change in the makeup of HISD's Board and, consequently, the future direction of HISD. We can't do it without your financial help and your effort in raising additional campaign dollars. Due to time constraints, I recommend that we go forward. Please call me if you have questions. I'll be calling you. (Edmonds, October 3, 1995)

The memo played perfectly into Arthur's hands. The *Houston Forward Times,* one of Houston's largest black newspapers, plastered the story across the front page, "PAC group targets minority HISD trustees: 'Fat Cats' will make money talk . . . but will black Houston let Arthur Gaines walk?" (November 1–7, 1995). An accompanying picture of Arthur was captioned, "Arthur Gaines fell into disfavor for fighting for HISD's 'have nots.'" The article described how the downtown business machine was pumping money into defeating black and Hispanic school board members who were "refusing to betray their communities." The plot was a "political hit" on Gaines and Jefferson. Much of the memo was quoted.

The Baptist Ministers Association of Houston and Vicinity, headed by the Reverend J. J. Roberson, the same group that had come out so strongly for Paige when his superintendency was threatened by the Hispanic Education Committee, condemned what it called a CIA-type operation to control politics in the African American community:

We regret and despise attempts by elements of the White business establishment to assume that we, as a community, cannot think for ourselves. We choose our own leaders and representatives at the ballot box. The big billboards and leaflets with pictures constantly flooding our community with your unknown, unsung candidates for the HISD school board race will be soundly rejected by our voters. They have paid no dues in our community. Our children and employees are special to us. School board members Arthur Gaines, Carol Galloway, and Robert Jefferson have consistently voted in our best interest. They are against privatization and contracting out services which will take thousands of jobs from the many workers we have in maintenance and operations. One wrong vote could send an economic recession through our community which we cannot stand. We are aware of the trickle down effect from the ultra conservatives. (*Forward Times,* November 1–7, 1995)

Arthur's public response was, I am "utterly shocked. I had always heard that 'downtown interests' had a hand in politics, but to see something in writing brings me to the reality that, hey, these people really do these things!" (Fleck, November 2–8, 1995, p. 8).

Election day was Tuesday, November 7. Arthur's victory was huge. He defeated Teddy McDavid 59 percent to 14 percent (two other candidates split the remaining votes). The leaked Jim Edmonds memo, everyone agreed, helped Arthur tremendously. And as it turned out, Teddy McDavid was not a strong candidate. So we would keep Arthur.

We would also keep Carol Galloway (no opponent) and probably Esther Campos. Esther had been forced into a runoff election, but with 49.2 percent of the vote seemed almost certain to win. Laurie Bricker, as expected, was easily elected over four opponents.

One election remained well up in the air. Robert Jefferson had come in second to Clyde Lemon in a very close three-way race.[8] There would be a runoff election on December 9. The reformers still had a chance to recapture working control of the board.

Jeff Offers a Deal

I was still mulling over the election results Wednesday afternoon when Ron Franklin called. "Don, you can't believe it! Guess who just left my office? Robert Jefferson! He has offered me a bribe!" Ron was almost shouting into the telephone. "That's right. He said if I would keep the COMAC Academy issue quiet, he would change his vote on River Oaks. Today is November 8. Don't you see. I gave my word to say nothing until November 8. Can you believe it? I'm appalled. The man's slime. I'm going to tell the whole story to the *Chronicle.*"

Two days later the story was on the front page. "Cover-up attempt claimed: HISD's Jefferson accused by Franklin of offering a deal," read the headline. "I am absolutely appalled," said Ron, "and I am about a hair away from resigning and saying I don't want anything to do with it."

Jefferson acknowledged that he had met with Ron, but said, "I really just thought we were talking generally as friends about issues that we would be handling." He denied any offer to exchange his vote on River Oaks for Ron's silence on COMAC. The board already knew about the COMAC issue, he said. "I didn't want them to make an issue of it, but everybody on the board knew already. This is no secret. It is brought up at this time for political reasons." As for COMAC, said Jefferson, "I wasn't responsible for COMAC Academy. If I would have been responsible, a lot of different things would have been done" (*Chronicle*, November 10, 1995, p. A1).

The article said little about the business irregularities at COMAC, but a week later the *Chronicle* printed a long story about the operations of COMAC Academy. The facts were clear. Jeff was directly involved in the management of COMAC, and COMAC was reporting students it did not have, lavishing high salaries on a bloated executive staff, and not paying teachers.[9]

Victory

We could never tell if Jeff's involvement with COMAC had any impact on the runoff election. It seemed to be quickly forgotten. Clyde Lemon was determined to run a positive campaign. He refused to mention either Jeff's school tax problem or COMAC. He just stressed his resume—former major in the U.S. Marines, J. D. from Texas Southern University, commissioner on the Texas Juvenile Probation Commission—and his commitment to teacher raises, drop-out prevention, alternative schools, and training for principals, teachers, and students in team building.

The runoff election was as hot as the general election. Once again Houston's business leaders and some River Oaks parents raised money for Lemon. Once again Cathy Mincberg and Laurie Bricker, who had strong political contacts in the white neighborhoods in the western part of the district, worked hard to mobilize parents to vote for Lemon. Once again Gayle Fallon pulled out all the stops for Jefferson. The union tried to make privatization the main issue in the election. A vote for Lemon was a vote to lay off thousands of HISD employees. Lemon was also attacked for being an active Republican. Pictures of him standing with Newt Gingrich were plastered on car windshields on the Sunday before the election at nearly every black church in the district.

Election day was December 9. It was a very cold day for Houston. Voter turnout, which had been very light on November 7—about 17 percent of the eligible voters voted—was even lighter.

About 8:00 P.M. I drove to Kaphan's Restaurant, the site of Lemon's election night party. I had never met Clyde before, but it was time. I was impressed, as Rod had assured me I would be. Clyde was a small, strong man with fierce eyes and a strong step. He looked every inch a United States Marine. It was clear that he did not see himself as Paige's candidate. He had received a lot of help from Paige, Mincberg, Bricker, River Oaks parents, and the business leadership of Houston, but it was clear he had his own network of friends and his own reasons for running. Clyde would be his own man.

About 10:00 the final returns came in. Clyde Lemon was the winner, with 3,138 votes to Jefferson's 2,683. Esther was also a winner in an election where less than 2,700 people voted. The room erupted in shouts and applause. The reform of HISD would continue.

NOTES

1. In 1995, average teacher salaries were about $30,000 per year. Most bus drivers, food service workers, school custodians, and unskilled clerical workers were paid between $9,000 and $13,000 per year. Principals and mid-level administrators made in the $50,000 to $75,000 range. Most top-level administrators made over $80,000. Teacher salaries were near the mean for teacher salaries in Harris County, and HISD's low-skilled employees were paid above marketplace rates. Principals and top-level administrators were paid less than people with comparable responsibility in the private sector.

2. Fifteen million new dollars would cover increased costs over which HISD had little control, basically inflation in the cost of purchased goods and services. Ten million dollars would provide additional staff in schools.

3. Eight million dollars for incentive pay was given to schools. A committee of teachers established criteria, which had to be weighted at least 25 percent for growth in student achievement. Teachers who met the criteria received extra pay.

4. All principals who were willing to accept these contracts and waive all claims to due-process and tenure rights would receive an additional $7,500 per year. Subsequently 219 of HISD's 247 principals accepted the new contracts.

5. On July 5, Gayle Fallon wrote a letter to board members charging that "An open-ended salary range could ultimately result in arbitrary placement up or down on an annual basis. There is not sufficient trust in administration at this point to believe that this will not happen. We can easily envision principals setting salaries 'at-will' for individual employees" (Fallon, July 5, 1995).

6. Gaines and Jefferson also had other opponents.

7. The Texas State Board of Education allowed school districts to pass on state per-student funding to public or private organizations for alternative education programs for students who met the state-mandated "at-risk" criteria or for students who had dropped out of school.

8. Lemon received 2,959 votes; Jefferson received 2,938; Mary Houston, a retired nurse who had run two years earlier against Paige, received 2,921; a fourth candidate received 892.

9. "He [Jefferson] was involved in all the meetings," said district superintendent Paul Ofield. "We talked to him and said he needed to disassociate himself from the COMAC Academy because he was on the school board, and it could be interpreted the wrong way. . . . He did not do that." In fact it was clear from the documents that though Jefferson had not signed the contract with HISD—it was signed by an executive assistant—Jefferson was in charge. HISD learned what was going on when the teachers complained that they were not being paid. Meetings between HISD and COMAC were held. An audit was conducted. What HISD discovered was that COMAC had collected about $16,000 more money than it should have by reporting more students than it

actually had. And the roughly $90,000 that had been collected had been used to pay handsome salaries to nine administrators (a *chancellor*—a close friend of Jefferson— and a *corporate staff*), help pay off a COMAC loan, and pay $2,000 for a banquet that was not school-related. Meanwhile, not only were salaries for COMAC's 10 teachers not paid, but COMAC was not paying federal payroll taxes to the IRS on the administrative salaries it was paying. HISD canceled the contract. The school was closed (*Chronicle*, November 16, 1995, p. A29).

12

Stop HISD Bonds

Finally, 1996 was the year for HISD's repeatedly postponed bond election. Many HISD schools were over 50 years old. Generations of HISD boards had underfunded maintenance to keep tax rates low and provide competitive salaries for teachers. HISD schools needed $1 billion for repairs and renovations. Also, because student enrollment had increased by 16,000 since 1988, several hundred million more dollars were needed for a dozen plus new schools.[1]

Voters had approved a $300 million bond issue, Phase A of Project Renewal, in March 1989. Fifteen new schools had been built, new building additions had been added to 22 schools, and 83 schools had been repaired and refurbished. Phase A had been completed on time and on budget. A hundred plus school communities not included in Phase A had been promised that a second bond issue to fund Phase B would be submitted to the voters for approval in 1993. But burned by the great 32 percent tax increase of 1992 and one controversy after another, the board delayed. It could delay no longer.

PREPARATIONS FOR THE BOND ELECTION

Arnold and Paige Begin Planning

The board president who would lead HISD through the bond election was Paula Arnold. The talk before the board elections was that Olga Gallegos had five committed votes for board president—all five minority board members. Some of us did not believe Olga would be a strong leader. Now, with Robert Jefferson's defeat, Olga had only four committed votes. Paula, seeing the opening and recognizing the need for strong leadership to obtain voter approval for a bond issue, stepped forward. On January 11, at the first board meeting in January, she was unanimously elected board president.

Almost immediately, Paula and Rod began planning for a spring bond election. For over a year, Rod had been meeting with the School House Committee—a small group of business leaders—to gather information on facilities needs, demographic changes, financial projections, public opinion, and election law. Much of the work had been done.

Now it was time to make decisions. When should the election be held? How should facilities renovation and new construction needs be prioritized? How big should the bond issue be? How much money would be needed to fund the election campaign, and who would raise the money? What specific election strategy should be followed and how and by whom should the campaign be managed?

Reversing the River Oaks Vote

We all knew obtaining voter approval for a significant bond issue would be difficult. Despite recent improvements, HISD was still viewed by most active voters as a failed school system. We also knew that a bond issue had no chance of passing if the board did not reverse the River Oaks vote. The decision by the board the previous June to keep River Oaks Elementary an all-Vanguard school had not only alienated River Oaks parents, it had divided the city. The majority of voters in a low turnout bond election would be white, many of them River Oaks residents. And it would be very difficult to raise money for the election campaign from Houston's business elite, many of whom lived in River Oaks. New board member Laurie Bricker had an idea for a solution.

Laurie, a white woman in her early 40s, was a life-long resident of Houston, educated in HISD schools and at the University of Texas. She also had a M.Ed. from the University of Houston. She had been an HISD parent activist for years, served as PTO board member or president of HISD schools at every level, and built up a small practice as an educational consultant advising parents on educational options for children with special needs.

Laurie was a whirlwind, short, on the heavy side, with flashing eyes, a great mass of thick, dark hair, and charm and energy to burn. I had never met anyone so busy. She attended every possible luncheon, reception, dinner, press conference, training seminar, performance, celebration, or whatever. She was constantly calling old friends, new friends, or strangers to obtain information, promote an idea, set up a luncheon appointment, or just gab. And everywhere she went, Laurie made friends, though sometimes her enthusiasm and self-promotion offended.

Laurie's plan for River Oaks was complicated, but the key point was simple. Neighborhood children would be phased in for non-Vanguard enrollment, and following the same phase in schedule, Vanguard parents could enroll their non-Vanguard children in the non-Vanguard classes. This plan would please many Vanguard parents and help fill non-Vanguard classes.

On February 28, the board met for a short planning retreat at the Omni Hotel. It was a tough meeting. The room was beautiful and spacious and the dinner excellent, but the River Oaks vote, the fight over the 1995–1996 budget, and the 1995 board elections were still fresh in our memories. There was not much trust in the room. Rod laid out all the issues and options for a bond election. After much discussion, we agreed to press ahead for an election in May for a nearly $600 million bond issue for a mix of facilities renovations and new schools.

Laurie made a passionate appeal for support of her River Oaks recommendation. She knew Clyde Lemon's vote guaranteed board approval, but she wanted a strong majority to demonstrate board unity and put a decisive end to the controversy. No such luck. Her phase in proposal with a sweetener for the Vanguard parents was unacceptable to the other minority trustees.

A month later, on March 21, the board approved Laurie's plan for River Oaks Elementary. The vote was 5–2. Arthur Gaines and Carol Galloway voted no. Olga Gallegos and Esther Campos abstained. Once again many of the River Oaks Vanguard parents angrily objected: The decision was driven by "power and politics, not solid educational considerations" (*Chronicle,* March 22, 1996, p. A1). But neighborhood parents were pleased, and most of Houston seemed relieved to put the issue to rest.

Securing the Support of the Partnership

We seemed as ready for a bond election as we would ever be. It was time to act. Rod and board members had already been visiting elected officials and community leaders making the case for a late spring bond election. One last essential step remained. HISD needed the blessings of the Greater Houston Partnership. Houston's major corporations were the main source for the $400,000 or so needed to fund the election campaign, and a proposed bond issue and tax increase without the partnership's endorsement would be viewed skeptically by Houston's professional and business classes and almost certainly be rejected by the *Chronicle's* editorial board. It would be difficult enough to win a bond election with the partnership's active support. It would be impossible to win without it.

So the courtship of the partnership began. During the last two weeks of March, Rod, sometimes with selected board members and top HISD officials, met repeatedly with representatives of the partnership. We wanted their support for a $597 million bond issue to be put before the public sometime in May. Approximately half would be for new construction and half for renovation and repairs. The partnership wanted to postpone the election for another year, keep the bond issue to the lowest possible amount, and spend most of the money on existing facilities. We emphasized the need. They emphasized the likelihood that the voters would say no.

The negotiations almost failed. At a hot meeting on March 25 in Rod's office, John Walsh, a former Exxon executive who had replaced Al Haines as president of the chamber of commerce division of the partnership, placed before us a proposed memorandum of understanding that promised the support of the partnership for a bond issue held to "the lowest reasonable amount" for an election in early 1997. In return, HISD would implement reforms in management, governance, organization, operations, and financing, and develop an all-funds budget that would "hold [the] tax burden to the minimum necessary to achieve academic and operational objectives."[2]

There was no way the board could accept the deal. The reform recommendations were great. They were exactly what Paige and the board reformers were trying to do. But the partnership was only offering to help meet a small fraction of HISD's facilities needs *next year*.[3]

In the end, we compromised on a May 28 bond election for $390 million in return for commitments by HISD to shared decision-making, decentralization, accountability at all levels, public school choice, outsourcing, merit pay, reduced administrative costs, and a continuous maintenance program.[4] The agreement was struck just hours before the board met on March 29—the last day the board could approve a bond election for spring 1996. Board approval was quickly given by a 9–0 vote. The gallery, mostly parents and school employees, cheered.

The $390 million would fund the renovation of 84 older schools and the building of 15 new schools. The tax increase required to fund the bonds would be 6.6 cents over a three-year period. At the end of the three years, the owner of an $80,000 home, who currently paid $816 in annual taxes to HISD, would pay an additional $38.94. Senior citizens with homestead exemptions would see no increase in their taxes.[5]

Mixed Support from Other Voting Blocs

We were fortunate to obtain the support of the partnership. We could not go forward without them. We were not so fortunate with some of the other power blocs in the city. The African American community was generally supportive. Rod had effectively made the case for the HISD bonds with the black ministers, and even though African American communities stood to gain little from the bond issue—there was minimal overcrowding in predominantly black schools—the black ministers openly and enthusiastically supported the bonds.

The Hispanic community was another story. Though most of the schools built in Phase A of Project Renewal and most of the schools planned in Phase B were in Hispanic communities, Hispanic opinion was split. Most of the elected officials strongly supported the bond issue. They knew that without the bonds no new schools could be built in Hispanic neighborhoods. The activists, however, opposed the bonds.

Their logic was hard to follow: Mexican American schools in the East End were overcrowded. Many of these schools were also low-performing ones. HISD was not meeting the needs of Hispanic students, therefore HISD could not be trusted. Until HISD built Chavez High, the school promised as part of the deal that brought Frank Petruzielo to Houston and for which land had already been purchased and architectural designs approved, HISD should not be given more money.

The real reason for their nonsupport seemed obvious. Since Paige's selection as superintendent, they had threatened that the price for their exclusion from the process would be their opposition to the coming bond election. In fact, this point was explicitly acknowledged in a *Chronicle* op-ed by Guadalupe San Miguel Jr., one of the plaintiffs in the Hispanic Education Committee lawsuit against HISD. Latino exclusion from decision-making, he said, citing the Paige selection and other examples, justified the Latino voting population withholding its support of the bond election (*Chronicle*, April 18, 1996, p. A35).

On March 19, at Carrillo Elementary School, 11 Hispanic elected officials tried to convince a crowd of about 150 Hispanic activists to support the bond issue. It was a tough sell. "We have lost faith in you guys on how you spend the money," said one activist. I will not support bonds until HISD improves its performance, said another (*Chronicle*, March 20, 1996, p. A24).

Another group that was divided over the bonds was HISD's own employees. Most of the employee groups were strongly supportive, but the HFT, though officially neutral, was decidedly nonsupportive. For two years, every time a major HFT issue was before the board, Gayle Fallon had threatened that if the board voted against the interests of teachers (read interests of the union), teachers would not support the bond election.

In April, Gayle made the threat once again. In an effort to block teacher contract revisions, HFT members deluged board members with letters and telephone calls telling them to vote no on the superintendent's teacher contract recommendations or teachers will not support the bond election. The staff in the board services office estimated that 432 calls making this threat were received on April 16–18. On April 18, the board approved the revised teacher contracts. Now it was virtually impossible for Gayle to support the bonds.

Republicans Officially Remain Neutral

The last key voting bloc in the city that could decisively affect the outcome of the bond election was the Republican Party. It was unheard of for party organizations to take positions on a school bond issue. But in recent years, Republicans had become the dominant party in Harris County, and after years of bitter feuding, the party appeared to have been captured by social conservatives. Many social conservatives were critics of HISD. For over a month, I had heard talk that Harris County Republicans were going to actively oppose the bonds.

On March 30, the day after the board called the election, I was a precinct delegate to the Texas Senatorial District 17 Republican convention. "Stop HISD bonds" leaflets were on every chair. "Stop HISD bonds" T-shirts could be seen throughout the great meeting room. Many delegates were pushing for a *stop the bonds* resolution. I left early, determined to devote the next two months to campaigning for the bonds among Republicans.

With a briefcase of printed materials to support my points, I began the circuit of Republican clubs: the Greater Houston Pachyderm Club, Houston Professional Republican Women, Daughters of Liberty Republican Women, Magic Circle Republican Women, Downtown Pachyderm Club, Memorial West Republican Women, Glenbrook Valley Republican Women, Republican National Hispanic Assembly, and on and on.

Nearly everywhere I had to debate opponents of the bonds. None of them denied that HISD schools were overcrowded and needed repair. That was never the issue. The issue was HISD itself. It was a failed school system. Children were not learning to read; schools were not safe; and most of HISD's revenue was being wasted on a huge, incompetent bureaucracy. Only by defeating the bonds could voters get HISD's attention and force it to reform. Reform, I discovered, meant privatizing all noneducational support services, lobbying the state legislature to abolish the state requirement of no more than 22 children in K–4 classes, and offering all students vouchers so they could attend private schools.

Again and again I pointed out that the reform had already begun. Test scores were up significantly. The drop-out rate had been cut in half. And schools were safer, thanks to the establishment of an HISD police department, zero tolerance for weapons, and numerous initiatives in student discipline and violence prevention. I talked about accountability, decentralization, the PEER audits, a significant decline in administrative spending as a percent of instructional spending, and HISD's low tax rate.

I made few converts. Few were interested in my data. Many just seemed to hate public schools. Some were abusive. It was clear to me that if the Republican Party turned out its most frequent voters, the social conservatives, the bonds would fail. Somehow we had to head off an antibond resolution at the May 6 Republican convention of county precinct chairmen.

Gary Polland, chairman of the Harris County Republican Party, agreed to meet me on April 22. When I arrived at his office, I found him gathered with a handful of party leaders around a small table in a small, crowded conference room. Gary, an attorney who had been elected county chairman in 1994 with the help of social conservatives, was a man of medium size, about 40, with thick dark hair and a beaming face. His advisors were mostly well-educated professionals and successful business people. They had high visibility in the party and access to large sums of money. They had no doubt they could kill the bonds. Why shouldn't they?

We had a spirited discussion that lasted well over an hour. I was astounded how little these Republican leaders knew about public education and HISD. As I made the case for HISD's facilities needs and reviewed HISD's improvements in recent years, I could see attitudes changing. Yes, we did teach phonics. We were privatizing, at least a little. Overcrowded and run-down schools were not just inventions of liberal educrats. And wasn't it Republican doctrine that education was a local responsibility? Furthermore, the leader of the reform of HISD was Rod Paige, a Republican. No doubt Republicans could defeat the bonds, but opposition to the bonds would hurt Houston's children, embarrass Paige, and paint Harris County Republicans as antichildren. Why give Democrats another chance to bash Republicans for not caring about children?

Not every one was persuaded. But I left the meeting with hope that most of the group would use their influence to keep the party from passing a resolution against the bonds at the upcoming county convention. Gary promised he would do his best to give me an opportunity to speak to the delegates.

In anticipation of the convention, Jo Konen, a Republican activist who had been hired by the School House Committee, and I began calling leading Republican moderates urging them to work against any resolution opposing the bonds.

The convention was at the J. W. Marriott on Westheimer. The large convention room was packed. The resolution against the bonds was moved and seconded. Gary Polland, a bit nervously I thought, introduced me to the delegates.[6]

I gave a short version of my standard speech. "Don't adopt this resolution," I concluded. "If the party takes a stand against the bonds and they pass, we become a paper tiger. If the bond issue loses with the party on record against it, then we are the bad guys. The last thing we need to do is say to the district, 'Sorry, we are not going to meet the needs of the kids.' "

My friend Jo Konen, who was a precinct chairman and official delegate to the convention, stood to address the delegates. Most of HISD's students, she noted, were African American and Hispanics. Official opposition to the bonds would result in the party being portrayed in news reports as biased against minorities. "We have never passed a resolution opposing bond issues in the white suburban districts," she concluded.

Some long-time party activists had different opinions. HISD had broken too many promises to the public. Students weren't learning. HISD had squandered some of the tax money it already had.

By voice vote the resolution was rejected.

The convention did not end on an entirely happy note. A few minutes later, the precinct chairmen approved a resolution denouncing the way HISD was conducting early voting. "They are basically trying to steal the election," said Larry Simon, who proposed the resolution (*Chronicle*, May 7, 1996, p. A21).

THE BOND ELECTION CAMPAIGN

Early Mobile Voting

Simon had a point. The strategy for the bond election was built around early mobile voting. It was legal, but was it fair? The School House Committee thought so. So did most parent activists.

Officially the School House Committee—a small group of business leaders—ran the campaign. They raised the money—about $325,000, mostly in large $5,000 to $15,000 contributions from Houston's major corporations and major HISD vendors—set campaign strategy, and made the major decisions on campaign expenditures. Most of the money was spent on direct mail and phone banks.[7]

The focus of the campaign was on getting out the yes vote. The strategists determined that changing the minds of negative voters was impossible and moving significant numbers of undecided voters to support the bonds would be very difficult. HISD's critics were legion, and the endless pounding of Channel 13 ABC TV on the Alternative Certification Program scandal the previous spring had damaged HISD's credibility even further. A bond election announced well in advance and held on a high turnout state or citywide election day would give HISD's critics time to mobilize and most likely lead to a crushing defeat.

To get out the yes vote and keep the no vote to a minimum, the committee determined to hold the election as a single issue election on a weekday before school was out and take advantage of a 1991 amendment to the state election code which allowed early mobile voting. Starting on May 8, voting machines would be set up at schools, sometimes for only a few hours at a time when large numbers of parents were expected. Parents coming to schools for band concerts, parent fund-raisers, award ceremonies, etc., would have the opportunity to vote early at over 200 schools. Almost the entire campaign apparatus was designed to get out the parent vote at early voting or on election day. Every school had a parent coordinator responsible for mobilizing parents, relatives, and friends to vote early for the bonds.

The strategy was legal and was being used with increasing frequency throughout the state. But it had never been used in HISD. The partnership did not like it—Harold Hook called it a stealth election—and in truth, neither did most board members. But we were persuaded that a low turnout election that maximized voting by HISD parents was our only chance to get the bond issue passed. We allowed the ends to justify the means.

The public reaction to early mobile voting was negative. Barry Klein, president of the Houston Property Rights Association, accused HISD of "rigging the election." Paula Arnold's response that the district was just trying to "make sure that people have as many opportunities to vote as possible," was certainly not the whole truth (*Chronicle*, April 20, 1996, p. A29). Nearly everywhere I went campaigning for the bonds, I had to face the charge that HISD was trying to steal the election. I put the best face I could on the procedure, but I was exceedingly uncomfortable.

The Sharp Audit

There was one other issue that was difficult to explain, a districtwide performance audit by Texas Comptroller John Sharp. In 1995, the Texas Legislature had ordered Mr. Sharp to conduct a massive Texas School Performance Review of HISD. At a cost of nearly $800,000, nearly 50 auditors would spend six months looking at everything in HISD for every conceivable way to eliminate waste and improve performance.

Sharp introduced the audit to the people of Houston on April 7 with an op-ed in the *Chronicle* (p. C5) and during April and May the newspapers were full of stories about the audit. The audit quickly became a major issue in the bond election. Why, asked business leaders, Republican activists, and many voters, did we not put off the bond election until after Sharp reported his findings and recommendations in October? "Let's see how much waste there is in the system before we give HISD more of our money," said the critics. It was a valid point, and one that we answered with difficulty.

We had three responses. First, the need was great and we had already waited three years. Second, we did not believe Sharp would find savings sufficient to meet even a small fraction of our facilities needs. Third, the city was abuzz with talk of a huge tax-supported bond referendum to finance a new major league baseball stadium. We thought it important that taxpayers vote on the school bonds before they voted on the stadium bonds. Most business leaders I talked to accepted this argument. Most of the Republican voters I talked to did not.

Turning out Our Base

While I was working with Republicans, Paula, Laurie Bricker, and Clyde Lemon were working practically around the clock to get out the vote of the traditional public school constituencies. There were literally hundreds of bases to cover, and from the periodic reports I got from Paula, the work was going well. Laurie was extraordinarily effective in West Houston, where a new high school was planned. The other board members, as far as I could tell, were doing nothing.

Blasts from the Media

Meanwhile, though the *Chronicle* endorsed the bond issue on May 4 and the black press was very helpful, HISD was taking a beating in the media. A *Chronicle* columnist, Thom Marshall, who had for years made fun of HISD's large, white concrete administration building—he called it the Taj Mahal—was writing a series of columns using incomplete and out-of-context data to ridicule HISD for administrative bloat and incompetence.

Questions like "How many HISD assistant superintendents does it take to change a light bulb?" were funny and for that reason very effective. Marshall's final column concluded that HISD got an F in his bond vote test. He would only support the building of new schools and fixing up old schools if all administrators above the principal level were eliminated. In short, Mr. Marshall did not want a school district, he wanted 250 plus independent, uncoordinated public schools (*Chronicle*, May 12, 1996, p. A31; May 19, 1996, p. A29).

The most damaging blast from the media came from Channel 13. May was sweeps month for the television stations—the month viewing ratings were established to set advertising rates. Undercover reporter Wayne Dolcefino and Channel 13 ABC TV had boosted their ratings in May 1994 by hammering away at HISD's Alternative Certification Program. This May the target was food service.

On May 1, 2, 3, 6, 8, and 9, Channel 13 *Eyewitness News* ran a series of reports that claimed to have uncovered "multi-million dollar waste and mismanagement" in food service. Employees were stealing food. Food was being wasted. Kitchens were overstaffed. School inspections were inadequate. In one report, a food service worker was shown leaving a school with a bag of what was presumed to be food. Another showed an employee leaving with a box of milk cartons. A third showed two food service employees leaving a school kitchen carrying pizza boxes.

Rod knew food service needed improvement. It was a huge $66 million per year operation that served nearly 200,000 meals each school day. It was not obviously dysfunctional, and it had been recognized for years for promoting a low-fat, low-sugar menu for children.[8] But costs seemed excessive, and complaints were frequent. In January, Rod had appointed a PEER review task force to examine all aspects of food service operations and recommend improvements.

The Dolcefino charges prompted an immediate investigation by HISD's internal auditors. Preliminary results indicated that most of the charges were unfounded. These reports were ignored by Channel 13.[9]

On May 20, Wayne Dolcefino also charged that Rod Paige had instructed Arthur Andersen to withhold release of a critical report of HISD's payroll and human resources functions until after the bond election. The next day H. Devon Graham Jr., Andersen's managing partner in Houston, sent a letter to James Masucci, general manager of Channel 13, informing him that Channel 13 had telecast "inaccurate information" even though Andersen had given correct information directly to Dolcefino and Channel 13 news director Richard Longoria prior to the telecast. The study was not complete. Dr. Paige had not asked for a delay. "Regardless of your opinions on the impending bond issue," concluded Mr. Graham, "we are frustrated and very disappointed that Channel 13 is using our name and information your personnel know is misleading to attack Dr. Paige's credibility on the issuance of our report. Accordingly, we have authorized HISD to use this letter to clarify the facts" (Graham, May 21, 1996). There was no correction from Channel 13.

Republican Activists Intervene

May 28 was almost upon us, and another great blow against the bonds was about to fall, though we did not know it at the time. The Republican Party was officially neutral, but a few powerful Republican social conservatives were determined to kill the bonds. Working with Barry Klein, president of the property rights association, and operating under the name Stop HISD Tax Hikes, they struck in the last few days before the election with 95,000 customized postcards mailed to HISD voters, mostly homeowners with high property taxes, and social conservatives.[10]

"Look how much your taxes will increase if this Bond Election is passed!" said the postcard headline. Then followed the recipients' address, current property tax amount, the cost of the 32 percent tax increase of 1992, and the total tax that would have to be paid if the $390 million bond issue were approved. "Are You Getting Your Money's Worth?" continued the postcard. And then in great bold letters, following the name and address of the voting location, "Tuesday, May 28th, vote No on the HISD Bond Election!" At the bottom of the card, in print so small it could hardly be read without a magnifying glass, were the words "homestead and other exceptions may not be included." There was no explanation that property owners 65 or older would be exempt from the tax increase.

To reinforce the postcard, Stop HISD Tax Hikes also used automated phone machines to place calls to 60,000 homes with a recorded message urging voters to reject the bonds (*Chronicle,* May 30, 1996, p. A1). The election was lost.

The final vote was 30,233 against the bonds, 26,808 in favor. Fifty-three percent of less than 10 percent of eligible HISD voters had killed the bonds.

PUBLIC RESPONSE TO THE BOND FAILURE

Why the Bonds Failed

The postmortem began the next day. Why had the bonds failed? Everyone had an opinion. Rod blamed himself. HISD had not effectively communicated its needs to the public. Dan McClung, the School House Committee's campaign consultant, charged that the antibond postcards were "misleading or deceptive—and very, very effective." But the main reason the bonds had failed, he said, was because they required a tax increase. Richard Hooker, associate professor of education at the University of Houston, agreed. The antitax sentiment was significant, particularly in a climate of negative publicity about the way HISD spent its money.

The bond opponents were ecstatic. Barry Klein characterized the vote as a victory for the taxpayers and a stunning defeat of the trustees and bureaucrats of HISD. "We believe that the public is ready for dramatic change in public education." HISD should now respond to the will of the people and implement aggressive privatization, elimination of teacher tenure, unrestricted vouchers, relaxed fire codes, and lobby the legislature for repeal of the provision in the Texas Education Code that limited class sizes in grades K-4 to 22 students. Klein and friends wanted to meet with Paige and other school officials to begin negotiations (*Chronicle,* May 30, 1996, p. A1; June 19, 1996, p. Z12–2).

The *Chronicle* editorial board believed the no vote was primarily a vote of no confidence in the board of education and administration. Voters acknowledged the need to bring schools up to fire code standards and fix leaking roofs, but many voters did not trust the trustees or administration to remedy these problems. "Voters apparently have serious doubts about where the school district is headed and about the ability of the district's administration to adequately manage" (May 30, 1996, p. A26).

For weeks the commentary flowed. Critics of HISD in newspaper columns and letters, on radio call-in shows, and in conversations everywhere chortled that HISD had gotten what it deserved, recounted anecdotes that proved HISD was incompetent, and offered prescriptions for reform. Save money by getting rid of bilingual education. Fire all administrators and sell the Taj Mahal. Break up the school district. The prevailing opinion seemed to be that because a narrow majority of voters in a low turnout election had voted against raising their own taxes, HISD was a failed school system that should somehow be put out of its misery.

In fact, no one knew why those who cast ballots voted the way they did. There were no exit polls. What one could say with assurance was that the bonds had been defeated by primarily older, more affluent, white, and most likely Republican, voters. Just over 5 percent of eligible black voters cast a ballot; 70 percent voted yes. Just under 5 percent of Hispanic voters cast a ballot; 61 percent voted yes. Just under 12 percent of eligible white voters cast a ballot; over 58 percent voted no.[11] The simplest explanation of the vote was that voters who did not have children in HISD schools, paid high property taxes, and did not want their taxes increased, voted. Voters who had the most to gain from the bonds—moderate- to low-income blacks and Hispanics—stayed home.

Republicans Propose a School Reform Agenda

The short-term political legacy of the bond loss was that, for a time, Barry Klein and a small group of property rights association members and conservative Republican and liberal Hispanic activists—a strange alliance indeed—thought they could use their new-found power over HISD to push their reform agenda on the district. The long-term political legacy was that the Harris County Republican Party became a player in the reform of Houston's public schools.

Gary Polland and the Republican leadership had taken the high road during the election campaign. They had kept the party out of the election. But they had tasted power. They knew a future bond election would be difficult without their support, and they saw an opportunity to impose a conservative school reform agenda on HISD.

Everybody did it. The partnership, the HFT, and the Hispanic activists all had their agendas for HISD. They offered or withheld their support depending on HISD's acceptance of their agendas, and they were very active in school board elections. Why should the Republican Party be any different?

At the precinct convention on May 6, following the voice vote to reject the resolution against the bonds, Polland had announced that he planned to form a committee to make recommendations to HISD on educational reform. "We're not Republicans who just 'oppose,' " he said. It appeared that the Harris County Republican Party was going to be a force in the 1997 school board elections.

A year later, on June 30, 1997, Polland and James Evans, chairman of the Harris County Republican Party Education Committee, published an op-ed in the *Chronicle* setting forth the Republican "plan of action" for the reform of HISD. For years, they said, the nonpartisan label on school board elections had led the Republican Party to ignore its duty to provide leadership in school reform according to conservative principles. Meanwhile, service on the HISD board had provided a springboard for ambitious Democrat politicians.

Times had changed. Republicans had a seven-point plan that would be used to evaluate candidates seeking the support of Republican voters for election to the HISD board of education. The seven points, said Polland and Evans, were common sense. Already the political winds had forced members of the HISD board at least to give credence to five of the seven points.

The seven points were: privatize everything possible; institute zero tolerance for disruptive students; actively pursue outstanding college graduates outside the education hierarchy to teach; hold teachers accountable for effectiveness and reward outstanding teachers with pay competitive with the private job market; reduce administrative positions by 40 percent; provide all students with total public school choice and partial vouchers for private schools; and abolish HISD and replace it with five or more independent school districts (*Chronicle*, June 30, 1997, p. A19).

HISD RESPONSE TO THE BOND FAILURE

Modified Vouchers

While others talked about why the bonds had failed and considered their political options, Paige and the board had to focus on the consequences. What should be done about overcrowding and old, inadequate, and sometimes unsafe buildings? On July 18, Rod presented his options to the board.

They included spending down further the fund balance; restructuring debt; selling off surplus property; raising taxes; possibly, through a specially created public facilities corporation, building new schools on a lease purchase contract; building more temporary buildings; eliminating special purpose classrooms for fine arts, music, physical education, and science; adjusting school attendance boundaries to move students toward underutilized, inner-city schools; reducing kindergarten to half a day for nonfree lunch children; closing all prekindergarten programs; and offering extended-day schedules and year-round schooling in some parts of the district (Paige, July 18, 1996). There were problems associated with every option, but in time the board approved partial implementation of most of them.

The option that generated the most public interest actually had little immediate impact on overcrowding, but it opened the door to the possibility later on of huge transfers of HISD students to private schools. It was a school choice proposal that offered modified vouchers to selected parents to place their children in selected private schools. The idea came to Laurie Bricker, Cathy Mincberg, and me in a conversation a few days after the election.

Rod called the plan contract placement. HISD already contracted with private schools for some special education students, and nothing in state law prohibited contracts with nonreligious private schools for the education of regular students.

Within weeks it was news all over America. The superintendent of Houston's public schools was proposing that district money be used to send HISD students to private schools. HISD residents who had been enrolled in a public school the previous year and who were zoned to a *capped* school, would be given the choice of being bussed to another HISD school, enrolling in a public school in another school district, or attending a private school with which HISD had a contract.

HISD would pay contracting schools 90 percent of the full per pupil per year operating cost of educating an average student in HISD—$3,575 in 1996. Contracting schools could not charge parents any additional tuition or fees. They would have to accept all HISD students who applied on a first-come, first-served basis or, if more students applied than could be admitted, admit students on a lottery basis. And they would have to take daily attendance and administer the TAAS to all students.

"It's a back-door voucher," charged Gayle Fallon in the July 23 *Chronicle* in a front page article headlined: "Some stamp 'voucher' on HISD plan." She went on, "It sure walks, looks, and smells like a voucher. They're not legal in Texas. That lost at the Legislature and they are trying to do it by local policy" (*Chronicle*, July 23, 1996, p. A1).

The board was divided. "It's a distant relative of vouchers," said Laurie Bricker. "We are subsidizing private schools," said Arthur Gaines; "you don't want to do that." "It's a contract for service to help solve our problem," said Paula Arnold, who hated traditional vouchers. "The truth is this district is in a crisis situation to provide facilities for kids. I'm forced to look at this as an alternative at this time with the failure of the bond election."

On August 15, after considerable public discussion, the board approved the contract placement policy and authorized the superintendent to develop and publish requests for proposals from private schools. On September 19, the board authorized the first contract under the new policy, a contract with the Varnett School.[12] On October 14, over 100 HISD students were placed at Varnett. "I feel really fortunate to have the private setting," said parent Patty

Randall. "It's something that I've always wanted but couldn't afford. It's a little more personal attention" (*Chronicle,* October 15, 1996, p. A14). By mid-November, HISD enrollment at Varnett was up to 158.

In December, the board authorized contracts with two more private schools, River Oaks Academy in southwest Houston and Wonderland Private School in south Houston. On January 6, 1997, nearly 200 HISD students began classes at River Oaks Academy.

A School Roof Collapses

At about noon on Monday, August 12, just three days before the board approved the contract placement policy, a portion of the roof at Houston Gardens Elementary School collapsed, leaving a 75-foot hole over the cafeteria. Fortunately no one was in the cafeteria. It was determined later that the roof collapse was caused by extensive termite damage to wooden beams coupled with heavy rains. Houston Gardens was one of the 84 schools targeted for renovation by the bond issue.

The immediate task was to confirm the safety of 124 other schools that contained wooden beams spanning large spaces. School opened in a week. HISD had only four structural engineers on its payroll. The next day, Paige put out a call to Houston's architects and engineers to help with an emergency inspection program. The response was magnificent. Starting at dawn on Wednesday, 10 teams of volunteer and HISD architects and engineers began inspecting schools. Fourteen showed damage that needed closer inspection. It was determined that five of these needed emergency repairs.

Over the weekend, a major construction firm, Brown & Root Services Corporation, sent teams of up to 35 workers to each school. Covered walkways were reinforced. Standing water was drained. And some partitions were reinforced. On Monday, every HISD school but Houston Gardens was ready for students. The 460 Houston Gardens students were bused to three neighboring elementary schools.

To HISD's friends and supporters of the bonds, Houston Gardens proved that HISD's facilities crisis was real. To HISD's critics, Houston Gardens was proof that HISD was, at best, incompetent. Barry Klein even charged that HISD had deliberately deferred repairs on buildings in order to build passion for the bonds. Paula responded with an angry letter calling Klein's charges "disgusting, shameless opportunism" and an "unforgivable affront to the thousands of hard-working professionals and volunteers in HISD who are doing their utmost to ensure students' safety" (*Chronicle,* August 16, 1996, p. A41; August 19, 1996, p. A21). Her meetings with Klein and his group to discuss their agenda for improving HISD came to an abrupt end.

Fire and Safety Code Violations

Two days after the roof collapsed at Houston Gardens, Houston Fire Department inspectors informed HISD that there were minor fire code violations at two schools that had to be corrected before school could open. The violations were corrected, and the schools opened.

But two days after school opened, Houston Fire Marshall H. G. Torres informed HISD that about 40 schools had received citations for fire and safety code violations and that at five schools the violations were serious. Closing the schools had been considered, but after meeting with Paige he had agreed to allow the schools to stay open. A few days later, Rod and his staff began negotiations with the fire marshall's office to develop a collaborative plan to make the required changes.[13]

The 1996–1997 Budget

The Houston Gardens roof collapse occurred on August 12. The first citations from the fire marshall became public on August 14. The next day, August 15, the board met to approve the budget for 1996–1997. Public interest was intense.

The voters had said no to a tax increase for facilities on May 28. And John Sharp was scheduled to report his recommendations for eliminating waste in HISD to the public in just seven weeks. There was no way Rod could recommend a tax increase. Yet money had to be found for facilities. Fifteen million additional dollars were needed to fund enrollment growth and some unavoidable continuing cost increases. And teachers were demanding a large pay raise.

Rod's response to these pressures was a no-tax-increase budget that freed up $39 million from debt restructuring for crisis facility repairs and increased the regular maintenance budget by $5 million. Staff cuts of $4 million and $29 million from the undesignated fund balance were budgeted for unavoidable continuing costs needs and an additional $12 million for performance compensation for teachers.

None of the teacher groups was pleased, and the HFT was furious. Teachers were being punished for not supporting the bond election. Teachers had been promised that if TAAS scores improved significantly they would receive a significant pay raise. TAAS scores were up. Where was the raise? "[Paige] has lied to this district," said Gayle Fallon. "He promised them a decent raise. I hope the board has more sense than the superintendent. They've got to live with these teachers. These teachers can vote yes or no on the next bond election" (*Chronicle*, August 1, 1996, p. A1).

Paige's budget passed on August 15, but only with a last-minute change.

In response to a plea from the Congress of Houston Teachers, Rod recommended using $8 million of the $12 million budgeted for teacher incentive pay to fund a 2 percent across-the-board raise for all teachers. Even then, the budget was only approved 5–4. No one was happy. Some of us wanted more money for facilities. Some wanted more money for teachers. Gayle Fallon voiced her displeasure by likening the budget to a penny tip. "We're not expecting a real good year this year" (*Chronicle*, August 16, 1996, p. A1).

The collapse of the roof at Houston Gardens, the fire and safety code crisis, and the 1996–1997 budget all focused attention back to the failed bonds. Thereafter the public and the district began to focus more on the future and the upcoming report of Texas Comptroller John Sharp.

But there was a legacy. The failed bonds left Houston's public schools in desperate need of repair and condemned thousands of children to overcrowded conditions that negatively impacted teaching and learning. It would cost the taxpayers more to do later what should have been done in 1996. On the plus side, the failed bonds, along with the Sharp Audit, gave Paige and the board reformers a powerful argument for accelerating the pace of reform. Nineteen ninety-seven would be a banner year for the reform of Houston's public schools.

Not quite two months later, on November 5, 1996, the voters of Harris County passed by a 51 percent to 49 percent margin a referendum to issue public bonds supported by tax dollars to build and renovate stadiums for keeping professional sports in Houston.

NOTES

1. At least a dozen schools had structural problems. One hundred and forty-five needed roof repairs. One hundred and fifty-six needed renovations to bring them into compliance with fire and safety codes. Nearly 900 HISD classrooms in grades K–4 were out of compliance with state law, which limited classes in these grades to 22 students. Almost 25 percent of the total HISD student population attended classes in nearly 2,100 temporary classrooms. Over 100 HISD schools were turning away children in at least one grade. Several high schools built for 2,500 students had nearly 3,500. Quite a few elementary schools built for 700 to 800 students had 1,200 to 1,400. For some children in these schools lunch started at 10:00 A.M. and bathroom visits were limited to odd or even hours.

2. The specific points in the reform agenda included a commitment to encourage both state and HISD charter schools; maximize choice for students among HISD schools and between HISD and other school districts; maximize outsourcing opportunities *immediately* in all areas of expenditure; compensate employees based on merit and performance, including bonuses, and eliminate automatic salary increases; implement *true* decentralization by giving more authority and responsibility to principals,

teachers, and parents; reduce administrative costs relative to academic costs; and pledge no new tax increases in excess of inflation plus student growth without voter approval (Walsh, March 25, 1996).

3. Negotiations continued. At one point Paula Arnold and I, who were doing most of the negotiating for the board, threatened to go ahead with the bond election without the support of the partnership. "Consider your position," we told them. "If the voters approve the bonds, the partnership is marginalized. If the bonds fail, you will be blamed for the failure and charged with being anti-public education." John Walsh and his team informed us that they had made their final offer, stood up, and walked out of the room.

4. The details of the agreement between HISD and the partnership were not worked out until late April. To follow through on its commitments, HISD agreed to establish an education performance review advisory committee and a facilities task force (Arnold, April 23, 1996; HISD, May 16, 1996). Perhaps partially because of the support of the partnership, the bond issue was also supported by the Houston Citizens Chamber of Commerce, the Houston Hispanic Chamber of Commerce, the Houston West Chamber of Commerce, the East End Chamber of Commerce, the Houston Association of Realtors, and the *Houston Business Journal*.

5. The agreement with the partnership was not well received by the parent activists in the overcrowded areas of HISD. They saw the overcrowded conditions in the schools and the state of many of the buildings nearly every day. They had been pushing for a bond election since 1993. They had written letters, circulated petitions, and addressed the board on numerous occasions. Southwest Houston was angry and far west Houston was almost in a state of rebellion. These parents considered the reduction of the bond issue from $597 to $390 million a sell out. Who were these business executives who presumed to make decisions for their children? Why did board members show them such deference?

6. Gary Polland did not take a position, but his body language said he was very uncomfortable. He repeated again and again that nonsupport of the resolution did not mean support for the bonds.

7. HISD officially did nothing. By law it could provide information to voters, but no HISD money could be spent on the campaign, and HISD employees, including Paige, could only campaign on their own time.

8. In August 1996, a nationwide study by doctors ranked HISD as third among big-city school districts for healthy meals (*Chronicle*, August 29, 1996, p. A34).

9. The final report, corroborated by independent investigations by the TEA, the Harris County district attorney, and the U.S. Department of Agriculture was not issued until August 8, by which time the bond election was history. It confirmed that except for incidents of limited petty theft and a number of minor managerial problems, the allegations were untrue. The milk cartons, for example, were not fresh. The pizza had been delivered by Pizza Hut. Food service actually had a net understaffing of 28 employees. HISD asked for a correction from Channel 13. None was given.

10. The Republican activists were Bruce Hotze, a Bellaire businessman who ran Compressor Engineering Corp., Robert Randall Sims Jr., David Wilson, Don Sumners, and Larry Simon. Of the total $32,000 spent by Stop HISD Tax Hikes, Compressor Engineering Corp. contributed over $12,000.

11. White voters accounted for nearly 54 percent of all votes cast. Voters with household incomes of more than $62,200 accounted for over 60 percent of all votes cast. Voters over 46 accounted for somewhat over 70 percent of all votes cast (Paige, September 9, 1996). It is not possible to determine the exact age of all voters because before 1971 voters' age was not required at registration.

12. It was a tough vote for Paula. "Putting public dollars into private facilities is a failure of the city of Houston to provide for students," she said. "It makes me very sad. I'm going to do it because there are children we can't provide for in our district and keep my philosophical views out of it." Ironically, both Olga Gallegos and Esther Campos, who had voted against the contract placement policy, now objected that Varnett, a predominately black school in Southwest Houston, was the only school receiving a contract. No schools had been found to relieve overcrowding in the Hispanic east end. "Are we finding anything in these areas? Are we looking? We need to find places for them. They can't continue to go to classrooms with 35 students," said Esther (*Chronicle*, September 20, 1996, p. A1).

13. Had HISD officials really allowed 40, or even five, schools to become fire traps? Not really. The buildings had met fire and safety codes when they were built, but the codes had changed. Even Torres acknowledged that the violations were the consequences, in part, of an absence of inspections for about 13 years. Other school districts within the Houston city limits were also being cited for safety code violations. The truth was that fire and safety inspections had recently resumed, the collapse of the Houston Gardens roof had stimulated the fire marshall to intensify his scrutiny of Houston's schools, and some HISD principals had been careless.

13

228 Ways to Save a Bundle

The $390 million bond election dominated the first six months of 1996. The Texas School Performance Review of Texas comptroller John Sharp dominated the second. Like the failed bond election, the Sharp audit gave HISD a black eye. But like the failed bond election, it positioned HISD for a great surge of reform activity in 1997.

SHARP IS COMING

John the Knife

John Sharp was elected Texas comptroller of public accounts in 1990. Almost immediately, he established himself as a great enemy of waste in government and friend of the taxpayer. A small-town conservative Democrat with sleepy eyes and a moon-shaped face, Sharp was naturally cheap. He did not waste a dime in his personal life, and he did not believe government should, either. His weapon of choice was the performance audit. State programs, state agencies, prisons, school districts, troubled hospital emergency rooms, all were subject to the scrutiny of John Sharp's auditors. *Texas Monthly* called him John the Knife (Jarboe, 1994).

Of course, the comptroller's office was a huge publicity machine. Cost-shifting to the federal government, one-time shifts in revenues, and other accounting tricks accounted for a significant percentage of the billions of dollars Sharp claimed to save the taxpayers. And calculated leaks, perfect timing, folksy press conferences, and brilliant packaging made Sharp's audit reports major public events. Everyone knew that someday Sharp would run for governor. Still, Sharp's audits were helpful, if sometimes painful, experiences for the agencies and institutions he audited, and Sharp was saving taxpayers significant amounts of money.

It was inevitable that sooner or later John Sharp would audit HISD. The plum was just too big to resist. For years, Sharp's staff had talked about an audit of HISD. How would they manage such a massive venture? Better start small and work up to it. By early 1995, the comptroller's office had audited 18 school districts, including Dallas, and recommended nearly $150 million in savings. They were ready for HISD. And thanks to State Senator John Whitmire (D-Houston), HISD was ripe for picking.

Senator Whitmire Demands an Audit

It was March 1995. The Texas Legislature was in session and its principal focus was a complete rewrite of the Texas Education Code. Whitmire, wanting to make a point about no pass/no play, staged a press conference to slam HISD for giving 55 percent of all secondary students Fs or incompletes on their six weeks report cards. To Whitmire, this was evidence that HISD was not teaching.

To some HISD principals, high midterm failure rates proved just the opposite: HISD maintained high standards and used low midterm grades to motivate students. Furthermore, charged one principal, Whitmire had misinterpreted the data.

Whitmire was angry. One just did not publicly embarrass state senators, or at least not this one. "I'm going to find out why you can't teach these children," he shouted to HISD's man in Austin, Larry Yawn. "I'm going to request that John Sharp do an educational audit of HISD." Larry tried to explain in vain that John Sharp did not do educational audits. His audits focused on business operations. Educational audits of school districts were the responsibility of the Texas Education Agency. No matter, Whitmire would have a Sharp audit, and by a rider to the new education code, Senate Bill 1, he got one.

Board president Arthur Gaines's reaction was negative. "It is nothing but purely an action on his part to continue to project himself in the media. If he wants to sit on the school board, let him run and get on the school board. I'm sure he'll find it much less remunerative than the office he holds."

"The bottom line is, I'm elected to represent the public," responded Whitmire. "It's my judgment that taxpayers need someone to be responsive to them. I'm not sure that's what Mr. Gaines is doing" (*Chronicle*, March 24, 1995, p. A35).

To the press, Rod Paige said: "I think we are pretty wide open to this [the audit]." To HISD employees he said: "Frankly, it is difficult to know how HISD is expected to maintain high professional teaching standards, yet be maligned for exercising those high standards in assessing students' classroom performance" (Paige, March 28, 1995).

HISD Prepares

In early June, the comptroller's office announced that the audit would likely begin in March 1996 and would cost about $600,000. HISD officials, said a spokesman for Sharp, had been very receptive: "In this early stage, we have had very close cooperation and have felt very welcome."

That indeed was our strategy from the beginning. We had nothing to hide. Since 1991, in addition to annual financial audits, various HISD functions and programs had been audited 12 times by professional audit firms. The TEA had conducted three massive accreditation reviews. Fourteen PEER task forces had evaluated most of HISD's major functional areas. Also, we had asked the partnership to help us decentralize. We knew we could not reform HISD by ourselves. We had always asked for the best advice we could get from the best experts we could find. We believed Sharp's auditors would do a very professional job. If they could find ways to save money, we would cheerfully save the money. "The bottom line," said Paige, "is come on" (*Chronicle,* June 10, 1995, p. A37).

Of course, we also recognized that the Sharp report would be a political document. John Sharp had built a national reputation for himself as a friend of the taxpayer. He was an ambitious politician with a great future. He was going to spend $600,000 of the taxpayer's money conducting the audit. His auditors had found $60 million of waste in Dallas. No matter what, they were going to find at least $100 million in Houston. That was a given. We all knew it. Key people in Sharp's office acknowledged it. So whatever we did, Sharp would find $100 million of waste in HISD. The public would say, see we told you so. Sharp would be a hero. HISD would be embarrassed.

What could we do about it? Nothing. It would be impossible to fight John Sharp. He had credibility. HISD did not. If HISD objected, resisted, or in any way seemed ungrateful, the media and the public would see it as denial. All we could do was prepare as best we could, welcome helpful recommendations, and continuously thank Senator Whitmire and Comptroller Sharp for their commitment to children.

Almost immediately, Rod put his senior administrators and internal audit staff to work reviewing previous Sharp audits, especially the one in Dallas, assessing HISD for potential Sharp recommendations, and where possible taking action. He also pushed his staff to implement as many PEER recommendations as possible, launched additional PEER task forces, and did all he could to develop a personal relationship with Sharp.

THE TEXAS SCHOOL PERFORMANCE REVIEW

The Audit

In November 1995, the comptroller's office began the process to select the contractor(s) to conduct the performance review by issuing requests for proposals. In February 1996, contracts were awarded. In March, the district began gathering mountains of documents and organizing them for easy access by the auditors. In April, the formal audit began.

The audit, known officially as a Texas School Performance Review (TSPR), was a massive undertaking. The project manager was Betty Ressel, director for school performance reviews in Sharp's office. The actual work was done by four management consultancies: Coopers & Lybrand, the prime contractor; Empirical Management; Neil & Gibson, student transportation; and, when a facilities review was added to the plan of work, MGT of America as a subcontractor to Coopers & Lybrand. Nearly 50 auditors worked on the project for about five months. The actual cost came to over $800,000.

Mr. Sharp introduced the audit to the people of Houston on April 7 with an op-ed in the *Chronicle*. It was masterful. Taxpayers deserved to know their schools were being held accountable, said Sharp. Teachers, parents, students, and others who lived or worked in the district knew what needed to be done to improve schools, but no one had ever asked for their ideas. "We will ask." School officials, by implication, were incompetents, as illustrated by horror stories of foolishness and waste in other districts—five maintenance workers sent to paint one board. And Sharp audits were the taxpayers' best friend: "So far," concluded Sharp, "we have offered more than 2,000 recommendations to improve operations in 21 school districts and saved taxpayers nearly $205 million—all without recommending laying off a single classroom teacher" (*Chronicle*, April 7, 1996, p. C5).

During the first week of the review, the auditors held 12 town hall meetings in schools throughout the city. Attendance was good. Giant flip charts were posted on walls for teachers, parents, and community members to write comments, complaints, and ideas. They had a lot to say. The TAAS test should be eliminated. Magnet programs should be at every school. Air-conditioners didn't work. Toilet paper was not provided in restrooms. HISD should put prayer back in the classroom. There should be a return to paddling. And on and on (*Chronicle*, April 17, 1996, p. A27 and May 1, 1996, p. Z14). Not much management improvement here, but great public relations.[1]

During the second and third weeks of the review, the auditors met with 28 focus groups: district superintendents, teacher and administrative employee group representatives, citywide PTA and PTO groups, the partnership, community partnership advisory committees, legislators and city- and county-elected officials, taxpayer associations, university education professors, civic leaders from Houston's four major ethnic communities, media representatives, juvenile courts and criminal justice personnel, labor employment agencies, youth groups, and so forth.

The primary emphasis of the third and fourth weeks was individual interviews with elected officials, school board members, and school administrators from all levels and functional areas.

Two weeks after the defeat of the bonds, on June 11, Sharp announced at a press conference in one of HISD's most run-down high schools that his office was adding a facilities review to the performance audit. This addition to the scope of work, said Sharp, had been decided prior to the May 28 bond election. It would help HISD find money to repair school buildings and recommend ways to maintain schools to prevent future major repairs (*Chronicle*, June 12, 1996, p. A33).

In June and July, the auditors organized, evaluated, compressed, and edited the information they had gathered. In August, they presented their findings, commendations, and recommendations to Sharp for his approval. And on September 5 and 6, they held extensive conversations with HISD officials to confirm the accuracy of their findings.

Public interest in the upcoming Sharp report built as the summer progressed. The audit would have commanded public attention under any circumstances, but because of the failed school bonds, public interest was intense. HISD's critics were confident Sharp would find mountains of waste and justify their rejection of the bonds.

The Audit Report

The first audit findings, released to the public on July 25, were the results of the opinion surveys. "Report: HISD suffers 'serious image problem,' " headlined the *Chronicle*. "Regardless of the accuracy of specific complaints, a widespread perception exists among teachers, parents and taxpayers that the district fails to live up to its promise," said the report. Criticisms included a topheavy and wasteful central administration, lack of accountability, poor student discipline, excessive paperwork and bureaucratic red tape, and overcrowded classrooms and outmoded equipment (*Chronicle*, July 25, 1996, p. A29).[2]

The early release of the opinion survey results indicated we were in the hands of a spinmaster. In the middle of Houston's hot, slow summer, but before the blistering heat of August that always drove a large number of Houstonians to Colorado and other cooler places, Sharp was keeping his audit before the public. The release of the full report confirmed Sharp's mastery of spin. A few days before the scheduled release in the first week of October came what appeared to be orchestrated news leaks to build interest in the big story.

On September 25, 1996 the *Wall Street Journal* reported that a not-yet-released audit of Houston's public schools by Texas Comptroller John Sharp had uncovered uncollected property taxes of $86 million, partially because of a long-standing district practice of not foreclosing on delinquent taxpayers' property (p. T1). Betty Ressel, from Mr. Sharp's office, refused comment. Almost none of the facts reported in the article were accurate.

On September 27, the *Chronicle* reported, under the headline "Release draws near for audit of HISD," that "State Comptroller John Sharp in a long-awaited audit set for release next week, is expected to critically address HISD's practice of paying employees who do not have job assignments." The article went on to review the history of the audit, outline HISD's problem with employee assignments, and repeat the story about the uncollected $86 million in back property taxes (*Chronicle*, September 27, 1996, p. A29).

The week of the official release, the week of September 30, was political theater at its best. The final report (Sharp, October 1996), a 663-page document entitled *Children First*, supported by a 314-page volume of appendices and a 41-page executive summary, was not released in one news conference. Executive summaries were released in parts over four days at four different news conferences in four different schools, and on the last day there was a public hearing in the evening at an HISD middle school for parents and community leaders.

Each day began with a Sharp op-ed in the *Chronicle* and beautifully crafted press releases from Sharp's office. Press conferences, masterfully staged for television, followed later in the morning. Sharp stood behind a podium covered with a large poster proclaiming "Children First," which showed two small handprints. Another poster listing the major recommendations of the day rested on an easel at Sharp's side. The media was present in force.

Each day, Sharp made a 15- to 20-minute presentation and then took questions from the media. Each evening, Sharp's face dominated the television news. Each day following, the *Chronicle* gave Sharp the lead story on the front page and, of course, space on the editorial pages for another opinion piece. For a week the failures of HISD and the wisdom of John Sharp were the talk of Houston.

Houstonians who watched the sound bites on the evening news and read Houston's only major newspaper, the *Chronicle*, would have never guessed that the report was actually quite positive. The report was organized into 12 chapters.[3] Each chapter presented findings, commendations, recommendations, suggested implementation guidelines, and estimated fiscal consequences.

In all there were 228 recommendations. Timely implementation of these recommendations, said the report, would, over a five-year period, cost an ad-

228 Ways to Save a Bundle

ditional $46 million and save an estimated $116 million. The net saving was $70 million. As a percentage of HISD's total budget, the gross savings was less than 2 percent.

Of the $46 million in additional costs, $35 million was in just two areas, instruction and transportation. HISD should add two or more days of training for teachers, administrators, and support staff to build teamwork and improve classroom teaching; develop curriculum guides; modernize the bus fleet; improve training for mechanics; and more aggressively recruit bus drivers. Most of the other additional costs were also for employee training and equipment upgrades.

Eliminating 320 positions, 114 administrators and 206 mostly low-paid clerical workers, custodians, warehouse employees, etc., accounted for about $30 million of the $116 million in estimated savings. Six major recommendations, which included a few of these staff cuts, accounted for another $60 million: outsource or reorganize food service ($16.7 or $12.5 million); maximize timely and efficient collection of delinquent taxes ($12 million); increase Medicaid reimbursement revenues ($8.8 million); eliminate payroll costs of employees awaiting assignment or placed in nonproductive positions ($5.6 million); improve process for competitive bidding for health insurance ($8 million); and reorganize human resource management and payroll ($8.8 million).

A key part of the report was a chapter on facilities which had been added at Paige's request just before the May 28 bond election. HISD should use $56 million of its undesignated fund balance for renovation and repairs and institute a long-term preventive maintenance program. It should also consider a multitrack, year-round school calendar as a pilot project for 10 percent of its elementary schools. Participation would be voluntary. Savings would be $14.5 million per year, enough to build two elementary schools.

The report also contained 91 commendations. Most had to do with innovative instructional programs, community partnerships, cost-savings initiatives, and revenue enhancements.

That was essentially it. The report was an impressive piece of work. It was professionally done, thorough, balanced, and mostly on target. Sure, some HISD administrators had complaints about recommendations in their area of responsibility, and there were a few places where the report did not get things quite right. But these were minor issues. John Sharp knew what he was doing. He was a master of his craft.

He was also a master at promoting himself. His performances at the four press conferences were smooth. He was comfortable in front of the camera and came across as fair-minded, sometimes funny, very knowledgeable, and totally honest. Rod, who had a long, pointed, and at times spirited discussion with him in a hangar at Hobby Airport just a few days before (September 25) was pleased. The hammering we had expected did not occur.

In fact, Sharp again and again resisted the media push for critical sound bites and used over half of his time to say good things about HISD. Improvement in student achievement was noteworthy. Instructional technology in HISD was as good as he had seen. HISD was an innovator in charter schools. Student transportation was a model for the nation. Medicaid reimbursements were probably the best in the nation. Business and community partnerships were unparalleled. There was no way to improve the management of HISD's investment portfolio. Schools were much safer than the public perceived. HISD had been extraordinarily effective in obtaining federal grants and maximizing state revenue.

The Sharp report confirmed that HISD was, on the whole, efficiently managed and making significant progress. Sharp's auditors had not found mountains of waste. And even if the downsizing recommendations were correct—at least a debatable point—less than 1.5 percent of HISD's full time workforce of 22,000 employees were redundant.

There were some excellent recommendations in the Sharp report. But it was not a silver bullet. It was not a break-the-mold document. It was not an agenda for school reform. Sharp had put no new instructional or management paradigm on the table. He had simply recommended ways to fine-tune the existing operation.

RESPONSE TO THE TSPR

Media Response

All this, of course, was not how the media viewed the audit. The front-page *Chronicle* headlines on October 1, 2, 3, and 4 were: "Audit of HISD urges job cuts; Audit targets food service; Use available money for repairs, HISD told"; and "228 ways to save a bundle."

Along with the front-page stories, the *Chronicle* printed numerous cartoons, editorials, and other related stories. The series of cartoons by cartoonist C. P. Houston were especially pointed. One, with the title "Thinker," showed a confused man sitting on a stump holding a book identified as *Sharp Audit/ HISD Opportunities Report*. "Decisions! Decisions!" he was thinking. "Do we want a fresh-slate, fresh-perspectives, vigorous, open-action world-class school district? . . . Or do we prefer the cash-burning, crisis-driven, old-habit, piddlin, politicin, bumfusslin system we've got?" (*Chronicle*, October 4, 1996, p. A36).

The major editorial by the *Chronicle*—there were several—was titled "Making Change: It will take guts to solve entrenched HISD problems." The key sentence read: "It is no secret that HISD is deeply troubled, and few Houstonians were surprised by the serious problems the auditors identified" (October 6, 1996, p. C2).

The clear thrust of the *Chronicle* coverage of the Sharp audit was that HISD was in shambles. Its only hope was to implement every single Sharp recommendation. These recommendations were the road map to the promised land. Any criticism of a Sharp recommendation by an HISD trustee or administrator would be shameless denial.

Television coverage was even more negative.

No one in the media ever probed Senator Whitmire's motives for asking for the audit. No one asked whether Sharp, a Democrat, held back from making sweeping outsourcing recommendations because he did not want to offend organized labor. No one ever pointed out that the audit was not an educational audit and that the report was not an agenda for school reform. To my knowledge, no news source reported on the $1,000 per couple fundraiser hosted for Sharp by 30 or so of Houston's richest and most influential business leaders on October 9 at the home of Diana and former lieutenant governor Bill Hobby. The Sharp audit begged for serious, thoughtful analysis. All it got from the media was cheerleading.

Not surprisingly, public opinion reflected the coverage of the media. Talk on the streets, letters to the editor, and comments from bond opponents and others was, "We told you so." Typical of the comments was a letter to the *Chronicle* editor from a resident of Conroe, a small town 30 miles from Houston. The writer's view was that Sharp had delivered a "scathing" audit of a "failing" school district managed by a "bloated, self-serving administrative bureaucracy and a politically motivated school board" (*Chronicle*, October 12, 1996, p. A37).

Paige's Response

The criticism hurt, but we had determined that no matter what Sharp or the public said, we would respond positively. Even before the report, Rod was sending out memos to all HISD employees and community leaders stating that he was looking forward to the report, that he intended to respond positively to the recommendations, and that employees should not be discouraged by negative media coverage (Paige, September 27, 1996). "I want to reiterate," he told employees, "that I view the TSPR as yet another opportunity for the district to continue the broad-based improvement efforts which began nearly two-and-a-half years ago in HISD" (Paige, September 26, 1996).

Rod's public comments at Sharp's first press conference were equally positive. He thanked Senator Whitmire for initiating the audit. He thanked Sharp for his professionalism and the spirit of cooperation that had prevailed during the audit. He politely declined from commenting on any of the recommendations, citing his lack of opportunity to study them. Thereafter, he tried to keep a low profile.

Privately, Rod was going through hell. HISD had become his child. Every criticism struck like an arrow in the heart. Early in the morning of Sharp's first press conference, in response to Sharp's op-ed in the morning paper, he called me to confess that he felt like someone in combat: "I'm alive, but wounded badly, and you guys on the board are dead."

Meanwhile, quietly and without public comment, Rod and his staff were putting into place a structure and process for examining and implementing as many as possible of Sharp's 228 recommendations. It was a massive undertaking, and it had to be done quickly. Sharp was coming back in mid-April to give HISD a report card.

The work began on October 7, the Monday following Sharp's week of reports to the people of Houston, with a meeting of Rod and his senior staff. By Friday, October 11, a steering committee had been formed and a plan of work outlined. The steering committee, chaired by Richard Miranda, an experienced business executive who Rod had recently hired as chief of staff for business services, included Susan Sclafani, chief of staff for educational services, and HISD's chief officers for technology, internal audit, quality improvement, and governmental affairs. Rod also assigned four technical advisors from research and internal audit to the committee.

By October 16, Rod was able to announce that HISD had already fully implemented 10 recommendations, would implement 17 more within a few weeks, and was making progress on implementing another 77. The remaining 124 recommendations were being evaluated. Betty Ressel confirmed to the press that HISD's rapid and strategic response to the performance review was impressive.

Responsibility for studying and implementing recommendations was assigned by the steering committee to 10 senior administrators. In most cases the administrator was responsible for a chapter in the Sharp audit. Rod called these executives champions. The champions assigned the specific recommendations in each chapter to 46 action teams.

In addition to putting into place a structure, the steering committee designed a process. Each action team would write a mission statement, agree on ground rules for teamwork, be able to request technical assistance from research and internal audit, and follow a specific plan for evaluating recommendations and implementing change. The lessons learned implementing PEER recommendations were now being applied to implementing Sharp.

The steering committee met 25 times between October 11 and April 4. The 46 action teams met nearly 1,000 times. The post-six-month report of HISD's responses to the TSPR was 551 pages long (HISD, April 18, 1997).

By the end of January, Rod was able to announce to the public that HISD was cutting 372 noninstructional positions over the next three years. One hundred and seventy would be cut by August 31, 1997. The total savings to the taxpayers over these three years would be $21 million. Over half of the savings from the first cut of 170 would come from upper- and mid-level staff at central office. Superintendent level positions were being cut by 20 percent.

By early April, when the comptroller's review team conducted its six-months review of HISD's responses, Rod and his staff were ready. The same could not be said for the board. Business recommendations were one thing. Political recommendations were quite another.

The Meddling Board of Education

There was a villain in the Sharp audit. It was the board of education. The first recommendation in the report called for two additional trustees, a president and vice president, to be elected districtwide. The second recommendation asked the board to modify its policies and practices to avoid micromanagement.

The problem, said Sharp, was that board members micromanaged and meddled in personnel decisions. "Numerous district staff reported visits or calls from individual board members who voiced an opinion about a certain individual, program or activity. Administrators, especially those employed on a performance contract, are placed in a very difficult position when these events occur" (Sharp, October 1996, p. 8).

It was true. Some HISD board members meddled in management. All over Texas, school trustees meddled in management. Public schools were in the middle of the political arena, and like elected officials at every level, school trustees were subject to the pressures of special interests. All board members were tempted to intervene in student discipline decisions, suggest personnel moves, or tilt toward a particular vendor. Most board members yielded to temptation on occasion. Some board members made getting jobs or contracts for those who could assist their reelection their primary business.

Were HISD board members particularly egregious meddlers? Would electing two additional trustees, a president and vice president elected districtwide, change anything? Perhaps.

Soon after his election as superintendent, Rod told me the pressure for jobs from board members and others was unbelievable. Since the early summer of 1995, he had been quietly promoting the idea of at-large trustees. Creating single-member districts, he said, had increased minority representation on the board, but there had been an unintended negative consequence. Board members felt accountable only to the group that had elected them. The result was a board plagued by racial, economic, and geographical divisions. Several board members appeared more interested in their trustee districts than in the district as a whole. This made it difficult to allocate resources and facilities fairly.

Also, since trustees were frequently elected in low turnout elections, a small group of activists could capitalize on any unrest in the district and propel the most zealous candidate into office. Once in office, zealous individuals concentrated on those issues which got them elected, making compromise for the good of the whole take a backseat to the rhetoric of extremism.

In the wake of the bond defeat, the *Chronicle,* perhaps picking up the point from Paige, had editorialized that HISD needed to restructure its board so that some trustees would be elected districtwide. The current structure "balkanized" the city, created a "parochial tug-of-war" on the board, and forced the superintendent to become a political deal-maker (July 7, 1996, p. C2).

Immediately following the Sharp report, the *Chronicle* began hammering away for at-large trustees. An October 6 editorial urged the board to approve a resolution at its next meeting calling for the legislature to allow the district to elect at-large members (p. C2). An October 20 editorial asked the board to meet with Houston's state legislators to draft a bill that would allow the board to have at least two at-large members on a board of nine or fewer (p. C2). A November 6 editorial again urged at-large trustees, but this time added that the board president and vice president should continue to be elected by the board (p. A36).

On November 11, the argument was pressed even further by David Langworthy, a member of the *Chronicle's* editorial board, in an op-ed headlined "A 'teachable moment' for HISD board." There were at least three open secrets in HISD, said Langworthy: "One is the crying need for an at-large component on the HISD board to help Superintendent Rod Paige and the too-slim majority on the present board with a big picture vision for HISD, fend off those trustees whose 'vision' does not extend beyond the next patronage job, teachers' union demand or vendors' contract." The second secret was that Paige did not want to enlarge the board. He is already pressed to the limit " 'babysitting' nine board members with egos and agendas who expect him to be at their beck and call." The third secret was the allegiance of several of the present board to "vendors, the unions and their own political power bases rather than the children of Houston and the district's taxpayers" (p. A22).

The Sharp audit, said Langworthy, had brought out "a serious minded commitment on the part of Paige and a majority of the HISD board to do what is necessary to bring change to the district." It was a "teachable moment." The newly elected Houston delegation to the Texas legislature had a mission. They should restructure the HISD board (p. A22).

The business community was equally committed to at-large trustees. Soon after the Sharp report, business leaders began talking about adding at-large trustees for HISD to their legislative agenda for the upcoming session of the Texas legislature. John Walsh, president of the chamber of commerce division of the partnership, told the press that: "Governance is, in our mind, the most powerful opportunity to enhance the performance and accelerate the pace of reform in the Houston Independent School District" (*Chronicle,* November 3, 1996, p. A33).

Early on November 15, over coffee, juice, and muffins in the conference room at the partnership's office in Two Allen Center, Walsh and a small group of Houston's business elite met with Rod, Paula, and me to discuss the issue. We all agreed that two or three at-large trustees would improve the board. We also recognized that the real issue was not at-large trustees. It was minority representation. The Texas legislature had moved HISD from seven at-large trustees to seven single-member district trustees in 1975—and expanded the number to nine in 1977—for the express purpose of increasing minority representation on the board. Currently HISD had three safe black seats, and two—soon to be three—safe Hispanic seats. We all knew it would be difficult to convince African American and Hispanic leaders to support at-large trustees and risk diluting minority representation on the board. Paula said it would be impossible. We concluded with a decision to gather opinions from 21 identified community leaders and meet again (Blake, November 20, 1996).

The committee met again on December 3. The results were what Paula had predicted. The response from minority leaders was "over our dead bodies." The committee did not meet again. In early February, the partnership decided to drop the issue from its legislative agenda (Walsh, February 14, 1997).

Board Response

While Paige pushed his staff to study and implement as many recommendations as possible and the *Chronicle* and the partnership pushed for at-large trustees, the board struggled with its own response. We were not united. Publicly, we all wanted management efficiency, but we were divided on privatization. Publicly, we all opposed micromanagement, but some board members would probably never quit trying to influence unduly personnel and contract decisions. And only Laurie Bricker, Ron Franklin, and I wanted at-large trustees. Still, we had to do something.

Paula worked hard to obtain consensus. At the November 7 board meeting, she introduced a resolution committing HISD to implement or improve upon each recommendation in the Sharp audit. The words "improve upon" gave board members the wiggle room to cast an affirmative vote. The resolution was approved unanimously.

Paula next recommended a policy to curtail board micromanagement. Though it did not put into place any mechanism for enforcement, it was explicit: "The Board of Education as a body, and as individual board members, shall be prohibited from engaging in activities which inappropriately interfere with the administrative responsibilities of the Superintendent of Schools and the administrative staff."[4]

This vote was not unanimous. Carol Galloway had been fidgeting uncomfortably in her chair during the presentation of the agenda item. Then she spoke, reading from a prepared statement. The gist of her statement was that the board had no authority over her private job responsibilities as an employee of the Houston Federation of Teachers. She intended to continue to intervene in personnel issues affecting HFT members. It was an astonishing admission. The media did not report it.

Also, at the November 7 board meeting, Paula announced the appointment of a citizens' task force to advise the board on the governance issues in the Sharp audit, particularly the at-large trustee issue, and serve as "scorekeepers" to confirm to the public that HISD was acting in good faith to respond to all 228 recommendations.

At the second meeting of the task force on January 22, the serious work began. A parent activist, Nancy Lomax, accepted the chairmanship. Twelve subcommittees, corresponding to the chapters in the Sharp audit, were established to review HISD's responses to the Sharp recommendations. The task force voted to hold public hearings in representative areas of the city to assess public opinion on at-large trustees. And the task force suggested that the board "establish a formal process for resolving complaints against board members with the board president as mediator" (HISD, January 22, 1997).

This last point had been discussed by trustees since the November 7 vote to ban meddling. What would happen to a trustee who continued to meddle? Paula had been keen to establish a formal process, possibly even appointing a retired judge to investigate and resolve complaints against board members. No, said the TSPR citizens' task force, that seems a bit too formal, just place that responsibility on the board president.

It fell to me to follow up on this suggestion. Two weeks earlier I had been elected board president for 1997. The task seemed simple enough. Surely most of my colleagues would jump at the chance to show themselves zealous opponents of meddling.

On Tuesday, February 4, I announced my policy recommendation for the February 6 board meeting at a press conference. The board was going to establish a formal process for complaints against board members. Persons could bring charges of board meddling to the board president who would "act to resolve the complaint with the board member or with the board as a whole." The president would advise the person registering a complaint of its resolution, and in resolving a complaint could utilize the services of an experienced, trained mediator as a consultant.

Two days later the board rejected my recommendation. Carol Galloway began the discussion with a strong statement decrying the attempt of one board member to govern another. "I will not be subjected to this Gestapo policy," she concluded. "This policy is designed to eliminate my free speech" (HISD, February 6, 1997, p. 1). The debate went downhill from there. In the end, Campos, Gaines, Galloway, and Gallegos voted no. (Franklin and Lemon were absent.) Seeing that the motion would fail, I also voted no and announced immediately that I had voted with the majority so I could move to reconsider at the next board meeting when, hopefully, all nine board members would be present.

For the next two weeks a battle raged over what was, in fact, a very limited check on board member meddling. The first shot was fired by State Senator Mario Gallegos, Olga's son, who threatened reprisals against the district if I did not drop the issue. I refused. Paula, who was a close friend of Mario, responded by getting in his face and telling him to drop it.

On February 16, the *Chronicle* struck with an editorial headlined "Don't Micromanage." Micromanagement added an "insidious, politically motivated element to district business." The proposed policy to establish a formal process for resolving complaints against board members was fair and should be approved. The article continued: "Meanwhile, there are disturbing assertions that legislators with close ties to the school board and/or school lobbyists have been applying behind-the-scenes pressures to have the item removed from the HISD agenda. This pressure, sources say, extends even to the point of threatening legislative reprisal against the district. Such is the worst kind of political game-playing and micromanagement from afar" (p. O2).

After all this, perhaps because of all this, the board approved my recommendation on February 21. The same motion, with a sentence added empowering the first vice president to resolve complaints against the board president, passed 6–3.

The second decision by the TSPR citizens' task force that required follow-up by the board was the decision to hold public hearings on the issue of at-large trustees. The hearings were held on February 17 and 24, and March 3. Almost no one came. Only four of 22 speakers wanted at-large trustees. The task force advised the HISD board to oppose any legislation to change the current structure of the board (Alvarado, March 21, 1997).

The issue was already dead. Though two state representatives had filed bills in the Texas House to give HISD at-large trustees, there was no chance the legislature would act against the vehement opposition of black and Hispanic legislators. The partnership had already dropped the issue from its legislative agenda. The public hearings just confirmed the death sentence.

The board and public response to at-large trustees and micromanagement said volumes about school reform in urban America. Those who had the most to gain from getting politics out of the schools—minority children and their parents—were often represented by school board members and legislators who were committed to keeping politics in the schools. White voters did not seem to care. Rod Paige, a few board members, Houston's business leaders, the *Chronicle,* a few legislators, and John Sharp understood very well that politics in the schools was an enemy of school reform. But even this coalition could only dent the status quo.

HISD'S SIX-MONTH REPORT CARD

On April 17, 1997, John Sharp once again addressed the people of Houston in a major press conference. This one was held on the lawn in front of the HISD central administration building. It was a beautiful spring day, though a bit windy. I had the opportunity to introduce Sharp. He was in high spirits. He praised Senator Whitmire again and heaped encomiums on HISD's Richard Miranda. Routinely, said Sharp, he issued report cards to school districts approximately one year after a performance review, but because HISD was so large, he had decided that Houston taxpayers deserved a six-month progress report in addition to a one-year report, which he would release in October.

"I'm pleased that HISD seems to have taken many of my proposals seriously," he said. "And while it may be too early to judge their ultimate success, I believe the district at this early stage has earned a grade of 'satisfactory, so far.'" He went on to confirm that 88 percent of his recommendations had either been completed or were in progress.[5] "Based on the same scale HISD applies to its students, the district deserves a letter grade of 'B' for its first steps toward implementing my recommendations." In 10 of 12 chapters HISD had made satisfactory response. Only in two areas, community involvement and facilities and energy management, did HISD still "need work."

Specific achievements were noted. HISD had already saved $4.24 million. The district had launched an overhaul of curriculum management and instructional training. Teacher and administrator evaluations had been modified to focus on individual performance. Job positions had been cut. Employees in questionable job categories unrelated to their professional backgrounds or abilities had been reduced from 40 to 24.

The board was also given credit for approving a policy forbidding micromanagement and for establishing a complaint process and peer censure for board member meddling. Noting that the district had chosen not to act on his proposal for an at-large president and vice president elected by voters districtwide, he went on to challenge the board again to get out of micromanagement (Sharp, April 17, 1997).

It was a long press conference. Rod expressed his appreciation, again, for the leadership of Senator Whitmire and the thorough work of Sharp's team. The audit was a great tool for HISD, and the district and the people of Houston owed Sharp a debt of gratitude. Reporters asked questions. Few were hostile. Sharp's six-month report was a triumph for HISD.

Sharp's final word to the press was that HISD had "in six months moved as fast or faster than the most exemplary districts that we have looked at in terms of the number of things that have been implemented" (Miranda, April 24, 1997). The next day's *Chronicle* carried an editorial headlined "HISD has made a good start on Sharp's recommendations" (April 18, 1997, p. A46).

There would be another report card in six months. Richard Miranda and his champions and chairpersons still had a lot of work to do. But no one doubted that the one-year report would be positive, and by then there would be numerous new issues to distract the public. The Sharp audit, after just one more day of attention, would be history.

The public would probably remember it as confirmation that HISD was a deeply troubled school district, inefficiently managed by a bloated bureaucracy and governed by a politically motivated school board. The reality was that the TSPR had not uncovered mountains of waste. Instead it had revealed an effective and rapidly improving urban school district with, not surprisingly, numerous opportunities for improvement. Sharp's 228 ways to reduce waste, increase revenue, and fine-tune the existing operation were a significant contribution to the improvement of HISD, but they had little to do with school reform.

Yet, perhaps inadvertently, the Sharp audit, like the failed bonds, gave a great boost to the reform of Houston's public schools. The reforms of 1997, as we shall see, would not have been possible without John Sharp.

On June 12, 1997, shortly after Texas Lieutenant Governor Bob Bullock announced he would not seek reelection, John Sharp formally launched his campaign for lieutenant governor (*Chronicle,* June 12, 1997, p. A33). Calling himself Mr. Texas Performance Review, Sharp claimed that he had saved the state $8.5 billion. Within hours of his announcement, Sharp had a website on the Internet. Above his picture was the slogan: "Act Sharp! Think Sharp! Vote Sharp!"

NOTES

1. Public opinion was also gathered through a published survey, via e-mail, and over a special toll-free telephone hotline.

2. Interestingly, 60 percent of the parents believed their children were receiving a good to excellent education; 71 percent of the students surveyed believed they were receiving a quality education; and 80 percent gave their teachers an A or B.

3. The chapters were District Organization and Management, Educational Ser-

vice Delivery and Performance Measures, Community Involvement, Personnel Management, Facilities and Energy Management, Asset and Risk Management, Financial Management, Purchasing and Warehousing Services, Information Services, Food Services, Transportation, and Safety and Security.

4. Following was a list of nine specific activities that were declared off limits, including assigning and evaluating district personnel, recommending selections and promotions of district personnel, and any other activities included as responsibilities of the superintendent of schools and administrative staff in the Texas Education Code.

5. The report card could have been even more positive. HISD had actually failed to act on only 3 percent of the recommendations. The other 9 percent of the recommendations that had not been acted upon were strategic in nature and involved the implementation of new systems that would require 18 to 24 months (Miranda, April 24, 1997).

14

A New Beginning for HISD

The defeat of the $390 million bond issue in May 1996 and John Sharp's audit report to the taxpayers in October were defining moments for HISD. The failed bonds proved to HISD watchers that the public had no confidence in Houston's public schools. The Sharp audit confirmed for most Houstonians that the bond vote was justified.

In the year that followed, however, attitudes changed. The public began to notice that most HISD performance indicators were improving significantly. Also, almost every month the board of education approved another bold reform initiative. HISD was getting better after all.

The prevailing opinion was that these improvements and actions were a response to the failed bonds and Sharp. The public had at last gotten HISD's attention. There was truth in this view, but the reality was far more complex.

The reform of HISD began with *Beliefs and Visions* in 1990 and the selection of Frank Petruzielo as superintendent in 1991. Frank's achievements were not insignificant: shared decision-making in every HISD school, school improvement plans, school-based budgeting, the establishment of a professional district police force, massive changes in school attendance boundaries, several significant management audits, and a start toward more effective employee performance evaluations.

But the real improvement of HISD began with Rod Paige. His election as superintendent in February 1994 was the single most important event in the reform of HISD. Without Paige, shared decision-making would never have taken root, accountability would not have become firmly established, and decentralization would never have happened. Also, without Paige, there would have been no PEER task forces, no performance contracts for administrators, no modified vouchers, no business outsourcing, and no incentive pay for teachers.

The reform of HISD started well before the failed bond election and the Sharp audit. But these two events accelerated the pace of reform. They focused attention on the politically driven behavior of board members. They pushed Paige into hiring an effective press secretary.[1] They gave Paige the opportunity to come forth with a fresh, bold reform agenda for HISD. And, perhaps most significantly, they put into the hands of Paige and the board reformers a powerful argument to obtain board support for Paige's agenda.

PAIGE'S NEW BEGINNING FOR HISD

By early 1996, Paula Arnold, Ron Franklin, and I knew *Beliefs and Visions* was history. We were the only ones with ownership. Except for Olga Gallegos, none of the other board members had even been on the board when *Beliefs and Visions* was approved. Also, the cutting edge of school reform in America had entered a new phase. The first wave of school reform—standards—had dominated the mid-1980s. *Beliefs and Visions* had caught the second wave of school reform—restructuring. Now a third wave was building—competition.

Rod and I talked about the need for a new vision for HISD in the days immediately following Sharp's report to the people in early October. He needed to act fast. Even if the board could reach consensus on a new vision statement, which was doubtful, it would take six months. And it was even more doubtful that the theme of a new vision statement by the current board would be competition. The reform leadership of HISD had moved from the board table to the superintendent's office. If a bold, new reform agenda for HISD were to be put before the city, it would have to come from Rod.

Rob Mosbacher played an important role in the development of the new reform agenda. Mosbacher, a lifelong Houstonian, oil company executive, and former Republican candidate for U.S. senator and Texas lieutenant governor, was an attractive public personality who looked even better when you got to know him. Weeks before the Sharp report, he began advising Rod on how to handle the district's public response. Shift the attention of the public from the failures of the past to the promise of the future, he told Rod. Praise Sharp, and then go beyond him with a reform agenda that emphasizes accountability, incentives, decentralization, and competition.

Paige and the board reformers were already there. In March 1996, the board had approved a contract with Integrated Healthcare Delivery Systems to provide workers' compensation claims service, saving taxpayers over $2 million per year. In June, Browning-Ferris Industries had taken over HISD's heavy waste disposal and recycling services, saving another $450,000 per year. A small incentive pay program for teachers was now in its second year. The district's first four charter schools had been chartered in June 1995. And the first HISD students using *modified vouchers* were already enrolling in the Varnett School.

Still, Mosbacher's advice was significant. He understood that having an aggressive reform agenda was not enough. Paige needed to distill the agenda into a few simple words and place it before the public as a bold new beginning for HISD.

This is exactly what Rod did. On October 16, he unveiled his *New Beginning for* HISD in a whirlwind of staged media events.[2] Rod's message was clear and strong. The district had been under enormous pressure. It had not been an easy time. The bond election and the Sharp audit had been wake-up calls. HISD did many things remarkably well, but there were a multitude of things HISD did not do well or should not even be trying to do. Almost everything could be done better.

Since 1990, board members and superintendents had changed. *Beliefs and Visions* had been largely overwhelmed by events and changing circumstances. The time had come to revitalize these beliefs and visions from 1990; Rod said, "I view the bond election in May and the Sharp Audit this month as providing us with precisely the right opportunity to outline some very basic, but bold, new principles which can guide this District well into the next century." Today, continued Rod, is "a new beginning for HISD."

Rod's four basic reform principles were Accountability, Best Efforts, Choice, and Decentralization. HISD would establish objective, believable measures of accountability so that the community could track progress. Teacher salaries would be based on direct measures of teacher skills, knowledge, and student performance. Where HISD could not perform a business function as cheaply as the private sector, the function would be outsourced. All HISD students would be allowed to attend the public school of their choice, as long as space was available. Students would have "academic free-agency" and schools would have to compete for students. Innovative proposals to manage schools from nontraditional providers would be welcome. Over the next three years, HISD would transition to a budget system that allocated money to schools on a weighted-per-pupil basis.

News coverage of Paige's media blitz on October 16 was disappointing. The media were far more interested in Paige's comments about HISD's response to the Sharp audit than they were in his new initiatives. Most employees and parents acted as if the new beginnings principles had never been announced. Paige's press conference of October 16 was largely forgotten.

It would have taken formal endorsement of these principles by the board of education, extensive promotion by the district, and widespread media coverage over many weeks to capture the attention of the public. That was not possible. Powerful interest groups—employee groups, organized labor, the NAACP, and others—opposed one or more of Paige's four principles. At best the board would have supported them five to four after a bitter vote.

THE REFORMS OF 1996–1997

But in the year that followed, month by month, agenda item by agenda item, by clever scheduling, a great deal of arm-twisting, enormous staff work behind the scenes, and very close votes—sometimes fights—at the board table, HISD began to embrace the principles of competition.

The policy changes and contracts approved by the board from October 1996 to August 1997 could almost be called a revolution. They were changes that could not have been imagined just a few years before. The board relinquished its authority to approve personnel appointments, promotions, and transfers. Within the constraints of HISD's overcrowded schools, an effective public school choice program was established. Nineteen charter schools were approved. A contract was signed with a private company for the education of at-risk adolescents. Several significant student achievement initiatives were launched. Employees became more accountable for their performance. And except for student transportation, the management of almost every major business activity of the district was contracted out to private companies.

Reducing the Board's Role in Management

Reducing the Number of Board Meetings. On April 17, the board approved a policy change that reduced regular board meetings from two to one per month. One board meeting each month would free up staff time and improve the quality of staff preparation. This was the reason Rod gave to board members.

It was the truth, but it was not the whole truth. Rod did not enjoy board meetings. Not infrequently an unbalanced person speaking to an agenda item or addressing the board at the hearing of citizens would rake the superintendent or the board over the coals. When this happened, the T.V. cameramen always jumped to their cameras.

But what Rod hated most was the carping, nagging criticism of board members. Ever since he had been superintendent, he had from time to time given me a look or passed me a note showing his frustration or even anger over a particularly stupid remark. Not infrequently, at the end of a hard day at the board table, he would say, "I don't need this. I can't take much more of this."

One meeting a month was great for Paige and his staff, and some board members jumped at the chance to cut down on the time required to be a board member. Others were not pleased. Board meetings were their opportunity to keep a close eye on the superintendent and posture for their constituents. Surprisingly, the one-meeting-a-month agenda item passed with minimal grumbling about how Rod was trying to eliminate the power and influence of the board.

   Waiving Board Personnel Authority. On June 4, the board approved a major policy revision that reduced the board's influence over personnel decisions. The previous November, in response to Sharp, the board had explicitly prohibited board members from pressing personnel recommendations on the superintendent, but the board still had the responsibility to approve all new appointments and promotions for both contract and noncontract employees.
   Every board agenda included numerous personnel recommendations. Frequently, in executive session, Rod's recommendations were challenged. Why was someone being paid so much? Why was a black principal being recommended for a Hispanic school? Why was so-and-so being transferred? We all had questions from time to time. Some were legitimate. Many were not.
   Rod hated the process. Except for his direct reports, he did not select personnel. Time and again he reminded the board that HISD was decentralized. His personnel recommendations were the recommendations of selection committees. Time and again he told me privately that a particular fight in closed session was really a last-ditch stand by a board member to influence a personnel appointment.
   The new Texas Education Code passed by the legislature in 1995 offered a way out. School boards could delegate final authority for selecting personnel and setting terms of employment to superintendents.
   "Do you think the board will approve this?" Rod asked me sometime in March. "The board will still have to open and close positions and approve the salary schedule. The board will still have ultimate control over the workforce. But I'll be able to fill positions without having to wait for the next board meeting, and it'll be easier for me to place the right people in the right positions."
   This approval also came much easier than I expected.[3]

Contracts, Choice, and Charters

   HISD'S First School Management Contract. On January 23, the board approved a contract with Community Education Partners (CEP), a private company, to educate middle school and high school students with behavior and academic problems. CEP agreed to educate 450 HISD students at $7,500 per student per year and improve each student's achievement by at least two grade levels per year or reeducate them at no cost to HISD.
   This was HISD's first contract for school management with a private, for-profit company, and it was a win for everyone. Up to 450 students would receive the attention they needed and would no longer be disrupting HISD class-

rooms. They would also be educated at a cost to the taxpayer much less than the per pupil cost at HISD's own alternative middle school for at-risk adolescents, and CEP guaranteed academic achievement.[4]

Within District Choice. On February 6, the board approved Paige's choice plan for 1997–1998. Any HISD student could attend any HISD school, provided space was available. Students zoned to neighborhood schools would receive priority admission to their zoned schools.[5] If applications for a school exceeded capacity, a lottery would be held.

District Charter Schools. Also on February 6, the board approved an aggressive plan for establishing district charter schools. The Education Code approved by the legislature in May 1995 authorized the state board of education to approve up to 20 state charter schools and allowed school boards to grant campus charters. HISD, said Rod, would grant as many as it could. Charter proposal would be solicited from school communities, principals, teacher organizations, teachers groups, universities, and other entities. Schools run by nondistrict entities would receive $3,575 per student, 90 percent of the average school spending per pupil for HISD students. HISD would provide oversight as required by law and district policy.

These would not be HISD's first charter schools. Even before the legislature convened in January 1995, Rod had proposed a charter for one of Houston's most famous principals, Thaddeus Lott. Since his confrontation with Joan Raymond in 1991 over alleged cheating at Wesley Elementary, Lott had won national acclaim. Year after year, with direct instruction and tight discipline, Lott turned poor, minority children into top academic achievers. For years, he had been wanting more autonomy from HISD.

The charter was granted on June 1, 1995, to a board of commissioners for a feeder pattern of three elementary schools and one middle school. The charter granted the board of commissioners—in effect Lott—autonomy over curriculum, instructional strategies, textbooks and teaching materials, student conduct and discipline, and personnel. HISD retained responsibility for business support services and building maintenance and repair.

By mid-July, 19 new charters had been added to Lott's four-school charter: seven whole school charters, four school within a school charters, and eight external charters. Every charter was innovative. Some were groundbreaking.

For example, The Pathway School—Academy of Academic Achievement would focus on high school students who needed more guidance and less structure. The Knowledge is Power Program Academy provided a standard curriculum with a powerful focus on character development for children in grades five through eight. Classes would meet from 7:30 A.M. to 5:00 P.M.

during the week, four hours on Saturday, and one month during the summer. Pro-Vision's Centripet Project would provide weekday or seven-day residential options for middle-school students with academic and behavior problems. Kaleidoscope School/Escuela Caleidoscopio at Cunningham Elementary would explore issues of identity and heritage for students in grades six through eight with multicultural, bilingual, and biliterate techniques. Project Chrysalis at Cage Elementary would feature morning classes and afternoon applications using the city as the classroom. The Dawn School, the first of its kind in the nation, would be a residential school for homeless children. There were others.

Most of the charter schools and programs were very successful. A few were not. The HFT supported enthusiastically HISD's contract with Community Education Partners and raised no objection to district charter schools.

Improving Instruction and Assessment

From the beginning of his superintendency, Rod emphasized again and again to anyone who would listen that HISD's core business was teaching and learning, but it was not until 1995—because of the flap over his appointment, the decentralization initiative, and the Alternative Certification Program scandal—that he was able to turn his attention to curriculum.

Curriculum Alignment. In January 1995, Paige launched a curriculum management audit to determine the degree to which the district's written, taught, and tested curricula were aligned and the extent to which the district's resources were organized to support the development, implementation, and monitoring of the curricula. Central and district office staff began training in the five standards for auditing curriculum management: control, direction, connectivity, feedback, and productivity. In February, school staff began receiving training. In the months and years that followed, curriculum alignment was a district priority. (Recall that February 1995 was also when Paige proposed and the board approved a new core curriculum for high school.)

Balanced Approach to Reading. Paige's next major curriculum priority was elementary school reading. In January 1996, Texas Governor George W. Bush announced a major campaign to improve reading instruction in Texas's public schools. Rod had been talking with me since October about reading instruction in HISD. Bush's announcement stimulated his immediate response. Why wait for the legislature? A few weeks later, Rod commissioned a PEER task force on reading.

The 22-member panel, chaired by University of Houston professor and nationally recognized reading expert Barbara Foorman, issued its final report just 10 weeks later, on May 3. The 85-page document, *A Balanced Approach to Reading,* defined balance as "a program that combines skills involving phonological awareness and decoding with language and literature-rich activities" (HISD, May 3, 1996). The essential components were phonological awareness, print awareness, alphabetic and orthographic awareness, comprehension strategies, and reading practice.

For HISD this meant a significant shift away from whole language to phonics. An enormous infrastructure needed to be put into place. In June, action teams were chartered and a three-year implementation plan developed. In August, the board approved a $3.2 million budget, mostly for training. Handbooks and benchmarks were developed. Software packages were purchased. During 1996–1997, 36 reading teacher trainers provided five days of training to more than 3,300 K–3 teachers. In addition, reading training was provided to middle and high school reading enrichment teachers. Dr. Foorman was retained to provide a minimum of four days per month of consulting support.

In March 1997, Rod obtained board approval to put an additional $2.3 million into reading improvement. This money was used in 17 schools to assist students in grades 3–6 who had never received balanced instruction in phonemic awareness and literature, provided additional support for below-level readers in secondary schools, and piloted intensive reading instruction programs in 12 elementary schools. From 1996–1997 onward, every child in HISD received instruction in phonological awareness and decoding.

Stanford 9. On December 9, 1996, the board approved for all appropriate students in grades 1 through 11, beginning in 1997–1998, the norm-referenced Stanford 9 Achievement Test program, or the Spanish language Aprenda 2. Since the crash of the Norm-referenced Assessment Program for Texas in 1992–1993, HISD had gone without a standardized norm-referenced test. Cathy Mincberg and I, and later Laurie Bricker, had pushed hard for one of the national testing programs, but to no avail. It was expensive—for HISD nearly $1 million a year—and many principals and teachers did not want to give up another instructional day for testing. (We suspected that some also feared that low scores would embarrass the district.) But at last Rod said do it, and it was done.

Improving Employee Accountability

Contracts, Terminations, and Grievances. On October 3, 1996, the board approved on first reading significant policy changes that governed employee contracts, termination hearings, and grievances. The new policies, made possible by changes in the Texas Education Code in 1995, were based on recommendations by a PEER task force on employee hearing procedures that reported to the board in July 1996.[6]

The old policies made it difficult to terminate incompetent employees, allowed grievances to become adversarial and disruptive, and wasted time and money. The average cost for a grievance hearing was $4,389. The average cost for a termination hearing was $20,824. Not counting staff time, HISD had spent over $600,000 the previous year in hearings. The new policies, said Paige, would "result in a more productive workplace, a less adversarial employment relationship, and generate savings of both time and resources" (Paige, October 3, 1996).

There were four major provisions of the new policy. (1) The district would no longer offer teachers continuing contracts. Teachers (after the probationary period) would be offered two-year term contracts. (2) Termination and nonrenewal of contracts for teachers and other term contract employees would be for *good cause* only and follow procedures mandated by state law. (3) Termination procedures for noncontract employees—salaried and hourly or daily rate employees—would no longer include an evidentiary hearing. Noncontract employees could appeal termination decisions to the next line supervisor, whose decision would be final. (4) Grievance hearings would be conducted as a conference without examination and cross-examination of witnesses, and one step in the appeal process would be eliminated.

Gayle Fallon was outraged. The new policies were "insulting" to teachers. "We have never drawn a line in the dirt and said that if you cross over it you may never again be considered a friend of teachers," she wrote trustees on October 1. "Because this proposal attempts to take employees back to the 1950's as far as their ability to settle grievances internally with any sense of equity and strips contract rights from all new hires and current probationary employees, we are doing it on this issue" (Fallon, October 1, 1996).

Richard Shaw, secretary-treasurer of the Harris County AFL-CIO Council, supported Gayle's letter the next day with his own letter to the trustees. The words he used to describe the treatment of HISD employees in the 60s and 70s included tyranny, oppression, authoritarianism, disgusting, belittling, harassing, and patronizing: "To say that HISD employed a plantation mentality, is about the kindest thing that I could say (and only in the sense that they did not do actual bodily harm to their slaves-employees)." Any action by HISD to reduce equity for employees would not be looked upon favorably by the AFL-CIO. "As the AFL-CIO Council's spokesperson, I can assure you that friends of our affiliated Unions are friends of the Council's" (Shaw, October 2, 1996).

The board approved the contracts and policy changes on second reading on October 17 with one small change. Current probationary teachers would be grandfathered and remain eligible for continuing contracts at the end of their probationary period.

HFT Lawsuit Dismissed. On January 27, 1997, State District Judge John Devine dismissed a lawsuit filed against Rod Paige, Paula Arnold, Esther Campos, Cathy Mincberg, and me by the HFT. The suit, which was filed on November 22, 1995, charged that we had conspired together to bust the union (*Dewey v. Paige*, November 22, 1995). What was the evidence? Such actions as adopting an ombudsman program to help employees resolve problems in the workplace, making available to teachers prepaid legal insurance as part of their benefits package, and a Paige memorandum to all employees asking them not to "sidestep the available process and go directly to individual board members to resolve personal job-related concerns" (Paige, November 20, 1995).

On May 22, 1997, Judge Devine ruled that the HFT lawsuit was frivolous and ordered the union to pay the district's legal fees, $59,000. Paige called it a victory for taxpayers and children.[7]

New Teacher Appraisal System. On March 20, the board adopted the state-developed Professional Development and Appraisal System (PDAS) as the official teacher evaluation system for HISD. The new Texas Education Code passed by the legislature in 1995 abolished the Texas Teacher Appraisal System (TTAS) and required school districts to adopt a new teacher appraisal system beginning with the 1997–1998 school year. Districts could adopt the PDAS or a locally developed appraisal system that met the requirements of the code.

The PDAS was an improvement over the TTAS. It linked teacher appraisals to student achievement and discipline. But the link was weak. To exceed expectations in Domain VIII, Improvement of Academic Performance, all a teacher had to do was ("almost all of the time") align instruction to TAAS objectives, analyze TAAS performance, sequence classroom instruction to incorporate TAAS objectives, select instructional materials that correlated with TAAS objectives, and provide feedback to students regarding their learning progress on TAAS objectives. Actual student performance still had little to do with the teacher's evaluation.

Since Gayle Fallon had killed the System for Teacher Appraisal and Review in early 1994, the teacher assessment issue had been complicated by new requirements of the Texas Education Agency. By March 1997, there were good administrative reasons to approve PDAS even though it was less rigorous than STAR.

Whistle-Blower Policy. On May 1, the board approved a new whistle-blower policy designed to help uncover employee mismanagement, unethical conduct, theft, and fraud. The policy was based on a PEER task force report received by the board on March 6.[8] The whistle-blower policy encouraged employees, parents, students, and others to bring forward complaints; provided guidelines for work supervisors; and prohibited retaliation against individuals who made reports under these procedures. The district committed itself to investigate all complaints through a centralized case-management and case-tracking system under the direct supervision of HISD's chief of staff for business services.

Improving Business Operations

Management Infrastructure. On January 23, the board approved a contract with Main Event Management Corporation to obtain consulting and training support for the installation of management operating systems and management training for HISD administrators. The cost to HISD would be $160,000 for licensing fees. American General Corporation would donate an additional $700,000 in consulting and monitoring services.

The man behind this was Harold Hook, the same man who had chaired the partnership's Houston Business Advisory Council and conceptualized the decentralization process for HISD in 1993. Hook, Paige had discovered, was more than the successful chairman of American General. He was a management theorist who had designed a powerful infrastructure of management operating systems and developed an outstanding management training program.

In September 1996, Rod and four of his direct reports began training in Model-Netics, the name Hook gave to his management training program. Rod loved it. Hook had not invented much that was new, but he had brilliantly synthesized the full range of management, communication, organizational development, and problem-solving principles into 151 two-to-five-word phrases, illustrated in most cases by a clever diagram. It was Management 101 plus a lot more, made easy and memorable. Within a year, every administrator from assistant principal up had been trained in Model-Netics.

In January 1997, HISD began installing four management operating systems developed by Hook: a directive and information system, a desk manual program, an approval control program, and a systems control program. The district also obtained Main Events Management training for some of its most effective school administrators to become internal consultants. Paige was determined that the management culture and systems of HISD match the best in the private sector.

Delivery Order Contracting. On March 7, the board approved HISD's first delivery order contract, a contract with Brown & Root to correct fire code violations and safety problems at 45 priority schools, with other schools to follow. Brown & Root agreed to deliver a wide range of major and minor building repairs for preset unit prices. The maximum that could be awarded under the contract during the performance period, March 6, 1997 to March 6, 1998, was $20 million (this was part of the $39 million in the 1996–1997 capital budget for emergency repairs). If the district chose, it could issue up to four annual renewal contracts under the same terms and conditions up to $100 million.

During the presentation and discussion of the agenda item, no one mentioned the word "outsourcing."

Outsourcing Facilities Management. On June 4, the board unanimously approved a contract with ServiceMaster Management Services Company to maintain and operate all HISD campuses and facilities. The contract was huge, for HISD did almost everything in-house: custodial services, grounds, landscaping, tree stump removal, paved service care, moving and storage, electrical services, plumbing, roofing, sheet metal, utilities management, temperature control, structural maintenance, construction and moving of temporary buildings, lock repairs, and so forth. It was a $40 million per year operation.

Facilities maintenance had always been a problem. Effective and efficient facilities management required an analysis of what, how, and when various functions were performed, appropriate procedures manuals that mapped best practices based on industry standards, training for employees in best practices, effective and well-documented preventive-maintenance systems, benchmarking against industry leaders, effective supplier relationships that guaranteed best quality and price in the acquisition of supplies and purchased services, and so forth. Without experienced facilities managers and the knowledge base available to a professional facilities management company, HISD could never do this well.

The ServiceMaster contract paid ServiceMaster $4.2 million per year, with four one-year renewable contracts, for an initial period of five years. Gross savings for HISD would be $8.3 million per year, for a net savings of $4.1 million per year. The two most important features of the contract were the performance guarantee and the protection of HISD's employees. ServiceMaster's performance would be measured monthly using new accountability and performance standards. Service quality and productivity had to reach prevailing industry standards. If they did not, ServiceMaster would bear the cost of making it so. Also, HISD employees would continue to be district employees, and not one would lose his or her job because of the contract.

There would be a reduction in force. Full-time equivalent employment in facilities management would be reduced from 1,053 to 749 over four years through attrition and retirement. Reduction in force by layoffs during the first year of the contract would increase net savings to over $7 million per year, but this was not acceptable to the board.

The ServiceMaster contract was hardly noticed by the media. Paige and his staff studiously avoided using the words "outsourcing" or "contracting out." Rod called it a partnership. The AFL-CIO said little. The NAACP said nothing. No one mentioned that at $20.5 million over five years, the saving to the taxpayer in the ServiceMaster contract exceeded John Sharp's most ambitious recommendation. No one asked why outsourcing facilities management was a recommendation Sharp failed to make.

Outsourcing Food Service. On July 17, the board approved a contract with Aramark Corporation to manage HISD's food service operations. The Aramark contract was the culmination of nearly two years of controversy about food service, and at the last moment it generated more fireworks at the board table than any issue since the selection of Rod Paige as superintendent.

HISD's food service operations were huge. Nearly 200,000 meals a day were served at 258 schools by over 2,000 food service employees. The annual operating budget exceeded $66 million.

Food service was also problematic. Students complained about the food. Participation was low. The management system was ineffective. The Sharp report recommended that food service be outsourced or reorganized. In January 1997, a food services PEER task force, which had been working for almost a year, recommended reorganization.

The decision was up to Paige. On February 5 he announced his decision: food service would be managed by a private company; no food service workers would lose their jobs; requests for proposals would be sent out in a few weeks. Rod acknowledged that good people who had taken a hard look at food services had reached different conclusions, but he believed that food service experts from the private sector could do the job better.[9]

The cascade of letters and phone calls from food services workers to Paige and board members began the next day. Food service workers had been wounded by character assassination. Privatization would cost more, not less. Food service was being asked to be the sacrificial lamb to change public opinion about HISD. A political chess game was being played at the expense of people losing their jobs. Paige had forsaken his people. And on and on.

The battle raged on through the spring. Orell Fitzsimmons, state director of the Texas United School Employees Union, was telling food service workers that many of them would lose their jobs. A majority of the food service workers were African Americans. Black ministers were being stirred up by their parishioners. At least four of the minority board members appeared to be firmly opposed.

Again and again Rod sent out letters to board members, food service employees, pastors, community leaders, and others. The district was planning to hire a private firm to *oversee* food service operations. Cafeteria workers would remain employees of the district. No current HISD employee would be terminated because of the proposed contract.

On April 1, Rod wrote Fitzsimmons charging him with personally and knowingly disseminating information absolutely contrary to the truth. "This letter serves as notice to you that any further disturbances caused by your dissemination of bad information will be dealt with by all legal means available to the district. While you may have your opinion about what could happen to our employees, your misstatement of the facts and blatant disregard for the truth will not be tolerated" (Paige, April 1, 1997).

On May 9, Fitzsimmons staged a protest in the atrium of the central administration building. All HISD food service employees were invited. Listed as hosts on the notice were board members Arthur Gaines, Carol Galloway, Esther Campos, and Olga Gallegos. Rod furiously responded with a flyer to all work locations. "No food service employee will be fired because of this contract," stated the flyer. "Food service workers will remain employees of the district, and their benefits will remain the same as for all other district employees. *Do not be misled by lies and misinformation from any labor organization. Your job is safe*" (emphasis in original).

Meanwhile another battle raged. Who would get the contract? It would be either Aramark or Marriott Management Services. Sometime in early June, the staff recommended Aramark. Aramark would bring in its own management team, but food service workers would continue to be employees of the district, and reductions in force would be made only through attrition or retirement. The contract would pay Aramark $2 million per year and guarantee HISD improvements in quality and participation. Again, Rod did not call it "outsourcing." It was a partnership.

Marriott, which had been aggressively lobbying board members, turned up the pressure on the board. There was wonderful irony in its strategy. Earlier, both Aramark and Marriott had been asked if they would consider a split contract, giving each company about half of the schools. Aramark had responded whatever works best for HISD. Marriott had said absolutely not (Sturm, June 13, 1997). Now, with the contract going to Aramark, Marriott suddenly discovered compelling reasons why HISD should split the district and hire both companies (McKenzie, June 20, 1997; Werner, July 2, 1997).

Both Aramark and Marriott had committed to meet HISD's minority participation guidelines, but Marriott had brought in as a partner a prominent African American restaurateur and obtained the support of many influential black Houstonians. Rod was practically being threatened. The three black trustees, I was told, were being pushed very hard. Clyde Lemon appeared to be the swing vote. My own conversations with Clyde were not encouraging, but the day before the meeting, Rod told me that both Clyde and Arthur would support his recommendation.

Suddenly at the board table, the majority for Aramark collapsed. Without any advance notice, before any significant discussion on the motion that had just been made in response to the superintendent's recommendation, Clyde moved an amendment to split the district and direct the superintendent to negotiate contracts with both Aramark and Marriott. There was no debate. The amendment passed five to four, with all five minority trustees in the majority.

I was stunned. The board was inserting politics into one of the largest contracts ever made by the district. Paula was outraged. "What are you doing," she almost shouted, glaring at the five yes votes. "We just recently voted a policy to ban micromanagement. We can't tell the superintendent that he has to do business with a specific company!"

Ron Franklin was trying to catch my eye. "Recess," he said. "Recess the meeting" (HISD, July 17, 1997).

We recessed for nearly an hour. Out in the gallery a very large crowd, including the Aramark and Marriott people, emitted a low roar and moved in random patterns like people at a cocktail party. Back in the board services office suite and in the small offices of board members, Laurie Bricker, Ron, and then Rod hammered away at Clyde. Brutal might be an understatement.

Back at the board table, Clyde moved to reconsider his amendment, then withdrew it, and then abstained as the original motion to award the contract to Aramark passed. Voting yes were Arnold, Bricker, Franklin, McAdams, and surprisingly Gaines. Voting no were Gallegos and Campos. Galloway had left.

Reengineering Human Resources Management. On September 18, the board gave final approval to a contract with IBM and other service providers to reengineer and manage HISD's human resources and payroll systems. HISD agreed to pay IBM and other vendors $15 million over two years. The projected net savings for the district over five years would be $20 to $25 million. The guaranteed minimum savings was $10 million. As part of the contract, IBM would reengineer HISD's computer software to solve the year 2000 problem, a project that would otherwise cost $4 to $6 million.

The contract with IBM was the (almost) last step in a long process to reorganize human resources management. It began with Paige's first PEER task force, personnel management, which reported in April 1995. The task force recommended that the district install a new human resources information system that could be fully integrated with the payroll process. This led to an assessment by Arthur Andersen of personnel and payroll information systems.

The Andersen report, presented to the board in June 1996, described a human resources department almost untouched by modern information technology. Record-keeping was fragmented. Employee data was kept in at least

40 different places, much of it on paper. Where computers were used, employees frequently had to print out data from one computer and then key it into another. In one year, the district spent $700,000 answering inquiries about its own data. The cost to cut a payroll check was several dollars more than that of the private sector, and HISD cut over 28,000 checks a month. Andersen recommended that HISD outsource payroll and as much as possible of the human resources department.

The Andersen report came one month after the bond election failed and four months before the Sharp report. For a week or so there was a lot of talk about privatization. Gayle Fallon was adamantly opposed. The *Chronicle* editorialized that the board should not wait for John Sharp. Jobs were a secondary issue. If privatization could do the work cheaper and better, it should be done (June 16, 1996, p. C2). Nothing happened. A few months later, Sharp recommended that HISD implement the Andersen recommendations.

The contract negotiations with IBM were complicated and prolonged. The deal with IBM was not finalized until just a few days before the September 18 board meeting.

The contract with IBM marked the end of an extraordinary year of nuts-and-bolts school reform. Collectively, and over time, the impact of these policy changes and contracts would have an enormous impact on the people of HISD. The driving force behind all these changes had not been the board of education. It had been Rod Paige.

A NEW BEGINNING FOR HISD

The last battle of 1997 was over the budget. By making hard choices, and with some good news from the Harris County Appraisal District, Paige was able to recommend a 1997–1998 budget that provided a 5 percent across the board increase in teacher pay plus another 1 percent for performance pay without a tax increase. There was a furious battle with the HFT over the 5 percent increase (HFT wanted 10 percent) and performance pay. But the board was unmoved and the city did not seem to notice. The budget was approved on August 29.

In the days that followed, talk among HISD watchers shifted from school improvement and taxes to the upcoming board elections.[10] Indeed, some community leaders and parent activists had been talking about the 1997 board elections for over a year. For at least two years everyone had known that neither Paula, Ron, nor I planned on seeking a third term. Clyde and Laurie's terms also ended in 1997, and though both were seeking reelection, reelection was not certain. Paige was managing with a narrow, unstable majority on the board of education. Changing even one trustee changed the dynamics of the board. In 1998, the board reformers who had started and sustained the reform of HISD would be gone. Everyone knew an era in the history of HISD was coming to an end.

As Ron, Paula, Cathy, Rod, and I reflected on our work together since the battle for *Beliefs and Visions* in 1990, we had reason to be proud. We had not achieved what we had hoped. We had not turned the pyramid upside down. Too many of Houston's children were still not receiving the quality education they deserved. But we had made a start.

We had not always worked together. Paula had opposed the negative appraisal of Joan Raymond and the initial decision to hire Rod as superintendent, and she had voted against several of Rod's most important recommendations. Rod, Paula, and Cathy saw Frank's limitations before Ron and me, and early on Ron and I were the only enthusiasts for outsourcing. Over the years we had disagreed on a host of minor issues. We were all quite different.

Yet we shared core principles, trusted and believed in each other, and happily deferred leadership to one another. We started as strangers with a common goal, developed into an effective power bloc on the board, and became friends. We had set out to transform Houston's public schools. We had not. But we had at least started HISD down a new path.

Of course, we had not done it by ourselves. Most of our policy initiatives were supported by other board members. We could never have deposed Joan Raymond without Felix Fraga and Wiley Henry. We could never have hired Rod Paige without Arthur Gaines. Clyde Lemon, following his election in 1995, was the key fifth (though sometimes it appeared reluctant) vote that enabled Rod to move forward with his reform agenda. And Laurie Bricker was as strong for the principles of *Beliefs and Visions* as Rod himself.

There were also scores of business and community leaders, parent activists, and district personnel who made critical contributions to the improvements in HISD: the members of the Coalition for Educational Excellence, the Hook committee, the decentralization commission, more than a dozen PEER committees, business leaders and business partners, Parents for Public Schools, thousands of parent and community volunteers, Paige's senior staff, thousands of HISD principals and teachers, John Sharp, and even John Whitmire. HISD was improving because the leadership of Houston and a great many parents and voters demanded that it improve and because district employees were able and willing to make it happen.

Finally, without the permission (and sometimes prodding) of the Texas legislature, many of our reform policies would not have been possible. We were fortunate to serve Houston at the same time that educational reformers like Senator Bill Ratliff (R-Mt. Pleasant) and a host of others were serving all of Texas.

Nevertheless, the leadership of the reformers on the board had been decisive. And this leadership was about to change. The upcoming board elections would fundamentally change the board. If Paige lost his slim majority, the further reform of HISD would probably come to an end and much of what we had accomplished would be at risk. Even if the voters elected strong, reform-minded trustees, the old *Beliefs and Visions* board would be history. Nineteen ninety-eight would be a new beginning for HISD.

In July, I decided to seek a third term on the board. The decision surprised me almost as much as it surprised others. For four years I had known I would not run again. Board service was not good for my family life or my business. I did not want to go through another election. And the endless controversies had left me tired and much too cynical. Eight years was enough. But in the end, the entreaties of Rod and others convinced me that I was needed. Perhaps as a link to the board of *Beliefs and Visions,* I could help the new board find its voice and continue the journey Cathy, Rod, Ron, Paula, and I had begun in 1990.

But even if I were reelected, my life in 1998 would be part of another story. The board elections of 1997 and the other events of autumn belonged to the future. The voters of Houston would decide what that future would be.

NOTES

1. In December, Paige hired a media consultant, Terry Abbott. In March, Abbott was appointed press secretary with a salary over $110,000 per year. Board members had been pushing for years for a professional to handle media relations. Most of us recognized that HISD was, in effect, in a continuous political campaign and that only a media professional with political experience had the expertise we needed. We also recognized that to hire a press secretary with political experience, HISD would have to pay $100,000 per year or more. Both Petruzielo and Paige had been unwilling to endure the criticism that would inevitably follow a decision to pay $100,000 per year to a press secretary, who HISD's critics would immediately dub a spinmeister. The defeat of the bonds and the Sharp audit convinced Paige that it had to be done. As expected, there was widespread criticism of Abbott's salary. But Abbott, who had been press secretary for former Alabama Governor Guy Hunt, was perfect for the job, and within months we could see that he was worth every dollar the district paid him. His work contributed in no small measure to the improvement of the district's image in the months that followed.

2. At 10:00 A.M. he held a major press conference at Mark Twain Elementary. At noon he addressed the Galleria Chamber of Commerce at the Hilton Hotel, Southwest. At 7:00 P.M. he met with parents at Will Rogers Elementary. To support his media blitz, Rod scheduled three additional evening meetings with parents at schools in different parts of the city and outlined his proposals in letters to community and parent leaders (Paige, October 18, 1996; Paige, October 21, 1996).

3. Gayle Fallon objected. She, who had previously charged that it was the board's involvement in personnel that caused patronage and corruption, now objected that taking the board out of the loop would lead to patronage and corruption (*Post,* June 10, 1993, p. A21; HISD, May 13, 1997, pp. 1–2).

4. The CEP program was built on a specially trained professional staff, a highly structured educational environment, individualized interactive computer instruction, and lots of tough love.

5. Specialized programs, such as magnet and Vanguard (gifted and talented) programs, would continue to maintain specific entry criteria.

6. The PEER Employee Hearing Procedures Task Force was chaired by Jeffrey A. Davis, an attorney with McGinnis, Lochridge & Kilgore, LLP.

7. The matter was later resolved on appeal.

8. The PEER Internal Affairs Task Force was chaired by Houston Police Department Assistant Chief for Special Investigations H. A. (Art) Contreras.

9. "HISD cannot quickly and effectively reengineer the food services program," said Rod. "Without outside support, we do not have the resources to effectively reorganize food services. And such a reorganization would detract from our primary mission of educating children" (HISD, February 5, 1997). This was the real issue with Rod. Even if HISD could manage food service as effectively and efficiently as a private company, which he doubted, Rod believed that managing noneducational business activities distracted HISD's top management from its core business—educating children.

10. Other important issues demanded the board's attention during 1997. In April, the district's guidelines for admission of students into magnet and gifted and talented programs—65 percent African American and Hispanic and 35 percent white and other—were challenged in federal court. But this issue and others really belonged to the future.

15

Lessons from Houston

What have I learned in eight years as a Houston school board member? What can elected officials, educators, business and community leaders, interested parents, and school reformers everywhere learn from the Houston experience? Obviously, the Houston story is unique. Time, place, circumstances, and individual actions shaped events.

But the issues and dynamics of school reform in Houston cannot be that dissimilar from the issues and dynamics in other American cities. Urban school reformers everywhere must deal with public opinion, the media, state education agencies, business interests, teacher unions, organized labor, political parties, taxpayer groups, neighborhood interests, discrimination and ethnic conflict, and the core educational issues of curriculum, teaching, learning, assessment, accountability, and management effectiveness. I believe urban school reformers everywhere can learn from the Houston experience.

First it is important to see the Houston experience in the context of school reform in America.

THREE WAVES OF SCHOOL REFORM

Americans have always been school reformers. On some core issues we have changed our minds again and again. Should teachers deliver knowledge or help students construct their own knowledge base? Should all students be taught a common core of academic subjects, or should they be allowed to take the academic and vocational courses that will keep them interested in school and help prepare them for the workplace? Should professional educators be given the freedom to manage schools as they think best, or should schools be placed under direct democratic control (Cuban, 1990)? These issues, debated for a hundred years or more, are part of the current debate about schools in America.

248

Standards

What is new in the debate is the recognition that in the high-technology global economy of today and tomorrow, the negative consequences of inadequate public schools are much greater than they used to be. This awareness sparked the publication of *A Nation at Risk* in 1983 and launched the so-called first wave of contemporary education reform.

The key to school improvement, said the first wave reformers—mostly business leaders, governors, and legislators—was standards. By the early 1990s the standards movement was having an impact on schools. The school calendar in most states was increased by three to five days, bringing most states up to the national standard of 180 days. High school graduation requirements across the country were strengthened. Most colleges and university admission standards were raised. Teacher salaries in almost every state increased at nearly twice the rate of inflation. Spending per pupil increased dramatically (Crosby, April 1993).

The first wave of school reform in Texas began in 1984 with House Bill 72. This bill, other legislation (there were 30 additional legislative initiatives between 1981 and 1991), and supporting state board of education rules, put into place scores of major reforms. Twelve curriculum areas and the essential elements related to these curriculum areas were established. Minimum competency tests for students and minimum requirements for high school graduation were implemented. Increased academic content for teacher certification was required, as were teacher competency tests (which nearly every teacher passed), a new instrument and process for teacher evaluation (the ineffective TTAS), and a professional career ladder (that ended up being totally ineffective). The reform that attracted the most public interest was *no pass, no play*, the controversial requirement that removed students who failed classes from extracurricular activities (Lyndon B. Johnson School of Public Affairs, 1993).

The Texas legislation of the 1980s set standards and mandated results. The reform initiatives were not a failure. Standards needed to be set. But the reforms were a disappointment to those who advocated them. School boards, superintendents, principals, and teachers were not stakeholders. A host of issues that affected student performance were not addressed. Local systems did not change.

Restructuring

By the end of the 1980s it was becoming apparent to state policy makers in Texas and throughout the nation that changing standards and mandating procedures and practices would not significantly improve student achievement.

A much more massive, systemwide effort was required. The first wave of school reform was giving way to a second wave: restructuring, alignment, or systemic reform.

Among the leading intellectual fathers of systemic reform were Ernest Boyer, John Goodlad, and Theodore Sizer. They, and many others, realized that to improve student achievement Americans would have to change their schools and the environment in which schools operated.

Systemic reform, said the second wave reformers, required changes in roles, rules, and relationships between and among students, teachers, and administrators at all levels, from the school building to the state level. The central elements of restructuring were: (1) decentralizing authority to the lowest appropriate level in the system, which meant school-based management; (2) shared decision-making at schools; (3) accountability for results, which meant clear goals and accurate and fair methods for measuring school performance; (4) curriculum alignment, which meant clarity on what students should know and be able to do linked to a curriculum, performance standards, and meaningful methods of assessment in every curriculum area; and (5) changes in instruction that were student-centered and enabled students to master higher-order thinking skills and construct knowledge.[1]

Competition

Since early 1990, a third wave of school reform has been building. The operative word is "competition." Reformers, mostly political conservatives, have decided that public schools are incapable of reforming themselves. Power must be taken from the public school establishment and placed elsewhere.

The theoretical foundation for this viewpoint was put forward by John Chubb and Terry Moe in 1990 in *Politics, Markets, and America's Schools,* one of the most influential books on school reform published since *A Nation at Risk.* The core issue, said Chubb and Moe, is direct democratic control. Public schools are public. This is their great strength and their great weakness. In a democracy, the people must directly or indirectly control their institutions. The military, the federal judiciary, and higher education are under indirect democratic control. Public schools are under direct democratic control.

This means that, mediated through the political process, society imposes its higher order moral values on public education. Public opinion, expressed by voters, filtered through state legislatures and boards of education, and interpreted and monitored by education bureaucrats, determines what happens in public schools.

The consequence is that, unlike private schools, public schools cannot focus on just satisfying parents and students. They must also satisfy the public. Schools must desegregate, provide multicultural awareness, teach children in

Spanish, meet ethnic guidelines for enrollment in gifted and talented programs, include children with learning or physical handicaps in regular classes,
teach sex education and AIDS awareness, forbid (in most states) corporal pun-
ishment, grant social promotions, keep all children in school regardless of
their behavior because putting them on the street is a worse alternative, and
so forth.

Making sure all these things happen requires administrators, implementation plans, teaching materials, training for principals and teachers, reports
to demonstrate compliance, program evaluations, and policies and procedures
to deal with noncompliance.

The negative consequences of direct democratic control are most pronounced in large urban school districts, say Chubb and Moe. Cities have a
disproportionate share of uninvolved parents and students who are difficult
to educate. Populations are ethnically and economically mixed. Tough environments and diverse populations lead to additional educational priorities
and conflicts over values. The result is more bureaucracy. All large urban
school districts, for example, have bilingual and affirmative action departments.[2]

Recognizing these realities, third-wave reformers argue that standards
and restructuring, while helpful, are not sufficient. Schools must be placed at
arm's length from direct democratic control. School boards should perhaps be
appointed rather than elected. All business and support functions should be
outsourced to private vendors. Charter and contract schools should be established as rapidly as possible. And children, at least those who are served by
low-performing schools, should be given vouchers so they can avoid the public schools entirely.

The third wave of educational reform is building, but it is too early to tell
if it will have significant impact on public education in America. The number
of charter schools is increasing rapidly, but it is not yet clear whether charter
schools will become a serious educational option for mainstream children or
remain a small side show serving primarily disadvantaged children (Vanourek
et al., 1997). Contracting out schools to private companies has been tried in
only a few cities, with mixed results. And there have been only limited, small-
scale experiments with school vouchers. The only trend that seems to be picking up speed is the abolition of elected school boards in major urban school
districts (Chicago, Cleveland, Boston, Baltimore, Washington, D.C., and most
recently Detroit).

Beliefs and Visions was approved by the HISD board in June 1990, just
as the second wave of school reform was reaching its crest. The reforms of
1991–1995—shared decision-making, school-based budgeting, accountability, and decentralization—were second-wave school reforms. Rod Paige's new
beginning for HISD was announced in late 1996, though it had been under

way for two years, and belongs to the third wave of school reform. We Houston school reformers were products of our time. The improvements we have made in Houston's public schools have been driven by standards, restructuring, and competition and are proof that all three waves of reform make essential contributions to improved public schools.

HOUSTON ACHIEVEMENTS

What has been achieved in Houston since 1990? A lot. Active shared decision-making committees at each school are now the rule, not the exception. At most schools they are meaningfully involved in developing school improvement plans and major campus decisions—budgets, schedules, uniforms, student discipline, and so on.

In 1990, Joan Raymond selected principals with input from her trusted advisers. As a courtesy, she informed trustees just days, sometimes hours, before presenting her recommendations to the board for approval. Sometimes upward of 25 principals were moved by one board action. School communities waited nervously to see who the superintendent had chosen as their leader. Political deals between the superintendent and board members were not uncommon.

Today most school communities, guided by a district superintendent, select, de facto, their own principals. The process is participative, open, and thorough. Board members are completely out of the loop. Selection decisions are better, for the most part. And school communities are now stakeholders in the success of new principals.

The HISD accountability system has had a huge impact on student achievement. In the years that followed its approval in 1993, behaviors changed. Principals, on whom the rewards and consequences fell most heavily, began demanding more control over their schools and better support from central office. All over the district, principals began adding more phonics to their instruction in reading, working on better curriculum alignment, examining student performance data student by student, and pushing to improve classroom instruction.

The impact of private-sector contracts for administrators has also been significant. Paige has exercised his option on a number of occasions to terminate principals and other administrators, including district superintendents, and the word from administrators is that the loss of job security has significantly sharpened their focus on student performance. New teacher contracts, teacher evaluations, and termination and grievance processes have also improved teacher accountability. Many of these changes have been made possible by changes in the Texas Education Code.

District decentralization has significantly shifted power away from central office, but real decentralization is still a dream. Some of the district offices have become little central offices instead of service centers for schools. And schools are still budgeted with staff positions, not dollars. The principal of a typical elementary school, with a total operating budget of nearly $2 million, usually controls less than $100,000. Also, because middle-class schools tend to attract and keep experienced teachers at or near the top of the salary schedule, and schools full of at-risk students are more likely to be staffed by young teachers at or near the bottom of the salary schedule, resource inequity still exists. Until schools are budgeted with dollars, based on weighted student enrollment, and given the freedom to configure their workforces as they wish, central office will rule.

Peer Examination, Evaluation, and Redesign task forces have made an enormous contribution to the improvement of HISD operations. PEER has also become the methodology of choice for addressing complex student services and instructional issues. PEER recommendations, the recommendations of Texas comptroller John Sharp, and the aggressive contracting out of most of HISD's major business functions have improved significantly the management of business operations and support services.

The bottom line for HISD is productivity: output divided by input. Productivity is difficult to measure, but consider HISD's key outputs (student performance, the drop-out rate, and school safety) and most easily measured input (money).

In Texas, the best measure of student performance is the Texas Assessment of Academic Skills.[3] Since 1994, the best baseline year for TAAS, state TAAS scores have improved, as one might expect. But HISD scores have improved even more (see Table 15.1). During this same period, the percentage

Table 15.1 Changes in HISD and State TAAS Percent Passing for Non-Special Education Students for All Tests Taken from Spring 1994 to Spring 1998

| | 1994 | | | 1998 | | | |
	HISD	State	HISD–State Gap	HISD	State	HISD–State Gap	Decrease in Gap
Grade 3	51	58	7	73	76	3	4
Grade 4	47	54	7	77	78	1	6
Grade 5	51	58	7	83	83	0	7
Grade 6	40	56	16	66	79	13	3
Grade 7	37	55	18	64	78	14	4
Grade 8	31	52	21	59	72	13	8
Grade 10	38	52	14	62	72	10	4

Source: Houston Independent School District (HISD) Research Office.

of Texas students eligible for free and reduced-price lunch increased from 45.1 to 48.4. The percentage of HISD students eligible for free and reduced-price lunch increased from 57.3 to 77.

These improvements in student performance have dramatically improved school accountability ratings. On the HISD accountability matrix, which measures schools against a fairly constant baseline, the number of exemplary schools has increased in five years from 10 to 84. The number of recognized schools has increased from 19 to 117. At the bottom of the matrix, the number of low-acceptable schools had decreased from 81 to 0. The number of low-performing schools has dropped from 68 to 2.[4]

HISD schools have also improved their ranking on the Texas Education Agency accountability rating system, which has increased performance standards since 1993 and measures subgroup performance as well as overall school performance. Since 1993, the number of exemplary schools has increased from 0 to 36. The number of low-performing schools has decreased from 55 to 8.[5] In 1998, HISD had a higher percentage of exemplary schools than any of the other six largest urban school districts in the state.[6]

Accurately determining the number of dropouts is difficult, and various ways are available to calculate drop-out rates, but by any measure, HISD has fewer dropouts. According to the Texas Education Agency, which calculates the drop-out rate by dividing the total number of annual dropouts by the cumulative enrollment for the year for students in the 7th through 12th grades, the HISD drop-out rate has declined from 10.4 percent in 1990 to 2.8 percent in 1997.

HISD schools are also safer than they were in 1990. School safety is hard to measure. HISD did not begin keeping uniform crime report data on police-related incidents until 1993–1994. And for the first three years, as principals—under a new Code of Student Conduct that required reports to local law enforcement—kept better data, the number of police-related incidents increased. But in 1996, Sharp's auditors, basing their opinion on focus groups, concluded that school safety and security had improved (Sharp, 1996, p. 632). And from 1995–1996 to 1997–1998 the number of incidents leading to arrest fell from 2,664 to 2,155 and the number of violent crimes—defined by the Federal Bureau of Investigation as rape, robbery, murder, or aggravated assault—fell 38 percent.

School finance is complex in Texas, as it is in most other states. But it is not misleading to note that HISD's tax rate, at $1.384 per hundred valuation, is the lowest among the 21 school districts in Harris County and 28 cents below the county average. HISD also has the lowest effective tax rate among the large urban school districts in Texas.[7] And weighted general fund spending per pupil per year in 1995–1996—$4,206—was third from the bottom among Harris County school districts and, when adjusted for inflation, less than in 1992–1993.

LESSONS FROM HOUSTON

Board and Superintendent Unity and Continuity

HISD is still a low-performing school district. But it has improved significantly in recent years. And it has managed reasonably well the monies entrusted to it by the taxpayers. The improvement of HISD is a success story that has in it lessons for the nation.

The first lesson is that urban school reform is not possible unless the superintendent and a majority of the board share a common vision and work together for an extended period of time. A unanimous board and complete agreement between board and superintendent is not possible and not necessary. But a working majority of the board must have a clear vision of what needs to be done and work closely with a like-minded superintendent for a few years before any significant improvements can be expected.

The reform leaders on the HISD board were never a bloc. We sometimes disagreed on major reform issues and frequently disagreed on minor issues. We were all different. But we shared core principles and a common vision for HISD. We did not always see eye to eye with our superintendent, even when our superintendent was Rod Paige. At one time or another, nearly every one of us had a vigorous disagreement with Paige. After becoming superintendent, Paige, as one might expect, changed. Superintendents naturally and appropriately see the world through different-colored glasses. Still, we always considered Paige one of us. We were on the same team. We trusted and believed in one another.

Superintendents Must Effect Change

The second lesson from Houston is that a board of education cannot reform an urban school district, probably not any school district. Boards can set forth a vision and mandate change. Only superintendents can effect change. Boards can create an environment in which reform can take place. Superintendents have to develop and implement the reform program. Boards need to put forward a clear vision of what they want and hire a superintendent who shares that vision (and has the leadership and management skills to make it so). Then they must stick with their superintendent through thick and thin and try to build public support for the reform program. All this is easily stated; it is not easily done.

Nontraditional Superintendents Are Best

A related third lesson is that nontraditional superintendents might be the most effective reformers. Paige was perfect for Houston. As dean of the school of education at Texas Southern University, he knew enough about public education not to be dependent on the bureaucracy. As a trustee, and in previous civic leadership roles, he had become acquainted with the centers of political power in Houston and earned the trust of Houston's business, political, and ethnic elites. And as a man with broad experience outside public education, Paige could think outside of the box.

School reform is political action and good management. A strong leader with broad experience, political and management skills, and enough knowledge of education to face confidently the bureaucracy of a big-city school system is more likely to be a reform leader than a traditional superintendent who has spent his or her entire professional life working within the system he or she is trying to reform. This certainly was the experience in Houston.

Minority Superintendents Are Preferred

The fourth lesson is that, with probably a few rare exceptions, only minority leaders can reform America's urban school districts. Urban schools are mostly minority schools. And race matters. Houston is a city where African Americans, Hispanics, Asians, and whites get along fairly well. But ethnic issues are always just below the surface. Sometimes they are right out on the table.

School reform is change, and many of the changes needed—higher academic standards, alternative schools, greater employee accountability, and outsourcing, for example—can be perceived as threats to minority self-esteem, minority jobs, and established centers of minority power. Only minority leaders have the credibility and trust to make tough decisions and lead minority communities through the uncertainties of change.

Most of the reform leaders on the HISD board were white. Without Paige, the board's voice would have been muted. And it would have been almost impossible for a white superintendent to implement Paige's new beginnings agenda for HISD. Only Paige could obtain support from a minority board—and from minority leaders throughout the city—for school choice, charter schools, contract placement of HISD students in private schools, new contracts and personnel management policies to significantly increase employee accountability, the virtual elimination of board influence in personnel appointments, the outsourcing of almost all major business functions, and numerous terminations and transfers of nonperforming minority administrators. One could not effectively play the race card against Paige.

Education Administrators Are Essential

The fifth lesson from Houston is that school district administrators and building principals are the people who develop reform policies, put them into practice, and make them work. Paige's accomplishments are the accomplishments of a team of hard-working central office administrators, district superintendents, and a large number of principals, mostly the same people who worked for Joan Raymond and Frank Petruzielo. What made the difference? Leadership.

Educrats, as they are sometimes derisively called, are people with jobs. Like most people with jobs, they want to keep them. Without strong leadership, they can be part of the problem. But without them, there can be no solutions. Outside consultants are useful, sometimes necessary, but district and school administrators are the only ones who know how the current systems work. They are the only ones who can design and operationalize new systems. HISD has been blessed with an extraordinarily talented and hardworking group of senior administrators.

Results, Not Methods

A sixth lesson is that the focus of school reform should be on results, not methods. The board reformers in Houston wisely focused on standards, accountability, management systems, personnel management policies, and operational effectiveness.

School reform works best when policy makers give educators clear objectives and an environment in which objectives can be reasonably achieved. Then policy makers can and must hold educators accountable for results. Most of the educators I have worked with in Houston are competent. Many are as competent as the best leaders and managers I have worked with in the private sector in the last 10 years as a quality management consultant. Given clear objectives, workable systems, and accountability, they can solve complex teaching and learning issues and obtain acceptable results. Policy makers who tell educators how to get results are as likely to be wrong as right, and by prescribing methods they inescapably transfer responsibility for results from educators to themselves.

High Expectations for All Students

A related seventh lesson is that school trustees must not accept low levels of performance from poor children. Educators repeat often the phrase "all children can learn" and then turn around and expect less from poor children. I have heard more than one policy maker say that it is not fair to compare the performance of poor (usually minority) children with middle-class (frequently white) children. The national data are consistent, poor children do not perform as well as middle-class children. But if we don't expect them to, they probably never will.

In Houston, the board of education takes the position that poor children can and will perform as well as middle-class children. We make no excuses for schools serving poor communities. We expect principals and teachers in these schools to develop teaching methods that meet the learning needs of poor children, and we hold them accountable for the performance of their students. The results confirm our expectations. In Houston, we have dozens of exemplary schools that are filled with poor children. The gap between white and minority children on the criterion-referenced TAAS is closing. We also expect to close the gap between poor and middle-class students on the norm-referenced Stanford 9.

No Partisan Politics Allowed

The eighth lesson from Houston is that partisan politics must be kept out of the board room. The reform principles that work are mostly commonly accepted management principles and an appreciation of the power of market forces. In Houston, Republicans (Rod Paige and I and later Clyde Lemon and Laurie Bricker) and Democrats (everyone else) worked together without regard for party affiliation. We were able to do this because none of us pressed or defended a partisan agenda. All of us tried to focus on teaching, learning, and effective use of the taxpayers' money.

Business Leaders Must Be Involved

The ninth lesson is that business leaders play a critically important role in urban school reform. Houston has a large cadre of powerful, active business leaders who have been tireless advocates for school reform. Business leaders provided most of the expertise on the PEER task forces. Business leaders were directly involved in the decentralization initiative. They have been helpful advancing HISD's legislative agenda with the Texas legislature. They have supported HISD's bond issues. And on a host of important policy issues, they have kept HISD's feet to the fire.

In addition, thousands of business volunteers have been active in schools. Currently, HISD has 395 business-school partnerships. In 1996–1997, business and community partnerships contributed $6.7 million and provided another $12.6 million of in-kind volunteer hours. Business volunteers have made a significant difference in many schools. Some of the business interventions have been extensive and sustained and have had enormous, positive impact on entire feeder systems.

Perhaps most critically, business leaders have been active in school board elections. For all the good business can do in individual schools, for all the advice business leaders can offer superintendents, only school boards and superintendents can reform school districts. Business leaders can most effectively reform urban schools by using their money and influence to elect reform candidates to boards of education. Houston's business leaders understand this and have significantly influenced the reform of public schools by supporting candidates committed to reform. Their influence is limited. They cannot guarantee victory to anyone. But they can tilt a close race. Business support was significant in the elections of what became the *Beliefs and Visions* board in 1989, and business support made Lemon's election possible, without which most of the reforms of 1996–1997 would probably not have happened.

State Reform Important

The 10th lesson from Houston is that urban school reformers need help from the state. The 1990s have been a good decade for school reform in Texas. The Texas Legislature mandated shared decision-making in 1991, called for accountability in 1993, and gave school districts significantly greater opportunities to innovate along with significantly more accountability for results in 1995. HISD has usually been ahead of the Texas legislature, but without doubt state reform has made possible and reinforced many of the reform actions of the HISD board.

CHILDREN COME IN LAST

Special Interests

There is one more lesson from Houston. It is the thesis of this book. The core issue in urban school reform is governance, the place where special interest politics intersects with direct democratic control. I became an HISD trustee in 1990 convinced that public schools, especially urban schools, were failing. The reasons were low standards in schools of education, inadequate teachers, entrenched state education bureaucrats, and superintendents and principals who did not know how to manage. Of course, like most people, I had no inside knowledge of urban school systems, and I had not read the literature on school reform.

My views have changed. Public schools, at least Houston's public schools, are better than I realized. Some are among the world's best. And educators deserve more praise than blame for the condition of America's public schools.

Of course school people are part of the problem. There are many turf-protecting bureaucrats. Teacher union leaders focus on higher salaries, job security, and nonthreatening work environments for their members, not the needs of children. And superintendents usually want control and career advancement.

But school people, I have discovered, are no different from the other special interests that have a stake in public education. Ideologues of the left and right want the school district to advance their agenda. Ethnic leaders want to advance the interests of their ethnic group. Vendors want contracts. Homeowners want school attendance boundaries that will protect or enhance their property values. Some parents press personal agendas ahead of school agendas. Most taxpayers want low property taxes. And trustees want to get reelected.

Of course, while pursuing their personal interests, everyone proclaims that they want what is best for children. They do. It is just that there is something else they want even more.

Direct Democratic Control

Many urban schools are failing, but it is not because educators have failed. And it is not because special interests have pressed aggressively their agendas on boards of education. It is not even because urban environments are problematic for children and schools. Educators have failed where boards of education have allowed them to fail. Special interests have prevailed over the common good where boards of education have not had the integrity to resist them. Urban environments are problematic, but where boards have demanded that educators develop methods to meet the needs of urban children, they have done so.

No, the root cause of failing urban schools is direct democratic control. Chubb and Moe are right. Schools are in the middle of the political arena. Children and schools are important to everyone who wants to change or protect the cultural, political, or economic status quo. Schools are where all the ills and divisions of American society are put under a looking glass. Schools are where many of the racial issues that divide America are most sharply focused. Schools are big business. Schools cost the taxpayers a lot of money. And school people, like all people, have personal and group interests that powerfully influence behavior.

Trying to mediate all these pressures, at least in Houston, is an elected board of education comprised of trustees representing single-member districts that in almost every case are safe African American, Hispanic, or white seats. Trustees have a political incentive to champion ethnic interests and avoid conflict with ethnic or racial extremists. They have a strong incentive to provide jobs and contracts for political friends to build support for reelection or election to higher political office. And like elected officials at higher levels of government, they have a strong incentive to bring home the pork.

Because voter turnout is frequently low at board elections, and because employees and their families nearly always vote, trustees pay very close attention to the wishes of employee groups. And since organized labor can deliver a significant number of volunteers and votes in the predominantly African American and Hispanic districts, minority trustees take very seriously the demands of the Houston Federation of Teachers, which delivers the support of the AFL-CIO to candidates it supports.

So is the problem the board of education? Not really. Board members are human, too, frequently all too human. The root cause of the problem is direct democracy and an apathetic citizenry which has to a significant degree abandoned the field to special interests. The majority of citizens do not vote. The small minority who do, for the most part, have a very limited understanding of the realities of urban education.

Most voters have little contact with schools and have not been served well by the media. Most of what they know they see on the evening news or read in the morning paper. What they see is controversy and, from time to time, mismanagement and scandal. The television stations and newspapers, which like to position themselves as the fourth branch of government and the guardians of liberty, are for-profit companies with their eyes on the bottom line. They believe in an informed citizenry, but they are also trying to attract viewers and sell newspapers. Controversy and scandal sell. School reform is boring.

This is the core issue. The media are giving the public what the public wants. With one or two exceptions, the media people I have come to know in Houston are well-informed, honorable people. The larger question is, why are most Americans so uninterested in real news about schools, or for that matter anything else? Why are citizens in a free society so unwilling to inform themselves about their own institutions and act in the best interests of these institutions? School reform is really only a part of a larger reform of society and politics that is needed in America.

Society gets more complex by the year, and government, which reaches inexorably deeper and deeper into the lives of Americans, gets more complex times two. Could any of our founding fathers, who in a far simpler age built a great deal of indirect democratic control into our constitution, have imagined how much time it would take citizens 200 years later to become informed on all the public policy issues that require attention by their elected representatives?

Public policy has become too complex for average citizens, most of whom have decided that voting is more trouble than it is worth. And those who vote act more and more as members of special interest groups rather than citizens responsible for the common good. Accordingly, elected officials cater to voting blocs and cultivate those with money so they can buy the sound bites on television to sway the uninformed. Is it any wonder that partisanship prevails and money talks? Is it any wonder that in urban America, all too often, children come in last?

We can blame educators or special interest groups for the problems in our schools. We can blame the system. We should blame ourselves. Diane Ravitch said it well when she titled her 1985 collection of essays on the educational crisis of our time *The Schools We Deserve.*

WHAT IS TO BE DONE?

Only an informed, participative citizenry can keep special interests in check and focus public institutions on the public good. Only high turnout elections of well-informed voters can guarantee the long-term welfare of America's schools. This state of affairs is not soon to be expected. Maybe it never existed and never will.

Maybe democracy works best when, as our founding fathers realized, it is balanced and checked and frequently indirect. Maybe urban schools, like other important public institutions, should not be under direct democratic control. One thing is certain, school reformers must design systems of governance that get politics out of the schools.

This is my final lesson from Houston. Urban schools must be placed at arm's length from direct democratic control. This is not a conclusion I have reached easily. Ultimately in a democracy, the people must rule. But must they rule directly? Some institutions—the military, the federal judiciary, the Federal Reserve Board, and public higher education, to name a few—serve the public better when they are buffered from direct democratic control. Urban schools, I believe, would also serve the public more effectively if they were taken out of the middle of the political arena.

So my prescription for school reform in urban America is fairly straightforward. All three waves of school reform since 1983 have contributed to the improvement of public education. Standards are essential. Restructuring is necessary. But only fundamental changes in governance can transform the nation's urban school systems.

Since we cannot change society we must change boards. Strong principals, involved communities, and business partners can improve individual schools, at least for the period of their involvement. But throughout urban America, if school systems improve, it will be because boards (and the superintendents they hire) make them improve. No one else can.

In Houston, a city with remarkable civic, business, and ethnic leadership, I believe all that is required is the election of at-large trustees. In Houston, even under the present governance structure, we have made significant improvements in our public schools. But reform has come slowly, victories have been won narrowly, all that has been gained is continuously at risk, and there is a great deal more to be done. Every two years, four or five trustees are elected. There is no assurance that the reform of Houston's public schools will continue.

In some cities appointed boards are probably needed. Where this has been tried in recent years the quality of board members appears to be high and improvements have been forthcoming.

Each city (and state) must decide for itself what will work best. But the objective in every case should be to get politics out of the schools. The ways to do this are obvious. Unless there are compelling reasons not to, all business and support functions should be outsourced to private vendors. The superintendent should have full and final authority for personnel appointments and the recommendation of contracts for goods and services to the board of education. The board should grant as many charters as possible and, wherever possible, contract with a variety of public and private agencies to manage schools. Also, a variety of innovative private school choice programs should be implemented to meet the immediate needs of children not being adequately served by the public schools. All these policies have the same effect: they insulate the education of children from direct democratic control.

A FINAL NOTE ON HOUSTON

One of the most intriguing recommendations in the literature on school reform, and one that I hope will be adopted in Houston, is the recommendation of Paul T. Hill (1995) that urban boards be transformed into contracting agencies. Hill suggests that public education is a concept, not necessarily an institution. School boards do not have to operate schools. They can contract with a variety of public and private organizations to manage schools.

In Hill's model, each school would have a school-specific contract with the board of education that defined its mission, guaranteed public funding, ensured accountability, and maintained public confidence. School boards would no longer make policies that constrained all schools. Rather, through school contracts, they would make educational decisions on a school-by-school basis. School boards would still retain ultimate responsibility for school quality. They could intervene, per contract terms, if necessary replace contractors that failed to deliver, and raise standards for renewed contracts as schools improved.

Hill's model would turn central office into a small group of financial professionals, contract negotiators, educational assessors, auditors, attorneys, grant writers, data collectors, research analysts, facilities and transportation experts, and so forth.

Obviously, there would be hundreds of details to work through, especially in the area of personnel management. And the devil is always in the details. For example, if teachers had contracts with schools rather than the school district, what role would the district have for recruitment, vetting, facilitating transfers, providing legal services, and so forth. And would all schools be required to conform to a districtwide salary schedule? Implementing Hill's model would be a challenge, but it could be done. And it would decisively place schools at arm's length from direct democratic control.

My goal for my third term as an HISD trustee is to implement a version of Hill's model in Houston. I want every HISD school to be, in effect, a charter school. A paradigm shift of this magnitude, I am confident, will transform nearly every one of Houston's public schools into a center of excellence. And there will be no turning back. Once school communities taste independence and the accountability for results that goes with it, they will never give it up.

NOTES

1. The literature on restructuring is extensive. I am following Lorraine M. McDonnell, Senior Political Scientist, The RAND Corporation, *Restructuring American Schools: The Promise and the Pitfalls* (1989), which includes an excellent bibliography; and Marshall Sashkin and John Egermeier, *School Change Models and Processes: A Review and Synthesis of Research and Practice* (1993), which also includes an excellent and extensive bibliography on restructuring. The most provocative book on restructuring is, in my opinion, Richard F. Elmore and Associates, *Restructuring Schools: The Next Generation of Educational Reform* (1991).

2. In suburban and small-town school districts, say Chubb and Moe, the problems of direct democratic control are less pronounced. Sometimes they are almost nonexistent. School districts are smaller. Communities are more homogenous. And there is broad community agreement on values. Principals and teachers, who spring directly from the community, can be trusted to impose the communities values on the schools. A large educational bureaucracy is not needed. Free from external controls, schools are free to focus on meeting parent and student requirements.

3. The Stanford 9 and Aprenda 2 were given for the first time in September 1997. The results, which will become baseline scores for HISD, were better than expected. Almost 134,000 students in grades 1 through 11 took the Stanford 9. More than 20,000 Spanish-speaking students took the Aprenda 2. Most percentile scores for most grades were in the high 30s or low 40s. The 11th grade percentiles on the Stanford 9 were reading, 42; math, 44; language subtest, 46.

4. Both low-performing schools are new, alternative schools.

5. Four of the eight are new, alternative schools.

6. Houston, 12.2 percent; Dallas, 2.8 percent; Ft. Worth, 5.1 percent; Austin, 8.5 percent; San Antonio, 2.1 percent; El Paso, 5 percent.

7. These numbers are for 1997–1998. In July 1998, the Board of Education approved a $.075 property tax increase per hundred valuation for 1998–1999, bringing the tax rate to $1.459.

Epilogue

The 1997 board elections returned Laurie Bricker, me, and three new trustees to the board of education. The new board appeared to have a five- or even six-vote majority intent on turning back the clock on some of the key reforms of 1997. For a few months in early 1998, it seemed that the reform of HISD had come to an end.

The old *Beliefs and Visions* trustees had *powered down* the board—that was the phrase the new majority used. Superintendent Paige was too powerful. The board had become a rubber stamp. It was time to reassert the board's authority over major personnel decisions. Other policy reversals would follow. Paige was quietly talking about leaving the superintendency.

But on March 19, after a furious behind-the-scenes battle for votes, the move to reassert the board's control of major personnel decisions was defeated at the board table by 5–4. Within a month, a reform majority was once again effectively controlling the board.

The key fifth vote for Paige on March 19 was Arthur Gaines. "King Arthur," who had caused Rod so much trouble in 1995 and opposed many of the key reforms of 1997, was now courtly; senior statesman Arthur Gaines; close friend of Rod Paige; and enthusiastic supporter of high standards, accountability, and business efficiency.

Arthur seemed to grow stronger in reform with each passing month. With his support, new reform proposals were welcome. Rod's agenda was assured. Five certain votes for reform frequently became seven, eight, or even nine votes at the board table.

Talk of turning back the clock disappeared. HISD's senior administrators breathed a sigh of relief and refocused their attention on improving the district. All three new trustees began to emerge as strong reform leaders for the future. The city celebrated the unity of the board. The reform of HISD was back on track. It continues to this day.

Three major reform policies were approved in 1998: a comprehensive no-social-promotion policy, a revision of the HISD accountability system, and an expansion of HISD's modified voucher program. The first has generated enormous activity to identify and assist children who are not mastering grade-level reading and math skills. The second has significantly increased the number of special education and limited-English-proficient students taking the TAAS reading, writing, and math tests. The third opens up to failing students in failing schools the opportunity to attend a private school at HISD's expense.[1]

In August 1998, the board approved a tax increase of 7.5 cents per hundred valuation, the first tax increase since Frank Petruzielo's famous 32 percent tax increase in 1992. The business community and the *Houston Chronicle* were supportive. There was hardly a peep of opposition.

In November 1998, the voters of Houston approved a $678 million bond issue for high-priority repairs in 69 schools and the construction of 10 new schools. Approved along with the bonds was a property tax increase, to be phased in over three years, of 4.92 cents per hundred valuation.

The business community enthusiastically supported the bonds and provided ample money to fund the election. The *Houston Chronicle* and nearly every center of power in the city, even the leadership of the Harris County Republican Party, supported the bonds. The yes vote was 73 percent!

So far 1999 has been another great year for school reform. On June 17, a PEER task force appointed by Paige in late 1998 recommended to the board that over the next three years HISD move from allocating staff positions to schools to direct funding of schools with dollars based on average daily attendance of weighted students. Principals, within appropriate guidelines, will have the freedom to configure their own workforces, pay actual labor costs, and buy services from the central office or elsewhere. They will also carry over operating deficits or surpluses from one year to the next.

The task force was chaired by old friend Al Haines, who as president of the Chamber of Commerce Division of the Greater Houston Partnership, chaired the decentralization task force in 1994. He is now chief administrative officer for Houston Mayor Lee Brown. Strongly supporting Al on the task force were other old friends from the business community—Harold Hook, now retired from the chairmanship of American General; and consultant Darv Winick, still active as the best connected business-education guru in Texas.

Providing professional staff support of the highest quality to the task force, and indeed subtly guiding the task force to the recommendations Paige wanted, was Robert Stockwell, Paige's link to the decentralization task force in 1994, PEER coordinator, and now an indispensable internal change agent for Rod.

The board unanimously adopted the task force recommendations, and Paige and his staff are now putting into place a structure and process for comprehensive implementation. The devil, of course, is in the details. The transition will be difficult. But if HISD can do it right, Houston's public schools will at last have the control over personnel and budgets that they were promised in *Beliefs and Visions*.

On June 17, the board also approved broadening eligibility for HISD's modified voucher program. Now students who fail to meet promotion standards will have the opportunity to attend a private school at HISD's expense.[1]

On July 22, after a month of intense negotiations and a great amount of public controversy, the board approved a new policy on multilingual education. The new policy requires children with limited English proficiency to "learn to read, write, and speak English as quickly as individually possible without sacrificing long-term academic success." English reading proficiency is the standard for transition to academic instruction in English, and once the transition has been made, all academic instruction will be in English.

The policy also commits HISD to encourage mastery of a second language by all students by providing students whose first language is not English the opportunity to continue language study in their first language through high school. English speakers will be given the opportunity to study a second language, starting in the elementary grades.

The reforms of 1998 and 1999 would not have been possible without the leadership of the three new trustees elected in 1997: Lawrence Marshall, Jeff Shadwick, and Gabriel Vasquez.

Marshall, an African American, is a retired HISD deputy superintendent. He knows education and business, embraces radical reform with enthusiasm, and is the most fiercely principled man I have ever known. I think he is a Democrat, but if he is he is certainly an independent one.

Shadwick, white, is a young attorney specializing in business bankruptcy. He is an active, conservative Republican, with a quick mind, a great sense of humor, and remarkable social skills. His pragmatic, flexible style has pleasantly surprised those who feared he would push a partisan agenda on the district.

Vasquez, a Hispanic, is an assistant professor of communication at the University of Houston. He is an active Democrat who is currently running for a seat on the Houston City Council and who most civic leaders believe has a great political future. He has embraced Paige's reform agenda and shown tremendous courage—and taken enormous political heat—by joining with Shadwick to write the new HISD multilingual policy.

As it turned out, the voters of Houston made excellent choices when they selected three new HISD trustees in 1997. It is now August 1999. In three months they will have an opportunity to vote again for four HISD trustees. The future of Houston's public schools and the children they serve continues to be in the hands of the people.

NOTE

1. HISD's expanded modified voucher program has, as of yet, resulted in no new contracts with private schools.

A Note on Sources

With only a few exceptions, the sources used in the preparation of this book are public. They are not, however, readily accessible.

The Houston Independent School District does not have an archive, nor does it practice effective records management. Board of Education agenda items, board meeting minutes, and other documents relating to the board of education are archived in the board services department. Important data is preserved by the finance office, human resources department, student transcript office, and research office, but copies of important reports, letters, and other documents are kept in the offices where they originate, and files are purged frequently.

Statistical and student performance information about HISD and HISD schools can be found on the HISD website, www.houstonisd.org.

Two major newspapers served Houston during the period of this book, The *Houston Chronicle* and *The Houston Post*. The *Post* was last published on April 18, 1996. It was purchased by the *Chronicle* and shut down immediately. The *Chronicle* maintains files for both newspapers, which can be searched on the *Chronicle*'s website, www.houstonchronicle.com.

This book is based primarily on HISD documents, public and personal letters, board minutes, newspaper articles, and my personal calendar. My complete file of sources is on permanent loan to HISD and stored in the board services archive.

I have given the dates and pages for board minutes. However, board minutes are sometimes summaries, not verbatim transcripts. Quotations from board minutes are sometimes taken directly from the tapes.

References

Alvarado, Carol. (1997, March 21). Letter to HISD trustees.

Arnold, Paula. (1996, April 23). Letter to HISD trustees.

Berryhill, Michael. (1995, August 31–September 6). Gayle Force. *Houston Press*. pp. 10–18.

Blake, Dayle. (1996, November 20). Memorandum to Willie Alexander et al.

Caldwell, Kirbyjon and others. (1993, October 5). Letter to HISD board members.

Chubb, John E. and Terry M. Moe. (1990). *Politics, Markets, and America's Schools*. Washington, DC: The Brookings Institution.

Crosby, Emeral A. (1993, April). The "At-Risk" Decade. *Phi Delta Kappan, 74*. pp. 598–604.

Cuban, Larry. (1990). Reforming Again, Again, and Again. *Education Researcher, 19 (1)*. pp. 3–13.

Curtis, Gregory. (1996, September). Charles Miller. *Texas Monthly, 24(9)*. p. 107.

Dewey v. Paige. No. 95–057397. (190th Dist. Ct. of Harris County, TX, 1995, November 22). Oral Deposition of Gayle Fallon.

Edmonds, Jim. (1995, October 3). Memorandum to HISD study group.

Educational Economic Policy Center State of Texas. (1993, January). *A New Accountability System for Texas Public Schools* (3 Vols.). Austin, Texas.

Elmore, Richard F. and Associates. (1991). *Restructuring Schools: The Next Generation of Educational Reform*. San Francisco: Jossey-Bass.

Fallon, Gayle. (1993, March 8). Letter to Don McAdams.

Fallon, Gayle. (1993, March 9). Letter to Harris County delegation to the Texas Legislature.

Fallon, Gayle. (1993, June 17). Letter to Don McAdams.

Fallon, Gayle. (1993, November 6). Letter to Frank Petruzielo.

Fallon, Gayle. (1995, July 5). Letter to HISD trustees.

Fallon, Gayle. (1996, October 1). Letter to HISD trustees.

Federation Teacher. (1995, September). Thank you, King Arthur (Gaines)! p. 1.

Fleck, Tim. (1995, November 2–8). The Insider. *Houston Press*. p. 8.

Fleck, Tim. (1997, August 21–27). What Went Wrong at the Rice School? *Houston Press*. pp. 15–21.

Graham, H. Devon Jr. (1996, May 21). Letter to James Masucci.

Haines, Al. (1994, October 26 and 27). Letters to Al Gonzales.

Haynes & Boone. (1994, July 29). *Report of Investigation, Houston Independent School District Bilingual Alternative Certification Program.*

Hill, Paul T. (1995). *Reinventing Public Education.* Santa Monica, CA: Rand.

Hispanic Education Committee v. HISD. (S. D. Tx. 1994, December 27). Final Judgment.

Hook, Harold. (1993, June 17). Letter to Don McAdams.

Hook, Harold. (1994, January 19). Letter to Don McAdams.

Houston Chronicle. (1990, November 15). HISD's mess. p. A36.

Houston Chronicle. (1990, November 28). Time to move on. p. A18.

Houston Chronicle. (1991, April 15). Cheating claim wounds school's pride. p. A1.

Houston Chronicle. (1991, April 16). Apology owed. p. A12.

Houston Chronicle. (1992, June 18). State lawmakers wrangle over planned HISD tax hike. p. A30.

Houston Chronicle. (1992, June 19). HISD tax hike. p. C14.

Houston Chronicle. (1992, June 21). Houstonians should accept tax increase for schools. p. E1.

Houston Chronicle. (1992, July 3). Ire against HISD at fever pitch. p. A1.

Houston Chronicle. (1992, July 5). HISD's bid for 47% tax hike is incredible. p. E1.

Houston Chronicle. (1992, July 5). Asking too much. p. E2.

Houston Chronicle. (1992, July 10). Avoidable mistake. p. A28.

Houston Chronicle. (1992, July 10). HISD likely to request Petruzielo trim budget. p. A1.

Houston Chronicle. (1992, July 12). Should HISD get its 47 percent tax increase? p. G1.

Houston Chronicle. (1992, July 15). HISD board will not back Petruzielo's tax hike. p. A1.

Houston Chronicle. (1992, July 17). Trustees turn down 47% HISD tax hike. p. A1.

Houston Chronicle. (1992, July 19). Tax hike a lesson in politics Petruzielo failed. p. D1.

Houston Chronicle. (1992, August 12). Railroad job. p. A20.

Houston Chronicle. (1992, August 26). Petruzielo's third budget well-received by trustees. p. A1.

Houston Chronicle. (1992, August 27). Poorly done. p. B18.

Houston Chronicle. (1993, June 8). Rusk school restaffing can happen elsewhere. p. A13.

Houston Chronicle. (1993, October 8). Accountability plan for Houston schools approved by trustees. p. A26.

Houston Chronicle. (1993, October 12). Rare praise for HISD's accountability plan. p. A17.

Houston Chronicle. (1994, January 22). Hispanics to protest appointment of Paige. p. A1.

Houston Chronicle. (1994, January 23). Changing HISD. p. E2.

Houston Chronicle. (1994, January 24). Hispanics seek new superintendent search. p. A9.

Houston Chronicle. (1994, January 26). Blacks split over furor concerning HISD's Paige. p. A17.

Houston Chronicle. (1994, January 27). Paige's decision to come today. p. A18.

Houston Chronicle. (1994, February 3). Committee chews out school board member. p. A19.

Houston Chronicle. (1994, February 19). HISD conduct in Paige hiring draws inquiry. p. A1.

Houston Chronicle. (1994, February 22). After latest maneuver, group says next move up to Paige. p. A13.

Houston Chronicle. (1994, February 23). Paige's first day on job. p. A17.

Houston Chronicle. (1994, April 1). Holmes sees no wrongdoing by HISD panel. p. A1.

Houston Chronicle. (1994, April 3). HISD hassle is a liability for governor. p. E2.

Houston Chronicle. (1994, April 5). Local NAACP gives Paige more support. p. A15.

Houston Chronicle. (1994, April 7). State won't intervene in Paige dispute. p. A1.

Houston Chronicle. (1994, April 8). Clergymen seek ouster of educator. p. A25.

Houston Chronicle. (1994, June 4). Political apathy hurts Hispanics. p. A29.

Houston Chronicle. (1994, July 24). HISD to ponder privatizing services. p. C1.

Houston Chronicle. (1994, August 27). HISD's lax standards scrutinized. p. A1.

Houston Chronicle. (1994, August 30). Groups fire "warning shot" at proposals to privatize. p. A9.

Houston Chronicle. (1994, August 31). HISD suspends two in continuing probe of stolen test copies. p. A24.

Houston Chronicle. (1994, November 11). HISD schools with low rating decline to 3 from 15 in one year. p. A34.

Houston Chronicle. (1994, December 22). Private sector-style contracts for HISD administrators Ok'd. p. A32.

Houston Chronicle. (1995, February 3). Paige ranks teacher raises as top priority. p. A29.

Houston Chronicle. (1995, February 7). New HISD board leader self-avowed traditionalist. p. A15.

Houston Chronicle. (1995, February 23). HISD begins budget debate, but tax hike seems unavoidable. p. A23.

Houston Chronicle. (1995, March 24). Trustees spar with senator. p. A35.

Houston Chronicle. (1995, April 5). Unions fighting HISD reorganization plans. p. A20.

Houston Chronicle. (1995, April 9). Not so elementary. p. O2.

Houston Chronicle. (1995, June 10). Legislature-ordered HISD audit is planned for March. p. A37.

Houston Chronicle. (1995, June 16). Proposal for dual campus in River Oaks is rejected. p. A33.

Houston Chronicle. (1995, June 24). Doing right at River Oaks Elementary. p. A36.

Houston Chronicle. (1995, July 13). Two HISD trustees say funds offered to alter vote. p. A1.

Houston Chronicle. (1995, July 14). Allegations by trustees to be probed. p. A1.

Houston Chronicle. (1995, July 15). HISD's special-ed lambasted. p. A30.

Houston Chronicle. (1995, July 21). District attorney's office closes HISD bribe probe. p. A1.

Houston Chronicle. (1995, August 22). More pay asked for HISD workers. p. A13.

Houston Chronicle. (1995, August 24). 11 teachers sue HISD over transfers. p. A37.

Houston Chronicle. (1995, September 10). Decentralizing. p. C2.

Houston Chronicle. (1995, September 18). HISD trustee delinquent in his taxes. p. A9.

Houston Chronicle. (1995, September 21). Clueless. p. A34.

Houston Chronicle. (1995, October 11). School board I. p. A26.

Houston Chronicle. (1995, October 15). School board II. p. C2.

Houston Chronicle. (1995, November 10). Cover-up attempt claimed: HISD's Jefferson accused by Franklin of offering a deal. p. A1.

Houston Chronicle. (1995, November 16). Concerns raised about contract. p. A29.

Houston Chronicle. (1996, March 20). Hispanic leaders press for big HISD bond issue. p. A24.

Houston Chronicle. (1996, March 22). Vote favors River Oaks residents. p. A1.

Houston Chronicle. (1996, April 7). HISD audit requires involved public. p. C5.

Houston Chronicle. (1996, April 17). Complaints and compliments. p. A27.

Houston Chronicle. (1996, April 18). Serious questions about HISD for city's Latinos. p. A35.

Houston Chronicle. (1996, April 20). HISD officials plan sites for early voting. p. A29.

Houston Chronicle. (1996, May 1). Note for school. p. Z14.

Houston Chronicle. (1996, May 7). County GOP won't take stand on HISD bond issue. p. A21.

Houston Chronicle. (1996, May 12). Has downsizing reached HISD? p. A31.

Houston Chronicle. (1996, May 19). HISD gets an F in bond vote test. p. A29.

Houston Chronicle. (1996, May 26). The no vote. p. A26.

Houston Chronicle. (1996, May 30). Outspent and outgunned, foes found way to prevail. p. A26.

Houston Chronicle. (1996, May 30). HISD looking at its options. p. A1.

Houston Chronicle. (1996, June 12). State to include facilities review in HISD audit. p. A33.

Houston Chronicle. (1996, June 16). School jobs. p. C2.

Houston Chronicle. (1996, June 19). Savoring victory. p. Z12–2.

Houston Chronicle. (1996, July 7). HISD redo. p. C2.

Houston Chronicle. (1996, July 23). Some stamp "voucher" on HISD plan. p. A1.

Houston Chronicle. (1996, July 25). Report: HISD suffers "serious image problem." p. A29.

Houston Chronicle. (1996, August 1). HISD chief's new budget expected to hold the line. p. A1.

Houston Chronicle. (1996, August 16). Funding dispute boils over in wake of school roof collapse. p. A41.

Houston Chronicle. (1996, August 16). $1.2 billion HISD budget includes teachers' raise. p. A1.

Houston Chronicle. (1996, August 19). HISD getting job done. p. A21.

Houston Chronicle. (1996, August 29). Meal study gives food for thought. p. A34.

Houston Chronicle. (1996, September 20). HISD approves contract with private school, raises. p. A1.

Houston Chronicle. (1996, September 27). Release draws near for audit of HISD. p. A29.

Houston Chronicle. (1996, October 4). Thinker. p. A36.

Houston Chronicle. (1996, October 6). Making change. p. C2.

Houston Chronicle. (1996, October 12). Political ramifications to HISD audit. p. A37.

Houston Chronicle. (1996, October 15). An extra-big first day of class. p. A14.

Houston Chronicle. (1996, October 20). School board. p. C2.

Houston Chronicle. (1996, November 3). HISD weighs audit's push to expand board. p. A33.

Houston Chronicle. (1996, November 6). Watch carefully. p. A36.

Houston Chronicle. (1996, November 11). A "teachable moment" for HISD board. p. A22.

Houston Chronicle. (1997, February 16). Don't micromanage. p. O2.

Houston Chronicle. (1997, April 18). HISD has made a good start on Sharp's recommendations. p. A46.

Houston Chronicle. (1997, June 12). Sharp opens campaign for lieutenant governor. p. A33.

Houston Chronicle. (1997, June 16). School jobs. p. C2.

Houston Chronicle. (1997, June 30). 7 points to help HISD do a better job of educating. p. A19.

Houston Forward Times. (1995, November 1–7). PAC group targets minority HISD trustees. p. A1.

Houston Independent School District. (1990). *A Declaration of Beliefs and Visions for the Houston Independent School District by the HISD Board of Education.*

Houston Independent School District. (1990, November 13). Minutes, Board of Education.

Houston Independent School District. (1992, May 21). Minutes, Board of Education.

Houston Independent School District. (1993, June 17). Minutes, Board of Education.

Houston Independent School District. (1993, October 7). Minutes, Board of Education.

Houston Independent School District. (1993, November). *System for Teacher Appraisal Review.*

Houston Independent School District. (1994, January 20). Minutes, Board of Education.

Houston Independent School District. (1994, February 3). Minutes, Board of Education.

Houston Independent School District. (1994, June 27). *Transcription of the Task Force for District Decentralization Open Forum.*

Houston Independent School District. (1994, August 25). Minutes, Board of Education.

Houston Independent School District. (1994, August 30). *Draft Report of the Decentralization Task Force to the Commission on District Decentralization.*

Houston Independent School District. (1994, November 17). Minutes, Board of Education.

Houston Independent School District. (1994, November 17). *Report of the Decentralization Commission to the HISD Board of Education.*

Houston Independent School District. (1994, December 1). Minutes, Board of Education.

Houston Independent School District. (1995, January 5). Minutes, Board of Education.

Houston Independent School District. (1995, March 30). Minutes, Instructional Consultation.

Houston Independent School District. (1995, April 4). Minutes, Combined Consultation.

Houston Independent School District. (1995, April 6). *Executive Summary, A Peer Review of the HISD Personnel Department, Presented to Dr. Rod Paige, Superintendent of Schools, Houston Independent School District, Submitted by the PEER Program Personnel Review Committee.*

Houston Independent School District. (1995, April 13). *A Peer Review of the HISD Transportation Services, Presented to Dr. Rod Paige, Superintendent of Schools, Houston Independent School District, Submitted by the PEER Program Transportation Services Review Committee, Supported by Texas Association of School Business Officials.*

Houston Independent School District. (1995, June 15). Minutes, Board of Education.

Houston Independent School District. (1996, May 3). *A Balanced Approach to Reading: A Peer Review of the Houston Independent School District's Reading Program.*

Houston Independent School District. (1996, May 16). Board Agenda Item A–6.

Houston Independent School District. (1997, January 22). Minutes, TSPR Citizens' Task Force.

Houston Independent School District. (1997, February 5). Superintendent Press Conference.

Houston Independent School District. (1997, February 6). Minutes, Board of Education.

Houston Independent School District. (1997, April 18). HISD *Post Six Month Report: HISD's Response to Texas School Performance Review by Texas Comptroller John Sharp.*

Houston Independent School District. (1997, May 13). Minutes, Instructional Consultation.

Houston Independent School District. (1997, July 17). Minutes (tapes and written summaries only), Board of Education

Houston Post. (1992, June 19). Just too steep. p. A26.

Houston Post. (1992, June 20). HISD tax hike plan brings fast reaction. p. A1.

Houston Post. (1992, June 21). HISD chief stands firm on tax hike. p. A1.

Houston Post. (1992, July 4). 49 cents nonsense. p. A28.

Houston Post. (1992, August 12). Grim outlook for HISD budget. p. A1.

Houston Post. (1992, August 12). It's just too much. p. A18.

Houston Post. (1992, August 28). HISD board OKs budget calling for 32% tax hike. p. A1.

Houston Post. (1993, May 24). This week: Frank Petruzielo. p. A1.

Houston Post. (1993, June 5). HISD cleans out "problem" school. p. A1.

Houston Post. (1993, June 10). "Death penalty" at Rusk shows real woes in public education. p. A21.

Houston Post. (1993, June 19). Gallegos claims no role in Rusk principal's case. p. A27.

Houston Post. (1994, January 22). Do it again, HISD. p. A28.

Houston Post. (1994, January 24). Hispanics threaten HISD suit. p. A1.

Houston Post. (1994, January 25). Board president outlines reasons for HISD superintendent vote. p. A15.

Houston Post. (1994, January 25). HISD process flawed, but Paige a good choice. p. A15.

Houston Post. (1994, January 26). Paige stays above fray in HISD flap. p. A1.

Houston Post. (1994, February 8). Clouds lifting on stormy transition. p. A13.

Houston Post. (1994, February 18). HISD asks state certification, but Paige still a step from helm. p. A25.

Houston Post. (1994, February 19). State to monitor Paige during first week as superintendent. p. A28.

Houston Post. (1994, February 23). HISD's Paige off to a good start. p. A13.

Houston Post. (1994, February 25). HISD Board thinks waiver solves problems for Paige. p. F2.

Houston Post. (1994, March 31). Wider probe requested in Paige hiring. p. A1.

Houston Post. (1994, April 1). The HISD mess. p. A30.

Houston Post. (1994, April 7). DA sees no merit in case against Paige. p. A1.

Houston Post. (1994, May 19). Starting with a clean slate. p. A31.

Houston Post. (1994, May 23). HISD's big test. p. A16.

Houston Post. (1994, August 27). Petruzielo in dark on unqualified bilingual hires, he says. p. A23.

Houston Post. (1994, August 31). HISD suspends 2 in probe of worker-test sales. p. A21.

Houston Post. (1994, September 29). Reviews send 8 HISD drivers packing. p. A29.

Houston Post. (1994, November 11). HISD rates 10 schools exemplary. p. A1.

Houston Post. (1995, January 15). Paige two. p. A39.

Houston Post. (1995, March 11). Parents upset over school's Vanguard status. p. A26.

Houston Sun. (1995, April 10). HISD moves away from seniority? p. A1.

Jarboe, Jan. (1994, March). John the Knife. *Texas Monthly, 22(3).* pp. 106–115.

Kerr, Irene. (1992, June 17). Letter to Frank Petruzielo.

Lyndon B. Johnson School of Public Affairs, The University of Texas at Austin, and Texas Center for Educational Research. (1993, February). *A Decade of Change: Public Education Reform in Texas 1981–1992,* Special Project Report. Austin, TX.

McAdams, Don. (1993, March 21). Letter to Gayle Fallon.

McAdams, Don. (1993, June 22). Letter to Gayle Fallon.

McAdams, Don. (1994, July 19). Memorandum to Rod Paige.

McDonnell, Lorraine M. (1989). *Restructuring American Schools: The Promise and the Pitfalls* (Background paper commissioned for *Education and the Economy: Hard Questions, Hard Answers,* a conference sponsored by the Institute on Education and the Economy, Teachers College, Columbia University, September 5–7, 1989, Brewster, Massachusetts.)

McKenzie, Naomi. (1997, June 20). Letter to Richard Miranda.

Meno, Lionel R. (1994, March 30). Letter to HISD trustees and superintendent.

Meno, Lionel R. (1994, April 6). Letter to Ron Franklin.

Miranda, Richard. (1997, April 24). Memorandum to Rod Paige.

Montgomery County. (1993, September). *Investing in a Commitment to Quality: A Report of the Corporate Partnership on Managerial Excellence in the Montgomery County (Maryland) Public Schools.*

Mora, Linda G. (1993, July 28). Letter to Frank Petruzielo.

Paige, Rod. (1994, March 28). Memorandum to principals and others.

Paige, Rod. (1994, November 21). Press conference statement.

Paige, Rod. (1995, March 28). *For Your Information: Communications from Dr. Rod Paige, Superintendent of Schools.*

Paige, Rod. (1995, August 1). Letter to community leaders.

Paige, Rod. (1995, November 20). Letter to HISD employees.

Paige, Rod. (1996, July 18). Letter to HISD trustees.

Paige, Rod. (1996, September 9). Letter to community leaders.

Paige, Rod. (1996, September 26). Letter to HISD employees.

Paige, Rod. (1996, September 27). Letter to community leaders.

Paige, Rod. (1996, October 3). Letter to Frank Michel.

Paige, Rod. (1996, October 18). Letter to community leaders.

Paige, Rod. (1996, October 21). Letter to PTA and PTO presidents.

Paige, Rod. (1997, April 1). Letter to Orell Fitzsimmons.

Petruzielo, Frank. (1993, April 21). Memorandum to HISD trustees.

Petruzielo, Frank. (1993, October 21). Letter to HISD trustees.

Ravitch, Diane. (1985). *The Schools We Deserve.* New York: Basic Books.

Raymond, Joan. (1991, March 28). Letter to HISD administrators.

Ross v. Eckels. No. 10444. (S. D. Tx. 1971, May 24).

Ross v. HISD. No. 10444. (S. D. Tx. 1981, June 17).

Sashkin, Marshall and John Egermeier. (1993). *School Change Models and Processes: A Review and Synthesis of Research and Practice.* Washington, DC: U.S. Government Printing Office.

Sharp, John. (1996, October). *Children First: A Report on the Houston Independent School District by the Texas Performance Review.* Austin: Texas Comptroller of Public Accounts.

Sharp, John. (1997, April 17). *Children First: A Six-Month Report Card on the Houston Independent School District by the Texas Performance Review.* Austin: Texas Comptroller of Public Accounts.

Sharp, John. (1997, April 17). Press Release of Texas Comptroller of Public Accounts.

Shaw, Richard. (1995, May 1). Letter to Rod Paige.

Shaw, Richard. (1996, October 2). Letter to HISD trustees.

Stockwell, Robert. (1994, October 27). Letter to Rod Paige.

Sturm, Leonard. (1997, June 13). Letter to Rod Paige.

Swartz, Mimi. (1994, September). Kaye Stripling. *Texas Monthly, 22(9),* p. 102.

Texas Education Agency. (no date). Texas Teacher Appraisal System Preliminary/Final Observation Form. Austin: Texas Education Agency.

Texas Education Agency, Department of Accountability. (1993, July 28). *District Report for Performance-Based Accreditation, Houston Independent School District.* Austin: Texas Education Agency.

Texas Education Agency, Governance Operations Division, Office of Accountability.

(1994, February 22–24). *Special Governance Assessment Report, Houston Independent School District.* Austin: Texas Education Agency.

Texas Education Agency, Office of Accountability. (1993, June). *Highlights of Senate Bill 7 Related to Accountability, Assessment, Public Reporting and Awards, Accreditation, Site-Based Decision Making.* Austin: Texas Education Agency.

Texas Education Agency, Office of Accountability. (1993, July). *Texas Education Agency, Statewide Accountability System: An Overview of the Accreditation Procedures as Revised by Senate Bill 7.* Austin: Texas Education Agency.

Texas Education Agency, Office of Policy Planning and Evaluation. (1994, April). *Accountability Manual: The 1994–95 Accountability Rating System for Texas Public Schools and School Districts.* Austin: Texas Education Agency.

Thomas v. HISD. (S. D. Tx. 1995). Oral Deposition of Gayle Fallon, October 17, 1995.

Vanourek, Greg, et al. (1997, June and July). *Charter Schools in Action, Final Report,* Three Parts. Washington, DC: A Hudson Institute Project.

Wall Street Journal. (1995, March 10). Schools tie salaries to pupil performance. p. B1.

Wall Street Journal. (1996, September 25). Houston taxes often unpaid, audit finds. p. T1.

Walsh, John. (1996, March 25). Letter to Willie Alexander, Harold Hook, Charles Miller, Don McAdams, Rod Paige, Charles Duncan, and Jonathan Day.

Walsh, John. (1997, February 14). Letter to Rod Paige, et al.

Werner, Chris D. (1997, July 2). Letter to Don McAdams.

Wright, Lance V. (June 8, 1990). *School Improvement Through Implementation of School-Based Management/Shared Decision Making at Selected Schools in the Houston Independent School District, a Concept Paper.* Unpublished manuscript, University of Colorado at Denver.

Index

Abbott, Terry, 246 n. 1
Accountability, 37, 250, 252
  Educational Economic Policy Center
    (EEPC), 71–73, 78
  HISD establishment of, 74–83
  Houston Federation of Teachers (HFT)
    and, 67–72, 89–94, 96–101, 237–238
  measurement issues in, 62–63, 72–77, 236
  Rusk Elementary School and, 67–71
  for schools, 62–83, 236, 253–254
  for teachers, 89–94, 96–101, 236–239, 252
  Texas accountability system, 71–74
Administrative performance planning and ap-
  praisal system, 94–96
African Americans. *See* Black community
Allocation Handbook, 28
Almaguer, Martha, 115
Alternative Certification Program (HISD),
  22, 140–146, 153, 158, 161, 198, 200,
  235
Alvarado, Carol, 225
American College Test (ACT), 62–63
American Federation of Teachers (AFT),
  102 n. 2
American General Corporation, 239
American Productivity and Quality Center,
  2–3, 146
Aramark Corporation, 241–243
Arnold, Paula, 2, 35, 39, 41, 73, 78, 81–82,
  113, 115, 154, 157, 159, 160, 161, 162,
  169, 172, 180, 181, 209 n. 3, 209 n. 4,
  210 n. 12, 223–224, 230, 238, 243, 244,
  245
  accountability and, 80, 82
  background, 11
  and bond elections of 1996, 191–192, 199,
    200, 205

  difficulties with Frank Petruzielo, 64,
    65–67
  hiring of Rod Paige as superintendent,
    109–111
  hiring of Frank Petruzielo as superinten-
    dent, 18–23
  as HISD board president, 16–23, 33
  HISD unity and, 18
  redistricting of HISD trustee districts,
    17–18
Arthur Andersen, 70, 147, 201, 243–244
Asian community, and redistricting of HISD
  trustee districts, 55–57
Ayers, Randy, 174–175

Balanced Approach to Reading, A, 235–236
Baptist Ministers Association of Houston
  and Vicinity, 111–112, 186–187
Barnes, Lee, 44, 45, 76, 160
Beliefs and Visions, Declaration of, 6–11, 24,
  25, 33, 34, 37, 62–64, 74–75, 92, 105,
  122, 124, 132, 136–137, 139, 155, 157,
  158, 159, 162, 164, 166, 229–231, 245,
  246, 251–252, 259, 267, 268–269
Bellaire, 20, 46–47, 57–58
Bellaire Area School Improvement Committee (BASIC), 57–58
Bellaire High School, 47, 48, 49, 54–55, 60,
  78, 134
Berryhill, Michael, 90
Black community
  appointment of Rod Paige as superinten-
    dent, 111–112, 115, 118–119
  and bond elections of 1996, 194
  and feeder systems, 134–135
  hiring of Frank Petruzielo and, 19–23

Black community (*continued*)
  magnet schools and, 59, 171
  and redistricting of HISD trustee districts,
    55–57
  Rice School/La Escuela Rice, 52, 53
Blake, Dayle, 223
Blitman, Hal, 143–144
Blueprint: Houston Schools of Excellence, 24–
  29, 30, 32–34, 37, 105
Bond elections of 1996, 191–208
  campaign for, 198–202
  and Greater Houston Partnership, 193–194
  and Harris County Republican Party, 195–
    198, 201–202, 203–204
  HISD response to failure of, 204–208
  and School House Committee, 191–192,
    197, 198, 202
Bond elections of 1998, 268
Bonfield, Gordon, 25
Bonner, James A., 183
Boyer, Ernest, 250
Braeburn Elementary School, 56, 59, 78
Brenner, Arlene, 130
Bricker, Laurie, 176, 183, 187, 188, 200,
  205, 223, 236, 243, 244, 245, 258, 267
  background, 192
  and reversal of River Oaks vote, 192–193
Brooks, Sylvia, 128, 132
Brown, Lee, 268
Brown & Root Services Corporation, 206,
  239
Browning-Ferris Industries, 230
Bryant, Faye, 22
Budget issues. *See also* Privatization
  bond elections of 1996, 191–208
  bond elections of 1998, 268
  budget of 1995–1996, 179–180
  budget of 1996–1997, 207–208
  budget of 1997–1998, 244–246
  in decentralization process, 28–29, 123,
    138
  school-based budgeting and, 28–29, 123,
    229
  tax battle of 1992, 34–45
Bullock, Bob, 227
Bush, George W., 101, 118, 120, 235
Business-school partnerships, 258

Cage Elementary School, 235
Caldwell, Kirbyjon, 79

Calloway, Ken, 186
Camp, George, 97, 98, 99, 101
Campos, Esther, 135, 157–162, 166, 174,
  179, 183, 187, 193, 210 n. 12, 225, 238,
  242, 243
  background, 158
  election to HISD board, 120
Carrillo Elementary School, 195
Cater, John, 128
Chandler, Walter, 115
Charter schools, 218, 230, 232, 234–235,
  251, 264
Chavez High, 195
Children First, 216
Choice, within district, 234
Choice, Lloyd, 68–69
Chubb, John, 250–251, 260, 264 n. 2
Class issues, magnet schools and, 59, 171
Coalition of Ministers Against Crime
  (COMAC), 183–184, 187–188, 189–
  190 n. 9
Code of Student Conduct, 254
Collins, Bonnie, 143–144
Commission on District Decentralization,
  127–133
Community Education Partners (CEP), 233,
  235
Condit, 55
Congress of Houston Teachers, 86, 99, 102
  n. 2, 208
Connally, Ben C., 20–21, 60
Contract schools, 251, 263–264
Contreras, H. A. (Art), 247 n. 8
Coopers & Lybrand, 214
Corruption. *See* Fraud and corruption
Covalt, Rosemary, 116
Crosby, Emeral A., 249
Cryer, Bill, 119
Cuban, Larry, 248
Culberson, John, 36, 37, 38
Cullen Missionary Baptist Church, 167
Cunningham Elementary School, 55, 59,
  235
Curtis, Gregory, 85 n. 10

Danburg, Debra, 118
Dauber, Joyce, 129
Davis, Jeffrey A., 247 n. 6
Davis High School, 134–135
Dawn School, 235

Decentralization, 122–139, 250, 253, 258–
    259. *See also* Privatization
    Blueprint: Houston Schools of Excellence,
        24–29, 30, 32–34, 37, 105
    Commission on District Decentralization,
        127–133
    components of, 127
    Decentralization Task Force, 128–133
    feeder system and, 57, 131, 133–135, 163,
        234
    Hook Committee and, 122–127
    Hook-Haines Plan for, 125–133
    under Rod Paige, 127–139, 178–179, 233–
        234, 239–244
    Peer Examination, Evaluation, and Re-
        design (PEER), 146–154, 163, 166,
        213, 235, 243, 245, 253, 258
    resistance by Petruzielo, 122–127
Declaration of Beliefs and Visions, 6–11, 24,
    25, 33, 34, 37, 62–64, 74–75, 92, 105,
    122, 124, 132, 136–137, 139, 155, 157,
    158, 159, 162, 164, 166, 229–231, 245,
    246, 251–252, 259, 267, 268–269
Declaration of Del Lago, 162–163
Del Lago Manifesto, 162–163, 166
Deloitte & Touche, 123, 139 n. 1
Deming, Edwards, 146
Democratic Party of Harris County, 6, 115,
    258
Department of Education, U.S., 138
    Office of Civil Rights, 114, 116
Department of Immigration and Naturaliza-
    tion Services, U.S., 141
Department of Justice, U.S., 18
Department of Professional Standards, 101,
    102 n. 4
Devine, John, 238
Dewey, Andy, 99
Dewey v. *Paige,* 178, 238
Direct democratic control, as problem,
    260–262
District superintendents
    contracts for, 94–95, 135–136
    performance evaluations and, 94–96,
        134–136
    staff and budget issues, 138–139
Dolcefino, Wayne, 140–141, 145, 155 n. 3,
    200, 201
Drop-out rates, 254
Dutton, Harold, 118

Edmonds, Jim, 184–187
Educational Economic Policy Center
    (EEPC), 71–73, 78
Educrats, 257
Egermeier, John, 264 n. 1
Ellis, Melody, 4, 13, 16, 17, 18, 33
Ellis, Rodney, 4
Ely, Jane, 118
Empirical Management, 214
Evans, James, 204
Expectations, for students, 67–71, 257–258
Eyewitness News, 200

Facilities management, 240–241
Fallon, Gayle, 15, 33, 38, 44, 84 n. 1, 84 n. 3,
    108, 132, 136, 155 n. 2, 166, 167, 183,
    188, 189 n. 5, 195, 205, 207, 208, 238,
    244, 247 n. 3
    accountability for schools and, 68, 69, 70–
        71, 75, 76, 78–80, 83
    accountability for teachers and, 89–94,
        96–101
    background, 70
    decentralization process and, 132–133
    Rusk Elementary School and, 68, 69,
        70–71
    war against Rod Paige, 163–164, 177–181,
        184, 237
Finder, Lawrence D., 141
Fire and safety code violations, 207, 208,
    239–240, 254
Fitzsimmons, Orell, 241–242
Fleck, Tim, 53, 184, 187
Food service management, 200–201,
    241–243
Foorman, Barbara, 235–236
Fraga, Felix, 10–11, 12, 13, 14, 16, 18, 107,
    108, 143, 157, 161, 175 n. 1, 245
    appointment to HISD, 4–5
    background, 5
Framework for Educational Excellence 1990, A,
    25
Franklin, Ron, 2–4, 16, 17, 22, 24, 41, 65,
    157, 166, 183, 187, 223, 225, 230, 243,
    245
    accountability and, 69, 76–77, 79, 80
    background, 10
    as HISD board president, 100, 101, 106,
        108, 110, 111, 115, 117, 118, 126–
        127, 135, 158, 161–162

Franklin, Ron (*continued*)
  and Rod Paige as superintendent, 106,
    108, 110, 111, 115, 117, 118
  resignation of Joan Raymond and, 10–14
  River Oaks Elementary School controversy
    and, 168–175, 176–177, 181
Fraud and corruption
  Alternative Certification Program
    (HISD), 22, 140–146, 153, 158, 161,
    198, 200, 235
  employees with criminal backgrounds,
    145, 150–151
  money and HISD board votes, 174–175
  selling of employment tests, 145
  whistle blower policy, 238–239
Frels, Kelly, 94, 117, 177
Friedberg, Tom, 39–40, 82

Gaines, Arthur, 37, 39, 41, 65, 82, 106–108,
    110, 115, 118, 125, 143, 159, 160, 162,
    166–168, 172, 173, 177–187, 189 n. 6,
    193, 205, 212, 225, 242, 243, 245, 267
  background, 33
  and HISD board elections of 1995, 178–
    181, 183–188
  as HISD president, 163
Gallegos, Mario, 18, 225, 243
Gallegos, Olga, 13, 16, 18, 41, 67, 68–69,
    71, 109, 113, 135, 157–158, 159, 179,
    183, 191, 193, 210 n. 12, 225, 230,
    242
Galloway, Carol Mims, 37, 41, 67, 69, 80,
    91, 99, 106, 108, 136, 159, 160, 162,
    164, 166, 168, 172, 178, 179, 183, 186,
    187, 193, 224, 225, 242, 243
  background, 33
  election to HISD board, 33
General Education Development (GED),
    183–184
Gibson, Ann, 147
Gingrich, Newt, 188
Gonzalez, Alberto, 128, 132
Gonzalez, Yvonne, 112–113
Goodlad, John, 250
Goolsby, Gary, 147
Gordon Elementary School, 57–58, 78, 130
Gottlieb, David, 25
Governor's Select Committee on Public Edu-
    cation, 37
Graham, H. Devon, Jr., 201

Greater Houston Coalition for Educational
    Excellence, 25, 35, 36, 39, 81, 82, 245
Greater Houston Partnership, 24–25, 37, 45,
    62, 71, 99, 122, 193–194, 268
Green, Al, 118, 161
Griffin, Richard, 152

Haines, Al, 79, 82, 123–132, 139, 147, 194,
    268
  Hook-Haines Plan and, 125–133
Harris County Appraisal District, 244
Harris County Democratic Party, 6, 115, 258
Harris County Department of Education,
    152
Harris County Republican Party, 195–198,
    201–202, 203–204, 258
Haynes & Boone, 141–146, 147
Henry, Wiley, 10–14, 16, 17, 18, 33, 245
Hernandez, José, 68–69
Herod Elementary School, 56, 78
Hill, Paul T., 139 n. 4, 263–264
Hispanic community
  appointment of Felix Fraga to HISD, 5
  appointment of Rod Paige as superinten-
    dent, 108–120
  appointment of José Salazar to HISD,
    107–109
  and bond elections of 1996, 194–195
  and feeder systems, 134–135
  hiring of Frank Petruzielo and, 19–23
  magnet schools and, 59, 171
  and redistricting of HISD trustee districts,
    17–18, 47, 55–57
  Rice School/La Escuela Rice, 53, 60
  and tax battle of 1992, 38
Hispanic Education Committee, 107, 109–
    110, 113, 114–120, 127, 128, 163, 186,
    195
Hobby, Bill, 219
Holmes, John B., Jr., 117, 118–119, 174
Hook, Harold, 122–127, 139, 139 n. 1, 199,
    239, 268
Hook Committee, 122–127
Hooker, Richard, 202
Hook-Haines Plan, 125–133
Horn, Don, 161
Hotze, Bruce, 209 n. 10
Houston, C. P., 218
Houston, Mary, 189 n. 8
Houston Area Urban League, 128

Houston Association of School Administrators (HASA), 38, 86, 95, 99, 102 n. 2,
  136
Houston Business Advisory Council, 81,
  108, 122, 239
Houston Business Education Committee, 81
Houston Chronicle
  bond elections of 1996 and, 193, 195, 200,
    204
  decentralization plans and, 127
  information-gathering by, 12
  Jefferson problems in election of 1995,
    182–184, 187–188
  modified voucher system and, 205
  money for trustee votes claim, 174–175
  privatization and, 159
  resignation of Joan Raymond and, 12–15,
    16
  River Oaks Elementary School controversy
    and, 170, 173
  Sharp Audit and, 199, 214–216, 218–219,
    222–223, 225, 227
  and tax battle of 1992, 37–41, 43
Houston City Council, 107
Houston Council of PTAs, 81
Houston Education Association (HEA), 44,
  45, 76, 86, 89, 91, 99, 102 n. 2, 160,
  167
Houston Federation of Teachers (HFT), 15,
  33, 80, 83, 86, 99, 102 n. 2, 166–167,
  178, 180, 195, 224, 261
  accountability for schools and, 67, 68, 69,
    70–71, 72
  accountability for teachers and, 89–94, 96–
    101, 237–238
  decentralization process and, 132–133
Houston Forward Times, and HISD board
  elections of 1995, 186
Houston Gardens Elementary School, 206,
  207, 208
Houstonians for Public Education, 81
Houston Independent School District
  (HISD)
  accountability system. *See* Accountability
  achievements, summary of, 252–254
  Alternative Certification Program
    (HISD), 22, 140–146, 153, 158, 161,
    198, 200, 235
  appointment of Felix Fraga, 4–5
  Paula Arnold as president, 16–23

at-large members, proposal for, 222–223,
    224, 225
  board elections of 1989, 1, 2–5
  board elections of 1993, 77–78, 104
  board elections of 1995, 181–187
  board elections of 1997, 244–246, 267
  bond elections of 1996, 191–208
  bond elections of 1998, 268
  constituent service, 47–48, 134–135
  decentralization and. *See* Decentralization
  disillusionment with Frank Petruzielo, 30,
    33–34, 43–44, 62–71, 74–75,
    104–108
  District Five neighborhood issues, 46–61
  District Nine, 55–56
  district-wide conventions, 25–27, 29
  division of board, 157–175
  ending micromanagement by, 221–222,
    225, 226–227, 232–233
  facilities management and, 240–241
  food service and, 200–201, 241–243
  Ron Franklin as president, 100, 101, 106,
    108, 110, 115, 117, 118, 126–127,
    135, 158, 161–162
  hiring of Yvonne Gonzalez as interim
    superintendent, 112–113
  hiring of Rod Paige as superintendent,
    105–120
  hiring of Frank Petruzielo as superinten-
    dent, 18–23
  human services management, 86–91,
    243–244
  importance of, 2
  lessons from, 255–262
  magnet schools, 52, 57, 59, 60, 168–175,
    214
  Cathy Mincberg as president, 6–15
  Rod Paige as president, 33–34, 40–42, 44,
    55–56, 64–65, 87
  Peer Examination, Evaluation, and Re-
    design (PEER), 146–154, 163, 166,
    213, 235, 243, 245, 253, 258
  privatization and, 158–161
  Project 10, 9–10
  redistricting of trustee districts, 17–18,
    53–61
  resignation of Tina Reyes, 4–5
  retreat at Del Lago resort, 162–163, 164
  retreat at Eagle Lake, 137, 164
  retreat at Pirates Cove, 65–66

(HISD) (*continued*)
  retreat at Walden Resort, 17
  retreat in Columbus, 110
  retreats at Cat Springs, 3–4, 17, 23–24, 35
  Rice School/La Escuela Rice, 49–53, 60
  River Oaks Elementary School controversy
    and, 168–175
  Sharp Audit, 199, 207, 208, 211–227, 231,
    233
  split over jobs, 166–168
  summary of achievements, 252–254
  tax battle of 1992, 34–45, 57
  Texas School Performance Review
    (TSPR), 199, 207, 208, 211–227,
    231, 233
  unity of, 18
  vision statement, 6–11. *See also Beliefs and
    Visions, Declaration of*
Houston Post, The
  decentralization process and, 129
  information-gathering by, 12
  and tax battle of 1992, 37, 38, 41
Houston Press, and HISD board elections of
  1995, 184
Houston Property Rights Association, 199,
  201, 203
Houston Schools of Excellence Steering
  Committee, 25–27, 32–34
Howard, Gloria, 130
Hughes, Lynn N., 119–120, 163
Human services management, 86–91,
  243–244
Hunt, Guy, 246 n. 1

IBM, 243, 244
Integrated Healthcare Delivery Systems,
  230

James, Nona, 154
Jane Long Middle School, 57 60, 134
Jarboe, Jan, 211
Jefferson, Robert Charles, 118, 135, 157,
  159, 161, 162, 166–168, 174, 177, 178,
  179, 181–189, 189 n. 6, 189 n. 8, 189–
  190 n. 10
  appointment to HISD board, 113
  background, 113, 158
  and HISD board elections of 1995, 181,
    182–184, 186, 187–188
Jiles, Jodie, 79

Johnston Middle School, 55, 56, 60, 134
Juran, Joseph, 146

Kaleidoscope School/Escuela Caleidoscopio,
  Cunningham Elementary School, 235
Kashmere High School, 134–135
Kerr, Irene, 38, 95, 136
Kirk, Ron, 119
Klein, Barry, 199, 201, 202, 203, 206
Knowledge Is Power Program Academy, 234
Konen, Jo, 197

Lamar High School, 24, 97, 134
Langworthy, David, 222
Lanier Middle School, 7
Laredo State University, 142
Lawson, Bill, 118
Lay, Ken, 184
League of United Latin American Citizens
  (LULAC), 114
Leland, Mickey, 11
Lemon, Wayman Clyde, 182–185, 187, 188–
  189, 189 n. 8, 193, 200, 225, 242, 243,
  244, 245, 258, 259
Lindsay, David, 151–152
Lomax, Nancy, 224
Longoria, Richard, 201
Lott, Thaddeus, 15, 22–23, 234
Lyndon B. Johnson School of Public Affairs,
  249

Macy, Sylvia, 136
Madison High School, 55–56
Magnet schools, 52, 57, 59, 60, 168–175,
  214
Main Event Management Corporation, 239
Malcolm Baldrige National Quality Award,
  152
Markley, Melanie, 163
Mark Twain Elementary School, 50, 129
Marriott Management Services, 242, 243
Marshall, Lawrence, 269
Marshall, Thom, 200
Martinez, Roman, 111
Masucci, James, 201
May, Eric, 84 n. 9
McAdams, Don, 10, 75, 84 n. 3, 102 n. 5,
  115, 159, 178, 243
  background, 2–3
  first term in HISD, 2–3

as HISD board president, 125, 224–227
second term in HISD, 77–78
third term in HISD, 246, 264, 267–269
McClung, Dan, 186, 202
McDavid, Teddy, 183, 184, 185, 187
McDonnell, Lorraine M., 264 n. 1
McKenzie, Naomi, 242
Meno, Lionel R. ("Skip"), 74, 99, 101, 114,
    116–119, 120
Metropolitan Achievement Test (MAT),
    14–15, 62–63
Meyerland, 54–55, 60
MGT of America, 214
Milby High School, 134–135
Miller, Charles, 37, 38–40, 44, 62, 71–73,
    78–82, 84 n. 8
Mincberg, Cathy, 3, 4, 16, 17, 21, 22, 34,
    100, 106, 108, 110, 111, 114, 115, 125,
    126, 136, 138, 157, 168, 169, 172, 178,
    180, 188, 205, 236, 238, 245
  accountability and, 76–77, 80, 81–82
  background, 6
  difficulties with Frank Petruzielo, 64,
    66–67
  as HISD board president, 6–15
  resignation from HISD board, 176, 181
  resignation of Joan Raymond and, 10–14
  vision statement of HISD and, 6–9
Mincberg, David, 6, 115
Mindiola, Tatcho, 115
Ministers Against Crime, 113
Miranda, Richard, 220, 226, 227, 228 n. 5
Mischer, Walter, 11
Mitchell Energy Company, 25
Model-Netics, 239
Moe, Terry, 250–251, 260, 264 n. 2
Mora, Linda G., 30
Moreno, Patricia, 142, 144
Morgan, Bill, 143–144
Mosbacher, Rob, 230–231
Murphy, Mary, 97, 99, 101, 103 n. 9

National Education Association (NEA), 102
    n. 2
Nation at Risk, A, xiii, 249, 250
Neil & Gibson, 214
Nelson, Myrtle Lee, 48, 78
*New Accountability System for Texas Public
    Schools, A*, 71–72
New Beginning for HISD, 231

Newberry, Robert C., 111
Norm-Referenced Assessment Program for
    Texas (NAPT), 63, 72, 73, 236

Ofield, Paul, 189–190 n. 9
Olivarez, Marcia, 113, 116, 117, 120–121
    n. 2
Olivarez, Ruben, 115
Onstead, Bob, 184
Open Meetings Act, Texas, 106–107, 114,
    116
Open Records Act, Texas, 19
Outsourcing. *See* Decentralization; Priva-
    tization

Paige, Rod, 2, 4, 10, 16, 17, 23, 78, 122, 139
    n. 3, 140–155, 157, 158–169, 176–185,
    188, 189 n. 8, 210 n. 11, 217, 219–223,
    226–227, 229–243, 246, 246 n. 1, 246
    n. 2, 247 n. 9, 251–252, 267–269
  accountability and, 236–239
  and Alternative Certification Program con-
    troversy, 144
  background, 6–7, 105–106, 255–256
  bond elections of 1996, 191–208
  charter schools and, 218, 230, 232, 234–
    235, 264
  choice and, 234
  curriculum improvements and, 164–166,
    235–236
  decentralization process and, 127–139,
    178–179, 233–234, 239–244
  Gayle Fallon's war against, 163–164, 177–
    181, 184, 237
  and fraud and corruption situations, 144,
    145, 150–151
  hiring as superintendent, 113–120, 229
  and HISD board elections of 1995,
    181–187
  as HISD board president, 33–34, 40–42,
    44, 55–56, 64–66, 87
  New Beginning, 230–231
  Peer Examination, Evaluation, and Re-
    design (PEER), 146–154, 163, 166,
    213, 235, 243, 245, 253, 258
  privatization and, 158–161, 164
  as proposed superintendent, 105–119
  reforms of 1996–1997, 232–244
  resignation from HISD board, 112
  resignation of Joan Raymond and, 10–14

Paige, Rod (*continued*)
River Oaks Elementary School controversy
and, 169–174, 192–193
and Sharp Audit, 212, 213, 231, 233
superintendent certificate and, 114, 116,
118
vision statement of HISD and, 6–9
Parent activists. *See also* Asian community;
Black community; Hispanic community
and feeder systems, 134–135
and redistricting of HISD trustee districts,
17–18, 48, 53–61
and tax battle of 1992, 42
Parents for Public Schools, 245
Pathway School Academy of Academic
Achievement, 234
Peer Examination, Evaluation, and Redesign
(PEER), 146–154, 163, 166, 213, 235,
243, 245, 253, 258
Performance-based accreditation, 29
Performance evaluations
for administrators, 94–96, 134–136
for teachers, 87–88, 89–91, 96–101, 238
Texas School Performance Review
(TSPR), 199, 207, 208, 211–227
Pershing Middle School, 58, 134
Petruzielo, Frank, 19–45, 78, 90, 101, 103 n.
7, 133, 139, 139 n. 2, 155 n. 1, 163–
164, 195, 257, 268
accountability for schools and, 62, 63–83,
67–71, 73, 74–83
accountability for teachers and, 92–101
as advocate for urban education, 29–30
and Alternative Certification Program controversy, 142–144
background, 21
Blueprint: Houston Schools of Excellence, 24–
29, 30, 32–34, 37, 105
decentralization and, 122–127
district-wide conventions, 25–27, 29
and Greater Houston Coalition for Educational Excellence, 25, 32–36, 81, 82,
245
hiring as superintendent of Houston
schools, 18–23
HISD member disillusionment with, 30,
33–34, 43–44, 62–71, 74–75,
104–108
redistricting of HISD trustee districts,
54–61

school-based budgeting and, 28–29, 229
school improvement plans, 27–29, 229
shared decision-making and, 25–27, 229
as superintendent in Broward County, 108,
112, 113, 126
tax battle of 1992, 34–45
Phipps, Bill, 149
Poindexter, Hilda, 92
Politics, Markets, and America's Schools (Chubb
and Moe), 250–251, 260, 264 n. 2
Polland, Gary, 196–197, 203–204, 209 n. 6
Prime Time, 15, 22–23
Privatization. *See also* Decentralization
and budget of 1995–1996, 179, 180
HISD board rejection of, 158–161, 164
modified voucher system and, 204–206,
230, 267–268, 269
Professional Development and Appraisal Sys-
tem (PDAS), 238
Project 10, 9–10
Project Chrysalis, Cage Elementary School,
235
Project Renewal
Phase A, 49–53, 191, 194–195
Phase B, 191, 194–195
Property taxes, 254
increase in 1998, 268
tax battle of 1992, 34–45, 57
Pro-Vision Centripet Project, 235
Public Education Patrons (PEP), 3

R. P. Harris Elementary School, 130
Randall, Patty, 205–206
RAND Corporation, 139 n. 1, 264 n. 1
Ranger Insurance Company, 39
Ratliff, Bill, 245
Ravitch, Diane, 262
Raymond, Joan, 1–15, 18, 19, 24, 26, 31, 42,
49, 54, 57, 90, 92, 102–103 n. 6, 110,
125, 164, 234, 245, 252, 257
background, 1
extension of administrator contracts,
94–95
and forced retirement of Myrtle Lee Nelson, 48
management style, 1–2, 9
resignation as superintendent of Houston
schools, 10–15, 16, 161
Wesley Elementary controversy and,
14–15

Reagan High School, 134
Reform. *See* School reform
Reich, Robert, 70
Reinventing Public Education, 139 n. 4
Republican Party of Harris County, 195–198,
    201–202, 203–204, 258
Ressel, Betty, 214, 216, 220
Restructuring. *See also* Accountability; De-
    centralization
  Blueprint: Houston Schools of Excellence,
      24–29, 30, 32–34, 37, 105
  curriculum alignment in, 164–166, 235–
      236, 250
  school-based management in, 9–10, 28–
      29, 123, 229, 250
  in second-wave reforms, 249–250
  shared decision-making in, 9–10, 25–27,
      104, 123, 229, 250
  student-centered approach in, 250
Restructuring American Schools (RAND Cor-
    poration), 264 n. 1
Restructuring Schools (Richard F. Elmore and
    Associates), 264 n. 1
Reyes, Ben, 4
Reyes, Tina, 4
Rice School/La Escuela Rice, 49–53, 60
Richards, Ann, 101, 117, 118, 119, 120
River Oaks Academy, 206
River Oaks Elementary School controversy,
    168–175, 176–177, 181, 188, 192–193
River Oaks Trust Company, 128
Roberson, J. J., 111, 186
Rodriguez, Lori, 173–174, 175 n. 1
Ross v. Eckels, 20
Ross v. HISD, 20
Rudy, Keith, 78, 79
Rupp, George, 49
Rusk Elementary School, 67–71
Russler, Rick, 147

Safety code and fire violations, 207, 208,
    239–240, 254
Salazar, José, 108–110, 112–113, 157–158,
    174
  appointment to HISD, 107–109
  background, 107
  resignation from HISD board, 120
Salvation Army, 67, 69–70
Sandoval, Monica, 143
San Miguel, Guadalupe, Jr., 116, 120–121 n. 2

Santos, Alfredo, 116
Sashkin, Marshall, 264 n. 1
Schecter, Sue, 118
Scholastic Aptitude Test (SAT), 62–63, 166
School-based management, 123, 250
  initiation of, 28–29, 229
  Project 10, 9–10
School Change Models and Processes (Sashkin
    and Egermeier), 264 n. 1
School House Committee, 191–192, 197,
    198, 202
School improvement plans
  Blueprint: Houston Schools of Excellence, 24–
      29, 30, 32–34, 37, 105
  initiation of, 27–29, 229
School reform. *See also* Accountability; De-
    centralization; Restructuring
  competition in third-wave, 250–252
  direct democratic control as problem in,
      260–262
  lessons from Houston, 255–262
  restructuring in second-wave, 249–250
  standards in first-wave, 249, 251
  state-level, 259
Schools We Deserve, The (Ravitch), 262
Sclafani, Susan, 75, 125, 220
Scott, George, 15, 36–37, 39–41, 44
Second language, requirements for, 269
ServiceMaster Management Services Com-
    pany, 240–241
Shadwick, Jeff, 269
Shadwick, Lana, 174–175
Shared decision-making, 123, 250
  Blueprint: Houston Schools of Excellence,
      24–29, 30, 32–34, 37, 105
  initiation of, 25–27, 104, 229
  Project 10, 9–10
Sharp, John, 199, 207, 208, 211–216, 218–
    222, 226–227, 230, 233, 241, 244, 245,
    253, 254
Sharp Audit/HISD Opportunities Report, 199,
    207, 208, 211–227, 231, 233
Shaw, Richard, 178, 237
Simon, Larry, 198, 209 n. 10
Sims, Robert Randall, Jr., 209 n. 10
Sizer, Theodore, 250
Sklar, Louis, 184
Smith, Keryl, 160–161
Solar, Michael, 79
Southside Place, 46–47

Southwest Houston, 55
Spantran, 141
Special education students, 268
Stafford, Delia, 142–144, 155 n. 3
Standards, for teachers, 92, 101, 102 n. 4, 249
Stanford 9 Achievement Test, 236
Star of Hope Women and Family Shelter, 67
STAR (System for Teacher Appraisal and Review), 98–101, 238
State Advisory Committee for Teacher Appraisal, 100
State Board of Education, 3, 100, 145–146
Stockwell, Robert, 128, 132, 148, 268
Stripling, Kaye, 51–52
Sturm, Leonard, 35, 43, 143, 242
Sumners, Don, 209 n. 10
Swartz, Mimi, 51
System for Teacher Education and Review, 238

Tapia, Richard, 53
Taxpayers Coalition of Greater Houston, 36–37
Tax Research Association of Harris County (TRA), 36–37, 41–44
Teacher Assessment Development Committee, 101
Teacher Development and Assessment Committee, 97
Teachers
    accountability of, 89–94, 96–101, 236–239, 252
    Alternative Certification Program (HISD), 22, 140–146, 153, 158, 161, 198, 200, 235
    contract requirements, 88–89, 95–96, 136, 195, 237
    grievance procedures, 89–90, 237
    hearing officers for terminated, 93–94
    performance evaluations, 87–88, 89–91, 96–101, 238
    professional standards for, 92, 101, 102 n. 4, 249
    terminating, 89–91, 237
Tenneco, Inc., 25
Termination of teachers, 237
    difficulty of, 89–91
    hearing officers and, 93–94
Texas Assessment of Academic Skills

(TAAS), 29, 63, 67, 72–77, 83, 99, 101, 153–154, 171, 205, 207, 214, 238, 253
Texas Association of Chicanos in Higher Education, 116
Texas Association of School Business Officials, 149
Texas Business and Education Coalition, 71
Texas Commissioner of Education, 74, 99, 101, 114, 116–119, 120
Texas Education Agency (TEA), 3, 27, 29, 30, 63, 67, 69, 74, 76, 77, 83, 99–100, 138, 212, 238, 254
    Alternative Certification Program (HISD) scandal, 142
    and appointment of Rod Paige as superintendent, 114–120
Texas Educational Assessment of Minimum Skills (TEAMS), 62–63
Texas Education Code, 87, 89, 90, 93, 114, 116, 118, 202, 212, 228 n. 5, 233, 234, 236–237, 238, 252
Texas Monthly, 51, 211
Texas Open Meetings Act, 106–107, 114, 116
Texas Open Records Act, 19
Texas School Performance Review (TSPR), 199, 207, 208, 211–227, 231, 233
Texas Southern University, 21, 105–106, 146, 255–256
Texas Teacher Appraisal System (TTAS), 88, 96–97, 99, 152, 238
Texas Term Contract Nonrenewal Act (TCNA), 88–89, 95–96, 136
Texas United School Employees Union, 241
Thomas, Johana, 68–69, 84 n. 2
Thomas v. HISD, 75
Topper, David, 153
Torres, H. G., 207, 210 n. 13
Transamerica Asset Management Group Inc., 37

Universidad Autónoma de Nuevo Léon, 142
University of Houston, 115
University of Texas Health Science Center, 153

Vanourek, Greg, 251
Vara, Richard, 147
Varnett School, 205–206, 230
Vasquez, Gabriel, 269

Vasquez, James, 115, 116, 118
Vetterling, Caroline, 125
Viator, Ray, 147
Vinson & Elkins, 128
Voting Rights Act, 17–18
Voucher system, modified, 204–206, 230, 267–268, 269

Wallace, Chris, 15
Wallace, Susan Besze, 163
Wall Street Journal, 216
Walsh, John, 194, 208–209 n. 2, 209 n. 3, 223
Werner, Chris D., 242
Wesley Elementary School, 14–15, 234
Westbury High School, 54, 55–56, 60, 134
West Houston, 20, 200

West University Elementary School, 49
West University Place, 46–47, 50, 52, 53
Westwood, 55–56
Whistle blower policy, 238–239
Whitmire, John, 212, 213, 245
Whitmire, Kathy, 12, 78, 219, 226–227
Williams, Charlotte, 70
Wilson, David, 209 n. 10
Wilson, Livy, 143
Wilson, Ron, 38
Winick, Darv, 72–73, 76, 79, 81–82, 268
Wonderland Private School, 206
Wright, Lance V., 9

Yawn, Larry, 212
Young, Felipa, 69–70

About the Author

Donald R. McAdams is serving his third four-year term as an elected member of the Houston Independent School District Board of Education. In 1993 and 1997 he served as president of the board. For the past ten years McAdams has made his living as an independent quality management consultant, with national and international clients in manufacturing, mining, travel, financial services, healthcare, and education. Previously, he served as executive vice president of the American Productivity & Quality Center, president of the Texas Independent College Fund, president of Southwestern Adventist College, and professor of history at Andrews University. McAdams, who holds a Ph.D. in British History from Duke University, has recently been appointed research professor and director of the Center for Reform of School Systems at the University of Houston.